D0787737

Darkness and Light

Darkness and Light

An Exposition of Ephesians 4:17—5:17
D. M. LLOYD-JONES

BAKER BOOK HOUSE
Grand Rapids, Michigan 49506

Copyright 1982 by Bethan Lloyd-Jones

Reprinted 1982 by Baker Book House Company
with the permission of the copyright owner

ISBN: 0-8010-5617-9

Printed and bound
in the United States of America

Preface

There is no particular reason for the order in which the eight volumes which make up Dr Lloyd-Jones's sermons on Ephesians have been published. It was because they did not appear in chronological sequence that the only portion of the Epistle which remained to be covered at the time of the author's death on 1st March, 1981, was Ephesians 4:17 to 5:17. This present volume now closes that gap and thus concludes a series which has already become remarkably owned of God across the world. The opinion, once heard, that the main call for Dr Lloyd-Jones's sermons would be from those who actually sat under his ministry, has long since been disproved. Large though the numbers were which attended upon his unforgettable ministry, far larger numbers have already benefited from his published works. And many more, we believe, will yet come under their influence.

Dr Lloyd-Jones was first and last a preacher. None of his Ephesians sermons, preached between 1954 and 1962, was written, except for a skeleton outline. Accordingly, their publication was only possible because full recordings existed on tape. From these tapes, transcribed by Mrs E. Burney, Dr Lloyd-Jones prepared the Exposition of Ephesians for publication and to this labour, although aided by his wife and Mr S. M. Houghton, he personally gave a great deal of time. It was harder work, he would often say, than preaching itself!

In the case of this present volume Dr Lloyd-Jones was unable to undertake any supervision of the preparation for publication prior to his death. Happily the editorial principles upon which he worked were clearly laid down in the preceding volumes and his helpers, already named – with additional aid from Lady Catherwood, the author's elder daughter – have followed them faithfully and closely. No effort has been spared to see that the final form of this volume is as he would have wished it to be.

In 1937 when Dr Campbell Morgan was in the latter part of his ministry at Westminster Chapel, he spoke of his confidence that when God's workers have to lay down their work then God is there, and there is the next man coming on. He did not then know that within twelve months Dr Lloyd-Jones was to join him.

Now, more than forty years later, this book will also surely serve as a part in the on-going work of God.

In 1955 Dr Wilbur M. Smith, after visiting England, was to write fully in *Moody Monthly* of what he heard at Westminster Chapel, mentioning particularly Dr Lloyd-Jones's series on Ephesians which had then only gone as far as sermon thirty-eight. Smith concluded: 'I wish every minister of the word in America could have heard the sermons I have heard from this anointed servant of the Lord this summer. My own language is utterly inadequate to communicate the experience of sitting under such Spirit-anointed proclaiming of the eternal truths of our holy faith.'

This volume, together with the whole series, will by God's blessing give the reader some idea of what Dr Wilbur Smith meant. May it also aid in advancing such preaching in all nations!

The author of these pages has now entered into the joy of his Lord. It remains for us who continue in this present scene of pilgrimage and service to remember those who have spoken unto us the Word of God, 'whose faith follow . . . Jesus Christ the same yesterday, and today, and for ever' (Hebrews 13:8).

Iain H. Murray
28th December, 1981

Contents

[7]

Darkness and Light

Ephesians 4:17—5:17

17 *This I say therefore, and testify in the Lord, that ye*
   henceforth walk not as other Gentiles walk, in the
   vanity of their mind,
18 *Having the understanding darkened, being alienated*
   from the life of God through the ignorance that is in
   them, because of the blindness of their heart:
19 *Who being past feeling have given themselves over unto*
   lasciviousness, to work all uncleanness with greediness.
20 *But ye have not so learned Christ;*
21 *If so be that ye have heard him, and have been taught*
   by him, as the truth is in Jesus:
22 *That ye put off concerning the former conversation the old*
   man, which is corrupt according to the deceitful lusts;
23 *And be renewed in the spirit of your mind;*
24 *And that ye put on the new man, which after God is*
   created in righteousness and true holiness.
25 *Wherefore putting away lying, speak every man truth*
   with his neighbour: for we are members one of another.
26 *Be ye angry, and sin not: let not the sun go down*
   upon your wrath:
27 *Neither give place to the devil.*
28 *Let him that stole steal no more: but rather let him*
   labour, working with his hands the thing which is
   good, that he may have to give to him that needeth.
29 *Let no corrupt communication proceed out of your*
   mouth, but that which is good to the use of edifying,
   that it may minister grace unto the hearers.

30 *And grieve not the holy Spirit of God, whereby ye are sealed unto the day of redemption.*

31 *Let all bitterness, and wrath, and anger, and clamour, and evil speaking, be put away from you, with all malice:*

32 *And be ye kind one to another, tenderhearted, forgiving one another, even as God for Christ's sake hath forgiven you.*

1 *Be ye therefore followers of God, as dear children;*

2 *And walk in love, as Christ also hath loved us, and hath given himself for us an offering and a sacrifice to God for a sweetsmelling savour.*

3 *But fornication, and all uncleanness, or covetousness, let it not be once named among you, as becometh saints;*

4 *Neither filthiness, nor foolish talking, nor jesting, which are not convenient: but rather giving of thanks.*

5 *For this ye know, that no whoremonger, nor unclean person, nor covetous man, who is an idolator, hath any inheritance in the kingdom of Christ and of God.*

6 *Let no man deceive you with vain words: for because of these things cometh the wrath of God upon the children of disobedience.*

7 *Be not ye therefore partakers with them.*

8 *For ye were sometimes darkness, but now are ye light in the Lord: walk as children of light:*

9 *(For the fruit of the Spirit is in all goodness and righteousness and truth;)*

10 *Proving what is acceptable unto the Lord.*

11 *And have no fellowship with the unfruitful works of darkness, but rather reprove them.*

12 *For it is a shame even to speak of those things which are done of them in secret.*

13 *But all things that are reproved are made manifest by the light: for whatsoever doth make manifest is light.*

14 *Wherefore he saith, Awake thou that sleepest, and arise from the dead, and Christ shall give thee light.*

15 *See then that ye walk circumspectly, not as fools, but as wise,*

16 *Redeeming the time, because the days are evil.*

17 *Wherefore be ye not unwise, but understanding what the will of the Lord is.*

I

Practice Rooted in Doctrine

'This I say therefore, and testify in the Lord, that ye henceforth walk not as other Gentiles walk . . .'

Ephesians 4:17

We come here to a fresh division in Ephesians, and reach a very important junction, because this is actually the last great division in the Epistle. Paul begins in verse 17 what will continue as a section right to the end of his letter. Therefore it is a most important turning-point, and that makes it necessary that we should understand exactly what it is he is going to do and why he is doing it. It is important, therefore, at this particular juncture that we should be clear about the connections, and have in our minds a general view, a kind of general conspectus of the Epistle as a whole.

The Apostle has laid down his great doctrine in the first three chapters, and then, having done that, he follows on with his appeal and exhortation to us, to realise that we are members of the body of Christ, and that, therefore, our first concern and consideration should be to endeavour to keep the unity of the Spirit in the bond of peace at all times. He has helped us to do this by reminding us again of the doctrine of the nature of the Church; and in particular he has pointed out to us how the Lord Jesus Christ Himself, the Head of the Church, when He ascended up on high, appointed offices in the Church and people to fill those offices, and He has gone on doing so, in order that we might be so instructed and led and exhorted as to preserve this great goal ever in our minds (Ephesians 4:8, 11). We have not merely been saved that we might escape hell; we have been saved in order that God may present a people which will astonish the whole world.

You remember how he said in the tenth verse of the third chapter, 'to the intent that now unto the principalities and powers in heavenly places might be known *by the church* the manifold wisdom of God'. So that more and more we must think of ourselves not in a kind of atomistic or individualistic manner, but rather as parts of the church, as members of the body of Christ, and our supreme ambition should ever to be grow up into Him in all things who is the Head, that together we may attain unto a perfect man, unto the measure of the stature of the fulness of Christ.

This, then, is what the Apostle has been saying, and he has pointed out that, in view of the provision that has been made – not only by the instruction through pastors and teachers, but also by this life that flows from the Head, through the bands and the joints of communication, into every part according to its measure and its capacity – we really are left without any excuse at all if we fail.

In the seventeenth verse of chapter 4, to which we now turn, Paul comes to the practical outworking of all his earlier teaching. He starts off again with the word *therefore* – 'This I say *therefore*', in the light of all that has gone before. And the question, in the light of all that has gone before, is, *how* are we to grow up into Christ in all things? How are we to arrive unto this perfect man? How are we to maintain the unity of the Spirit in the bond of peace? From this verse to the end of the Epistle, Paul gives us his answer, and that in a very practical and detailed manner. Therefore it seems to me that it might be a good and a helpful thing if, at this point, I give a general analysis of the remainder of the Epistle, so that we shall see the scheme; and then we shall have to come to the various component parts and work them out. This is always a very good way of proceeding with Scripture. Incidentally, it is a very good way of proceeding with whatever problem may be confronting us. Physicians and clinicians and others who have been trained in the medical profession will tell you – at least, it used to be so when medicine was perhaps more clinical and less scientific, in a sense, than it is now, and less dependent upon mechanical aids and devices – that the old physicians, the old clinicians, always taught that the first thing a doctor must do with a patient is to look at him as a whole; he must not rush at once to the particular complaint, but must take a general view, and not until he has done so must he come to the particular. It is the same with a problem in mathematics, for example, or in chemistry. If you are trying to discover, by an analysis of a particular substance, what particular chemicals there are in a mass that is put before you, you apply your general tests first, excluding certain big groups before you come to a particular analysis within the groups. And it is exactly the same with respect to the Scriptures. So I suggest that it is good and wise for us, at this point, to take a general view of the remainder of this Epistle.

Here, it seems to me, is the division. In this fourth chapter, from verse 17 to verse 24, Paul tells us that we must realise that we are entirely new creatures in Christ. In moving on to matters of practical conduct and behaviour, he starts by saying, 'This I say therefore, and testify in the Lord, that you henceforth walk not as other Gentiles walk'; 'but rather', as he says later, 'that you put off the old man and put on the new man'. In other words, as Christian people we must realise that in Christ we are *entirely* new creatures. Having said that, in verses 25 to 29 he points out the obvious implication of that in practice, with practical illustrations. Notice the logic with which he does it: he says, 'Therefore' – to connect your practice, then, in the light of the doctrine – 'Wherefore'. If you have not realised the importance of the *therefores* and the *wherefores* in the writings of the Apostle Paul you do not know him at all – 'wherefore, putting away lying' – having put off the old man and put on the new, you put away lying – 'speak every man truth with his neighbour. Be ye angry, and sin not; let not the sun go down on your wrath', and so on. So the pattern is, doctrine first, followed by obvious, practical implications worked out in detail. Then in verse 30 Paul goes back again to doctrine. 'Grieve not,' he says, 'the Holy Spirit of God whereby ye are sealed unto the day of redemption'! In other words, we must always remember that the Holy Spirit dwells within us. The Apostle is talking about practical, day-to-day conduct, and has begun by putting down as his first reminder,

[13]

the fact that we are entirely new; the second follows quickly. 'Never forget', he says, 'that the Holy Spirit of God *dwells* within you' (verse 30), 'and because of that' (verses 31, 32) it is obvious, he says, that we must avoid anything and everything that will grieve the Holy Spirit that is within us. Therefore 'let all bitterness, and wrath, and anger, and clamour, and evil speaking, be put away from you, with all malice', and 'be kind one to another, tender-hearted, forgiving one another'. Why? Because if you do not you are grieving the Holy Spirit.

Then we come to chapter 5, verses 1 and 2. Never forget, Paul says, that Christ died to make you a child of God. You are dear children of God, because Christ hath 'loved us, and hath given himself for us an offering and a sacrifice to God for a sweetsmelling savour'. Doctrine again! And because of that doctrine, you and I must live in such a way as to be constantly manifesting its truth. So he gives again his practical illustrations: 'Fornication and all uncleanness, and covetousness, let it not be once named among you, as becometh saints'! Christ has died to make us saints. He so loved us that He *died* for us in order to present us to God as saints. Therefore, get rid of these ugly things. 'Neither filthiness, nor foolish talking, nor jesting, which are not convenient: but rather giving of thanks.' It follows, Paul says, of necessity, from the doctrine. But he works it out for us in practical details. In verses 6 to 17 of chapter 5 the Apostle does an interesting thing. He has been laying down doctrine, drawing out the practical implications. He now feels he must pause for a moment, as it were, and just drive his points home. He realised that it was very necessary for him to do so, because of certain false teachers that were visiting the churches – Antinomians, such as the Nicolaitans that are spoken of in the book of Revelation, men who had completely misunderstood the gospel and who were virtually teaching, Let us do evil that good may come; men who were turning the grace of God into a kind of excuse to do what you like and sin as you like. The Apostle says, therefore, 'Let no man deceive you with vain words', and he is so concerned about this and so alarmed for the future of the church at Ephesus that he devotes considerable space to it (verses 6–17). He warns the Ephesians against all false and specious arguments that would keep them from the practice of the Christian life, and enforces his warning by another positive statement of the truth concerning Christian men in Christ. Then he goes back again to the practicalities – that was a sort of digression, driving it home, clinching it as it were, making sure of it; he always does that.

In verses 18 to 21 the Apostle lays down another great principle of doctrine, namely, that we must always remind ourselves that our lives are to be lived in the Spirit and fully under the control of the Spirit. 'Be not drunk with wine, wherein is excess; but be filled with the Spirit, speaking to yourselves in psalms and hymns and spiritual songs, singing and making melody in your hearts to the Lord; giving thanks always, for all things, unto God and the Father, in the name of our Lord Jesus Christ.' The life of the Christian is to be a life entirely under the control of the Spirit, filled with the Spirit, controlled, dominated by the Spirit. This, clearly, is doctrine. Then from verse 22 to verse 9 of chapter 6 he applies it. Having laid down this truth that the Christian is a man living his life in the Spirit and filled with the Spirit, he then shows that, obviously, this again is something that must be worked out in practice; it must govern all our relationships. So he takes up the relationships between wives and husbands, and husbands and wives; children and parents, and parents and children; servants and masters, and masters and servants. Notice how in each case in all these sub-divisions he has the appropriate doctrine; he picks out the aspect of the general doctrine that is particularly relevant. And so, when he is dealing with the life in the Spirit it is these human personal relationships – husband, wife; children, parents; masters, servants – that he brings to view.

In the final section of the Epistle, from verse 10 to verse 20 in chapter 6, Paul says in effect, There is the programme, that is the sort of life you have got to live. Do you think that it is easy? Whatever you may think, he continues, it is not easy. You need strength infinitely greater than your own. There is a powerful adversary: 'We wrestle not against flesh and blood, but against principalities, against powers, against the rulers of the darkness of this world, against spiritual wickedness in high places.' There is a mighty antagonist who will do everything he can to keep us from this programme. Why? In order to ridicule the work of God and the grace of the Lord Jesus Christ. If Satan can make any Christian, or even the whole church fall into sin, how happy he is! So he will attack you, says Paul, at every particular point; and if you do not realise that, you are already defeated. There is only one way in which to act: 'Put on the whole armour of God.' God, he says, has made provision; God does not call us to fulfil a programme and then leave us to ourselves. Not at all! He has already provided for us perfectly, in great detail. So we find in chapter 6, from verse 10 to verse 20, a description of God's provision for the Christian in this fight of faith – the whole armour of God! And having said that, Paul ends, as is his custom, with personal salutations and words of remembrance.

There, then, is the analysis of the last section of this wonderful Epistle to the Ephesians. We have found that the Epistle can be divided into three main sections: first, chapters 1, 2 and 3, where Paul lays down the great doctrine of salvation; then, next, in chapter 4, verses 1 to 16, we find the doctrine of the Church and all that brings us into the Church; following that, in the third section, we have the outworking of the doctrines in our daily lives and conduct and experience, and in all the contacts of life. What a wonderful scheme it is, and how the Apostle works each section out in detail so that there shall be no room for mistakes!

Let us now look briefly at the general character of this last section, because, quite apart from the detailed teaching, there are certain principles taught here, which are of very great importance. We shall go wrong in our detailed application unless we approach it in the right way in terms of the principles that are obviously implied by the Apostle's whole method.

The first thing that we must of necessity notice is that the Apostle Paul never leaves anything to chance. He is a careful teacher and he is never content with the mere enunciation of principles. He always does that first, but he never stops at that, he never leaves it at that. He invariably applies his teaching. I could expand that almost endlessly. There is a school of Bible teaching which makes no attempt to apply the teaching. To me this is a contradiction of the Scriptures. One has no right simply to divide up this Word of God and leave it, saying, as it were, I am lecturing now and not preaching. It is a travesty of the use of the Word of God. This Word is always to be applied, and any intellectual understanding we may have of the Scripture could be a snare to us if we fail to do so. The Apostle compels us to apply it. And we have no right to look at the application simply as a general heading and say, There Paul is applying his doctrine, so let us move on to the next Epistle. Not at all! He means us to face up to every single detail; he compels us to do so by the detailed application of the truth.

Paul does this, of course, so that there is no excuse, as I have said, for failure. And that applies to us, not only in general, but in particular. You and I must apply what we know in detail. The Christian life is not a mere general philosophy; it is that, but it does not stop at that! It is a life to be lived, and it is a life that is to be lived in *particular details*. And if our Christian life is not being lived out in details, we are denying the very truth that we claim to believe. This can never be enforced too strongly. The whole purpose of this section is to show that very thing. Our Lord Himself stated this once and for ever when He said – to me, some of the most terrifying words in the whole of Scripture – 'If ye know these things, happy are ye if ye do them' (John 13:17). And let us never forget that it is according to the measure of what we have that it shall be given to us. 'Whosoever *hath*, to him shall be given, and he shall have more abundance' (Matthew 13:12; 25:29). Let us also remember that *to know* is a tremendous responsibility. James makes a very strong point of this when he says at the beginning of his third chapter, 'My brethren, be not many masters, knowing that we shall receive the greater condemnation.' *To know* is a great responsibility, because if we know without applying it, we shall have to answer for it. Our Lord again teaches this plainly and clearly, when He talks about the master coming back and investigating the conduct of his servants during his absence: He says that some are going to be beaten with many stripes, and some with few stripes. And the servants who will be beaten with many stripes are those to whom much has been given! Therefore, I say, if we have been grasping and revelling in the doctrine of this Epistle, our responsibility is enormous. We are to APPLY the truth. 'This I say, therefore.' And notice how he drives it home by saying, 'and testify in the Lord' – calling the Lord as my witness, is what he means. The truth is to be applied, and nothing must be left to chance, we must not stop at generalities; the application must come down to every detail of our lives.

At this point we come to a second principle. The life of the church and life in the church is not to be a detached kind of life. In other words, all we do and all we say is a part of our Christian life and living. Our lives outside the church and inside the church are essentially one and must always be inter-related, for one affects the other. There is nothing more fatal than to have a kind of break or gap or sudden change between life in the church and life outside the church. The man on the street really says that this is the reason why he is on the street today and not in the church. I am not saying whether he is right or wrong, but what he does maintain is that that was the position of our Victorian grand-fathers. Look at them, he says, in their churches and chapels on Sunday; but then look at them from Monday to Saturday outside. Look at the devotion and the reverence and the apparent god-liness on Sunday; look at them in the mart and in the shop and amongst men, and they are different men. Well, if that was true, and if it is true still, it is a valid criticism.

Alas! one finds this tendency sometimes in the present-day Church. There are men who, as it were, suddenly have to pull themselves up and put on a kind of uniform or mask, and suddenly become serious, who normally are frivolous. They seem to be two different men: they are one thing out on the street, then they cross the threshold of a particular building and suddenly they become serious and solemn. That is the kind of behaviour that the Apostle is denouncing. We are to be as reverential outside as inside; our lives are not to be determined by buildings. The life of the Christian is *one*, he is a new man! He is not a man who simply puts on a different suit of clothes when he comes to church and shortly takes it off again, or picks up religion like a bag and puts it down a little later. Not at all! He *is* something; and because he *is* this something, he is this something not only in the church

[18]

but wherever he is, in the market, in the shop, in the business, in the profession, in the home, living with his neighbours next door, everywhere. Of course! The whole doctrine proves that the Spirit is in this *new* man in Christ Jesus. The Spirit is not only in the man when he is in the church, the Spirit is in him when he is on the road, everywhere. There must be no sudden break between what we are outside and what we are inside the church. It is one. There is a glorious unity about this life.

But we must move on to consider the third principle. And here again we find it – the constant linking of doctrine and practice. We saw it in our analysis of this great section of the Epistle. We saw the alternative passages of doctrine and application, doctrine and application. I am not trying to press some artificial interest here; all I have done is to give you an exposition, an analysis, of what the Apostle says – it is his method. To me it is astounding that people can ever miss this. Here we find Paul turning to the practical section of his Epistle, and you might have said, Ah, there will be no more doctrine now at any rate; you have been keeping us to the doctrine for a very long time, but at last we have finished with doctrine; thank God, we have become practical at last. But, no, you cannot get away from it. He brings you back to it every time. Doctrine followed by practice is the distinct characteristic of his method. Even here in verse 17 – 'I say therefore . . . you must not walk as other Gentiles walk.' You and I would have stopped there probably. We would have thought that was enough. Not so Paul! He is bound to tell you about that walk of the Gentiles – 'in the vanity of their mind, having the understanding darkened, being alienated from the life of God', and immediately he is in the midst of his doctrine again, and he remains in it to the end of verse 24. Then he comes to its practical application in detail. Oh! doctrine and practice are so intimately related and connected that they must never be divided; Paul cannot deal even with the most practical matters except in the light of doctrine.

Now I want to subdivide this truth in this way. Our conduct must always arise from and be dictated by and controlled by our doctrine. In other words, the Christian life is not a code which is imposed upon us and which we do not understand. But I am afraid that that is done, and done today, even in evangelical circles. People come under the sound of the gospel and are converted. Then they are given a kind of code, and they try to practice it; they do not know why, and they do not understand the reason for it. I cannot be bothered, they say, with doctrine, I am not that sort of person; and often the people who are leading them may say the same thing. They try to conform to the code, as men do in other walks of life; but they do not understand why, and they are often very miserable and unhappy. They get bogged down in details, and there is a great fight going on within them. Sometimes they even have a nervous breakdown – I have had to deal with many such people. And it is all because they have never had doctrine. They have had a code. They are told that as a Christian, of course, you do not do this and you do not do that; but they do not know *why*, they do not see the *reason* for it. We must never leave people in such a position, never, it is very wrong. The Christian life is not a code that is imposed upon us. As it follows out of doctrine we must understand what we are doing and what we are not doing. Or, to put that still more plainly, we should never do things merely because other people are doing them; and we should not refrain from doing things simply because other people refrain from doing them. We must *understand why* we do them, or why we refrain. You are no more children, says Paul, you must learn, you must grow, you must have understanding!

I sum up the matter by putting it like this. Our conduct should always be to us something which is inevitable in view of what we believe. That is the way I like to think of it. If my Christian living is not quite *inevitable* to me, if I am always fighting against it and struggling and trying to get out of it, and wondering why it is so hard and narrow, if I find myself rather envying the people who are still back in the world, there is something *radically* wrong with my Christian life. Christian conduct and behaviour should be inevitable – there is no argument about it. And when we are in that position, we have really got the truth of the matter clearly.

Perhaps we shall find it helpful to draw a distinction between morality and Christian living. There is a great difference between the two. Morality is concerned about the goodness and the rightness of the thing done, in and of itself, and in terms of its social consequence. It asks, is it a good thing? is it a bad thing? what does it lead to? how does it affect other people? There is a sense in which morality is a very insulting thing to a human being, because, in the last analysis, it is not really interested in me, it is only interested in my behaviour. Ah, that is where Christianity is so different! Christianity is interested primarily in me; and it is interested in my conduct, not in and of itself and in terms of its social consequence; it is interested in my conduct and behaviour because of its interest in Christ, in God, in the church, in the plan of redemption, in the whole scheme of salvation, in the fact that God will, through the church, astound the principalities and powers in the heavenly places. Not conduct in itself, but conduct in terms of this vast scheme; God nullifying the effects of evil, destroying the works of the devil, and restoring and re-uniting in one all things in Christ. Christian conduct and behaviour always has a specifically Christian reference and it is only rightly viewed in terms of the grand purpose of redemption.

But we move on to another principle. Failure in the living of the Christian life, therefore, must ultimately result from a failure somewhere or other to understand the doctrine and the truth. That does not need any further demonstration. In the light of all I have been saying, if any one of us is failing at any point in conduct and behaviour, it is because we have not understood the doctrine. If there is anger and malice and hatred and bitterness, and an unforgiving spirit, in any of us, it is there because we do not realise that the Holy Spirit of God dwells within us, and that we are grieving Him. That is the doctrine! We cannot go on being like that if we comprehend the doctrine. It is failure to understand doctrine that causes failure in practice. Therefore – and I want to emphasise this – nothing is worse than to ignore doctrine and to talk about being practical. The biggest failures I know in the Christian life are the people who decry doctrine and say, I am a practical man, I am not interested in your theology, practice is everything with me. They, of all people, are the ones who fail most of all, as they must, because conduct is determined by doctrine and understanding. There is nothing, I repeat, that is more fatal than to say that you must contrast the practical with the doctrinal.

To put it another way, there is nothing that is so wrong and so unscriptural as to be making constant, direct appeals to the *will* without inculcating doctrine. The will is never to be approached directly; the will is to be approached through the mind and through the heart. So to appeal to people to take decisions and to come forward and receive something is a denial of the whole of the last section of this Epistle. It is utterly and absolutely wrong. You do not appeal to the *will* of people to make them holy; instead, you get them to understand the doctrine! It is not a matter of decision, it is a matter of understanding and outworking.

Therefore I do not hesitate to say that every method of teaching sanctification which is not based directly and immediately upon an understanding of doctrine, followed by an exhortation to us to apply that doctrine logically, is a false teaching of sanctification. The Bible teaches sanctification; the Apostle is teaching it here from this seventeenth verse to the end of the Epistle, and that is his method. But there are ways of teaching sanctification that by-pass completely the passage we have been studying. They do not pay any attention to it at all. You get sanctification for nothing, they say; you receive it as a gift; you do nothing. But the Apostle is exhorting us to work out in detail, logically, what we claim to believe, and to realise why we must inevitably do so if we really have understood and grasped the doctrine.

And that brings me to my final word, which is this. Our concern as Christian people should not just be a desire to be good, not a desire even to be better than we have been; it should not merely be a desire to get rid of certain sins and to stop at that, or to have happiness, or to have victory, even, in our lives: all that is too self-centred. And that is where, again, teachings of holiness go wrong. They say, Are you in trouble? – come to the clinic. Are you failing at any point? – come, we can put you right. The fact is, they are starting with *you*; *you* are everything. No, says Paul, that must not be your concern; that will follow. Our concern should be to function fully and perfectly as members of the body of Christ. What should worry me is not so much that *I* fail or that

I have got a problem in my life, but that I am failing *Him*, I am failing the *church*, I am failing *God* and His great and wonderful purpose. It is all too subjective and self-centred; we must see ourselves – the Apostle has given us this sixteenth verse to enable us to do so – as members in particular of the body of Christ. And that should be our concern, we are letting down GOD, as it were, and His glorious purpose; the church is being let down; Christ is being let down. He has *died* to make His people perfect and entire and whole, and here are we failing! Oh, if only we would look at it like that! So often I find that people are concerned about themselves and their particular sin; and they spend the whole time in praying to be delivered from this sin. Then I ask them, Have you considered it in terms of your relationship to Christ? have you ever considered it in terms of your membership of the Body of Christ? And they have not! They have been negative in their approach, and they go on in failure. We must be positive, our desire should be to show forth the praises of Him who has called us out of darkness into His marvellous light. Our desire, our objective, should be to show the glory of Christ and of His Church in this present world.

Let me put it in the words of our Lord Himself in the Sermon on the Mount: 'Let your light so shine before men, that they may see your good works' – and say what a wonderful person you are, how good and how holy? Not for a moment! 'Let your light so shine before men, that they may see *your* good works, and glorify your *Father* which is in heaven.' We are to live in such a way that people coming into contact with us will not understand us, will be puzzled by us, will feel that we are some sort of an enigma, and will be driven to say, Well, they are as they are because they belong to that Christ of whom they speak; they are different, they are new people. This personal reference is all-important. We must see it all in terms of our high calling, of our privileged position, of our being joined together to the Head in this wonderful Body, through these bands of supply. The life of the Head is flowing through us, so that as men and women look at us they should be compelled to think of Christ. We are followers of Him, we are imitators of Him, we are to be like Him. 'We are in this world,' says John, 'as He is', and as He was, and we are ever to live to the praise of the glory of His grace.

In these ways, then, the Apostle has put us on right lines, and, God willing, we shall follow him as he leads us through the particular applications of the one great, glorious and central truth.

2

The Emptiness of the Christless Life

'This I say therefore, and testify in the Lord, that ye
henceforth walk not as other Gentiles walk, in the
vanity of their mind, having the understanding
darkened, being alienated from the life of God
through the ignorance that is in them, because of the
blindness of their heart: who being past feeling have
given themselves over unto lasciviousness, to work
all uncleanness with greediness.'

Ephesians 4:17–19

We continue with our consideration of words to be found in
Paul's Epistle to the Ephesians, in the fourth chapter, verses 17,
18 and 19.

We shall concentrate now particularly on verse 17.

I would remind you that the particular matter here is, that as
Christians, we are entirely new men and women, that regeneration
is the profoundest change in the world, and that therefore we
must always keep this in the forefront of our minds. A Christian
is not just a man who has decided to be a little bit more moral
than he was, or who has decided to join a church, or who has
decided this or that, whatever it may be. What makes a man a
Christian is that he has been born again, he has been given a new
nature, he is a new creation, he is altogether different from what
he was before. That is the first principle which the Apostle takes
up in this section of the Epistle, and in this verse he is beginning
to apply it. Remember that truth about yourselves, he says, and as
you do so, you will find that certain things are quite unthinkable;
they are impossible, and you will never look at them again,
because you now see so clearly that you have been separated once
and for ever from all that you were before.

But now let us look at the matter in the exact words which the Apostle himself uses. He begins by addressing them in a most solemn manner. He wants to call attention to something that is of vital importance to them. 'This I say therefore, and testify in the Lord.' He is not content with saying 'This I say therefore'; that would be strong, but he adds to it – 'This I say therefore, and *testify* in the Lord.' What does he mean by this word *testify*? The word really means *solemnly to enjoin*. It is as though he were invoking a witness. When you give a testimony you are bearing witness to something. A man is put into the witness-box and he testifies. And that is exactly what the Apostle is saying. He is anxious that they should not think for a moment that he is merely stating his own personal opinion, for there were people then (as there are now) who were only too ready to say, That is only *Paul's* opinion; that is what *Paul* thinks. You must not say that, says the Apostle; this is not just a personal foible of my own, it is not just something that I, because I happen to have a narrow mind, am saying or am thinking; it is not said because I was a Pharisee and trained in the law. Not at all! It is not merely I who am speaking, 'I say therefore, and *testify in the Lord*.'

By that expression '*in the Lord*' he does not mean so much that he is invoking the Lord as his witness although you do find that sometimes in the Scripture – 'As God is my witness', a person says, or 'In the presence of God'. But here it does not mean exactly that, although the idea is probably present. Surely what Paul means is that he is testifying to this as one who is *in* the Lord; he is one who is in communion with the Lord, he is delivering therefore what is a definitely authenticated commission; he is one who is daring to say that he is speaking as one who has access to the mind of the Lord. You remember how in his First Epistle to the Corinthians in the seventh chapter, he draws that kind of distinction; at a given point he says, Now this is what *I* think, I have not the mind of the Lord here. He was expressing his own personal opinion, and when it is Paul's own opinion he tells us plainly that it is so. But when he does not speak in that way, he is speaking *in the Lord*. In other words he is speaking with the full authority of an Apostle. Not only was the great and glorious doctrine revealed to him, as he tells us in the third chapter of our Epistle, but these details about conduct were also revealed to him; they have the same apostolic authority, the same divine authority, therefore, as have his expositions of the doctrines. Here, then, he is speaking as one who has been clothed with the unique authority that belonged to the apostles. Christians are built upon the foundation of the apostles and prophets. Christ gave these apostles to the church, and when they spoke and taught they spoke with a unique authority, their words were definitely inspired, they have the authority of God. 'I testify,' he says, '*in the Lord.*'

To what, then, is he testifying? What is this injunction which he puts to them in such a solemn manner, having arrested their attention, and having made them realise that they are listening to the word of the living God? You notice that he puts what he has got to say, first of all negatively. 'This I say therefore, and testify in the Lord, that ye henceforth walk *not*. . . .' We are so busy today, are we not, that we do not like negatives, we have not really got time for negatives, we want the positive truth and we do not like criticisms of that which is wrong. We must always be positive! Do you see the utter folly of such idle, vacant talk? Here is the divine authority speaking through the Apostle, and the first thing we have is *negative*, NOT! It is not enough to tell men and women, in a world like this and in the flesh, simply what they are to do. We all know perfectly well how inadequate that is. We must be taught first and foremost what we are not to be and not to do. The idea that if you just hold the ideal before men, they will at once conform to it, has been so completely disproved by the history of the human race, that it is almost incredible that anybody should still believe it. Here we are told first of all what we must not do. What is that?

'You must not,' Paul says, 'walk as the other Gentiles do.' The very words are wonderful; each one really is conveying some important meaning to us. Take the word *walk*, for instance: 'that ye henceforth *walk* not as the other Gentiles *walk.*' This refers to the whole life and conversation. Often in the Authorised Version you will find the word translated as *conversation* – 'only let your *conversation* be as becometh the gospel of Christ', says this same Apostle to the Philippians. He says 'our *conversation* is in heaven'.

[27]

He means the whole life, the general tenor of the life, and at the same time the life in detail. The *walk*, as used in Scripture, means the whole of a man's life, inward and outward. We must remember that our *walk* is not confined to the outward, it involves the inward also. This is important and I shall be stressing it later, because, according to this whole argument, what determines the outward is the inward. A man is as he thinks, and his walk in life tells you what he is thinking, because his walk is an expression of his philosophy.

We next meet with the significant word, '*henceforth* ...', meaning 'from now on' or *no longer*. Here at once Paul is introducing us to his doctrine. I am telling you, he says, and testifying in the Lord that you must *no longer* walk as the Gentiles do. You see the implication – you once did walk like that, but you are to do so no longer. Why? Because of the tremendous change that has taken place in you. So in a sense, the word *henceforth* contains the whole of the gospel. *Henceforth* tells us this: there is the past, that is what they once were, there is the unregenerate life; but *henceforth!* – something has happened; now there is the future and it is going to be altogether different. Immediately, you see, we are told what a profound change regeneration produces, how the Christian man is indeed a new man; old things are passed away, behold, all things are become new.

Then consider Paul's next phrase: 'that ye henceforth walk not' – as it reads in the Authorised Version – 'as *other Gentiles* walk'. But you will find that the Revised Versions at this point do not have the word *other*, but, 'that ye no longer walk as *the Gentiles* walk'. Well, this is purely a matter of documents, and it seems that the oldest and most authoritative documents have not got the *other*. It does not make the slightest difference, because in any case what Paul is saying is this: You Christians of Ephesus must no longer walk as the Gentiles walk, though you are Gentiles, and you did once walk like them. The translators of the Authorised Version have certainly grasped the point and they have also caught the spirit of the expression. What the Apostle is really saying is this: Look here, you are Gentile Christians, but as Christians you do not any longer walk as the *other* Gentiles walk. At this juncture, therefore, the Gentiles can be divided into two groups – the Gentiles who have become Christians, and those

[28]

who have remained where they were, the *other* Gentiles, the non-Christian Gentiles. So whether we take it as *the Gentiles* in general, or *the other Gentiles*, it is referring to exactly the same thing. But the word *other* certainly helps to bring out the tremendous change that has taken place. In other words, by every word that he is using, Paul is enforcing upon the minds of these Ephesian Christians that they are no longer what they once were. And this is the place where they rise up and praise God and sing their anthems. 'Whereas I was once blind, now I see'! – henceforth! no longer! Thank God for a gospel that enables us to speak like that and to say, Henceforth we have a new beginning, a new start, a new life!

What then are we no longer to do? What are we to refrain from? The Apostle here tells us how the Gentiles, the *other* Gentiles, still walk, and he puts it in the tremendous phrase, *'in the vanity of their mind'*. This is the phrase that introduces the terrible description which the Apostle gives here of the life of the unregenerate, the life of the pagan world at that time. It is, I say, a tremendous and a terrible description. We cannot read it without being reminded immediately of what Paul said at the beginning of the second chapter: 'You hath he quickened who were' – *were*, once upon a time, before the Gospel came to you, you *were* – 'dead in trespasses and sins, wherein in time past' – you see how he goes on repeating it – 'ye walked according to the course of this world, according to the prince of the power of the air, the spirit that now worketh in the children of disobedience; among whom also we all had our conversation in times past in the lusts of our flesh, fulfilling the desires of the flesh and of the mind; and were by nature the children of wrath, even as others.' Is he then just repeating himself? No, he is not. There is a sense, of course, in which he is, but there is a marked difference between what he says at the beginning of the second chapter and what he says here. And the difference is this. In the second chapter he is giving an objective description of the life of the unregenerate Gentiles, the life of the pagan world. Here he gives an inward or psychological analysis of it. Chapter 2, general description: here, dissection, analysis, exposure, showing us the source and the fount of it all. There is no more profound analysis anywhere of the unregenerate life than that which we find here. And as I say that, I have in my mind that other tremendous passage in the Epistle to the Romans, chapter 1:18–32, which is another of Paul's masterly, profound analyses of the life and outlook of the pagan world of his time. Read it, read every one of these passages. There is yet another in 1 Corinthians 6:9–11, and similar analyses are to be found in the Acts of the Apostles, chapters 14 and 17. They are all full of importance and of significance. Here it is that we find the most masterly descriptions of life without Christ that can ever be encountered. And here it is really all contained in one phrase: 'in the vanity of their mind'.

I am emphasising this matter, not because it is a matter of theoretical or academic interest, not because I am interested in the psychology of human nature and of behaviour. They are fascinating themes, I agree, but I am not calling your attention to them because I am animated by some theoretical interest like that. Still less am I moved by some kind of antiquarian interest in those ancient times, fascinating though such a study may be. Anthropology, as it is called, leads us back to a study of conduct and behaviour, to the investigation of civilisations and what has happened to them; and from the purely intellectual standpoint there is nothing more captivating and thrilling. But I am not pausing at this point because I am animated by any such motives or ideas. The reason why I am so urgent about this and why I am holding your attention to it, is because it seems to me that here we have a perfect description, analysis and explanation of what is increasingly becoming true of life in the modern world in which we are living. The principles which the Apostle teaches here are always true, and I suggest that our world is becoming more and more what it is for the reason given here, and because of the failure of modern man to realise the truth of it. So as we read his words, we are not simply looking at pagan society in Ephesus nearly two thousand years ago; we are also looking at London today, Paris, New York, any one of them; here is modern life, here is the modern world.

These things do not change. They are eternal principles. And therefore, if we are really concerned about the life of society and about the world, the first thing we must do is to understand the Apostle's teaching. We evangelicals are constantly being charged with not being practical. Ah, they say, there you are, you spend your time in discussing the Scriptures and talking to one another; but as for the great world outside, you do nothing about it. What I am emphasising here, therefore, is that we can do nothing until we begin to understand the teaching of Scripture. It is this alone that enables one to do anything about it. And all organisations that do not start from this, not only are failing and have failed, but must inevitably fail. That is the tragedy about purely *moral* societies. They have existed now, some of them, for nearly a hundred years, and yet in spite of their activities the position goes from bad to worse. Why? Because they have forgotten these apostolic principles.

In this Epistle the Apostle shows us the origin of the evil kind of life that he describes. Before he describes the life in detail he shows us why it is that anybody should ever live such a life. Or in other words, what the Apostle is asserting here is that you cannot have morality without godliness. There in a phrase, it seems to me, I have indicated the whole trouble during the last fifty years in particular. There are good people in the land who are very much concerned about morality; but they are not concerned about godliness. You simply cannot have morality, finally, without godliness. And the last half century has proved that to the very hilt. If we go back a hundred years and more we find that the great emphasis was upon godliness, and that the morality came out of the godliness. But then a generation came which said in effect, Morality is very good and it is most essential for the country, but of course we do not want this godliness any longer; we no longer believe in the supernatural, we do not believe in miracles, we do not believe that Christ is the Son of God – He was no more than a great moral teacher – and so, of course, we must shed all this godly part of it. And they did so. They thought they could preserve the morality without the godliness. But you see what has happened. Though you have got education and everything you can provide, if there is not godliness at the back of it your morality will collapse. And the modern world is just an illustration of that truth. In other words the Apostle is here concerned, not only with the fact that the Gentiles lived in a certain way, he is much more concerned with the reason why they did so. And that is still the position with us. All good, thinking, decent people must be alarmed at what is happening in this country. The slow but steady decline in morals must be evident to all. And clearly, decent-living people are tremendously concerned about the matter. But here is the great and inevitable question: Why is this happening, and what can be done about it?

Now the most futile and foolish thing of all is merely to denounce the evil. That is the simple and easy thing to do, as we meet it in the streets and in our newspapers; just to feel a sense of disgust, to turn away and say, How horrible! how terrible! Obviously that is not going to help anybody. The business of the gospel is not simply to denounce; it is not simply to restrain. The business of the gospel is to deal with the situation in the only way in which it can be dealt with radically, and that is, to preach the gospel of regeneration, this power of God unto salvation, that can deal even with this seemingly hopeless situation and insoluble problem. That is the whole story of the New Testament. There, then, is our over-riding reason for pausing at this point and going into the matter so carefully. This is the only hope for society. And let men do what they will, let them multiply their educational and moral and social organisations, they will not touch the problem. You can have your teetotal organisations, your morality crusades, and your moral councils, and a thousand other things, and you will not touch the situation. The evil involved is in the *heart* of men, and it is only a message that can deal with the *heart* of men that is adequate to meet the problem. What, then, does the Apostle Paul say about it? Let us follow his line of thought.

He divides the matter up into three sections. In verse 17 he makes a general statement about the condition of men – '*the vanity of their mind*'. In verse 18 he tells us the cause of the vanity. In verse 19 he gives us the consequence of the vanity. First, then, we must look at the general state and condition as he describes it: Here it is, 'that ye henceforth walk not as other Gentiles walk, in the vanity of their mind'. What does he mean by this? What does he mean by the *mind*? It is important that we should be clear about this because our first instinct would be to regard it as a description of the intellect. But he does not refer to the intellect only, for he makes reference to the intellect in the next verse (18), where he talks about the *understanding* being darkened. So when he says 'mind' here, he is not thinking of the intellect and the understanding only. 'Mind' here means something much bigger. It means the mind with its emotional capabilities included. It means thought, will, and susceptibilities. It means reason, understanding, conscience, affections. Indeed, it means the whole soul of man. In many other places in Scripture the term *mind* is used in this sense, as descriptive of the whole soul of man: intellect, affections, conscience, will, the entire personality. To put it another way, it means the Gentiles' entire outlook upon life, their whole reaction to it and their way, therefore, of living their lives.

The mind! The total personality! Paul tells us that these other Gentiles walk in the *vanity of their mind*. To understand what he means by vanity let me give you some alternative terms – what it really means is *emptiness* – emptiness! The Revised Standard Version translated it well: 'in the *futility* of their mind'. Utterly empty, absolutely futile! Indeed the word the Apostle actually uses, in its origin, means that which does not lead to the goal. It means, therefore, something which is aimless, pointless, lacking direction, it does not bring you to any goal, and of course it leads in the end to utter futility, to that which is absolutely empty. That, then, is his description in general of the life of the pagan Gentile world. But what a description that is too of the modern world, what a description of what so many regard as real life today! The life of London, especially in its highest circles! Life! Here it is, they say. The Apostle says it is empty, futile, aimless, utterly vain. Is he right?

We can certainly justify his description of that ancient world, so let us now apply it to the life of today and we shall see that it is equally true, and a perfect description of modern life apart from Christ. It is a life that leads nowhere, it never gives real satisfaction. Look at the ancient world. Ah, but you say, what about the great philosophers? Yes, let us be fair, let us look at them! In a life of darkness, there may be an occasional flash. In the darkness of their times, these great philosophers must have seemed like a flash of light. But did the flash lead to anything? They talked in a very learned manner about truth and goodness and beauty. These were their favourite themes – the search for truth, the search for goodness, the search for beauty. Goodness, beauty, and truth! These wonderful flashes! But what did they lead to? That is the question the Apostle is asking. What is the aim, what is the goal, what is the objective? Did they bring the people to any desired goal? Paul says No – they were pointless, futile, and aimless. But is he right? Let us put this philosophy to the test. Where did it bring men in a religious sense? We see from Paul's description of the people in Athens in Acts 17 that they were very much concerned about religion, about the gods and about worship. They talked a great deal about the First Cause, and the Uncaused Cause; they were seeking for God, they put up their altars to 'The Unknown God'; they were looking for an explanation in a religious sense. But what did it lead to? Read even the secular accounts of those ancient times, and you will find that they absolutely confirm the Scriptures. A large majority of the people were atheists who did not believe in God at all; some were pantheists, that is to say, they believed God was in everything and that everything is God. Others were polytheists. They believed in a multiplicity of gods – Jupiter, Mars, Mercurius – you will find them mentioned in the Book of the Acts of the Apostles, and people built great temples to them, as Acts 17 reminds us. Paul says, As I walked round your great city I came to the conclusion that you are much too religious, your whole city is cluttered up with temples. Polytheism! Here they are, the great philosophers, these great men searching after God. Where does it all lead to? Futility! They do not know Him. 'Whom ye ignorantly worship,' said Paul to them, 'Him declare I unto you.' In the vanity of their mind, aimless, futile; it does not lead to anything in the religious sense in which they were so interested.

But what about it more generally, intellectually? The answer is the same. They had no satisfaction whatsoever. They had no real understanding of men and of life and of the purpose of life in this world. They were very interested in history, and the problem of history, but they viewed it in terms of cycles. History, they said, just goes round and round in cycles, there is no advance, no direction, no goal; in your intention, perhaps, you seem to be going up, as it were, but you soon find that you are going down. In other words, events go round and round in a perpetual circuit. Such was their view of history; they had never had the biblical conception of this 'one far-off divine event, to which the whole creation moves'! Ecclesiastes, chapter 1, expresses it all so perfectly: 'Vanity of vanities'; 'the thing that hath been, it is that which shall be'. 'All the rivers run into the sea; yet the sea is not full'; why? Its waters are absorbed by the sun, formed into clouds and rained back into the rivers again – 'unto the place from whence the rivers come, thither they return again'. Just another example of the cycle that is history.

And then, what about death? what was their view of death? These great philosophers, had they any view of death? To many of them death was merely the end; the grave was the last word. Others believed in what they call the transmigration of souls, a series of reincarnations. Others held the view that the state of man beyond death was elusive, vague, indefinite and shadowy. Read Greek mythology and you will see what I mean. There they are, as it were, endlessly going about in a kind of gloom and darkness, without light, with all their passions still within them. Unhappiness! That was their idea of death, and of any life that might be beyond death and the grave.

What were they like morally? Complete failure here also! Read again the latter part of the first chapter of the Epistle to the Romans, and there you will find an account of life as lived in the moral sewers and gutters of the time with all the perversions and the foulness conceivable! Is it surprising that the Apostle describes it all as being vain and empty, futile and aimless? Furthermore, the leading philosophers were often the leaders in the immorality. Some of the greatest philosophers have praised the love of a man for a man as being beyond the love of men for women; they justified the perversions philosophically. Read them for yourselves. Before you listen to the modern philosophers who say we do not need Christ, and that Plato and Socrates and Aristotle are sufficient, just read them and you will find that they justify these perversions in that particular way. And the result of all this, of course, was that suicide increased, and continued to increase at an alarming rate.

[35]

So, in spite of all the flashes, the brilliant intellects, and all the interest in goodness, beauty and truth, life remained meaningless, vain, empty, futile. It is not only Solomon in the Book of Ecclesiastes who says this so many centuries before Christ. Go back again, I say, to Acts 17, look at the learned people in Athens – Stoics and Epicureans – men who met together to discuss these things. They met together, as we are told, 'to tell or to hear some new thing'. What's the latest? what's the latest craze, the latest fashion? – not merely in clothing, but in intellect, in thought, in ideas and in philosophy. They were always rushing after the latest and the last. What a confession of futility, what utter emptiness, a going round and round in circles, flashy, exciting, brilliant, but in the end, what? Nothing! No understanding of life; no knowledge of how to live; no understanding of death; nothing to cheer them beyond death and the grave! 'Let us eat, drink, and be merry, for tomorrow we die.' What is the use of anything! That was the life of the ancient pagan world.

In the Name of God I ask you, Is it not a strictly accurate description of life in this modern world without Christ? The television life! The cinema life! The drinking, gambling life! The life of society, high or low! And the apparent brilliance, marvel and show! But what is there in it? What is there for your soul? What is there for manhood? What does it tell you about life? What does it lead to? It leaves you at the end empty, indeed with nothing at all. Vanity! – 'in the vanity of their mind', empty, aimless, futile! In spite of our sophistication, in spite of the fact that nearly two thousand years have passed since these words were penned by Paul the Apostle, it is as true today as it has ever been. Let us see to it that we are not fooled and deluded by the gaudy show around us with all its talk about art, and with all its intellectual interest, and its sophistication – what is there in it? Look at its devotees. What have they? They have nothing. All is vain and empty. They talk about art for art's sake! Is that the way to solve the problem? Does that give direction? Does that build up the soul? Does that produce morality? Does that hold out hope for people who have failed and who have fallen? Of course it does not; they have nothing themselves, it is all make-belief. Life goes round and round, like a satellite, but it can stop at any moment, and civilisation can collapse as it has so often done in previous history. Life without Christ is always empty, it is always vain, it takes from you, it takes out of you, and it leaves you at the end the empty husk. It leaves you exhausted, with nothing to lean on, nothing to be proud of, and nothing whatsoever to look forward to.

Altogether then, the Apostle is saying, You are no longer to be controlled and influenced by an outlook and by a mentality like that. You who have been born again, are you looking back with longing eyes to that kind of life? Does the world appeal to you? Is that your conception of living? Out upon the suggestion, he says, it is utterly empty, futile, aimless and pointless. 'I say therefore, and testify in the Lord, that you henceforth walk not as the other Gentiles walk, in the vanity of their mind.' Thank God for ever having opened our eyes to that, to the world and all its glittering prizes. 'This,' says the Apostle John, 'is the victory that overcometh the world, even our faith.' It is faith, it is the gospel, that opens one's eyes to the vanity and futility of this world and its mind, its life, and its outlook. Thank God that in His infinite grace He has ever caused the beams of His Spirit to shine into our hearts and to give us an understanding. Thank God!

3
Darkness and Light

'This I say therefore, and testify in the Lord, that ye
henceforth walk not as other Gentiles walk, in the
vanity of their mind, having the understanding
darkened, being alienated from the life of God
through the ignorance that is in them, because of the
blindness of their heart: who being past feeling have
given themselves over unto lasciviousness, to work
all uncleanness with greediness.'

Ephesians 4:17-19

We have been considering the great Apostle's account of the kind
of life that was being lived by the Gentiles, those pagans who had
not become believers in and followers of our Lord Jesus Christ.
We have seen that it can be characterised in general as a life which
is walked in the vanity of their minds, an empty, useless, pointless
life that leads to nothing. It is like a bubble, and a bubble to look
at is very wonderful and attractive. Look at the perfect roundness
of it, look at the colours – all the colours of the rainbow – how
beautiful it is! And yet, suddenly it disappears, there is nothing
there; it is full of air, nothing else. That is the sort of life men and
women were living, the life of a bubble, with an apparent beauty,
an apparent charm and excitement, but with nothing in it; the
bubble bursts, and you are left empty-handed at the end with
nothing at all. *'In the vanity of their mind.'*

But Paul is not content with merely stating it in general. In
verses 18 and 19 he proceeds to analyse this, especially to show
why people come to live such a life. Very plainly and in detail he
shows us what it is that has ever produced such a mentality and
such an outlook. He gives us, we must agree, a most accurate
description of the life of the ancient, pagan world, and, as we

have seen, an equally accurate description of the life that is being lived by the vast majority of people today. And the question that must arise in our minds is, What is it that can account for the fact that anybody should live such a life, such a completely empty and vacant life, a life that promises so much and in the end gives nothing? What can account for the fact that a human being should ever be attracted by such a life and should ever want to live it?

The Apostle here supplies us with the answer. And again I must emphasise that I am calling attention to this, and following his analysis through carefully in detail, because what he says here is still the simple truth today. There can be no doubt at all that the reason why people live such a life is that they have never understood exactly what it is. The final masterpiece of Satan is to keep his serfs so busy that they have no time to think. And, as we shall see, even when they do stop to think, he prevents their thinking straightly and truly. Here then we have a picture of what unbelief really means. Here we have a masterly, intellectual and psychological analysis of the life of the unbeliever, the life of the person who is not a Christian. I defy anybody in any literature anywhere to produce such a masterly analysis as this; for profundity and clarity it is quite unequalled; and if you are interested in psychology, you will find it here. This section of the Epistle is just a psychological analysis.

What a condition! Listen to it again! 'Having the understanding darkened, being alienated from the life of God through the ignorance that is in them, because of the blindness of their heart.' Such is the condition, not only of the pagans of nearly two thousand years ago, it is an exact description and analysis of the condition of the clever, sophisticated people in this modern world who laugh at Christianity, who deride the Christian faith, and who boast of their knowledge and learning, their intellect and understanding. This is the truth about them. That is the amazing thing. Let us follow it out, let us see how it comes to pass that people who really pride themselves on their intellect and on their understanding are nevertheless really in the condition described here by the Apostle.

In this eighteenth verse there are four phrases, and each one of them is part of the description. But they seem to fall into two pairs. The first pair describes this condition in general; the second (and this is where we must be careful) the second pair explains the second phrase only of the first pair. Let us look at it in detail. What is the position of these people who walk in the vanity of their mind? The two chief things to be said about them, says the Apostle, are, firstly, that their understandings are darkened; secondly, they are alienated, they are estranged, from the life of God. And then he immediately tells us why they are estranged from the life of God. It is because, firstly, they are alienated from the life of God through, or because of, the ignorance that is in them; and secondly, because of the blindness, or rather the hardness, of their heart. So the second pair of clauses really gives us an account of, and the explanation of their estrangement from God; and yet in a very wonderful way the last two are also connected with the first. Why is it that these people are ignorant? why is it that their hearts are hardened? The answer is, because their understandings are darkened! So this, then, is the order: because their understandings are darkened they are full of ignorance, their hearts are hardened, and those two things in turn lead to their estrangement from God. The classification is of some importance, because if we said that the second two clarified and explained the first two, we should be saying something that is quite wrong. We must never say that their understandings are darkened because of the ignorance that is in them. That is putting it the wrong way round. They are ignorant because their understandings are darkened. So that is the fundamental statement: the darkening of the understanding leads to ignorance, to hardening of the heart, and these two obviously lead to an estrangement from the life of God. Let us look then at this description of the non-Christian and see exactly what it amounts to.

Shakespeare also knew something about this vain, empty, aimless life. He writes about a kind of person who spends the whole of his time in 'seeking the bubble reputation' and who is ready to seek it 'even in the cannon's mouth'. In this vain world, there are many who are always seeking some kind of reputation – a reputation for knowledge, for wit, for some kind of artistic or executive ability, for courage and for bravery – 'seeking the

bubble reputation'. Always the bubble! – and men will seek it
even at great danger to themselves. Thus they live, because their
understandings are darkened; it is the only explanation. What,
then, does Paul mean by *understanding*? In this context he means
particularly the intellect. Earlier in dealing with the word *mind*
(verse 17), we pointed out that *mind* there is a comprehensive
term which includes not only the reason but the affections and
the conscience, the whole man, the whole soul's activity. Here,
however, *understanding* really does mean *understanding*; it means,
in other words, the intellect, as opposed to the feelings and the
sensibilities. I am amazed and full of admiration, at the perfection
of this analysis, and to see how Paul works it out in every section
of a man's life; he puts the whole first, then the component parts.
The understanding, the intellect, he says, is darkened in these
people; their intellects are blinded. And what a terrible thing
this is! A kind of pall has descended upon and is covering the
minds of all people who are not Christian.

This is a great theme with this Apostle, as it is indeed of the
whole Bible. Notice how he puts it to the Corinthians in the
third chapter of his second Epistle to them, where he is comparing
and contrasting the Jews who remain unconverted with the Jews
who have become Christians. He says that the trouble with the
unconverted man, whether he is Jew or Gentile, is that there is a
veil over his heart and over his mind and understanding; he
cannot see. And the result is, adds the Apostle, that even when
the Jew listens to the reading of the Old Testament Scriptures as
he does every Sabbath day in his synagogue, he does not see the
meaning; he hears the letter but he does not get the spirit of the
teaching. There is a veil, he says, blinding them; they think they
know the truth, they spend their time in discussing it and in
talking about it, but they do not see it. Why is this? It is because
something is standing between them and the truth, so that they
cannot see it. Then, in the fourth chapter of this same Epistle, he
becomes still more specific. He talks about himself as a preacher
and an evangelist, and then he says, But everybody does not
believe what I say, and he puts it in these words: 'If our gospel
be hid, it is hid to them that are lost: in whom the god of this
world hath blinded the minds of them that believe not, lest the
light of the glorious gospel of Christ, who is the image of God,

should shine unto them.' The god of this world has *blinded the mind*! It is precisely another way of saying that their *understandings have been darkened.*

Now go through the whole of your Bible and you will find that this is what it says everywhere about man in sin and about man outside Christ. It describes the kind of life people live, and then it asks its question, Why do they live like that? There is, says the Bible, only one explanation: the failure is in their minds, their intellects, and their understanding. The highest faculty in man has become blunted and blinded; he cannot see because of this pall that has descended upon him; he is surrounded by darkness. But let me put this a little more theologically. The most disastrous effect that the Fall of Man produced upon man was in his understanding. That is the whole of the biblical explanation of why man is as he is and why the world is as it is. God created man perfect, endowed him with amazing faculties, made him lord of creation and of the universe; and yet we see something so entirely different. Why the difference? What has happened is that man sinned, he disobeyed God, and he fell. And the Fall has had the most disastrous consequences upon man and upon his whole life and living; and of all its terrible effects the most disastrous and devastating is upon the mind of man. It has darkened his understanding.

There is no word that the Bible uses more frequently with respect to the man who is not a Christian than the word *fool*. The sinner is just a *fool*. A fool is a foolish man, a man who lacks understanding, a man who does a thing because he does not know better; he blunders into something without thinking at all. What a fool! you say, What a fool to have gone into that! If only he had thought for a moment, if only he had got eyes in his head! Surely he lacks understanding! That is the word the Bible uses about the sinner, the man who is not a Christian. It is the *fool* who has said in his heart, There is no God. Of course! It is because he has not got understanding. Listen to Paul putting it in that great parallel chapter, the first chapter of the Epistle to the Romans, where he has the same sort of analysis. He says that what has gone wrong with mankind is that, though God has made them

[42]

in His own image, though creation ought to be speaking to them about God, and though they started by worshipping the Creator, they are now worshipping the creature. Why? Because, he says, 'their foolish heart was darkened'. And again he says, 'professing themselves to be wise, they became fools'! I remind you again that is the whole explanation of the modern world.

But Paul also uses another word. He describes the state of the unbeliever as one of *darkness*. He is a man who is walking in darkness even at noonday, groping about in the dark. Listen to some of the typical expressions of the New Testament. At the very beginning of the gospel we are told that the coming of the Lord Jesus Christ has fulfilled a prophecy spoken by Isaiah – 'The people that sat in darkness have seen a great light' (Isaiah 9:2; Matthew 4:16). Picture the human race *sitting in darkness*; it has been trying to find a way out but it cannot, and at last it has sat down in utter hopelessness and despair. It sinks into cynicism – 'the people that *sat* in *darkness*' – no light, no knowledge. They sit hopelessly and helplessly in darkness. At last, men see a great light, that is, the gospel. Or think of the Apostle's constant and familiar comparisons and contrasts. In writing to believers he says, Look here, you should not be living a life like that any longer; you are no longer of the night, you are children of the day! you are no longer in the darkness, you belong to the light! Children of darkness and children of light! night and day! Sin is always associated in the Bible with darkness.

Listen to our blessed Lord Himself again putting it in these words: 'This is the condemnation, that light is come into the world, and men loved darkness rather than light, because their deeds were evil' (John 3:19). The trouble, He says, is loving the darkness rather than the light. And then again, it is not surprising that the Apostle Paul should use these terms, because of what we read concerning his call on the road to Damascus. The Lord told him that He was calling him to be a witness both to the people and to the Gentiles, and with this particular commission, 'to open their eyes, and to turn them from darkness to light' (Acts 26:18). It is the business of preaching, it is the whole gospel of evangelism, that men's eyes should be opened; not that they should be entertained, or made to laugh or to weep; but to open their eyes, to turn them from darkness to light and to knowledge.

[43]

They were the very terms in which the Apostle was called. We must remember, too, that our Lord described Himself as the Light of the world – 'I am the Light of the world; he that followeth me shall not walk in darkness, but shall have the light of life' (John 8:12).

I have given you these quotations in order that we may see that this is what we find through the Bible about the life of an unbeliever. He is a man who is in darkness, he is blind, his understanding has become darkened. We all follow the Bible's example in this matter, do we not? For example, we have all tended in the past to describe the continent of Africa as 'The Dark Continent'. That is how we describe people who live in ignorance and in paganism – the Dark Continent! But, you know, William Booth was equally right when he wrote his famous book, *In Darkest England*. He wrote it in the Victorian era, and yet that is the title of his book, *In Darkest England* – and how dark was that darkness! That was the origin of the Salvation Army.

But it is important that we should realise that this applies to everybody who is not a Christian. That is why all philosophy and all speculation, brilliant and clever though it often is, in the end leads to nothing. The Apostle was able to tell the philosophers in Athens that their life was really one of seeking only and never finding, seeking 'if haply they might feel after Him, and find Him'. But they did not find Him, in spite of their mighty brains and intellects. Plato, Socrates, Aristotle, and the rest of them, never found God; they still ended in darkness. I am never tired of quoting the dying remark of the great German philosopher and poet, Goethe. His was a brilliant intellect, but you remember what he said on his death bed – they were among his last words – 'More light'. He said he needed more mental light! He had spent his lifetime thinking, analysing, discussing – great philosopher! But no! he ended in darkness, and he admitted it – 'More light!' And an almost infinitely smaller man, called H. G. Wells, virtually confessed the same thing at the end of *his* life; the title of his last book was *Mind at the End of its Tether*. He had trusted the mind all his life; he admitted at the end, in the middle of the Second World War, that he did not know where he stood, and that he

[44]

did not understand. His understanding was darkened! Of course he did not understand! He did not believe this Book! If only such people read the Old Testament! If, for example, they read the sixtieth chapter of Isaiah's prophecy, they would find this in the second verse: 'For behold, the darkness shall cover the earth, and gross darkness the people.' It is a literally accurate description of man's mind as the result of the Fall; it is darkened and blinded; he cannot think aright, he is incapable of understanding spiritual things. And, of course, that is why he regards spiritual things as foolishness, as folly, and scoffs at them and dismisses them.

But the height of the tragedy, and what seems to me to be the saddest part of it all, is that while he is in this condition, there is nothing that he boasts of so much as his intellect and his understanding. This explains why I am giving such attention to this problem. I find it very difficult to understand why many Christian people are really troubled and worried by the fact that so many great and intellectual people do not believe in Christianity, but dismiss it and deride it. You know them, I need not mention their names, they often speak on the radio; they write in the journals and they produce their books, *Why I am not a Christian*, and so on. Yet there are Christian people who are troubled by that and frightened by it. That, I repeat, is the thing I cannot understand, for if Christians understood this one text from Isaiah, they would never be surprised again. The understandings of unbelievers are darkened! They boast about intellect – of course! They say, I am not a Christian because I have got a brain; I can think, I am not taken in by sobstuff, I am not given to this kind of brain-washing; I still am in control, I am rational and I can think and reason, and because of my understanding I am not a Christian! That is their position. And, there, you see the masterpiece of Satan and the height of the deception. He has succeeded in deluding such people primarily about themselves, and the whole time they cannot see that their real trouble is in their understanding! This, to me, is almost a matter for humour and divine laughter. The chief of all the slogans of the Greek philosophers, the pagan Greeks, was 'Know thyself'! In that knowledge, they said, was the whole art of life and living. 'Know thyself!' I say it is laughable for this reason, because there was no other point at which they failed so completely and disastrously.

Now it is as true to say that today as it was two thousand years ago. The philosophers did not know themselves, for they thought their intellects were big enough and great enough to discover God and to encompass God and to understand God! But a man who starts thinking he can do that is nothing better than a fool, he does not know himself. And men are still doing it! And here I do want to emphasise that this statement about the understanding being darkened is true of all men who are not Christians. Do not think that this is simply a reference to illiterate, uneducated people. It is equally true of the most erudite, the most knowledgeable, the most cultured person in the world today. His mind and his understanding, are utterly darkened. And his whole difficulty about the Gospel is that this darkness exists between his mind and the thing he is looking at.

Perhaps a simple illustration will make this plain and clear. Have you not often observed that what is said in derision about Christianity by these supposed great thinkers and philosophers is also said in exactly the same way by Tom, Dick and Harry, by the man standing at the street corner? What makes the first man dismiss it is not his intellect; the other people may not be intellectual at all, but they still say exactly the same thing. The great philosopher writes his book on *Why I am not a Christian*, and he gives you the impression that his unbelief is the outcome of his powerful intellect. But go and listen to the man on the street corner, who says, 'I am not a Christian', and he will give you exactly the same reasons; there is no difference at all. It is played out, he says, it is bunkum, it is out of date. His terminology is slightly different, but the essential argument is precisely the same.

This is a very important matter for us all to grasp. Look at it like this. I remember having an experience a few years ago; I was being driven by a friend of mine through a part of Northern Ireland, and he had been telling me how, at a given point in our tour, we should be able to see Scotland. Eventually we came to that point, but we could not see Scotland. Why not? A mist had come down! I looked, with all the intensity I was capable of, and still I could see nothing but a mist. My friend kept on saying, 'Scotland is just over there', but I could not see it. Now why

[46]

could I not see Scotland? Was it because I suddenly began to
suffer from some terrible disease of the eyes? Had I suddenly
developed cataracts? Had my optic nerve suddenly become
paralysed? Was there some defect in my mechanism? Not at all!
My mechanism was as normal as it had ever been, but I could not
see Scotland. Why? It was the mist – the darkness of the mist.
But the fact that I could not see Scotland did not mean that
Scotland was not there. And had I started to say, I do not believe
that Scotland is there, I do not believe it can ever be seen, I am
looking and I cannot see it – what would you have said of me?
You would have said that I was a fool, and you would have been
right. That is precisely the position with all who are not Christians. Their understandings are darkened! I am not saying that
the mighty philosophers do not possess great brains. But the
greatest brain in the world cannot see through a mist and when
the pall of darkness comes down, as it has come down upon the
whole human race, then the greatest mind in the world is useless.

The Apostle is saying exactly the same thing in the first two
chapters of the first Epistle to the Corinthians. 'You see your
calling, brethren,' he writes, 'how that not many wise men after
the flesh, not many mighty, not many noble, are called.' And why
not? Because they are trusting to their own understandings;
they are darkened, they are blinded and they cannot see. The
princes of this world, when the Lord came into it, did not know
Him. They said, 'This fellow', this carpenter, 'away with him,
crucify him!' Why did they do it? Because they did not know
Him, 'for had they known him they would not have crucified the
Lord of glory'. How then do *we* know that He is the Lord of
glory? Ah, says, Paul, 'the Spirit hath revealed it unto us', 'the
Spirit that searcheth all things, yea, the deep things of God'.
'The natural man receiveth not the things of the Spirit of God,
for they are foolishness unto him; neither can he know them,
because they are spiritually discerned' – he cannot help it. Brilliant
though he may be, if there is a mist, he cannot see! Are you still
surprised that these people are not Christians, that they ridicule
the Incarnation and the miracles and the two natures in One
Person, and that they pour their scorn upon the sacrificial, substitutionary atonement, and the idea that God should punish our
sins in His Son? It is unreasonable, they say; it is irrational and

[47]

immoral; I cannot accept it. There is only one appropriate reply when they say that, and it is this: Of course you cannot! Did you ever expect that you could? Have you not realised that your whole mind is darkened, that your whole nature is perverted, that the pall of ignorance has descended upon you as upon everybody else, that you are in the same position as the merest child, the lowliest, most ignorant man in the world, and that your whole mind and understanding are darkened? And we as Christians must not be surprised at this, we must not be disturbed by it. Thank God that this is the truth! Thank God that it is not, primarily, a matter of understanding. Thank God, I say, for this good reason, that the greatest philosopher in the world at this moment is in exactly the same position as the most ignorant tribesman in a primitive jungle. The great philosopher has no advantage over the pagan in this matter of the gospel. Until both of them come under the influence and the power of the Holy Spirit of God, neither will see it. But thank God, when the Holy Spirit comes upon both, both will see it; not only the philosopher, not only the pagan, but both together! Come back to my illustration again. Take the greatest philosopher in the world this morning, and take an ignorant and illiterate man; let them join me as I stand there in Northern Ireland looking in the direction of Scotland. And none of us can see anything at all. But then the mist rolls away, and the three of us can see Scotland. It is not a matter of intellectual ability, be it small or great; it is a matter of this power of vision; man has lost it, his understanding is darkened, and that is the effect of the Fall.

Then, if we look at it another way, we see that the effect of the coming of the gospel is always described in terms of light. 'The people which sat in darkness saw great *light*'! (Matthew 4:16) And let me complete my former quotation from Isaiah 60:2 and 3: 'But the Lord shall arise upon thee, and his glory shall be seen upon thee. And the Gentiles shall come to thy light, and kings to the brightness of thy rising.' Or listen to Paul saying it once and for ever: 'God, who commanded the light to shine out of darkness, hath shined in our hearts, to give the light of the knowledge of the glory of God in the face of Jesus Christ'

[48]

(2 Corinthians 4:6). There it is! It is like the coming of the light into the darkness.

Let me at this point ask a simple question. Do you believe this gospel? Is this everything to you? If it is not, it is because your understanding is darkened. You think you know, you think you understand, but you do not. This is the only reason why people do not believe the gospel and why they are not Christians, But oh! let me put it like this. You are a Christian, but are you perfectly clear in your mind as to what is wrong with others who are not Christians? Have you become a little impatient, perhaps, with a husband or a wife or children or parents who are still in unbelief? Do you lose your temper when you talk to them about these things? Do you feel like shaking them because they do not see it? If you do, it is because you still do not fully understand that the trouble with unbelievers is that their understanding is darkened! You can demonstrate the truth, you can argue and reason and put it before them to perfection, and they will see nothing at all in it. And that is simply because of this darkness of the understanding, they cannot help themselves, they cannot do it.

There is a story which, to me, illustrates all this perfectly. It is about William Pitt the Younger, one of the greatest Prime Ministers which this country has ever had. He was a friend of William Wilberforce, the liberator of the slaves. But there was one great difference between them: William Wilberforce had undergone an evangelical conversion, and had become the saint that he was; William Pitt, of course, was a nominal Christian but it did not mean anything to him. Now in London at that time there was a great evangelical clergyman and preacher in the Church of England called Richard Cecil, and it was the delight of Wilberforce's life to go and listen to the preaching of this man. He was also anxious that his friend Pitt should go with him. He often invited him and there was always some excuse, affairs of State, being busy, and so on. However, a day came when William Pitt said to William Wilberforce, I find I am free and that I can come with you next Sunday. Wilberforce was eagerly looking forward to it and was praying for his friend, praying that a shaft of light might come to him. When Sunday morning came they went to the service. Richard Cecil was preaching at his best, under the unction of the Spirit, and Wilberforce was lifted up to

[49]

the highest heavens. He revelled and gloried in the truth, having a feast for his soul, his whole man being moved to its depths; occasionally he wondered what was happening to his friend. However, the service ended and as they were walking out together, and even before they had got out of the vestibule, William Pitt turned to William Wilberforce and said, 'You know, Wilberforce, I have not the slightest idea what that man has been talking about.'

I have no doubt at all that William Pitt was a greater man, as we judge men in the flesh, than William Wilberforce, a greater brain and a greater statesman. But that is not the thing that really matters. The heavenly, spiritual truth spoken by Richard Cecil meant nothing at all to him; he did not know what it was all about; he was bored by it, waiting for it to end! The other man was revelling and rejoicing! You see what makes the difference? it is the darkness! And it is a darkness that none but the Holy Ghost can take away.

What, then, is the point I am making? It is that we Christian people must realise this, as we think of others who are still not Christian. Do we recognise the cause of the trouble, that it is this appalling darkness that has come over and enshrouded the understanding? And even though we do everything we can, it will avail nothing. There is only one thing that can move the mist, and take away the pall, and that is the gale of the Spirit. We have tried almost everything else, have we not? We have organised and arranged and used means and methods that even we ourselves have felt to be doubtful. We have resolved that we will use anything that will bring the people in and lead to their conversion. But it does not! How can it? The darkness in the understanding, the pall of sin is the cause of the trouble. And there is only one thing that can deal with it. Thank God, says Paul to the Corinthians, it has happened to us; 'the things which God hath prepared for them that love Him . . . God hath revealed unto us by His Spirit' (1 Corinthians 2:9 and 10). 'Now we have received, not the spirit of the world, but the Spirit which is of God; that we might know the things that are freely given to us of God.' And to anyone who has found this whole subject boring I would say:

If you do not know what I have been talking about, if you do not understand these things, I say it is because your mind, your understanding, is darkened, you are under the dominion of the devil and of Satan, you are enshrouded by this darkness of evil and of hell. I say, realise it, and cry out for light, ask *God* to open your eyes! See the appalling condition in which you are.

I also say another word to those who are Christians and who enjoy and see these things. Your supreme duty and mine is to pray for revival, to pray that the Holy Ghost will so descend upon the Church that we shall speak in such a manner that men *will* see. I cannot do it; I am like this Apostle, even worse, 'in weakness, fear, and much trembling'; I have no confidence in myself, nor in the church, nor in any organisation, nor in anything else. No human agency can do it. But the Spirit can – 'in demonstration of *the Spirit* and of *power*'. Do you pray day by day for your minister that he might be filled with the Spirit of power, that he might preach in demonstration of the Spirit and of power? Do you pray like that or do you leave it all to him? Do we pray for the Spirit to possess us? Do we pray for revival? We know the state of society, we know the state of London, we know the state of the world, we are talking about it. But that is not enough! We must not rely on any man or numbers of men. We need the Spirit of God, we need a visitation in revival power, and we are called to pray for that, every one of us. We are only Christians because the Spirit of God has opened our blind eyes, and has taken away the darkness. And that is the need of all others. What a word, what a phrase is used by the Apostle! Men 'walk in the vanity of their mind, having the understanding darkened'. Poor, benighted fools, despite their sophistication and cleverness, their arguments and disputes on the wireless and the television, and their articles and their books! How brilliant! But it is the brilliance of a bubble! There is nothing in it. And their blindness is the result of the darkness. Have compassion upon them. Do not be content with denouncing them, pray for them. Above all, pray that the Spirit of God may come in such power that their darkness may be removed and their eyes may be opened.

4

Aliens from the Life of God

'This I say therefore, and testify in the Lord, that ye
henceforth walk not as other Gentiles walk, in the
vanity of their mind, having the understanding
darkened, being alienated from the life of God
through the ignorance that is in them, because of the
blindness of their heart: who being past feeling have
given themselves over unto lasciviousness, to work
all uncleanness with greediness.'

Ephesians 4:17–19

We continue our study of this remarkable analysis which the
Apostle gives us here of the life of the unbeliever, the life of any
person who is not a Christian. Paul was actually analysing and
giving an accurate, detailed description of the life of pagan
Gentiles in his own day and generation. But as we have seen, it is
equally true today, as it has always been true in all ages and
generations, of all who are outside the life of God.

We are looking at this for certain specific reasons; the first, of
course, is the one that the Apostle puts in the forefront, namely,
that having a true understanding of that kind of life we may hate
it, and avoid it, and get as far away from it as we possibly can.
A second reason is this: the more we understand the character
and the nature of that kind of life, the more we shall come to
understand and to appreciate what God has done for us in His
infinite grace in delivering us from such a life. How could He
ever look upon us in that condition? But He did! And that is one
of the best ways of extolling God's matchless grace. It is people
who have the deepest understanding of sin and what it means
who have the greatest understanding and appreciation of the
love and the grace and the mercy and the kindness of God. A

superficial view of sin leads to a superficial view of salvation, and to a superficial view of everything else. So we follow the Apostle as he shows us the depths of sin and iniquity, in order that we may be enabled to measure the height and the depth and the breadth and the length, and to know the love of Christ which passeth knowledge. And thirdly, we are doing this, as I have already said, in order that we may have a true understanding of the condition of those known to us, and among whom we live, who are still not Christians.

This is the first thing, surely, in connection with evangelism, and we are all evangelists if we are true Christians; we are all living among other people. Christianity spread in the early days of the Church through individual Christians who, when they were persecuted and scattered abroad, went everywhere and told people why they had been persecuted and what it was to be a Christian. And in the same way in days and in times like these, this question of evangelism becomes more and more one of our personal life and experience and witness. Therefore, we must have a true understanding of this pagan state, because it will determine our method. If we realise the depth of iniquity, if we realise that this is nothing but the simple truth about all who are not Christian, then, I say, it will drive us to our knees; it will help us to see that nothing short of the mighty power of God's Holy Spirit can possibly deal with such a situation. We shall spend more time in prayer; in particular we shall spend more time in praying and pleading for a mighty religious revival, an outpouring of the Spirit of God upon us. I therefore do not hesitate to say that if you and I are not praying for revival there is only one explanation. It is that we do not realise the nature of the problem confronting us. We think that we can still do it by means of organisations or other activities, but once we see what man really is in sin, we know that nothing short of the power of God can possibly deal with him. And I see no hope today apart from a mighty spiritual awakening such as God has graciously granted in past centuries. He granted one a century ago, in 1857, 1858 and 1859; another in the 18th century; and earlier still, the Protestant Reformation in the 16th century. I say that if we really do understand the condition of the world at this present time we shall all of us be on our knees pleading with God to send forth His Spirit in

[53]

mighty reviving power. There, then, are our reasons for going into these matters in detail. We have already seen the general description of 'other Gentiles' who 'walk in the vanity of their mind' – and we have begun to consider Paul's analysis of the situation. We have seen that one reason for the vanity of their minds is the darkening of the understanding. But that is not the only thing. Now we come to look at the second thing said by the Apostle: 'being alienated from the life of God'. That is why these 'other Gentiles' are walking in the vanity of their minds; their understandings are darkened, and they are alienated from the life of God. This is another tremendous statement, and it is important that we should understand what the Apostle is saying here. What exactly does it mean to be alienated from the life of God? What is the *life of God*? There are some who think that the words mean the kind of life which God approves, and certainly that is included, but much more is meant. The life of God is not merely the godly life, the life which God commands, the life which God indicates to us in the Scriptures as being the right life. The life of God does not mean a virtuous life only, or a life lived according to God's way, and according to His holy law. It includes that, but this phrase goes well beyond that. Let me prove this to you.

If the Apostle had meant only the godly life, the good life, the virtuous life, then he would not have used the word that he actually uses here when he talks about the life of God. Two words are used in the Greek language for *life*: one is the word *bios*, the word that we use when we talk about *biology*. Biology is the study of life in the sense that it is the study of the organisation of life, the general course or the general tenor of a life. Now here the Apostle did not use that word. 'Bios' is the lower of the two words. It indicates life in general, as it were, life as it exists in plants, and animals, and in man himself. But the Apostle did not use that word, so we must not interpret 'the life of God' as just meaning the good life, the godly life, the virtuous life. Instead, he uses the other word for life – *zoe*. This is the high word, that he always uses, and that the Scripture everywhere uses, when the subject is life itself, the life principle. It really means, in a sense, God's own life, the divine life as a principle within us. When he says, therefore, that men are alienated from the life of God, he is

[54]

referring to the life which is in God Himself, and to that principle of life which God gives to those who believe in Him.

Let me illustrate what I mean. The Apostle Peter in the early part of his Second Epistle writes like this: 'Whereby are given unto us exceeding great and precious promises: that by these ye might be partakers of the divine nature, having escaped the corruption that is in the world through lust.' There Peter is saying in his own way exactly what the Apostle Paul is saying here. They both say the same thing. That is why, if you really understand and study thoroughly one great Epistle, like this Epistle to the Ephesians, you really know the whole doctrine of the Bible. The Bible is *one* Book. Paul speaks of 'the life of God'. Peter tells us that God's children are 'partakers of the divine nature'. So what Paul is referring to here is the life that comes *from* God, the life which God gives. Pagans, unbelievers, non-Christians, he says, are utter strangers from that life, entirely separated from it, aliens.

The tragedy of man in sin, the man who is not a Christian, is that he is outside the life of God, does not participate in it, does not know it, does not enjoy it. Our Lord Himself really put this once and for ever, plainly, clearly and perfectly, in His great high priestly prayer, recorded in the seventeenth chapter of John's Gospel. This is how He prayed: 'This is life eternal, that they might know thee the only true God, and Jesus Christ whom thou hast sent.' He says: I have been sent into the world by Thee, and I have been sent to give unto Thy people this gift of eternal life! That is eternal life. The man who is without it does not know the only true God, neither does he know Jesus Christ. That, says Paul, is the trouble with these 'other Gentiles'; they are walking in the vanity of their mind, they are chasing bubbles. And not only because their understandings are darkened, but because they are absolute strangers from the life of God; they do not know it, they are not participating in it.

Here we must notice a very interesting thing (every word is so important!): 'Having the understanding darkened, *being* alienated . . .' This word really should be translated as '*having become* alienated'. An important and illuminating difference! It is not that they *are* alienated from the life of God, they *have become* alienated from the life of God. Here is a further reference to the Fall of man. We have already seen that man's understanding is darkened because of the Fall; man lost that understanding when Adam fell into sin. Here is another consequence. Man has become estranged from the life of God. Originally he was in fellowship with God; God made man for Himself and man was destined not only to know God but to enjoy fellowship with Him. God made him in His own image for this very reason. And that was the position at the beginning. We read about God coming down into the garden. Man looked at God with an open face, and he enjoyed God. He was in perfect communion and fellowship with God, and was sharing something of the everlasting and eternal life of God.

And that is why the Fall of man is the greatest tragedy in his history, and why the doctrine of the Fall is essential to any understanding of life in this world today. Why do we see man 'walking in the vanity of his mind'? Because he has fallen from the life of God! He fell in Adam and he has remained in that condition ever since. He is outside the garden, and the cherubim and the flaming sword are guarding that eastern gate of entrance. Man cannot get back there, he is outside; and life has become a wilderness because of this fall and the loss of the life of God. As the result of the Fall man was cut off from true life, was cut off from the source of his being, and he has been like that ever since. So that what you and I call life is not life, it is mere existence. Man in sin does not live, he exists, he is living like an animal, he is chasing vanities. He has become cut off from the life of God, the source of his being, and he is merely existing. He is no longer in paradise, he is outside in a wilderness – restless, troubled, and dissatisfied. He still has a vague memory within him that he was meant for something bigger; he cannot get rid of it; there is a sense of God within him. He is conscious of a contradiction. 'He feels he was not made to die', as the poet puts it. He has got some vague recollection of another existence and another type of life, and the result is that he has a longing for a paradise he has lost. He is ever seeking, but he cannot find it. He has become alienated from the life of God.

And yet, having this sense of God within him, man must

worship something, so he makes his own gods, he makes his idols. In the ancient times they made them of wood and of stone and of precious metals. Men still do that in some places, but we have got other ways of doing it today, for we are idolatrous by nature, every one of us. We worship ourselves, we worship our family, we worship our country, we worship our wealth, position – we must have a god! And man has ever been making gods. There is a sense of worship within him and he is trying to satisfy it. But all this does not satisfy; he has a feeling at the end that he has been fooling himself. And the gods he makes for himself do not satisfy. He is ever searching for 'the unknown God' and he cannot find Him. He has tried with his philosophy, as we have seen, but he has never succeeded. 'The world by wisdom knew not God.' Man thus, I say, is in this wilderness, and his life, his existence, is unhappy and unsatisfying. He is miserable and he is wretched, and having lost his contact with God and the life of God he has lost his sense of values; he does not realise his own true nature, he does not realise what is really of value. So he spends his time in chasing vanities, will-o'-the-wisps, and finds neither peace nor rest, and never satisfaction.

Oh, how busily man has been engaged in trying to find that satisfaction! Read the history of the centuries, read your secular history books, read the story of the great civilisations that have risen and have gone down. What does it all mean? Take a hurried view of the whole story of the human race, and what do you find? It is the story of man trying to find a place of rest, trying to find somewhere or something where at last he will find the answers to his questions, and the ultimate satisfaction for which he longs. But always, ever, at the end of all his highest endeavours, in one way or another he has to admit and to confess, 'I tried the broken cisterns, Lord, but ah! their waters failed.' Most men, if they are not Christians, become rather hopeless as they grow old. Cynicism and despair grip and enter in, because everything seems so futile, and all endeavour leads to nothing. What is the matter? The real trouble is just this very thing that the Apostle is speaking of. Man does not see and does not know that his one need is his need of God, the knowledge of God, sharing in the life of God! Man does not realise what the author of Psalm 42 realised so clearly when he said 'As the hart panteth after the water brooks,

[57]

so panteth my soul after thee, O God. My soul crieth out for the living God'! That is a man who knows, who has discovered his need and is on the track of the solution. If I have God, he says, I have all. But man in sin, in the vanity of his mind, does not know that, does not realise it; his understanding is darkened, and thus he has become alienated from the life of God.

My friends, I make no apology for putting a simple question to you at this point. Do you know God? Are you sharing the life of God? Have you found peace and rest for your soul? Let us quote once again that immortal statement of Augustine, 'Thou hast made us for Thyself, and our hearts are restless until they find their rest in Thee'! Have you got heart rest, soul peace? Having tried the broken cisterns and having found them to fail, have you found the Fount of living water, the Source of life and of every blessing? That, you see, is the difference between people who are not Christians, and those who are. The non-Christian is alienated from the life of God. The Christian, by definition, is a man who is no longer alienated and estranged; he knows that life, he is enjoying it, he is in it.

But we must go further. Why is the unbeliever, the ungodly man, thus alienated from the life of God? The Apostle gives us two answers to that question, and they are both found in this eighteenth verse. The first is this: 'through the ignorance that is in them'; secondly, 'because of the blindness (or hardness) of their heart'. We must look into them, because if there is anyone who does not know God and who is not enjoying the life of God, I must tell him why it is so. This is to me the essence of evangelism, to show people why they are not enjoying the life of God. It is, says the Apostle, because of the ignorance that is in them. We have seen that this ignorance is in them because their understandings are darkened. Ah, yes, but the vital question here is, what exactly are they ignorant of? It is the contention throughout the Bible that the real trouble with mankind is *ignorance*. We are living in a day and age when we boast of all that we know. We read our encyclopaedias, and little snippets in the magazines. We do not read big books any longer but try to know a little bit about everything with our summaries and our digests. Then we listen to these endless quizzes, and people seem to know everything! And yet we are told that the main trouble with the world today is ignorance! – 'through the *ignorance* that is in them'! What are they ignorant of?

The first and the chief thing of which they are ignorant is God Himself. Why are they alienated from the life of God? There is only one answer. It is because they do not know Him and the truth about Him. If only men knew the truth about God their whole situation would change, but they are ignorant about God, ignorant of His character, ignorant of His being, ignorant of His attributes. Why does man spend his time in Vanity Fair? Why does he spend his time juggling with these mere bubbles, these vanities that disappear and vanish? What is the matter with him? I say the trouble with him is that he has got such a depraved and low taste, he knows nothing better; he does not know God and the character and the being and the attributes of God. What are they? First and foremost, the glory of God! That is finally the supreme attribute of God. That is what makes God God, His Glory! He dwells in the light which no man can approach unto, which no man hath seen nor can see. 'Lord, Thy glory fills the heavens, earth is with its fulness stored.' The angels and archangels and all the glorified spirits spend the whole of their time in ascribing glory unto God. The glory of God! Oh, if we but had a glimpse of this, if the whole world had but a glimpse of it, the whole situation would be revolutionised; but men and women do not know the glory of God. They are interested in glory, of course; they will ascribe glory to one another and to great men, and they will stand for hours to see them and applaud them. So they give glory to kingdoms that are passing away, with the earth and all its glory. Why do they do that? It is because they have never known the glory of God!

And then think of God's majesty and of His eternity. God is the Father of lights with whom is no variableness, neither shadow of turning. From everlasting to everlasting, He is the same. Someone once put it in a graphic phrase: 'Time writes no wrinkle on the brow of God.' Everlasting and Eternal! The Eternal, the ever-blessed God! Does mankind ever pay any attention to that? Does mankind think of the holiness of God? Have you ever noticed how it is expressed in the song that was sung by Moses and the children of Israel? 'Who is like unto thee, O Lord, among the gods; who is like thee, glorious in holiness, fearful in praises, doing wonders?' Have we any conception of the holiness of God? Then again, think of His justice and His righteousness. Listen to the psalmist speaking of these attributes. 'Thy righteousness is like the great mountains; thy judgments are a great deep'! God is the God of all the earth. And have you thought of His power? 'In the beginning GOD created the heavens and the earth.' God spake and it was done; God said, 'Let there be light, and there was light.' Yes, says the song of Moses and the redeemed Israelites, 'He is glorious in power'; it is the power of His own glory. God not only made everything, He sustains everything. As Psalm 103 puts it, if God were to withdraw His Spirit even for a moment the whole cosmos would collapse; every tree, every animal, every human being. Everything is sustained and maintained by the Spirit of the Lord, and were He to withdraw, at once the whole creation would collapse and fall. He is not only the Creator, He is the Sustainer of everything. It is His power that keeps everything going.

Think, too, of God's love and His mercy, His compassion and His grace. We know something about this, do we not? Studying this Epistle to the Ephesians in the second chapter we read: 'But God, who is rich in mercy, for his great love wherewith he loved us . . .' and then the further phrase . . . 'that in the ages to come he might show the exceeding riches of his grace, in his kindness towards us through Jesus Christ'. Paul has spoken, too, about the 'unsearchable riches of Christ', and about God's wisdom and His power – the great attributes of God!

Now the trouble with the people who are living a life of vanity and who are alienated from the life of God is that they do not know Him. If only they could see these things, they would turn away from everything else and would spend their time in looking upon Him, in gazing upon Him, in meditating upon Him, in seeking to know more and more of Him. But they do not, they are ignorant and so they spend their time following after follies and vanity. Is not this the very thing that Paul said to the pagans at Lystra? They were about to worship Paul and Barnabas and to

[60]

offer sacrifices to them. Stop! says the Apostle in effect. We are men like you and preach 'that you should turn from these vanities unto the living God. . . .' It is because you do not know God that you think that we are gods; it is your ignorance!

Furthermore, men are not only ignorant of His character, His being, and His attributes, they are ignorant of His purposes and of His dispensations. They are ignorant of the fact that He is still the Governor of this world, and that He has a plan and a purpose for the world and for this life. They do not know the Old Testament, they do not know the New. They do not know that God has appointed an end to time as certainly as He started it, and that there is a day coming when God will bring this world to an end and wind up its affairs. And still more serious and important, they do not know that God is determined to destroy His enemies and all who are opposed to Him. They do not realise that this is God's world and that God is determined to bring it back to what it was. He made it perfect; the devil came in and he has marred it and ruined it. Will God leave it like that? Of course not! God has initiated this great movement of salvation, and the day is coming when the devil and all who belong to him shall be cast into the lake of fire and everlastingly destroyed from the presence of the Lord. They do not know that. They think that, because they can split an atom and harness its power, they can control life, the world and everything else. But they cannot! The whole world is in the hands of God. 'The Lord reigneth; let the people tremble.' He is almighty. He brought the world into being out of nothing, and He will end it when He chooses, and nothing can stop Him. Ignorant men do not know that they are in the hands of the living God, and that 'it is a fearful thing to fall into the hands of the living God'. If they only knew it they would not live as they do. They are ignorant of what God has done in Christ, they are ignorant of His great purpose of redemption and of restoration, and of the time of regeneration when Christ will come back and destroy with the breath of His mouth all His enemies. And, of course, they are ignorant of the fact that they themselves are involved in all this. They do not know that 'it is appointed unto men once to die, and after this the judgment'. They are ignorant of the fact that if they die in sin and outside the life of God they will spend an eternity as they are now but even worse, because

[61]

they will see the folly of it all. They are ignorant of all these truths! They are 'alienated from the life of God because of the ignorance that is in them.'

But I do not want to leave you with the negative. I rather want to emphasise that this is the tragedy, the pathos, of man in sin. Our hearts ought to bleed for all who are not Christians, because they do not realise what they are missing; they do not realise that even in this world, as it is at this moment, they can begin to know God. They do not know that they can be reconciled to Him and can have this knowledge of Him, and that they can begin to enjoy God here and now. 'The chief end of man is to glorify God, and to enjoy Him for ever.' Is it not tragic that they spend their time running after this world's tawdry trinkets? If they but knew this great truth they would give up these worthless things at once. But they do not know it, because of the ignorance that is in them. They do not know that they can become children of God, heirs of God and joint-heirs with Christ. They do not know that it is possible for them to spend their eternity, not in woe and wretchedness and unhappiness, but in indescribable glory in the presence of God, with a glorified body, entirely perfect in every respect, looking into the face of God and enjoying Him for all eternity. They do not know it! 'Eye hath not seen, nor ear heard, neither have entered into the heart of man, the things which God hath prepared for them that love him.' 'My people', says God through the prophet Hosea, 'are destroyed for lack of knowledge.' And that is still the trouble! Unbelievers are alienated from the life of God because of the ignorance that is in them. Oh! if they but knew Him! The business of the gospel is to open our eyes, to cry, Awake! awake! to sound an alarm, to tell men and women to flee from the wrath to come, and to come to *know* God, and to begin to enjoy Him. And that is your business and mine. We are to tell men and women about this life of God. This is evangelism! We are not merely to tell them that they will have this or that, or that they will have a new kick in life! No, it is to *know* GOD. The cults can give happiness and a temporary peace, and a thousand and one things, but there is only one thing that can bring a man to *know* God, and that is the Christian gospel. It does not give

me a lighthearted jauntiness; on the contrary, it makes me speak
in the words of W. T. Matson's great hymn:

> Lord, I was blind! I could not see
>   In Thy marred visage any grace;
> But now the beauty of Thy face
>   In radiant vision dawns on me.
>
> Lord, I was deaf! I could not hear
>   The thrilling music of Thy voice;
> But now I hear Thee and rejoice,
>   And all Thine uttered words are dear.
>
> Lord, I was dumb! I could not speak
>   The grace and glory of Thy name;
> But now, as touched with living flame,
>   My lips Thine eager praises wake.
>
> Lord, I was dead! I could not stir
>   My lifeless soul to come to Thee;
> But now, since Thou hast quickened me,
>   I rise from sin's dark sepulchre.
>
> Lord, Thou hast made the blind to see,
>   The deaf to hear, the dumb to speak,
> The dead to live; and lo, I break
>   The chains of my captivity.

May this be the testimony of us all.

5
Sin in a Pagan World

'This I say therefore, and testify in the Lord, that ye henceforth walk not as other Gentiles walk, in the vanity of their mind, having the understanding darkened, being alienated from the life of God through the ignorance that is in them, because of the blindness of their heart: who being past feeling have given themselves over unto lasciviousness, to work all uncleanness with greediness.'

Ephesians 4:17–19

We continue our study of this description – alarming because it is so accurate – which the Apostle here gives of the ungodly life, the life of the non-Christian. He was particularly describing the paganism of his own day and generation, but as we have seen, we have abundant evidence that it is an equally accurate description of the life of the ungodly at this present hour. The Apostle's concern is that the Ephesians to whom he is writing and who, having become Christian, had been emancipated from the pagan way of life, should no longer live like that; on the contrary, they should look at it with horror. To use a term used elsewhere in the Scripture, they should *eschew* it, shy from it as a horse does when he is frightened by something. That is his great object. But also, as I have been indicating, he would have them see what a glorious salvation they were enjoying. It had delivered them from such a condition and introduced them to something which was essentially different. And it is important, I feel, that we should realise that this is one of the problems confronting the Church. It is the problem of men and women who are still in that condition. And the moment we see that, we shall realise that in and of ourselves we can do nothing, and that the greatest need of the hour is the need for a spiritual revival and reawakening. I trust, therefore, that we are all praying more and more for a visitation of the Spirit of God upon the Church in these terrible times through which we are passing.

Now we have seen that men and women are chasing worthless vanities because they do not know God, His being and His attributes; and as we take up our study at this point, I want to emphasise this little word *in*. You notice that Paul says, 'being alienated from the life of God, through the ignorance that is *in* them'. Now that is not something that we can slip over. The Apostle deliberately uses that word 'in', in order that he might bring home to his readers at Ephesus, and to all who should ever read these words, the fact that this ignorance of which he is speaking is not something superficial, it is not merely a lack of knowledge in an intellectual sense; it is that, but it is much worse than that! It is something which is deep-seated in man as the result of the Fall and of sin. So we must not think of it as a mere lack of intellectual knowledge which can be easily rectified by giving information, – just as you might give men information about politics or about science or something else. That is not the problem here; this ignorance is *in* them. It is something that grips them and has become part of the very warp and woof of their whole life and outlook.

It is extraordinary how Christians can forget this, or seem to be entirely unaware of it. I have known Christian people, very zealous in Christian work, who really have believed that all that was necessary was that people should be taught. They felt that if London was plastered with texts there would be a tremendous response. The people just do not know, they said, therefore let texts of Scripture be put before them, as it were, everywhere they go. And they thought that as a consequence there would be a great turning to God. They failed to understand that the ignorance is *in* men. It is not merely intellectual, it is not information alone that people need; they need that, of course they do, but we have to realise that this ignorance is something which is down in the very depths of the personality. And it seems to me that there is a very simple way of proving that. There are many learned, intellectual, very knowledgeable people who have read the New Testament, but they still see nothing after reading it. This is because of the ignorance that is *in* them, below the level of the intellect, and the mere reading of the letter avails nothing; it is of no profit to them whatsoever. Therefore, I say, it is essential for us to realise that the ignorance is something that is down in the depths and gripping them; it is an ignorance that masters them. If I may borrow a phrase, from another section of the Church which I do not commend, it is a kind of *invincible ignorance*; the ignorance is *in* them. We shall see this more clearly by taking Paul's next phrase, because in a sense it partly expounds this one.

They are alienated, says the Apostle, from the life of God through – on account of – the ignorance that is in them, *because of* (here is the explanation) *because of the blindness of their heart*. I am here using the Authorised Version which, unfortunately at this point, is quite wrong in translating this word as 'blindness'. Of course, it amounts to *blindness*, but the word the Apostle used is not *blindness*, and the Revised and the Revised Standard versions are undoubtedly right at this point. The word means *hardness*, or *hardening*: 'because of the *hardening*', or, 'because of the *hardness* of their heart'. The ignorance that is in them is in part the explanation of the alienation, but in addition there is a *hardening* process taking place in the *heart*.

What Paul means by this word is not merely that the heart is hard, but that it has become callous; a kind of callosity has covered it. Most of us know the meaning of callosity. When the skin becomes thick on the sole of your foot, for instance, you have got a callosity. That, says the Apostle, is the kind of thing that has happened to men's hearts. The covering, the lining, has become thick and hard, indurated and fibrous; use any of these terms as you wish. But that is the expression that is used here; it is a kind of medical term. The whole thing is a picture, of course. The heart itself does not feel anything; but the heart is regarded as the seat of the affections and the emotions, and even more than that, in Scripture it is generally taken to stand for the very centre and seat of personality. But here undoubtedly the Apostle is thinking primarily of the emotions and the sensibilities. He has been dealing more with the intellect under the terms *understanding darkened*, and *ignorance that is in them*, but here he says that as we track the trouble further we shall discover that the ignorance that is in people and which controls them is ultimately

[66]

due to the fact that a hardening process has taken place in the very depths of their heart, and because of this thickening and hardening and callosity there is an absence of feeling; and the result of the absence of feeling is that men are no longer susceptible to the truth. Not only do they not believe, but they are no longer susceptible to truth, for their hearts are hard.

Our Lord surely was thinking of something like this in His parable of the sower. He spoke of stony ground where some of the seed fell, and again of the wayside, the hard-trodden path. The seed could not sink into it at all, and so was immediately eaten up by the birds. This is the kind of picture we have here, reminding us that throughout the Scriptures, both Old Testament and New, this condition of the heart is always put before us as the ultimate trouble with man in sin. This is why people can sit and listen to the Gospel and not be affected by it; this is why people can read the Bible and see nothing in it; it is this hardness of the heart. Now let me give you one or two examples of what I mean.

Take, for instance, that great lyrical, evangelical passage which is to be found in Ezekiel 36, beginning at verse 17. Now let me quote to you verse 26 in particular, which is the promise that God gives to the people concerning what the gospel is going to do: 'A new heart also will I give you, and a new spirit will I put within you; and I will take away the stony heart out of your flesh, and I will give you an heart of flesh.' There it is, perfectly stated. The heart is no longer supple, no longer sensitive, but indurated and hard; it has become like a stone; and the promise of the gospel is, 'I will take away the stony heart out of your flesh, and I will give you an heart of flesh', a heart that can feel, a heart that is warm, a heart that can respond, a heart that is supple. Next let me give you an example from the New Testament to balance the one that I have given you from the Old Testament. Here we turn to the Epistle to the Hebrews, and to a quotation there from a psalm. 'Wherefore (as the Holy Ghost saith), Today if ye will hear his voice, harden not your hearts, as in the provocation, in the day of temptation in the wilderness: when your fathers tempted me, proved me, and saw my works forty years. Wherefore I was grieved with that generation, and said, They do alway err in their *heart*; and they have not known my ways. So I sware in my wrath, They shall not enter into my rest.' At this point the

[67]

quotation ends, and the writer goes on to say, 'Take heed, brethren, lest there be in any of you an evil heart of unbelief, in departing from the living God. But exhort one another daily, while it is called Today; lest any of you be *hardened* through the deceitfulness of sin. For we are made partakers of Christ, if we hold the beginning of our confidence stedfast unto the end; while it is said, Today if ye will hear his voice, *harden not your hearts*, as in the provocation. For some, when they had heard, did provoke: howbeit not all that came out of Egypt by Moses.' There it is again, stated at length, and repeated, you observe, in an Epistle which is full of threatenings because of the danger of apostasy. The thing to look after is the heart! 'Son, give me thine heart', says the Old Testament. Guard your hearts, says another writer, The trouble, according to the Scriptures, eventually and finally is in the heart.

I am anxious to make this perfectly plain and clear. The difficulty with the unbeliever is not merely in his intellect; the whole person is involved, the feelings and the sensibilities as well. One of the great sources of trouble and of error is that we will persist in dividing up the human personality in a thoroughly artificial manner. We make a false dichotomy, which is always frowned upon in the Scripture. The tendency today is for people to regard themselves as pure intellect, excluding the sensibilities and the feelings. Belief, they say, is purely a question of the intellect, and they come to it with a scientific approach. But a man is not a mere intellect in a vacuum! Whether he believes it or not, the fact is that he is a strange combination and amalgam of quite a number of things – lusts, passions, desires, feelings and sensibilities. Though he may deny them, they are there, and he is always acting as a whole. That is why it is almost amusing, if it were not so tragic, to see the way in which people who pose as pure intellects are constantly displaying the fact that they are really being gover- ned by their prejudices and their feelings the whole time. They talk about Free Thought and so on. But there is no such thing as free thought where people are not allowed to reply.

I give as an illustration the way in which the whole Theory of Evolution has gripped the minds of men, and until very recently there was no opportunity for those who do not believe it to reply. The British Broadcasting Corporation would not give an opportunity to the other side; they would not allow it to be debated over the air. That which they call Free Thought is nothing of the kind, it is prejudice – the heart is involved. The fact that this rigidity is now somewhat relaxed is because the evolutionists are not quite as dogmatic as they once were! But they are still teaching as fact something which is nothing but a theory. And these men who would depict themselves as cold, detached, dispassionate scientists are thus showing before our very eyes the way in which the heart comes in and governs them and controls them. From beginning to end the Scripture emphasises this; it says that man is one, that his personality is indivisible, and that it is an utterly false view of man and of life when you try to isolate these things and to develop one part at the expense of another.

But let us go back to the beginning. The Bible tells us that at the very dawn of history the original trouble with Adam and Eve was in their hearts, not in their heads. The devil knew that very well. He did not come and have a theoretical discussion with our first parents. It was not a purely intellectual point that the devil put to Adam and Eve. The point he put to them was this, *Hath God said*, Ye shall not eat of every tree of the garden? His suggestion was, of course, that God, by a certain limiting prohibition, was really insulting them. Thus, the devil's temptation left the realm of intellect, and penetrated into the realm of feelings. God wants to keep you down, said the devil to Eve; He knows perfectly well that the moment you eat of that fruit you will be as a god yourselves and you will be equal with Him. In other words he was playing on her pride. But it is not intellect, when you appeal to people's pride and passion and desire for their own greatness! You have left the realm of intellect altogether; it is no longer scientific, it is no longer argumentative. But the devil knew that this was the point at which man was likely to fall, so he concentrated all his power and his attention upon it. The original sin, the original fall of man, was due to trouble in his heart, his sensibilities, his feelings, his passions; and it has continued and persisted like that ever since.

Do we not all know as a fact of experience, our own experience and observation of others, that persistent disobedience of God's will and God's ways always produces a hardening? Every time you commit a sin you become less sensitive. Every time you repeat a sin your conscience troubles you less than it did before. The first time, there is an agony, there is a kind of crisis, there is a regret, a remorse, and a sense of shame; but is it not true to say that as you go on repeating the same act there is less and less shame, less and less regret, less and less remorse? What is that due to? Oh! that is the hardening, the hardening of the heart! It becomes less and less capable of response, less and less capable of a reaction, less and less sensitive to appeals. There is nothing in life that I know of that is more tragic than to watch the gradual decline and hardening of a soul. Have you not seen it? Any person over fifty years of age must, alas! have seen it many a time; how a man you knew as a young man has just gradually become harder and harder and colder and colder, and seems now to be utterly insensitive. Hardening of the heart! It is an appalling thing, it is one of the saddest things in life. And what makes it even worse, is that men quite deliberately cultivate it.

As the quotation in Hebrews 3 points out to us, for the purposes of sin men and women deliberately harden their hearts. And of course you have got to do that if you want to enjoy sin. While the heart is tender and supple you cannot enjoy sin because your heart is protesting the whole time, and the remorse follows, and it takes away all your pleasure. So that if you want to enjoy a life of sin you have got somehow or other to do something to your heart, you must harden it, lest, in spite of all the modern theorising, it should keep on asserting itself. A man says, I have come to the conclusion there is no God; this talk about morality and religion is all nonsense, and I am going to live as I like. But, although he decides that, his heart goes on telling him that there *is* a God. When he breaks the sabbath he remembers; he wishes he did not remember, but his heart goes on speaking; he does wrong things, and his heart speaks. A battle goes on within him. There is only one thing to do, he must somehow try to silence his heart! Long after the intellect has capitulated the heart goes on making its protests! And so men discover that the only way to enjoy sin is somehow or other to silence the heart, to harden it.

If I were asked to state what, in my opinion, is the most out-standing characteristic of life outside Christ today, I would without any hesitation say that it is the hardness of the heart of man. There are too many people walking about with mask-like faces. And they have deliberately put it on. But before they put on such a face they put this hardness on to their hearts by crushing feelings deliberately, putting on this pose, this attitude towards life, deliberately crucifying things within them, silencing protests and stamping upon any softness or tenderness. They have decided to go in for that sort of behaviour. The hardness of life! How unfeeling some people have become, almost incapable of sympathy! To live such a life you have to come to a deliberate decision. If you allow your feelings to interfere it will spoil it all for you, so you put this casing around yourself, as it were, which is the hardening of the heart. Then, whatever comes, you take no notice, you continue to put on that bold front, and you go through with it. It is done deliberately, a kind of false crucifixion of the very life and nature that God has given to us. And it is, I say, being enacted before our very eyes. Do you not feel that with so many of these people you never really get to know them? You are meeting the mask, you are meeting this appearance that they put on, you never seem to be able to get at *them*. There is a steel casing around them and they are just acting as robots, as it were. It is a mechanical kind of life; and they are all doing the same thing in exactly the same way. They put on the same accent, they use the same phrases; it is all artificial. The hardening of the heart! It must be done, if they really want to enjoy that kind of life, because if the sensibility remains they cannot enjoy it, there is a protest the whole time, so the heart must be hardened.

What follows? Having done this for some time – this is the terrible thing! – these people who cultivate hardness find that they have really become hard, and though they would occasionally like to feel, they cannot. So for example when death visits the family they are incapable of tears, they cannot feel any longer, they have crushed their feelings so much that in the end they have none. And so life becomes cruel. Old people become an encumbrance. Let them go into an old people's home, they say. Thus it is that the things that used to make life sweet and noble and happy are rapidly disappearing, and we are all living this curiously hard, isolated life, in which the main desire is not to be troubled, not to be bothered. Thus it is, I say, that men find themselves incapable of feeling. And all this, of course, applies supremely in the attitude towards God. The hardening eventually leads to an utter enmity, and so the Bible says that the natural mind is 'enmity against God'; it hates God. Tell men about the glories of the gospel and the life of God and of Christ and they say, It leaves me quite cold! Of course it does! How accurate they are! The most glorious things in the universe, the most wonderful, uplifting, thrilling things – they leave me quite cold, says the unbeliever, I couldn't care less! What an awful phrase, what a tragic confession! Incapable of feeling, left quite cold, unmoved!

If you want a great classic example of all this, you will find it in the New Testament in the case of the Pharisees who could look in the face of the Lord Jesus Christ, hear his words and see His miracles, and yet hate Him. What was their trouble? Oh! He says, these people honour Me with their lips, but their heart is far from Me! – hardened! cold! insensitive! filled with bitterness and hatred, finally leading to violence! And as I have been saying, it is exactly the same today! If people just said, Well, I do not believe that Gospel of yours, and left it at that, it might not be so bad, but they can never stop there. They are bound to show their contempt, their scorn, their cold laughter, their chilly disdain, their steely, icy glance. Have you not seen it, this hardening of the heart, which shows itself above everything else in their relationship to God and the Lord Jesus Christ.

There it is, says the Apostle, men's understandings are darkened, they are alienated from the life of God because of these two things, the ignorance that is in them and the hardening of their heart. I have given you Paul's psychological analysis of them, and it is perfect. You will never find anything better, or more profound. As analysis it is devastating. But we must ask the question, What does all this lead to? Being what they are, how do men live? Here again the Apostle gives us the terrible truth: 'who, being past feeling, have given themselves over unto lasciviousness, to work all uncleanness with greediness'. Let us examine the phrases.

'Being past feeling.' That simply means they have got into a state in which they are beyond shame and beyond regret. Jeremiah knew something about this, for people have always been the same in the life of sin; that is why there is nothing more farcical and nonsensical than to think that man changes. Jeremiah writes about some of his contemporaries who had departed from God and who were in the same kind of phase through which the world is passing at the present time, even as it was when our Lord Himself was here. There are particular phases and epochs in the history of the world when sin seems to be more open, and then swift destruction comes. It was like that in the time of Jeremiah. The prophet tells us that his contemporaries were guilty of certain things, but the worst thing of all about them was that 'neither could they blush' (Jeremiah 6:15). They had become incapable of blushing. While you can blush there is hope for you; your heart is still working if you can still blush. It is a wonderful thing to see a young person blushing. I do not believe in the Peter Pan view of life, but there is this process of hardening which I have been describing, and while we are still young, it has not gone very far and we can still blush. The blush of shame, the blush of modesty! When did you last see it in anybody over twenty, I wonder? What a terrible calamity has happened to the human race! – 'neither could they blush', no sense of shame, incapable of blushing any longer, no matter what happens!

The Apostle Paul, when writing his First Epistle to Timothy, puts it like this: 'speaking lies in hypocrisy; having their con-science seared with a hot iron' (4:2). Here is another medical term. What does he mean by a conscience *seared with a hot iron*? The actual word he used was '*cauterised* with a hot iron'. You put the iron in the fire, it gets red hot, then you put it on the wound and it cauterises it, that is to say, it hardens it. Cauterised! And that is what has happened, Paul says, to men's consciences; they have been seared with a hot iron, the nerves are destroyed, the sensitivity has gone, they can no longer feel, they can no longer react. That is how they have dealt with their consciences, and that is how this kind of life is always lived. If you want to enjoy it in any shape or form it is essential to deal very forcibly with the heart and with the conscience; you have got to drown it or sear it or cauterise it, or somehow or another try to silence it. And according to the Apostle there is this terrible step at the end

[73]

when you have been so successful at it that you really are beyond feeling. Even though you would like to feel, you cannot, you have become totally insensitive, you seem to have lost your moral sense, you have become more or less like a beast. And the almost incredible thing is that men and women do this cauterising of the conscience deliberately.

How do they do it? A very common method is to argue as to whether there is such a thing as conscience after all, and to conclude that there is not; 'conscience' is only certain habits, mere traditions, which we have inherited; there is no such thing as an inward monitor placed there by God. You argue it away intellectually. Another way is to argue against the Bible and the biblical view of sin. All that, you say, is only a throw-back from primitive conditions, we do not believe that sort of thing any longer. You reject the whole biblical view of life and say, Man was made like this after all; he was given these powers and obviously he was meant to use them; do not listen to the taboos and the prohibitions and vetoes and restraints; they are only a part of the relics of paganism and of religion which we ought to be sloughing off. That is another way of cauterising the heart and the conscience.

Again, positively, you take up the cult of self-expression. Of course, you say, we are meant to express ourselves, and if we want to get any kick out of life, we must rid ourselves of all this nonsense of religion and so on; we must express ourselves and our personalities. I know of nothing so pathetic in life as people trying to express themselves and to be something that they were never meant to be. People who were meant to be naturally quiet and modest want to enjoy the social round or whatever it is, and in order to do so they put on this self-expression. But they are not really expressing themselves at all, they are expressing the model, the standard type, to which they are trying to conform. They call it self-expression, but they are crucifying their own personality, they are denying their real selves and are putting on this façade; they are trying to be bold, trying to do the daring thing. They probably do not want to at the beginning, but they gradually harden themselves into conformity. And thus they get into the state in which they are past feeling altogether. They finally reach a stage in which they have ignored their conscience for so long, and have been so diligent and assiduous in silencing it and cauterising it, that in the end they become incapable of feeling.

And so, in that state, says the Apostle, this is what they do; they 'give themselves over unto lasciviousness', which means they abandon themselves to it. Or, to use modern phraseology, they let themselves go. They abandon all restraint, all attempts at self-control and at discipline; they care nothing at all for conscience or for public opinion, tradition, decency, morality, or anything else. Divine threatenings, thoughts of death or of judgment, leave them unmoved. Nothing matters! If they have to face it, well, they fortify themselves with alcohol or something else, and deliberately put on the façade. They become quite lawless, nothing can restrain them or hold them back. 'Being past feeling, they have given themselves over unto lasciviousness.' The Apostle's language at this point reminds us of what he tells us in the first chapter of his Epistle to the Romans – 'And even as they did not like to retain God in their knowledge, God gave them over . . .' God abandoned them. Yes, that is the final stage, and here in Ephesians we have the stage before that. First of all, men and women give themselves over, and then eventually even God gives them over. That is the story of Sodom and Gomorrah. Thank God, I do not think we have quite reached it yet in this country; I am doubtful at times; but I do not think we have *quite* got there! But the world has reached that stage many times before; it had reached it at the time of the Flood; it had reached it when Sodom and Gomorrah were destroyed; it had reached it just before the captivity in Babylon; it reached it about A.D. 70; it has reached it since in certain dark periods. Is it going to reach it again? We are seeing very much of this 'giving themselves over'. The First World War did not stop it; nor did the Second World War. You would have thought they would have done! Nothing seems to stop it – thoughts of man, decency, God, eternity, nothing seems to avail, they 'give themselves over'. Unless something happens to arrest them, unless there is a mighty revival, there is only one thing that can follow, and that is that God will give them up, and give them over, and abandon them to a reprobate mind.

What do men give themselves over to? 'Lasciviousness'! This means wantonness, open and unrestrained and shameless lust! Have you not been watching it all since about 1940? The conduct of people even on the streets, the brazenness, the openness of it all! There are certain things which belong to private life, surely, and were never meant for public display. But more and more of this is seen in public – lasciviousness, unrestrained, outrageous conduct! 'the working' says Paul, 'of all uncleanness with greediness'! *Uncleanness* means lewdness, unchastity, all the foulness of life in a moral sense.

And all this, he says, is accompanied with *greediness*, the spirit of covetousness and of extortion. It really means that self is everything, nothing matters but self. I must have what I want, and the more I have the better! So I want money, because you cannot do this sort of thing without money. Everything is self-centred. Men will spend fortunes on the gratification of their lusts, and at the same time they display their selfishness and greed. If they have decided on a night of pleasure and somebody very dear to them is taken ill, it must not be allowed to interfere; nothing must be allowed to interfere with the pleasure. Greediness! Always out for self, and anything that stands between me and pleasure must be pushed into a siding, must be brushed out of the way! Here is this hardness, manifesting itself in greediness. The selfishness of the life of sin! It seems hale and hearty, and bonhomie seems to be the most evident feature. But go right into it and you will find that everybody is out for himself; it is all play-acting; they are not cheerful and bright at all; true love is absent; they pretend there is love; but there is not, it is lust, and it has its price. The whole thing is in terms of self and self-aggrandisement, and self-gratification. The Apostle is perfectly right. Men have abandoned themselves in the blindness of their hearts and the hardness of their conscience, being past feeling; they have given themselves over to lasciviousness, to work all uncleanness with *greediness*.

It is out of this kind of life, Paul tells the Ephesian believers, that they have been saved and emancipated. God forbid that any of them should ever look back to it with longing eyes! He does not

[76]

say, of course, that every single member of pagan society was guilty of the whole gamut of evil always and at the same time. Not at all! But he is describing pagan life as a whole, you see. Though you may, in your spirit of fear, be merely paddling on the edge of the ocean, do not forget that you are in the ocean, and that you are paddling in the same sea that the others are swimming and sinking in. The point is that you should not even want to paddle among them! That is the life – Out of it! says Paul, keep your feet dry and clean, have nothing to do with it, have nothing to do with the unfruitful works of darkness.

Christian people, the world you and I are living in today is the world that the Apostle describes in these verses 17, 18 and 19 of this fourth chapter of the Epistle to the Ephesians. Do you not see it? Can you not see it? Do you not see it everywhere, round and about you? Do you not see it in your newspapers? I say we should not only avoid it in every shape or form and in its every appearance, but we should realise that unless the Spirit of God comes upon the Church in mighty power and does extraordinary deeds, we are utterly helpless face to face with it. No man-organised campaign will ever deal with this; it cannot. It may produce individual results, but it cannot touch the evil as a whole. The whole of the history of the Church bears eloquent testimony to this fact, that nothing but a great outpouring of the Spirit of God upon the Church can ever deal with it. That can! It has done so in ages past. Thank God, it can still do so! If we have really grasped what the Apostle is telling us, we will prove it by praying unceasingly for revival.

6

Christian and Non-Christian

'But ye have not so learned Christ.'

Ephesians 4:20

Here we come to a dramatic and almost an abrupt statement. The Apostle has been describing the kind of life which is lived by the 'other Gentiles', the kind of life that these Ephesian Christians themselves used to live – the life still being lived by those of their compatriots and fellows who had not believed the gospel of Jesus Christ. And having finished his description he suddenly turns, and uses this word *But*. Now to get the full force of this, let us look at the statement again as a whole. 'This I say therefore, and testify in the Lord, that ye henceforth walk not as other Gentiles walk, in the vanity of their mind, having the understanding darkened, being alienated from the life of God through the ignorance that is in them, because of the blindness of their heart: who being past feeling have given themselves over unto lasciviousness, to work all uncleanness with greediness. *But* you have not so learned Christ'; and then Paul goes on to say, 'if so be that you have heard him, and have been taught by him, as the truth is in Jesus'.

We come, then, to this extraordinary, dramatic, vivid, almost, I say, abrupt statement which the Apostle makes here. And it is obvious that he put it in this form quite deliberately, in order to call attention to it and to shock them, and in order to bring out the tremendous contrast that he has in mind. And therefore the emphasis must be placed both upon the *but* and upon the *you*. 'But you' – '*you* have not so learned Christ': the *you* in contrast with those other Gentiles; and the *but* standing here as a great word of contrast to bring out this marked antithesis. What then do those two words suggest to us?

[78]

The first thing, surely, that they should convey to us is a feeling of relief and of thanksgiving. I start with this because I think that it is the thing that we should be conscious of first of all. We have followed the Apostle's masterly analysis, his psychological dissection of the life of the unbeliever, the pagan, the man who is not a Christian, and we see how it goes from bad to worse because his mind is wrong. He is in a state of darkness, the heart is affected, and he is alienated from God. We have also seen men giving themselves over, in their foulness and lasciviousness, to work all kinds of iniquity and uncleanness with greediness. We have been looking at it all and seeing it. And then, Paul says, 'But you'! And at once we say, Well, thank God! we are no longer there, that is not our position. And this, I repeat, is the thing that must come first; we must feel a sense of relief and profound gratitude to God that we are covered by this *But*, that Paul is here turning from sin to salvation, and that we have experienced the change of which he is now going on to speak.

I emphasise this point because it seems to me that there is no better test of our Christian profession than our reaction to these words 'But you'. If we merely hold the truth theoretically in our minds this will not move us at all. If we have looked on at the description of sin merely in a kind of detached, scientific manner, or as the sociologist might do; if we have put down groups and categories of people, and have done it all in an utterly detached way, then we will have no sense of relief and of thanksgiving as we come to these words. But if we realise that all that was true of us; if we realise that we were in the grip and under the dominion of sin; if we realise that we still have to fight against it, then, I say, these words at once give us a sense of marvellous and wonderful relief. It is not the whole truth, of course, there is more to be said. But as we respond to these words, in our feelings, in our sensibilities, as well as with our minds, we are proclaiming whether we are truly Christian or not. We read these words of Paul, and then we read our newspapers, and as we look at what is going on all around us, we say, Yes, it is absolutely right and true, that is life in this world. And then we suddenly stop and say, Ah! but wait a minute, there is something else! – there is the Christian, there is the Christian Church, there is this new humanity that is in Christ! The other seems to be true of almost everybody

in the world, but it is not, for 'there is yet a remnant according to
the election of grace'! Thank God! In the midst of all the darkness
there is a glimmer of light. Christianity is a protest in that sense;
something has happened, there is an oasis in the desert. Here it is;
thank God for it! And therefore I am saying that we test ourselves along these lines. Here we have been travelling in this
wilderness, in this desert, and it seems to be endless. There seems
nothing to hope for. Suddenly we see it – 'But you'! After all,
there is a bridgehead from heaven in this world of sin and shame!
But you! Relief! Thanksgiving! A sense of hope after all!

The words, 'But you', of course, also mark the entry of the
gospel. And I must confess that I am increasingly moved and
charmed by the way in which this particular Apostle always
brings in his gospel like this. We see him doing it in the fourth
verse of his second chapter. He always does it in this way. There
we read that terrifying passage in the first three verses, then
suddenly, having said it all, Paul says, 'But God'! – and in comes
his gospel. And he is doing exactly the same thing here. This *but*,
you see, this contrast, this disjunction, this is the Gospel, and it is
something altogether different, it has nothing to do with this
world and its mind and its outlook; it is something that comes in
from above, and it brings with it a marvellous and a wonderful
hope.

The Gospel always comes as a contrast. It is not an extension
of human philosophy, it is not just a bit of an appendix to the
book of life, or merely an addition to something that men have
been able to evolve for themselves. No! It is altogether from God,
it is from above, it is from heaven, it is supernatural, miraculous,
divine. It is this thing which comes in as light into the midst of
darkness and hopelessness and unutterable despair. But it does
come like that; and thank God, I say again, that it does.

The position we are confronted with is this. We are looking
at the modern world in terms of this accurate description of it,
and we see that everything that man has ever been able to think
of has failed to cope with it. Is political action dealing with the
moral situation? Is it dealing even with the international situation? Can education deal with it? Read your newspapers and you

[80]

have your answer. Hooliganism is not confined to the uneducated. Take all your social agencies, everything man has ever been able to think of. How can it possibly deal with a situation such as that which we have been considering in verses 17, 18 and 19? When you are dealing with a darkened mind, with a hardened heart, with a principle of lasciviousness controlling the most powerful factors in man, all opposed to God, all vile and foul, what is the value of a little moral talk and uplift? What is the power of any legislation? You cannot change men's nature by passing Acts of Parliament, by giving them new houses, or by anything you may do for them. There is only one thing that can meet such a situation; and thank God it can! 'I am not ashamed of the gospel of Christ,' says this great Apostle, as he looks forward to a visit to the imperial city of Rome with all its grandeur and its greatness, as well as its sin and its foulness. 'I am not ashamed of the gospel of Christ', he says, and for this reason, 'it is the power of *God* unto salvation'. And because it is the power of God it holds out a hope even for men and women who have given themselves over, abandoned themselves, to the working of all uncleanness with greediness.

I have often said that there is nothing so romantic as the preaching of the gospel. You never know what is going to happen. I have this absolute confidence that if the vilest and the blackest character in this city of London today hears this message, even if he is the most abandoned wretch in the foulest gutter, I see a hope for him, because of the gospel, this *but* that comes in, this power of God! The gospel comes into the midst of despair and hopelessness; it comes in looking at life with a realistic eye. There is nothing, apart from the gospel, that can afford to be realistic; everything else has to try to persuade itself like a kind of self-hypnotism. Here is the only thing that can look at man as he is, at his very worst and blackest and at his most hopeless, and still address him. Why? Because the power of *God* is in it. And this is a power that can make men anew and re-fashion them after the image of the Lord Jesus Christ, as the Apostle is about to tell us. It is the work of the Creator. So the Gospel comes in this way, and the words '*But you*' remind us of the whole thing.

But even more, and this is the point in particular that the Apostle himself is stressing here – these two words *But you* at once provide us with a perfect and a comprehensive description of the Christian. Paul has described the 'other Gentiles'; he is now describing the Christian. What does he tell us about him? Obviously, in the first place, he tells us that the Christian is one who by definition has been separated from and taken out of that evil world. The 'other Gentiles'? – that is how they are living. 'But you'! There has been a separation, the Christian has been laid hold of, he has been dragged out of that, and he has been put into another position. He was once like others, but he is no longer like them. Clearly, becoming a Christian is the profoundest change in the world. That is where, I suppose, the final enemy of the Christian faith is morality. And that is why I sometimes feel that Thomas Arnold, of Rugby fame, was perhaps of all men in the last century the one who did the greatest harm. His teaching and the teaching of his followers has obliterated this particular point, this complete change, this translation, this movement. But it is this truth that is emphasised everywhere in the Bible about God's salvation. You find the Psalmist speaking of it; he talks about being lifted up out of the horrible pit and the miry clay, and his feet being established upon the rock. He has had to be hauled up out of the slime, the horrible pit! the miry clay! taken hold of, lifted up, and set upon a rock, while his goings have been established on a different level. Now that is Christianity, and it is only as the Church comes back to the realisation of it that there is any hope for revival at all.

To establish the point I am making, let us hear Paul, at the beginning of his Epistle to the Galatians. He is thanking God for His wonderful grace in the Lord Jesus Christ, and he puts it like this: 'Who gave himself for our sins that he might deliver us from this present evil world' (1:4). That is why Christ died. The first object of His dying on the cross was that He might deliver His people from this present evil world; He takes hold of them and pulls them out of it. Listen to the Apostle again as he writes to the Colossians: 'Who hath delivered us from the power of darkness and hath *translated* us into the kingdom of his dear Son.' When you become a Christian you change your realm, you belong to a new kingdom; you are no longer in the kingdom of Satan, you belong to the kingdom of God and of His Christ;

you are no longer in the kingdom of darkness, but you are in the kingdom of light. These are Paul's terms and every one of them emphasises this movement, this translation. You are not simply improved a little bit just where you are; that is never the business of Christianity; it never does that. It is something new. And it is going to end in a new heaven and a new earth, wherein dwelleth righteousness.

The business of Christianity is not to improve the world. No! it is to take men out of the world, to save them from it, and to form this new realm, this new kingdom, and this new humanity. We must get hold of that idea. It is not a kind of Christianisation of the world that is taught in the Bible. People are to be taken *out of it*, to be separated from it, and to be translated into a different position. Peter puts it like this in the second chapter of his First Epistle: 'Who hath called you *out* of darkness *into* his marvellous light.' The Lord takes us out of Egypt, and puts us into Canaan! It was not an improvement of the conditions in *Egypt* that happened under the Old Testament dispensation: on the contrary, the Israelites were taken out of Egypt, taken on their journey, and brought into Canaan. Peter very rightly goes on to address Christians as 'strangers and pilgrims'. 'Dearly beloved', he says, 'I beseech you, as strangers and pilgrims, abstain from fleshly lusts, which war against the soul.' We are only strangers in this world if we are Christians. Paul says the same thing to the Philippians in his third chapter: 'Our citizenship is in heaven.' Someone has translated it, 'We are a colony of heaven', which amounts to the same thing. It means that our polity, as it were, our homeland, our seat of government, is *there*; our citizenship is in heaven! We are in this world still, but if we are Christians we do not belong to it; we do not belong to its mind, its outlook, its organisation; we are strangers and pilgrims, we are people away from home, we are people who are simply living here on a passport; we do not belong here. Our Lord has said it clearly for us in His great high-priestly prayer; He says, 'They are not of the world, even as I am not of the world.'

We must be clear about this. I am not saying that because of all that I have been quoting a Christian should not take part in politics or anything like that. It does not mean that at all, but it does mean that he is entirely separated in his being, in his essence and in his outlook. Because the Christian knows that this is still God's world which God is finally going to redeem, he believes that sin and evil must be controlled. In his view, politics and the whole of culture are negative and are simply designed to keep sin and evil within bounds, and to keep their manifestations from running riot. But what he does, he does as a stranger; he does it as a man who belongs to another realm, but who has pity upon this realm; and thus he gives his time and energies in an endeavour to keep evil within bounds. He does not put his faith in earthly things, he does not think that you can bring in a new Jerusalem by Acts of Parliament, as so many foolish people thought at the beginning of this century. He has no use for the 'social' gospel, because it has always failed and always must fail: for it is based upon the fallacy of not realising that man's heart is hardened, and that his whole outlook is darkened. It is of all teachings the most fatuous. But the Christian has been separated from all such hopes. He has been translated out of the kingdom of darkness into the Kingdom of God's dear Son.

But these words of Paul show us another thing about the Christian and his character. Because of this translation that has taken place, the life of the Christian is to present a complete contrast to that other life. 'But you; you have not *so* learned Christ.' Paul puts the emphasis on the word *so*. It is not *thus* that you have learned Christ, says the Apostle. You have not learned Christ in such a way as to say, Well yes, I believe in Christ but I still go on living as I did before. Impossible! he says, Out upon the suggestion! He again uses litotes, one of his favourite figures of speech. 'You have not so learned Christ' – that is a negative, is it not? What he means is something very positive. Litotes is a very good figure of speech to employ if you are anxious to bring out emphasis. Let me give you another familiar example of it. Take the one I have already quoted from in Romans 1:16 where the Apostle says, 'I am not ashamed of the Gospel of Christ.' What he means is that he is tremendously proud of it, that he has absolute confidence in it, and that he makes his boast in it. But he expresses it by an emphatic negative, *not ashamed*. Similarly, he says here, 'You have *not so* learned Christ.' By which he means that the very

[84]

suggestion is utterly impossible; it is unthinkable; the thing is ludicrous, he says, you cannot possibly hold it for a moment if you have really understood these things. The Apostle is emphasising that the life of the Christian is to be altogether different from that of 'other Gentiles'. It is to suggest and to present the most complete and striking contrast to everything that is represented by that kind of worldly life. The life of the Christian is not to be something vague and indefinite, not something which is difficult to define, and difficult to recognise. According to Paul's teaching, and the teaching of the entire Bible, it is clear-cut and obvious – it stands out, it is perfectly definite, and anybody should be able to recognise it at a glance.

Let us look at some of the terms which are used in the Scripture to bring out this very point. Take the words that were used by our Lord Himself. He says that the Christian is to be the 'salt of the earth'. He says also that Christians are to be 'the light of the world'. The Apostle Paul uses similar words in writing to the Philippians. In the second chapter he tells them that they are to 'shine' as 'lights in the world' (A.V.). The picture is that the whole world is in darkness, absolutely dark, and would be universally dark were it not for the occasional star here and there shining. Lights in the heavens! The contrast between Christians and people who are not Christian is the contrast between light and darkness. Again, Christ says that when a man lights a candle he does not put it under a bushel, but on a candlestick that it may light the whole house. And He also says that His disciples are like 'a city set upon a hill, which cannot be hid'. It is there for all men to see. A Christian should be as impossible to hide as a city set on a hill. The whole terminology is designed to bring out these very contrasts. The whole thing is put again so perfectly in the passage in 2 Corinthians 6, where Paul writes, 'What fellowship hath righteousness with unrighteousness? What communion hath light with darkness? What concord hath Christ with Belial? Or what part hath he that believeth with an unbeliever? Or what agreement hath the temple of God with idols?' So the Christian is one who stands out in society because he is a Christian. This does not mean that he will be angular or delight in being odd or make himself eccentric or foolish, but it does mean that as we read about our Lord that 'He could not be hid', it is equally true about the Christian. When purity appears in the midst of impurity there is no need for it to exaggerate itself or to send a trumpeter before it to announce its presence, as the Pharisees did, as they made broad their phylacteries. No! Purity advertises itself: the contrast does it all.

Now this is the kind of thing that the Apostle is here stressing and impressing upon the Ephesians. He says, as it were, to them: It is unthinkable that you should live as the unbelievers do; your whole life and behaviour, your demeanour and deportment should suggest something which is marvellously and strangely different. I am emphasising, you see, that it should not be difficult for people to know that we are Christians. But I wonder whether it is? I wonder whether sometimes they are surprised when they are told that we are Christians? Is not this one of the tragedies of the age in which we live, that the line of demarcation between the church and the world has become so obscured and ill-defined and uncertain? I know that there is undoubtedly a reaction against a false Puritanism and I am not here to defend a false Puritanism; God forbid that I should! You notice that I call it a *false* Puritanism – a mere morality that has really lost contact with the truth.

It was much in evidence at the end of the Victorian era, and God forbid that we should have that mechanical religion back! But I am suggesting that in our reaction we have gone altogether too far to the other extreme and we have obscured something that is absolutely vital in the New Testament, namely, this line of demarcation between the world and the Church.

At one time it was customary for Protestantism to criticise Roman Catholicism on the ground that it mixed the two, and it undoubtedly does; but alas! Protestantism has followed suit and has done the same! The modern Christian seems to think that he is doing something wonderful when he behaves very much like the man of the world; he tries to argue that this is the way to win him. But he is not winning him! Our Lord could mix with publicans and sinners, but He was never mistaken for one of them; He was called the friend of publicans and sinners, but the contrast was there even in the criticism. And the point is that the true Christian, because of what has happened to him, because of this

[86]

regeneration, because of the work of the Spirit, because he has been made anew, is of necessity a different man, and should show himself to be a different man.

But I will go further. Not only does the Christian know that he is different, the non-Christian also knows it. At once the Christian and the non-Christian are aware of a difference between themselves. They are aware of a lack of affinity. I want to press this, because it seems to me to be one of the most thorough-going tests we can ever apply to ourselves. Unless we are conscious of a lack of affinity with people who still belong to the world I cannot see that we are Christians at all. That does not mean that we cannot share certain things with them, that we cannot be pleasant, that we cannot pass the time of day with them, as it were. But it does mean that we are aware of a difference, of a barrier, that we belong to different realms and to different positions entirely. We can have social relations with non-Christians, but the whole time we are aware of this difference, we are not at home in that atmosphere. We may, for various reasons, have to be with them occasionally, but we are aware that we do not belong to their world. And they too are equally aware of the fact that we do not belong to it. And that is the thing that is so valuable, that even the non-Christian, the man of the world, expects the Christian to be different.

One of the greatest fallacies I have ever encountered in this respect was one that came in during the First World War. I describe it without mentioning the man most responsible for it; the individual as such does not matter, for we are not concerned with personalities but with principles. There was an outlook propagated by this particular man who argued like this. 'Take those men in the trenches in the first world war; now' he said, 'if we are going to influence those men when we go back into civilian life, we must show them that we really belong to them; so the way to do that, the way to win men to Christ, is to sit down and smoke Woodbines with them, and to use their language. If they curse and swear, let us curse and swear too; we are doing it for a good object, with a good intention; we will fraternise with them, we will show them that we are, after all, all of the same bunch, we belong together; and then if we only do that with them they will come crowding to our churches to listen.' But, you know, they did not! And thank God they did not! The man of the world, the man who is still a sinner, expects the Christian to be different, and he does not respect very much the kind of Christian who is *not* different. We read the Gospels and we find that the most desperate cases drew near to the Lord Jesus Christ. Why? Because He *was* so different! I am not suggesting that there is a spark of divinity in fallen human nature, but I am suggesting that there is always a hopelessness in the life of sin, which somehow or another pays its tribute to purity and holiness and Christ-likeness. It knows it is different. And so you will often find in novels and stories that when certain brutal men are trying to make fun of a Christian, perhaps the greatest bully of all will come along and stop them and say, You must not do that, he is a good fellow. There is the difference, and I say that it is recognised on both sides.

But what are the things which thus differentiate us? Let me give you John Bunyan's answer to my question. I am saying that the Christian, because he is a Christian, is altogether unlike the man of the world and that he *and* the man of the world are aware of it. Let John Bunyan say it in his *Pilgrim's Progress*.

'Then I saw in my dream that when they were got out of the wilderness, they presently saw a town before them, and the name of that town is *Vanity*'; (Paul speaks of men walking in the *vanity* of their minds!) – 'and at the town there is a Fair kept, called *Vanity Fair*; it is kept all the year long; it beareth the name of Vanity Fair, because the town where it is kept is lighter than Vanity; and also because all that is there sold, or that cometh thither, is vanity; as is the saying of the wise, "All that cometh is vanity".

'This Fair is no new-erected business, but a thing of ancient standing. I will shew you the original of it' (and he then quotes Ecclesiastes 1:2 and certain particular verses) 'Almost five thousand years ago, there were Pilgrims walking to the Celestial City, as these two honest persons are; and Beelzebub, Apollyon, and Legion, with their companions, perceiving by the path that the Pilgrims made, that their way to the City lay through this Town of Vanity, they contrived here to set up a Fair; a Fair

wherein should be sold *all sorts of vanity*, and that it should last all
the year long. Therefore, at this Fair, are all such merchandise
sold, as houses, lands, trades, places, honours, preferments, titles,
countries, kingdoms, lusts, pleasures, and delights of all sorts;
as whores, bawds, wives, husbands, children, masters, servants,
lives, blood, bodies, souls, silver, gold, pearls, precious stones,
and what not. And, moreover, at this Fair, there is at all times
to be seen, juggling, cheats, games, plays, fools, apes, knaves, and
rogues, and that of every kind.' (This is wonderful literature, is it
not? It is still more wonderful spiritually.) 'Here are to be seen
too, and that for nothing, thefts, murders, adulteries, false
swearers, and that of a blood-red colour.

'And, as in other Fairs of less moment, there are several rows,
and streets, under their proper names, where such and such wares
are vended; so here likewise you have the proper places, rows,
streets (*viz*. countries and kingdoms), where the wares of this
Fair are soonest to be found. Here is the Britain Row, the French
Row, the Italian Row, the Spanish Row, the German Row,
where several sorts of vanities are to be sold. But as, in other
Fairs, some one commodity is the chief of all the Fair, so the
ware of Rome and her merchandise is greatly promoted in this
Fair; only our English nation, with some others, have taken a
dislike thereat.' (That was, remember, three hundred years ago!)

'Now as I said, the way to the Celestial City lies just through
this Town where this lusty Fair is kept; and he that would go to
the City, and yet not go through this Town, must needs go out
of the World. The Prince of princes himself, when here, went
through this Town to his own Country, and that upon a Fair-day
too. Yea, and as I think, it was Beelzebub, the chief Lord of this
Fair, that invited him to buy of his vanities; yea, would have
made him Lord of the Fair, would he but have done him reverence as he went through the Town; yea, because he was such a
Person of Honour, Beelzebub had him from street to street, and
shewed him all the kingdoms of the world in a little time, that he
might, if possible, allure that blessed One to cheapen and buy
some of his vanities: but he had no mind to the merchandise, and
therefore left the Town without laying out as much as one farthing upon these vanities. This Fair, therefore, is an ancient thing,
of long standing, and a very great Fair.

[89]

'Now these Pilgrims, as I said, must needs go through this Fair. Well, so they did; but behold even as they entered into the Fair, all the people in the Fair were moved, and the Town itself, as it were, in a hubbub, about them, and that for several reasons; for,

'*First*, The Pilgrims were clothed with such kind of raiment as was diverse from the raiment of any that traded in that Fair. The people, therefore, of the Fair, made a great gazing upon them. Some said they were fools; some, they were bedlams; and some, they were outlandish men.

'*Secondly*, And as they wondered at their apparel, so they did likewise at their speech; for few could understand what they said: they naturally spoke the language of Canaan, but they that kept the Fair were the men of this World; so that, from one end of the Fair to the other, they seemed barbarians each to the other.

'*Thirdly*, But that which did not a little amuse the merchandisers was, that these Pilgrims set very light by all their wares; they cared not so much as to look upon them; and if they called upon them to buy, they would put their fingers in their ears, and cry, "Turn away mine eyes from beholding vanity"; and look upwards, signifying that their trade and traffic was in Heaven.'

Notice Bunyan's three reasons. I believe they are as true and as valid today as they have ever been! The Christian is careful even in the matter of dress and appearance. He is not governed by Vanity Fair, with all its sex appeal so-called, and all its enticements to evil and all the inflaming of the passions. The Christian is careful and modest in dress. And likewise in speech: not only in the things he talks about, but the way in which he talks about them. And thirdly, the Christian is not interested in the vanities and the trinkets that are being sold still in Vanity Fair. He is interested in the merchandise of heaven. His treasure and his heart are in heaven. 'But you have not so learned Christ!' Thank God for the gospel of salvation that delivers us from the enticements of Vanity Fair!

7
Knowledge of the Truth

'But ye have not so learned Christ; if so be that ye
have heard him, and have been taught by him, as the
truth is in Jesus.'

Ephesians 4:20-21

The Apostle Paul has been reminding us that to become a
Christian means that we have undergone the profoundest
operation that ever takes place in the whole of the universe. To
be a Christian means that we are born again, born of the Spirit,
born from above; that we are partakers of the divine nature;
that we are a new creation. That is essentially the New Testament
definition of what a Christian man really is. But what has brought
this to pass, what is it that accounts for this tremendous contrast,
this essential change? In verses 20 and 21 of our chapter the
Apostle answers the question himself. First of all, in the twentieth
verse he puts it, as it were, as a whole, in the two words *'learned
Christ'* – 'But you have not so *learned Christ'*. And then in the
twenty-first verse he analyses that expression and puts it in detail,
so that there should be no doubt or question at all about his
meaning. It is a kind of parenthesis: 'But you have not so learned
Christ' – a dash – 'assuming that you have heard him, and that
you have been taught by him, as the truth is in Jesus'. Now this
verse 21, I repeat, is really an exposition of verse 20. The Apostle
is fond of adopting this particular method; he states the thing as a
whole, then he divides it up for us in order that we may be quite
clear in our minds as to what he is saying. Let us now follow him
and look at the very terms that he employs.

In the first place the Apostle tells the Ephesian Christians that they had *learned Christ*. What does he mean by this? Both the terms are important. This *learning Christ* is always the key to the Christian life. In other words, Christianity is not a vague, indefinite, nebulous kind of feeling or experience; patently it is something which can be defined and described; it is primarily a matter of knowledge. That is the thing that obviously comes out here. Paul says to the believers, You are no longer there, in a world of sin; you are here, in the Kingdom of God. But why? Because of that marvellous experience you had? That is not what he says! He says it is because you have *learned Christ*. Christianity is primarily and essentially a matter of knowledge; it is the knowledge to which these people had come. He is bound to put it like this, in a sense, because, as we have seen already, the real trouble with the non-Christians is that their minds are darkened. You remember how Paul kept on emphasising that fact. Their essential trouble was in their minds, in their understanding. Obviously, therefore, a Christian is a man who primarily in the first place has received something in the realm of understanding. *Learned Christ*! This is a tremendously important point, because we are living in an age which does not like this emphasis. The whole trouble, it seems to me, today in the church and in the world is that this element is not given the priority that it should have, and that people are saying, Ah! well, as long as a man loves Christ and loves God ... It is always put in terms of sentiment, whereas in the New Testament the whole emphasis is always upon *knowledge*; upon *learning*, and upon *understanding*.

We must consider, therefore, what Paul means by this term 'ye have not so *learned Christ*'. Previously, the understanding of the Ephesians was darkened; they were alienated from the life of God because of the ignorance that was in them; and, coupled with that, was the hardness of their hearts. But now, says the Apostle to them, all that has been overcome and you have a knowledge of the Lord Jesus Christ. He frequently uses this very phrase; for example, in the second chapter of his First Epistle to Timothy he writes like this: 'It is the will of God that all men be saved, and come unto a knowledge of the truth.' 'To come unto a knowledge of the truth' is how he defines being saved. The Christian therefore, by definition, is a man whose eyes have been opened, while the unbeliever is still blinded by the god of this world. What then can he now see? First and foremost, he becomes aware of his own state and condition. And that is obviously the first thing that must happen to any man who becomes a Christian. So far he has been living a worldly life, following the crowd, doing what everybody else does, trying to persuade himself that life is wonderful. He may have read his Bible occasionally or may have been taken ill and people may have spoken to him about Christian things; but they have meant nothing to him, he is irritated, annoyed by them, and sees nothing in them. Now, the first thing that happens to such a person is that he begins to examine the position, his eyes are opened and he begins to see his own state and condition, and the condition of the world and the society in which he finds himself. He begins to ask questions and to say to himself, Is this earthly life going on for ever? is it going to last? what is its real value? He had never thought about that before. If he was a little unhappy before, he plunged into more pleasure; if troubles came, he turned his back on them and tried to drown them. But suddenly he finds himself facing these things and asking certain questions – what does a man do with himself when he has lost his health or his money? or when he has lost a loved one, and bereavement and sorrow come? What happens to a man when he is on his death bed? where is he going? what lies beyond? He begins to consider all these things. His eyes are opened, and he sees the utter folly and futility of his old position. He says, This is madness; I am not thinking, I am not facing facts, I am not facing life, I am acting on assumptions, I am not facing the big and the eternal issues. He begins to look at them and to examine them. And he sees, of course, that he is in a hopeless and perilous condition.

Next he begins to think about his relationship to God! He realises something about the being and the nature and the character of God! He sees his utter hopelessness and helplessness again. And then he begins to see the meaning of the gospel; he is *learning Christ*. He begins to see that Christ is the Messiah, the Deliverer, the One who has come into the world in order to deal with people in Vanity Fair and to get them out of that vanity of their minds in which they were walking, and to put them into His own Kingdom and introduce them to this other Realm. All this is what is meant by *learning Christ*.

Or again we can put it like this: the Apostle Peter in the third chapter of his First Epistle has a similar phrase; he says you must be 'ready at all times to give a *reason* for the hope that is in you' (verse 15). But the only man who can give a reason for the hope that is in him is a man who understands why he has such a hope in him. You do not give a reason for it merely by saying, You know, I used to be very miserable but now I am happy. That does not explain anything, because a man may say to you, 'Ah well, of course, you say that, and you say that it is because you are a Christian, but yesterday I was talking to a Christian Scientist who denies most of what you believe and he said the same thing; and then a little earlier I met another man who was not either of these things, held neither of these beliefs – he really was just a bit of a psychologist – and he said that he had found this marvellous release by what he called *positive thinking*!' You do not give a *reason* for the hope that is in you by just saying that you feel better than you once felt. Not at all! Before you can give a reason you must be able to give explanations, you must have understanding; and that means *knowledge*, it means that you must have *learned* something. And that is why the Apostle tells the Christians, 'You have . . . *learned Christ*'. It is nothing less than this wonderful knowledge of Him, and the knowledge concerning him. Now that is what makes us Christians at all. If we do not know what we believe, how can we be Christians according to the definition, 'Ye have not so *learned Christ*'? This, says the Apostle to these Ephesians, is the astounding thing that has happened to you, that whereas once you were in gross darkness, with obdurate, hardened hearts, where nothing of divine truth could touch you or penetrate, now the whole position is entirely changed; you have received the knowledge and the learning, and your hearts are softened; you now have hearts of flesh and they can feel and be moved.

How then has it all happened? There is only one explanation – this is the work of the Holy Spirit. Nothing else, nobody else, can do this but the Holy Spirit. It is His special, His peculiar work. It is He alone who can remove the veil from the heart. The perfect exposition of this, of course, is in 1 Corinthians chapter 2, where the Apostle explains that the princes of this world did not know God's purpose in the Lord Jesus Christ, for, he says, 'had they known it, they would not have crucified the Lord of glory. . . . But God hath revealed them unto us by his Spirit; for the Spirit searcheth all things, yea, the deep things of God.' 'For we have received', he says in the twelfth verse of that same chapter, 'not the spirit that is of the world but the Spirit that is of God, that (in order that) we may *know* the things that are freely given to us of God.' This work is of necessity the work of the Holy Spirit. Everything the Apostle has been saying about the godless, evil, sinful life makes this an absolute necessity. No-one but the Holy Spirit can enlighten the darkness, soften the heart, and enable the truth to penetrate and to grip and to master a man or woman. But it does, the Holy Spirit does this.

The Apostle John makes two wonderful statements about this in the second chapter of his First Epistle. He says, 'But you have an unction from the Holy One, and you know all things.' Here is the old Apostle at the end of his life writing to young Christians. They were very ordinary people, most of them were probably slaves and he is going to die and leave them, but he knows that there are many antichrists, false teachers, surrounding them and propagating their pernicious doctrines. What is his comfort? Well, he says, this is the only comfort, 'You have an unction from the Holy One, and you know all things.' Further on he says, 'But the anointing which ye have received of him abideth in you, and ye need not that any man teach you: but as the same anointing teacheth you of all things, and is truth, and is no lie, and even as it hath taught you, ye shall abide in him.'

This truth is the most glorious thing we can ever realise together. It is not primarily man's natural ability that matters. That must not be discounted, but to become a Christian does not depend upon one's natural ability and understanding. Thank God for that! If it were a matter of accepting or understanding a philosophical teaching, what an unequal salvation it would be! People gifted with brains and understanding, who have the leisure to read, and who have had academic training, would be in an entirely advantageous position, and there would be very little hope for the busy housewife or the man who has no natural ability and has never had any teaching or training or education. Thank God, that is not God's way of saving people! It would be utterly unfair and unjust, it would not be an equitable way of dealing with the situation. But God's way is quite different. No man, whatever his understanding, can really accept and believe and grasp this truth in and of himself. On the other hand the Holy Spirit of God can give the understanding to anybody! It does not matter how ignorant or how illiterate a person may be, He can give this insight, this anointing, this unction, which opens the understanding and the mind. The history of the church is full of this kind of thing. It shows how some of the simplest, most illiterate people have had a knowledge of the truth which some of the greatest brains have lacked. Not only that, sometimes it has been the case that a simple, illiterate person has been enabled to lead a great brain into a knowledge of the truth because of the Spirit's anointing!

This, then, is what is meant by *learning Christ*, and coming to this wonderful and blessed knowledge. It is the thing that accounted for the moving of these Ephesian Christians from the old position to the new. And it is something that you will find running right through the Scriptures. Take the case of Lydia, the first convert in a sense on the continent of Europe. You remember what we are told about her in Acts 16:14. Paul had joined a prayer meeting of women in Philippi on the afternoon of a Sabbath day. He sat down and preached to them, speaking unto them the word of the Lord; and then we are told about this woman Lydia, a seller of purple from the city of Thyatira, 'whose heart the Lord opened, that she *attended* unto the things that were spoken of Paul'. – Attended! If the Lord had not opened her heart she would not have attended. Many people hear the Word, but they do not attend to it; it means nothing; it bounces off them because of the hardness of their hearts. But we read of Lydia, 'whose heart the Lord opened', this was the softening, the preparation; and once the heart was opened she attended unto the things that were spoken of Paul, and so was saved and became a Christian. It is always the work of the Holy Spirit.

But let us look at the other term in the verse. 'But ye have not so learned *Christ*.' Why does the Apostle express himself in this way? He does it very deliberately, in order to impress upon us that the knowledge obtained by a man who has become a Christian is indeed a knowledge of Christ. Let me put it negatively. Why is it that this man who once walked after the vanity of his mind and who, being past feeling, had given himself over unto lasciviousness to work all uncleanness with greediness – why has he stopped living like that, why is he now a saint in the Church? What is the knowledge that has come to him? Certainly it is not a mere knowledge of morality and of ethics. Take any of the phrases found in the Apostle's tremendous list in the sixth chapter of the First Epistle to the Corinthians – 'Know ye not that the unrighteous shall not inherit the kingdom of God? Be not deceived: neither fornicators, nor idolaters, nor adulterers, nor effeminate, nor abusers of themselves with mankind, nor thieves, nor covetous, nor drunkards, nor revilers, nor extortioners, shall inherit the kingdom of God. And such were some of you: but ye are washed, but ye are sanctified, but ye are justified in the name of the Lord Jesus, and by the Spirit of our God.' There they were, many of the Corinthian as well as the Ephesian pagans – that is the sort of life they were living; guilty of these ugly, foul, bestial things; but they are no longer doing them. Why? Because they have learned something! What have they learned? Is it morality and ethics? Never! The teaching of morality and ethics alone has never been capable of changing such people. And this is why this must be emphasised with all the power that one can command and all the power of the Holy Spirit. Why did that drunkard cease to be a drunkard? Was it because temperance lecturers had convinced him of the evil effects of alcohol? What a monstrous suggestion it is! The mere knowledge of the consequences of sin has never been capable of restraining men from sin. The very men who know all about this are sometimes most guilty of these things, because their desire is stronger than their knowledge and their learning! No, this is not a matter of morality, it is not a knowledge of ethics: it is CHRIST they have learned.

But let us put it like this. What these people had learned was not merely and not only that their sins were forgiven. That is a wonderful knowledge, is it not? But if the gospel merely informed men that their sins were forgiven in the death of Christ, it would not deliver them from the horrible things which had been holding these Ephesians captive. They would probably say, Then it does not matter how much we sin, everything is going to be forgiven – the love of God is so great and so wonderful – even if we continue in sin, it will all be blotted out. There is nothing more misleading than the teaching which says that the gospel is no more than an announcement of the forgiveness of sins. Thank God, it *is* an announcement of the forgiveness of sins! – but it is not *only* that! That is the Apostle's whole point here. 'You have not *so* learned Christ', not so as to say 'That is all right, it is a kind of insurance policy, I can do what I like, I am covered.' No! says the Apostle, 'You have not *so* learned Christ'.

But I must add another negative, and with equal emphasis. The learning that is given to believers is not merely a learning about doctrine and theology in a purely intellectual and theoretical manner. Such learning is of no value to us at all, indeed it may be a curse to us. I remember a man under the influence of drink arguing with me about the doctrine of the Atonement. Theology was his great interest, the passion of his life; he was a great student of the Bible. But that did not make him a Christian. It is not what is meant by *'learned Christ'*! Do not misunderstand me at this point. This knowledge, this learning of doctrine and theology, is not only important, it is essential. A man cannot be a Christian without doctrine; he does not know what he believes otherwise; but you can have it in your mind, you can have it in theory, but as such it will be of no value to you at all; it is outside you, it has not moved you, it has not gripped your life, it has not changed you, it has not made you more and more conformable to the pattern and the example of the Lord Jesus Christ. So Paul does not say that the Ephesian Christians have merely learned the theory and the doctrine; they have not only come to an academic acquaintance with these great intellectual truths.

We can never repeat this too often; a mere knowledge of doctrine, which does not lead to a new life, is of the devil. The devil as an angel of light is very ready to get people interested in doctrine if that means that their lives are going to be unaffected. If he knows that they are going to become harsh and hard and intolerant in that way he will encourage them to read and to study doctrine and theology. So it is not only that! The Apostle puts it quite plainly, 'Ye have not so learned *Christ*,' CHRIST Himself! A knowledge, a personal knowledge of the Saviour, is the end and object of all doctrine. And if an increasing knowledge of doctrine does not bring us to an increasing knowledge of the blessed Person Himself, there is something radically wrong. And if it does not have a corresponding effect upon our conduct and behaviour, equally there is something radically wrong. The essential knowledge is a knowledge of Christ Himself as the Saviour, as the Deliverer, as the Messiah, as the One who came into this world to destroy the works of the devil, to redeem us from all iniquity, and to separate unto Himself a peculiar people zealous of good works. In other words, by using the comprehensive term here the Apostle means everything that is true of the Lord Jesus Christ Himself and also of all that He does. This is what he means by *learning Christ*.

But Paul subdivides the matter. And here he introduces it, as I have already pointed out, with the quaint expression 'if so be'. We must be clear about the meaning there. He does not mean that he is uncertain about them or their knowledge. He has already told them in chapter 1 that they have got it. By '*if so be*' he means, *assuming that*. He is saying, '*On the assumption that* you really have heard Him and that you have been taught by Him, as the truth is in Jesus.' But he wants to make this quite plain, so he divides it up for us. The best way of approaching it is to start with the thing that he puts last. It means that we have a knowledge of 'the truth as it is in Jesus'. It means in the second place that we really have heard that truth and heard Him. And it means in the third place that we really have been taught by Him. Now let us look at these points in turn.

The first thing is that we have this knowledge of the *truth as it is in Jesus*. The Apostle here introduces a very interesting change. First of all he says, 'Ye have not so learned *Christ*'; now he talks about 'the truth as it is in *Jesus*'. Why not *Christ* again? Why *Jesus*? Why does he say *Christ* in verse 20, and *Jesus* in verse 21? There is in that difference a most profound truth, which we ignore and neglect at our great peril. It illustrates what I would call the particularity of the gospel. Paul is really saying that we must not think of salvation in loose, vague terms; we must not talk about some great cosmic Christ who exerts an influence upon men in this world; we must not hold on to salvation merely as an idea and as a concept and as a thought. Not at all! The Apostle says we must think it all out in terms of *Jesus*. Now this Apostle of all men is fond of using the full term *the Lord Jesus Christ*, but here he says, 'as the truth is in *Jesus*'. And for this good reason, that the Christian is not saved by a philosophy of redemption; he is saved by that historic Person, Jesus of Nazareth, Son of God!

Here is a very great and a very real danger. It is one thing to hold on to the notion of forgiveness, the notion of renewal, the notion of divine life. You can hold on to all that without the Lord Jesus Christ! But the Apostle is not going to let us do that. He says, This knowledge of Christ is the truth as it is in *Jesus*. In other words you are tied to your New Testament, you are tied to your four Gospels. That is why they are given. There was Christian preaching and people became Christian before we had the four Gospels and before the rest of the New Testament was written and circulated; Why, then, were they ever written? The answer is that the devil became active immediately and tried to turn these great facts into mere ideas and into mere theories, and thereby their real meaning was evacuated. So the Apostle says that the knowledge of Christ is the truth that is in JESUS, 'as it is in JESUS'. And thereby we are brought face to face with this most profound truth about Christianity, that it is a faith that belongs to history. And thereby it differs from the world's religions.

All religions – Buddhism, Hinduism, Confucianism, and the rest – are built upon teachings and ideas. They say that if you accept them and follow them and put them into practice you will be helped and your life will be changed, and so on. That is not Christianity at all! Christianity is an announcement of certain facts and events which have taken place in history. It tells us that our salvation is based upon them; that in the fulness of the time God sent forth His Son, made of a woman, made under the law, to redeem them that were under the law – the historic Jesus of Nazareth. He is essential! It is not my application of His teaching that saves me, it is HE that saves me. So I am tied to the truth *as it is in JESUS*.

The Apostle means a number of things when he uses this expression. In a sense, the most important of them is that the truth is *only* in Jesus, and that it is nowhere else. In using these words Paul is only repeating a favourite theme of his. For instance, in writing to the Colossians he says: 'I would that ye knew what great conflict I have for you, and for them at Laodicea, and for as many as have not seen my face in the flesh; that their hearts might be comforted, being knit together in love, and unto all riches of the full assurance of understanding, to the acknowledgement of the mystery of God, and of the Father, and of Christ; in whom are hid all the treasures of wisdom and knowledge' (2:1–3). It is in Christ Jesus that are hid *all* the treasures of wisdom and of knowledge. All the truth is in Jesus, and there is no truth apart from Him, for everything is in Him and He alone *is* the Truth.

All the Apostles taught this. We read in the fourth chapter of the Book of Acts how Peter and John were put on trial by the authorities because they had healed a lame man at the Beautiful Gate of the temple. They were put on trial for that and also because they were preaching 'this Jesus'. You remember the reply that was made by Peter: 'This is the stone which was set at nought of you builders, which is become the head of the corner. Neither is there salvation in any other: for there is none other name under heaven given among men, whereby we must be saved' (verses 11 and 12). There is no truth apart from the truth that is in Jesus. And He has said it Himself, once and for ever. You will find it in John's Gospel, chapter 14, verse 6: 'I am the way, the truth, and the life: no man cometh unto the Father, but by me.' This is exactly what the Apostle is saying in this verse. You are what you are, he says, because you have learned Christ, because you have come to a knowledge of the truth which is in Jesus. God forbid, I say again, that we should ever separate our doctrine from His Person! God forbid that we should become academic and theoretical and detached, and forget even for a second that salvation has come in a Person, in this particular Person, Jesus, in whom God has stored all the treasures of His own wisdom and His own knowledge.

This is the thing that makes a man a Christian; this is the thing that delivers a man and changes his whole condition, and takes him out of the world and its vanity of mind and puts him into the

Christian Church and makes him a child of God and an heir of glory and of everlasting bliss.

Have you *learned Christ*? Do you *know whom* you have believed? Do you know *Him*? And in addition do you know *what* you have believed? Can you give a reason for the hope that is in you? The man that has learned Christ can do so; he knows Him and he knows the truth as it is in Jesus.

8

Hearing Christ and Learning Christ

'But ye have not so learned Christ; if so be that ye have heard him, and have been taught by him, as the truth is in Jesus.'

Ephesians 4:20-21

We come back once more to these striking and dramatic words addressed by the Apostle to the Ephesians who once had been pagans but who now had become Christian. Paul's teaching is that the gospel preaches holiness; it preaches Christian living over and against the pagan and sinful living that is still characteristic of the life of the world. If you have heard Him, he says, if you have been taught by Him, as the truth is in Jesus, you cannot possibly continue in sin. Obviously, therefore, as well as being wrong and utterly unscriptural, there is nothing that is more ridiculous than to say that you can be justified without being sanctified, that you can receive one blessing without the other, that you just believe in Christ and are saved and then later you go to certain meetings in order that you may learn about holiness and sanctification. This is patently wrong. If you know *anything* about Him it must lead to holiness. That is why, personally, I have never been able to understand how you can have *Movements* for evangelism, *Movements* for holiness, *Movements* about the Second Coming, *Movements* about temperance, and various other things. It is an utterly wrong and false division of the Scripture, it is a sheer manifestation of muddled thinking. Everything in the Gospel leads to holiness. So that at no stage in the Christian life can we say, Ah, yes, I have not yet become interested in holiness; that follows later – as if these were special departments with only a very loose connection between them. Paul maintains that if we have 'so learned Christ' we cannot possibly continue to live as we were once living. Let us follow him then as he works this out.

The great thing, says Paul, is this knowledge of the truth which is in Jesus. As we have seen, this means, first of all, a knowledge of the historic person of Jesus of Nazareth, and that our faith must be based solidly in Him. We must have no vague, philosophical ideas of salvation; they must all come out of Jesus, this Person who belongs to history. The old Creed was perfectly right – 'born of the virgin Mary, suffered under Pontius Pilate, was crucified, dead, and buried'. Hold on to the history! Once we lose the history we have lost everything. That is why the modern tendency in theology on the Continent of Europe is so dangerous (it is coming into this country and indeed has already come). It says that the facts do not matter; we hold on to the message, the truth. This supposedly *new* approach to the Bible tells us that we can hold on to the Higher Criticism and reject all miracles and all facts that do not fit in with modern science, and yet still hold on to the 'truth as it is in Jesus'. This, surely, is of the devil because this truth is all in Jesus, this historical person, and in Him alone.

The gospel is exclusive, and any man who objects to the exclusive character of the gospel is again denying it. 'There is none other Name under heaven given among men whereby we must be saved.' He himself said, 'I am the way, the truth, and the life. No man cometh unto the Father but by me.' We are not interested in a World Congress of Faiths. Christianity needs no help, it needs no addition, it is *all* in Him and there is nothing anywhere else. It is exclusively in Him, Jesus, this Person who belongs to history.

At the same time, however, we must be very certain that we accept the truth about Jesus Christ as it is. Not only is it true to say that the whole truth is in Him, we must accept the whole truth as it is in Him. I mean by this the very thing that John frequently mentions in his First Epistle. In the early days of the church, even before the end of the formation of the New Testament canon, there were false teachings about the Lord Jesus Christ. John talks about antichrists who had already crept in, and in opposition to them he elaborates on this theme – the Truth as it is in Jesus. The whole of the First Epistle of John is really nothing but an exposition of this one phrase. It is the opposite of everything false. John exposes these liars, who are teaching in the Name of Jesus, but who are in fact denying the truth. Who is it, he asks, that is born of God? And this is his answer: It is he who believes that Jesus Christ is come in the flesh! He writes in this way because the antichrists, these false teachers, were saying that the Christ had not really come in the flesh. They said that He had taken on a phantom body, that it was not a real body of flesh and blood. They did not believe in the Incarnation, they did not believe in the Virgin Birth. The eternal Christ, they said, took on Him a kind of phantom body which He used while He was here on earth, and He went out of it before Jesus was crucified on the cross.

That is what is called a *False Dualism*. It was in a sense, the first heresy of the Christian era – a kind of gnosticism. It had many names, usually Gnosticism or Docetism, but the exact terms do not matter. The point is that these men who were professing to be Christians were denying the gospel, saying that Jesus had not really come in the flesh. So as we read the First Epistle of John we find that he keeps on talking about the *flesh* and the *water* and the *blood*, the reality of these things as over against those false teachers. We must be certain, then, that we are really believing the truth about the Lord Jesus Christ as it is expounded in the Bible, and not this false mystical teaching.

But there were many other heresies creeping into the early church, such as the sin of the Nicolaitans mentioned in the book of Revelation and these led to sin and Antinomianism, teaching that any who professed Christianity could live a sinful life and yet believe they were saved. As is to be expected, John and Paul sound the same warning note. They both assure Christians that salvation issues in holiness, and that a believer's everyday life is related to, and must correspond with, the truth as it is in Jesus. Everything about the Lord Jesus Christ at once leads to holiness; so that if an evangelistic service does not lead to holiness it has failed. If there is not a message for every Christian in an evangelistic service it is not New Testament evangelism. Why? Because everything about Jesus leads to holiness.

What is the truth that is in Jesus? Think of it as a revelation of God. 'No man hath seen God at any time; the only begotten Son, which is in the bosom of the Father, he hath declared him.' We remember that our Lord said, 'He that hath seen me hath seen the Father'! But what did He teach about the Father? He had come to declare Him, to reveal Him, to expound Him. He also said that He had come 'to bear witness to the truth'. And this is primarily the truth about God! What is it? It is the truth that we all learned – most of us at any rate, I am sure – when we were little children, and we did not understand what we were saying, but it was all found in the Lord's Prayer – 'Our Father, which art in heaven'. That is what you teach a child, is it not? Not some benevolent 'daddy', smiling indiscriminately, but 'Our Father, which art in heaven'! Not even like an earthly father, but in heaven! Then, 'Hallowed be Thy Name'.

This is what we teach *children*! And yet people say, Ah, this is an evangelistic service: other services are concerned with holiness; holiness is not the subject now, there is nothing here for Christians, so Christians need not listen; they can be praying that others may be saved while the evangelist goes on with his sermon! You are familiar with the teaching, but what a denial of scriptural truth! The very mention of the Name GOD teaches holiness at once! 'Our Father which art in heaven, hallowed be Thy Name.' That is why joking and laughter in evangelistic services is out of place, for GOD is present, and where God is present, 'Hallowed be Thy Name.' Oh! how we deny the Scripture in practice!

What else? The Lord goes on to say, 'Thy kingdom come, Thy will be done on earth as it is in heaven.' It is because His will is not done that evangelism is necessary. I must not stay with this. But listen to Christ Himself praying to the Father; and this is what you hear. 'Holy Father'! 'Holy Father'! He was the only begotten Son; He had come out of the eternal bosom; yet that is how He addresses Him – 'Holy Father'. To Christ, then, is committed the revelation of God.

But what does He say about Himself? What are we told about

Him? Before His birth into the world Mary was told in the annunciation that, 'That holy thing which shall be born of thee shall be called the Son of God'! The Virgin Birth pronounces His sinlessness. He was not born out of natural wedlock, He was not born as everybody else has been born. Mary is told, 'The Holy Ghost shall come upon thee, and the power of the Highest shall overshadow thee.' There was need of a cleansing process. He had not a sinful human nature. The human nature was cleansed for Him, it was perfect. His very birth is holy. So you cannot mention His Name without at once realising that you are directed to holiness and to a new type of life. 'That holy thing which shall be born of thee. . . .'!

And then, follow our Lord's life; notice how separate it was, how unusual; so that He is able to say at the end, 'Who accuseth me of sin?' Again He says, 'The prince of this world cometh, and findeth *nothing* in me.' Nobody could find anything against Him. As the author of the Epistle to the Hebrews puts it, 'He was holy, harmless, undefiled, and separate from sinners.' You cannot preach Jesus Christ without preaching holiness; it is inconceivable! And if you attempt to do it you are denying Him. You cannot separate the message from the Person, in any sense. Ah, but, you say, people are not interested in Jesus Christ; what they want is peace or happiness or comfort. Well, if they are going to get satisfaction in Him, they have got to face Him, and He is holy, harmless, and undefiled, separate from sinners. You cannot preach Jesus Christ without preaching holiness.

And then take Christ's teaching. What is His teaching? The Sermon on the Mount! 'Blessed are the poor in spirit.' 'Blessed are they that mourn.' Some people say, Come to Jesus; do not worry about repentance now, that will come afterwards. But Christ starts with it! 'Blessed are the poor in spirit', that is to say, people who realise how helpless and weak they are. 'Blessed are they that mourn', that is to say, those who are conscious of their sinfulness. 'Blessed are they that do hunger and thirst after righteousness.' 'Blessed are the pure in heart, for they shall see God.' This teaching is found throughout the Lord's ministry. Listen to Him addressing the Pharisees and others. He says, You people who are so careful and punctilious about paying tithes of mint and rue and anise and cummin, you are negligent about the greater and weightier things of the law. You believe you should make clean the outside of the cup and the platter, but your inward part is full of ravening and of wickedness! That is His teaching! 'This people', He says, 'honoureth me with their lips, but their heart is far from me.' He is not interested in superficial, glib religion which is on the lips only; He is interested in the *heart*. 'Ye are they', He says again to these people, 'which justify yourselves before men, but God knoweth your hearts; for that which is highly esteemed among men is abomination in the sight of God.'

Ah! says many a modern man, I am not interested in these Epistles, I am a man for the Gospels, I am a believer in the simple gospel. Well, there is the gospel! There are your simple Gospels, packed from beginning to end with the importance of the heart, and its purity and cleanliness, because God is God, and God is Light, and in Him is no darkness at all. And then we read how a poor woman, a notorious sinner, comes to Him. She washes His feet with her tears, and He is kind and compassionate, and says concerning her to a Pharisee, 'Her sins, which are many, are forgiven.' To another such woman He says, 'Go, and *sin no more*'! He does not stop at saying, 'Thy sins are forgiven thee' but adds 'go, and sin no more'. And to yet another healed person He said, I have done this for you, 'Go and sin no more, lest a worse thing come unto thee'! And so it is always. He did not come merely to give people a little happiness and to assure them that their sins were forgiven, or to heal their sicknesses and diseases. He always emphasises this other side: 'Thy faith hath *saved* thee, go in peace', where the word *saved* means much more than physical healing. And then, too, we possess His teaching about Dives and Lazarus – it is His teaching – about the separation of the good and the evil, and of heaven and of hell.

Look now at our Lord's death. Why does He say that He *must* go to Jerusalem? Why did He set His face stedfastly to go there? He knew what was happening; He talks about 'that fox, Herod'. He knew all about the plotting and the machinations of His enemies, and yet He goes; He 'set His face stedfastly to go to Jerusalem'. Why? Because He had come to give His life a ransom for many. His death is essential to our salvation. It is essential because of the sinfulness of sin and the holiness of God. No other reason! So if you preach the death of Christ, how can you preach it without preaching holiness? The truth that is in Jesus is a condemnation of the life of sin; it shows the enormity of sin. There is nothing that preaches holiness so strongly as the cross on Calvary's hill. It is because God is holy and just and righteous, that the cross had to happen. It would involve a contradiction in the Being and the nature of God if He had forgiven sin without punishing it. So a man cannot preach the cross without preaching the holiness, the righteousness and the justice of God; it is the supreme manifestation of it. And what is the purpose and the object of His death? The Apostle Paul, in writing to Titus, puts it very plainly: 'Who gave himself for us, that he might redeem us from all iniquity, and purify unto himself a peculiar people, zealous of good works.' That is the whole message of the cross. And if we ever preach the cross without emphasising that it was meant to make us holy – 'He died that we might be forgiven, He died to make us good' – we are not preaching a full gospel.

And again, Christ's resurrection preaches the same thing. He rose to justify us, to say that God and His holy law were satisfied. He rose in order to present us to God, to present Himself for us and then to present us. He is seated at the right hand of God; for what purpose? 'He ever liveth to make intercession for us', that we might be holy. The whole process is directed to this one end.

And then, finally, we come to the last great doctrine in these acts of salvation, the sending of the Holy Spirit. What is the work of the Holy Spirit? It is to sanctify us. It is to prepare us for the glory that is awaiting us. The whole object of every part of salvation is to deliver us *from* Satan and *from* a life of sin, and to bring us *to* God; in other words, to take us out of, to separate us from, one kingdom and to put us into another. We are God's people and we no longer belong to the world. So we see that the whole truth concerning the gospel is that, as God's people, we should be holy.

It is not surprising, therefore, that the Apostle expresses himself in the words, 'But you have not so learned Christ', meaning, as we have seen, that a believer is brought out of a life of sin, and enabled to live a holy life. Does anybody still dispute it? I have simply picked out some of the big and the obvious things in order to show how inevitable is the radical change. But I will put it as a challenge. I defy any person to give me a single detail about the life of the Lord Jesus Christ – His coming, His living, His actions, His teaching, His dying, His rising again, His sending of the Spirit – which does not inevitably and as it were automatically direct attention to holiness and to the life which belongs to the realm of God. There is nothing which is so sinful and which so denies the gospel as to make a separation between salvation and a life of holiness. The most terrible of all divisions is the division which we make when we separate what we believe from what we are, and explain and excuse what we are doing by what we claim to believe. It is impossible, it cannot be done. 'You have not *so* learned Christ'; no man who has so learned Christ can possibly do it. So, says the Apostle, if a person is living a sinful, worldly life, the question to ask him is, Have you learned Christ, have you heard Him?

Hearing Christ, knowing the truth as it is in Jesus, depends upon two things. They are very simple, and very practical; at the same time they are very profound. The first is, to hear Christ. '. . . if so be that you have *heard* Him'. What does Paul mean? Obviously he does not mean to say, 'If you Ephesians really did hear the Lord Jesus Christ preaching . . .', because he knew perfectly well that they had not heard Him. They had never been in Palestine, they had never seen the Lord Jesus, they had never heard His message as such from His own lips. These were pagans, Gentiles, far away from Jerusalem and from Palestine. So it does not mean that. It does mean, however, that they had heard the message of the gospel. They probably had not heard any of the apostles apart from Paul himself, so *learning Christ* and *hearing Him* refer here to the apostolic message. Paul says, 'I am an ambassador for Christ', so that as you hear me you are hearing Him. The ambassador speaks for the king, the head of the kingdom, and Paul is an ambassador saying, 'We beseech you in Christ's stead, be ye reconciled to God.' So hearing the Apostle is hearing Christ; it always means hearing the message.

What then does the word *hearing* actually mean? '. . . if so be that you have *heard* Him'. The words of the Apostle imply a difference between *listening* and *hearing*, which can best be illustrated by words that our Lord Himself spoke: You will find it in John's Gospel, chapter 5: 'Verily, verily, I say unto you, he that *heareth* my words and believeth on Him that sent me shall not come into condemnation, but is passed from death unto life'. 'He that *heareth* my words'. The people to whom He was preaching were all listening to him but despite their listening, they did not *hear* Him: 'He that *heareth* my word and believeth on Him that sent me shall not come into condemnation.' Hearing is a tremendous thing. Let me give you another illustration of the same point. It belongs to that wonderful, lyrical story of the first convert that Paul had in Europe – Lydia, a seller of purple from the city of Thyatira. What we are told about her is this: 'whose heart the Lord opened, that she *attended* unto the things that were spoken of Paul' – she not only listened, but she attended. Men and women can listen to gospel sermons without hearing Christ. There are people who can sit and listen to the gospel the whole of their lives and never hear it. They do not attend to it.

It is the same distinction as we make between seeing and perceiving. You can look at a thing and see nothing but the thing itself. You can look at a marvellous landscape and see trees and grass and animals and mountains and rivers, and no more. As Wordsworth says of Peter Bell:

> *A primrose by a river's brim,*
> *A yellow primrose was to him,*
> *And it was nothing more.*

Just a primrose! Are there not plenty of primroses? And as far as Peter Bell was concerned there was nothing more to it. To him a primrose was a primrose, nothing more! But, says Wordsworth in another of his poems,

> *To me the meanest flower that blows can give*
> *Thoughts that do often lie too deep for tears.*

One man looks at a little violet in a hedgerow and he sees the mighty Creator, and he worships Him! The other man – Huh! just another flower, there are so many thousands of them! Or, if he is a botanist, he comes and dissects it – petals, stamens and the rest! You see my point? To *hear* Christ does not just mean that you listen to sermons or listen to the gospel. It does not even mean enjoying them. You can enjoy preaching and still not hear Christ. If a man is a preacher worthy of his salt you ought to enjoy his preaching; but there is a danger even so – you can enjoy the preaching and not *hear* Christ! It does not even mean being aware of what He has said. We can be aware of what He has said in the Four Gospels and still not hear Christ! It is possible for a man to take this subject up intellectually; there is nothing to stop him; and if he has got a good intellect he can divide up the books of the Scripture perfectly easily. But he may never *hear* Christ! He can tell you perhaps the content of the Epistle to the Ephesians; maybe he can do it in five minutes! But he may never have heard *Christ*! An intellectual knowledge, an awareness, is not enough. Indeed, I go further, and say that to accept the truth with the intellect alone is not the same thing as hearing Christ.

To hear Christ goes beyond all these things. It means that a listener to the gospel not only listens, but believes it to be the truth, understands what it says, and even understands what it *implies*. Furthermore, it includes the anointing, the unction that the Holy Ghost gives, that gives us a spiritual apprehension. It is not a glib and facile believism; it is something that takes up the whole personality. In other words, we realise its significance, and its significance for *us*. A man who *hears* Christ is a man who says, This is the most important thing in the world, this is everything; I know many other things and I am not detracting from their value, but this, this is truth, this is *the truth*! He has heard Christ! He says, 'I will let everything go rather than this; I will sacrifice everything as long as I can have the eternal life which this gospel promises the believers.' The message has gripped him, it has apprehended him, and he is apprehending it. It means that he surrenders himself to it. When a man has *heard* Christ, Christ and His gospel become the chief things in his life, he is mastered by them. he is governed and controlled by them, he surrenders himself to them, he lives to obey Christ and to obey the gospel. Indeed, it is quite obvious from the whole context and from the whole of the New Testament, that to *hear* Christ means that Christ controls and determines our lives. It cannot mean less than that! 'If so be that ye have heard Him,' I know who He is, says the believer, and I know why He has come, and I know that the gospel of Christ is truth, the truth of *GOD*; this, then, must be first and supreme in my life. That is what is meant by hearing Him. So much, then, for the first condition!

Let us pass on to the second condition. 'If so be that ye have heard Him *and have been taught by Him.*' So reads the Authorised Version; but it should be, 'if so be that ye have heard Him *and have been taught in Him*', taught *in* Him – a very important difference. What does the Apostle mean? He does not merely mean 'taught in the doctrine concerning Him', because he has already said that; this is an addition, meaning that we have been taught *in union* with Him. In other words, the teaching about which he is speaking is not a detached kind of teaching. To hear Christ and to be taught in Christ means that you are no longer an outsider, you are *in* Christ. That is why this kind of teaching is so different from every kind of teaching carried on in the world. A man can lecture to you on history, or poetry, or on science, or anything else, and of course the whole time there is this detachment, not only as between the people listening and the one who is speaking, but between those who are listening and even believing what is taught and the truth itself; you are not *in* it. But the meaning conveyed to us by Paul here is, that if you have *heard* Christ you are *in* Christ, and so you are learning from the inside. This is a tremendous thing and to some extent we have already been dealing with it. The Apostle introduces this kind of learning at the end of his first chapter. He prays for the Ephesian Christians, 'that the eyes of your understanding may be enlightened'; he prays 'that the God of our Lord Jesus Christ, the Father of glory, may give unto you the spirit of wisdom and revelation in the knowledge of him: the eyes of your understanding being en-lightened, that you may know what is the hope of his calling, and what the riches of the glory of his inheritance in the saints, and what is the exceeding greatness of his power to us-ward who believe, according to the working of his mighty power, which he wrought in Christ, when he raised him from the dead, and set him at his own right hand in the heavenly places, far above all prin-cipality, and power, and might, and dominion, and every name that is named, not only in this world, but also in that which is to come: and hath put all things under his feet and gave him to be the head over all things to the church, which is his body, the fulness of him that filleth all in all'. And again in this fourth chapter, Paul has been telling us that we are in Christ, in the body. He has been making tremendous statements – 'from whom the whole body, fitly joined together and compacted by that which every joint supplieth, according to the effectual working in the measure of every part, maketh increase of the body unto the edifying of itself in love'; and his prayer is that we all 'may grow up into him in all things, which is the head'.

What does it all mean? It means that we are being taught *in* Christ! The life of Christ is in us! It is not theory, it is a life-giving teaching, it is a life-imparting teaching. If I am preaching in the Spirit, as I pray God I am, I am not only uttering words to you, I am imparting *life* to you, I am being used of God as the channel of the Spirit and my words bring life and not merely knowledge. Do you accept that distinction? I am almost afraid sometimes for those of you who take notes, that you may just be getting the words and not the Spirit. I am not saying that you should not take notes, but I do warn you to be careful. Much more important than the words is the Spirit, the life; *in* Christ we are being taught, and built up in Him. So that in a sense, though you may forget the words, you will have received the life, and you go out aware of the life of God, as it were, pulsating within you. It is all the result of the indwelling of the Holy Spirit within us, and of the existence of bands of supply (as we have previously seen) by which the nourishment comes from the Head to every part of the body. Therefore, says the Apostle, if you really have heard Christ and have been taught in Him, you cannot possibly go on living 'according to the course of this world', because I have taught you already (he says) that you are parts of the body of Christ, you are members – as he will say in the next chapter – of His flesh and of His bones. His life comes percolating right through the bands of supply to *you*, and if that life is in you, how is it possible for you to go on living as do the unbelievers? 'Ye have not so learned Christ'!

I sum up the Apostle's teaching, then, in the following way. To *hear* Christ and to be taught *in* Him means that I have learned that God has so loved me that at a given point in time He sent His only-begotten Son into this world, out of eternity into the virgin's womb. He humbled Himself and was born as a helpless Babe and laid in a manger. He lived and He taught; He rendered a perfect obedience to His Father and His most holy law. And then, though He might have commanded more than twelve legions of angels to attend Him, and might have returned to heaven immediately, He deliberately went to the cross and suffered the shame and the spitting and the indignity of it all; and this He did to bear my sins; to receive my punishment; to suffer the penalty that my guilt had deserved; and infinitely more important, to deliver me from the bondage of sin and of Satan; to separate me unto Himself; and to make of me a man zealous of good works, delighting in holiness. He died; He was raised from the dead; He returned to heaven, and He sent down the Holy Spirit on the day of Pentecost, in order that I might have the assurance of my faith, and the joy, and the power. He has given me a new life and a new nature; He has joined me unto Himself; I am a member of His mystical body; I am a child of God, I am an heir of heaven.

That is what knowing Christ means, learning Him, hearing Him, being taught in Him! I believe the teaching that nought that defileth shall be allowed to enter into heaven; that heaven is eternally pure and holy, the antithesis of this world and sin, the opposite to hell. That is how I have learned Christ, that is how I have heard Him, that is how I have been taught in Him – that I am in Him the living Head, and a part of Him; and that beyond this life and death and the veil, I am going to be with Him for ever and for ever. If you believe these things, says Paul, you will 'have no fellowship with the unfruitful works of darkness'. If you believe these things, says John, 'He that hath this hope in him purifieth himself, even as he is pure.' The logic is inevitable and only one deduction is possible, namely, everything about Christ and our relationship with Him makes the old life unthinkable as well as impossible.

9
Putting off and Putting on!

'That ye put off concerning the former conversation the old man, which is corrupt according to the deceitful lusts; and be renewed in the spirit of your mind; and that ye put on the new man, which after God is created in righteousness and true holiness.'

Ephesians 4:22–24

In these verses the Apostle is reminding the Ephesian Christians of what it was they had learned in Christ Jesus. You see how logically he moves on. He reminds them first of all of the kind of life they used to live, and then he tells them that to 'learn Christ' is to learn that you do not go on living like that any longer. But again, lest there might be any uncertainty about this, or any failure on their part to understand it truly, he comes down to the practical level and reminds them of what the truth is in Jesus – this truth which they have already learned, and heard, and been taught.

The three verses we are now to consider have an unusual importance in a theological sense, and particularly with regard to the doctrine of sanctification. They are crucial verses with regard to a true understanding of the New Testament teaching on the all-important matter of holiness, and therefore we cannot pay too close or careful attention to them, were it merely for that reason. But in addition, and in some ways even more important, they are of great importance to us from the practical standpoint. The Apostle, as always, combines his doctrine and his practice. Unlike many of his followers, he is never guilty of separating them; the two always go together. If I may put it in a phrase – far too often the Christian Church today gives the impression that she is some kind of departmental store, having a whole series of departments with a very loose connection between them. But the Church was never meant to be like that. The Church is one, and there are certain things which must never be divided. Doctrine and practice: justification and sanctification: evangelism and building up. All go together, and it is all in terms of the truth.

The Apostle's statement, then, must be taken as a whole, because it is a whole. And yet we see that the whole is divided into parts. There are two parts here, with a kind of connecting link. The first part is negative; the second is positive. In verse 22 we have the negative, 'you put off, concerning the former conversation, the old man'; then comes the connecting link – 'Be renewed in the spirit of your mind' – and that brings you to the positive: 'that you put on the new man, which after God is created in righteousness and true holiness.'

There is a whole series of very remarkable contrasts here in these two verses 22 and 24. We have, for instance, the old man and the new man; the old man is going to destruction, the new man is created anew. Exact opposites! The old is rotting under the power of lust, the new is increasing under the power of God. The old is controlled by deceit, the new is controlled by truth. In other words, the contrasts are absolute contrasts. And that is what Paul is concerned to show, namely, that the two things are so essentially and entirely different that no Christian man who really has learned Christ can ever dream or think of continuing in the old way and on the old level. And this is the New Testament way of teaching holiness. It is simply asking us to be logical, to realise what we have believed, and therefore to put it into practice. It is a great appeal to reason and understanding and logic – *learned* Christ! *heard* Him! *taught* in Him as the truth is in Jesus! And any other presentation of sanctification and of holiness is not New Testament teaching; it is not scriptural; it savours more of the psychological.

As we come then to look at this great statement, there are one or two general points which must be dealt with first of all. As we have already seen, the two things in our verses must always be taken together. In other words the Apostle does not just give us the negative and leave it at that. He does not merely tell us to put off the old man, and then stop, for that is only part of an action; there is the other side, and they must always go together; we must put on as well as put off. We are not to remain naked, as it were. There is no kind of in-between neutral position. The two things must always be done together.

This is precisely the difference between Christianity and morality. Morality stops at the negative. It tells us, Put off the old man! you must not do this, and you must not do that. Then it is finished. That in essence is morality; it is always negative, it is only concerned with the putting off of the old. But that is never Christianity. Our Lord Himself once and for ever made this thing perfectly plain and clear. In the eleventh chapter of Luke's Gospel He speaks about the evil spirit that is gone out of a man. But because the man has merely driven out the evil spirit in a negative manner, and has not welcomed in the positive Spirit, the Holy Spirit, although his house is cleansed and swept and garnished, the evil spirit that has gone out soon returns with others much worse than himself; and the last state of that man, says our Lord, is worse than the first. From the spiritual and Christian standpoint there is nothing more dangerous than merely putting off the old man, cleansing your house, sweeping out the rubbish, as it were; for if the Holy Spirit does not come in, the last state, Christ says, will be worse than the first.

Historically speaking this is one of the most important things that we can ever grasp. I am one of those who hold the view that the real damage was done towards the end of last century when the Christian Church began to form organisations to deal with particular sins. She dropped unconsciously from the spiritual to the moral level. Now it is no part of my business to denounce these things, but I am just asking you to look at the facts. In spite of our having special organisations with regard to Sabbath observance, temperance, gambling, and many other matters – all carried on by excellent people who have worked very hard – what have they really achieved? I think the present facts show that they have achieved very little. And I am not surprised. That is not the way to deal with these things. The way to deal with them is to have the positive truth of the gospel. That is what happened in the 18th century. And I sometimes think that the high-road to revival is just to realise that the sooner we forget the 19th

[118]

century and go back to the 18th, the better it will be. The
positive preaching of the gospel in the power of the Holy Spirit
dealt with these various problems, inevitably; it always does.
That is the sort of point that emerges here. We do not merely
put off the old and stop at that; no, it is a combined action. We
put off the old, we put on the new; we are never to remain in a
neutral, naked condition. The two things must always be taken
together. And yet we do realise that they have to be *considered*
separately, in order that we may have a full understanding of
them. But though we consider them separately that does not
mean that we make isolated and discrete actions of them, as if we
said to a man, Well now then, for the time being, just put off the
old, and then later on, perhaps, we will take you to a meeting or a
convention where you can put on the new. Never! never! These
things must never be divided. We consider them separately,
merely for the sake of convenience and understanding, but we
must never divide them in that utter, absolute sense in our thought.

My second general comment on these verses is that the putting
off and putting on, according to the way in which the Apostle has
expressed himself here, are to be actions performed once and for
ever, although the connecting link, the renewing in the spirit of
the mind, is continuous. The A.V. translation, unfortunately,
does not bring it out quite as clearly as it should. 'That ye put off
concerning the former conversation the old man' is put by the
Apostle in the aorist tense, which indicates a once-and-for-all
action; the Christian puts off once and for ever the old man, he
says, and he puts on once and for ever the new man. Yes, but you
go on being renewed in the spirit of your mind; that is a continuous
action, it is in the continuous present; it never stops. But the
other is once and for ever, as I hope to show you. This difference
is important to the understanding of the doctrine of sanctification.

One further explanation is necessary at this point. It concerns
the word translated '*conversation*'. In the Authorised Version the
word always means conduct and behaviour, mode or manner of
living. We have various illustrations of this. The Apostle, in
writing to the Philippians, says, 'Only let your conversation be as
it becometh the gospel of Christ'. But he did not mean what is

always meant by *conversation* today; he was not confining it to speech. No, he meant the whole of the life. Later he again says to the Philippians, 'Our conversation is in heaven', which means our *citizenship*. So here he means by 'the former conversation' the old way of life which he has been depicting in verses 17 to 19. And this is how he puts it: I am therefore saying that what you have learned in Christ is that with regard to the old life which you once lived, you must put off the old man, once and for ever.

To get the exact meaning of this we must start by looking at the terms Paul uses – 'put off' and 'put on'. This is clearly a figure, and it is an obvious one. It is the figure of putting off a garment. You take off your gown and lay it aside. Or you put it on. Paul chooses this particular analogy in order to give us the sense of the finality of the action. Either you take your gown off or you put it on. It cannot be half on and half off. It is either something that you put aside – there it is, you have finished with it, thrown it away, as it were – or you take it up and put it on. It is a strong and graphic figure of speech, and it was precisely what the Apostle wanted at this stage. It conveys the full idea of forsaking and renouncing, laying a thing aside, not using it any more.

But what are we to put off? 'Put off', says Paul, 'as concerning the former conversation the *old man*'. 'Old man' is a kind of technical term that he uses, and it is a very important one. You will find it constantly in his Epistles, and it is essential for us to grasp its meaning. By *man*, of course, he means the *personality*, the totality of the personality. That is the *man*. So what he means here is the unregenerate person that we once were, who was dominated by a depraved nature, and to help us he calls that the *old* man, There is nothing difficult in these terms. We talk about our better self, and so we make a kind of division of ourselves, and in the same way Paul uses this expression, the *old man*. Why *old*? One reason is that he is contrasting something that used to be true of the believers of Ephesus, but is so no longer. He refers to the *former* conversation, and that is old because it belongs to their way of life in the past; it is what they once were – *former*.

But there is more than that in Paul's use of the term 'old man'. I think that he uses it in the sense of what the Bible means by original sin, because the old man that is in us is very old indeed;

he is in fact as old as Adam. And therefore 'the old man' really must be thought of as the old man that we all were by our birth and as the result of our descent from Adam. It speaks of all that we have inherited from Adam as the result of the Fall. So that there is a sense in which the old man is the same in every single one of us. We are all born with a corrupted nature, with a defiled nature, with a polluted nature. Surely nobody wants to dispute that! There is nothing so obvious as the fact of the universality of sin. Everybody sins, and everybody sins as soon as he is capable of taking any decision for himself. The smallest child likes doing what you tell it not to do; it likes doing what is not good for it to do. That is sin, original sin; it is a manifestation of the pollution in our nature, the depravity, the defilement that has been in human nature ever since the fall of Adam. We can see the universality of it today. You read your Bible and you find it everywhere there; it appears from the very beginning and that is why Genesis is such an important book. The classic passage on all this is the fifth chapter of the Epistle to the Romans where we read about our being 'in Adam' and then our being 'in Christ'. It is the same theme here. The *old man*, then, is what we all are by birth and by nature: fallen, polluted, depraved, corrupt, sinful, with a bias against God and towards evil. Sin is universal. Therefore, says the Apostle, I am telling you to put off that old man. Put him off!

Why then must we do this? Here again there is a preliminary point that seems to me to be of very great interest indeed, for people often stumble here, and feel that there is almost an inconsistency in the teaching of the Apostle. Here, they say, in the Epistle to the Ephesians, Paul is telling us to put off the old man, whereas in Romans 6, verse 6, he says, 'knowing that *our old man is crucified* with Christ'. How do you explain that? The argument in Romans 6 is that the old man was crucified with Christ and he *died* with Christ. Paul keeps on saying it, 'you are dead to sin', 'you are dead to the law', your old man has died with Christ. And yet, they continue, here in Ephesians 4:22 he is telling us to put off the old man. How can you put off the old man if the old man is already dead?

There is then, an apparent difficulty, but really it is no difficulty at all if you take the teaching just as it is. Romans 6:6 states something which is a fact. It is a description of what is true of us in our relationship to God. Every one of us, as I say, is born a child of Adam, every one of us is born in Adam, we belong to Adam, and we suffer all the consequences of Adam's fall. Yes, that is quite true, but it is also true to say of the Christian that the man that he was in Adam is dead. If a man is in Christ he is no longer in Adam, and if I am a Christian the man that I was in Adam has gone for ever. God does not recognise him; I have been justified freely by God's grace in Jesus Christ. God no longer looks upon me as a man in Adam, because I am a man in Christ. So it is perfectly right to say that the old man *was* crucified and has died with Christ. That is an absolute statement of fact.

Very well then, you say, if that is true, how can Paul here exhort us to put off the old man? The answer is this: It is because the old man is dead that I am to put him off. The only person who can put off the old man is the one who knows that, in his case, the old man is dead. Let me put it like this. Although in my relationship to God it is true to say that my old man is dead, nevertheless, from the experimental standpoint, because of habits and practices and lack of knowledge and understanding, many of the characteristics of the old man still cling to me as the new man. So the Apostle can say to me now, Have nothing to do with the old man, do not go on doing the things that he used to do, because he is dead! That is the argument, and it is perfectly consistent. The old man must always be thought of, as I say, in terms of our position, our relationship to God. We all start as in Adam; then if we become Christian, and are born again, we are in Christ; and if we are in Christ we are no longer in Adam. It is either one thing or the other, and the fact that we are in Christ means that we are dead to the Adamic nature, dead to sin, dead to the law, dead to any possibility of condemnation; we are new creatures in Christ.

In other words, what the Apostle is really telling us here is that *we ought* TO BE WHAT WE ARE. Does that make sense to you? *Be what you are.* Realise what you are, and be that! An illustration may help here. It seems that after the American Civil War and the liberation of the slaves in the South, some of them, very naturally, kept forgetting that they were now free men, and they went on living and behaving exactly as if they were still slaves. The same servile spirit and the same fear were there. Now actually there was a proclamation which stated that they were no longer slaves, but were completely free. That was the thing positionally and legally; that was justification. The former slave was no longer a slave; the same man was still alive, but the slave that he once was had gone for ever and was dead. Yes, but the poor man, out of habit and practice and custom, would go on living as if he were still a slave. So the thing to say to him was, Put off the slavery! you are no longer a slave! You are a free man; live as a free man, stop living as a slave, stop behaving as a slave, you are free! Be what you are! Now that is exactly what the Apostle is saying here.

There is no contradiction between Romans 6:6 and Ephesians 4:22. It is because the old man has been crucified and has died that we are exhorted to put him off. Never does the New Testament tell an unregenerate man to put off the old man; it would be monstrous and it would be illogical. But the regenerate man has to do so, and has to get rid of the memories and recollections and habits that belong to him and still tend to persist in him. I do hope that this is clear, because I admit that the teaching is somewhat difficult. It you want to know something still more difficult, read the seventh chapter of Paul's Epistle to the Romans; there you will find that he seems to be talking about three people at the same time! He talks about the *old man*, and the *new man*, and *I myself*. And he is perfectly right.

Let me illustrate what Paul is saying. When I become a Christian I find myself virtually like a man who is driving a pair of horses. I myself am the driver, with the reins in my hands; there is the horse on the right; there is the horse on the left; I am driving both these horses. The old man, the new man, and I myself! And we operate together and are conscious of doing so. I am conscious of the old man that I once was, I am conscious of the new man that I have become, and yet I myself, as it were, am able to consider these two. There it is. It may help to carry that picture in your mind. And so the Apostle says to *me*, put off that old man! Put off all that belongs to him, he is not really you any longer, so put off all that appertained to him; and put on the new man.

But there is another difficulty. There are those who are in trouble because they say that in the Epistle to the Colossians (chapter 3, verse 9), the Apostle says, 'Lie not one to another, seeing that you have put off the old man with his deeds.' Here he is saying that we *have* put off the old man with his deeds, and yet in Ephesians 4 he says, Put off the old man with all that belonged to him. Is this a contradiction? Of course it is not. Though I say that this action of putting off the old man is a once-and-for-all action, I do not mean that you only do it once in your life and never have to do it again. The moment a man becomes a Christian, or becomes conscious of the fact that he is a Christian, he *is* putting off the old man and he obviously arrives at certain conclusions and decisions. He says, Because I am a Christian there are certain things I can no longer do, and I am going to do other things. I am putting off the old man and putting on the new.

In the early days of the Church, when a pagan became converted and asked to be baptised, it was an obvious sign that he was doing this very thing. And that had happened to the Ephesian believers. The profession they had made in their baptism, or in any other form of admission into the Church, was definitely putting off the old and putting on the new. How, then, does it happen that Paul tells them to do this again, when they have done it once for all? The answer lies in what I have just been saying. Though each of them at the time said, I am finishing with the old life and I am taking up the new, yet as the years passed, and perhaps temptations came, and sin, they found themselves forgetting these things, and unconsciously at first drifting back to that old kind of life. So the Apostle writes to them and says, Where are you going? what are you doing? Don't you see that you are more or less back where you used to be? Put off the old man! and put it off once and for ever! So that, although it is meant to be a kind of once-and-for-all action, alas! in experience we find that we have to repeat the action many times. So there is no contradiction! Paul is saying to the Colossians, You are being inconsistent, you said that you were finishing with the old life, but I see that you are still carrying on with it – put it off! So there is no contradiction even at this point. Each time the need arises, there must be a complete and an entire action, without any reservations whatsoever.

There, then, we have looked at one reason for putting off the old man and putting on the new. We are to do so because of the new man that is in us, and because of what has happened to us. Take for instance Paul's argument in Romans 6 which is in a sense an extended commentary on the verses that we are considering. The Apostle says, Why do you not realise these things? why do you not realise that you yourselves are now dead to your past manner of life in sin? 'Therefore', he says, 'reckon ye yourselves to be dead indeed unto sin, but alive unto God'; then he continues, 'Let not sin, therefore, reign in your mortal body, that ye should obey it in the lusts thereof.' He says, Realise the truth about yourselves! Christ died to sin once and for all, and you are in Him and you have died with Him, and you are therefore dead to sin; put this logic into practice and into operation, 'neither yield ye your members as instruments of unrighteousness unto sin: but yield yourselves unto God, as those that are alive from the dead, and your members as instruments of righteousness unto God'. And then, you remember, having delivered his great argument, he says – 'I speak after the manner of men because of the infirmity of your flesh.' That is Paul's way of saying, I am now going to use an illustration in order to try to make it plain and simple for you. He says, 'For as you have yielded your members servants to uncleanness and to iniquity unto iniquity, even so now yield your members servants to righteousness unto holiness.' The whole argument amounts to this: because of what has taken place within us and has happened to us, we must now follow it out, and renounce and finish once and for ever with the old man and all his ways and habits and practices. We must realise the truth about ourselves in Christ Jesus. We must remind ourselves of what we have learned in Him. Furthermore, we must remember that we really are members of His flesh and of His bones, that we are parts of His body. And therefore, says the Apostle, everything that belongs to the old man must be forsaken, and must be given up once and for ever. Are we dealing here with what we are compelled to call a theological point?

Undoubtedly! But need one apologise for theology? God forbid! It is a failure to understand these things that leads to so much trouble in practice.

So I would put a question to all who are believers. Do you know, do you realise, that your old man has been crucified? Have you risen to the glorious realisation that you are no longer a child of Adam, that you are no longer in Adam? Have you realised that the man that you were in Adam has been blotted out of God's sight to all eternity? That is the meaning of justification by faith. God makes the pronouncement in a forensic sense. He tells us that we are just and righteous in His sight, because we are *in* Christ. The man I was has gone, has ceased to be. It is the most glorious thing a Christian can ever realise. He no longer thinks of himself as a man trying to make himself a Christian, or hoping that he will be a Christian. This is God's action, it is God who takes him out of Adam and who puts him into Christ; and it is His judicial pronouncement. As slavery was abolished, and the slaves were declared to be free, so it has happened to every Christian, to all who truly believe in the Lord Jesus Christ; God pronounces them to be free from original sin, from all they have inherited in Adam, from all the sins they have ever committed themselves. It is a legal pronouncement from the Judge of the universe Himself. The old Adamic man has ceased to be, the old man was crucified with Christ, he *is dead*; you are never called upon to crucify the old man, you are not told to try to kill the old man; God alone in Christ can do that, and He has done it! And we are the new man in Christ Jesus. There is nothing that I know of that is so strengthening to faith, so strengthening in the daily living of the Christian life, as to realise that the old man has gone for ever. And it is because of that that I am to put away from me for ever anything and everything that belonged to him or that in any way suggests him.

10

Corruption, Lusts, Deceits

'That ye put off concerning the former conversation the old man, which is corrupt according to the deceitful lusts; and be renewed in the spirit of your mind; and that ye put on the new man, which after God is created in righteousness and true holiness.'

Ephesians 4:22–24

Paul is here applying the fundamental doctrines of the Christian faith to the daily life of the Ephesian Christians, and his great point is that they no longer are to go on living as they once did. 'You have not so learned Christ', he assures them. Everything about the Lord Jesus Christ, he says, teaches us that we are to put off the old man and leave the life of sin. Think of His incarnation, and the reason why He came into the world. As the angel said to Joseph, His object was to deliver His people from their sins, and all He did was designed to that end. He came in order to die for us, to 'taste death for every man', that He might deliver us and emancipate us.

In this hymn, adapted from his work, Jeremy Taylor shows the 'cleansing of the Temple' to be a picture or parable of what the Lord intends to do in us.

> *Hosanna! welcome to our hearts! for here*
> *Thou hast a temple too, as Sion dear;*
> *Yes, dear as Sion – and as full of sin;*
> *How long shall thieves and robbers dwell therein?*
>
> *Enter and chase them forth, and cleanse the floor;*
> *O'erthrow them all, that they may never more*

Profane with traffic vile that holy place,
Where Thou hast chosen, Lord, to set Thy face.
       – variant from Jeremy Taylor 1613–67.

You notice how he puts it: when Christ entered into Jerusalem at the beginning of His last week on earth, He went into the temple and turned out the money-changers, these people who had made the house of God a den of thieves; He went into Jerusalem to cleanse and to clear out the temple. And, as Jeremy Taylor puts it, He came into the world to do the same thing for us, for we are meant to be temples of the living God. 'Know ye not that your body', says Paul to the Corinthians, 'is the temple of the Holy Ghost which dwelleth in you?' We see then that everything in this teaching concerning the Lord Jesus Christ leads to the inevitable conclusion that we are to put off the old man, our former conversation, our former way of living.

We have already seen that the most important reason for putting off the old man, is that he is already dead – crucified with Christ, he has died with Him. We are far too often like those poor slaves in the United States – the edict was given, the promulgation was made, that slavery had been abolished, yet some of them were so accustomed to the life of a slave that they could not realise that they were free but went on living as if they were still slaves. We are like them when we do the things that belonged to the old life. I can think of another illustration of this point. In dealing with a friend, an adult person, who is afraid of something, pain or anything else, how often do we say, 'Don't be a baby'? Now we are saying this to someone who is not a baby and what we mean, of course, is, 'You are no longer a baby, well, then, don't behave as though you were one.' That is to say, Put off the old man, you have left childhood; you *are* a man, well then, put off behaving like a baby. Now that is exactly the kind of thing that the Apostle is saying here. The old man has died with Christ, was crucified with Him, he is gone. Therefore put him off, do not go on being a baby.

But there is another reason for putting off the old man, and that is his condition, and the direction in which he is going. Put off the old man, says the Apostle, which is *corrupt* according to the deceitful lusts. Have nothing more to do with him because of his nature and his character. Everything, says Paul, which belonged to that old life is offensive. Have nothing to do with it, take it off, throw it away! As you take off a garment and put it on one side, do that with this old habit, this old nature, which he thus describes as the old man. Why should we do this? Paul, here, continues with his analysis.

First, in calling attention to the condition of the old man, and to the direction in which he is travelling, he uses the one word, *corrupt*. But this is a very big word, which we must split up into its component parts. According to the Bible, all of us inherit a corrupt nature. There is nothing of the Peter Pan theory in the Bible. 'Behold, I was shapen in iniquity; and in sin did my mother conceive me.' [Psalm 51:5] The nature that we inherit is corrupt and defiled. The whole of life bears eloquent testimony to that. The smallest infant gives abundant proof of it. We are born with a nature already corrupt, yes, but, according to the Apostle here, it is even worse than that, for that nature becomes even more corrupt! We read here in the Authorised Version, 'which *is corrupt*'; but a better translation would be, 'which *is being corrupted*', or 'which is *becoming corrupt*', getting even worse than it was at the beginning.

But there is another shade of meaning in the word that the Apostle used, and that is, *tending to destruction*. Normally, as we use the word *corrupt*, we carry that meaning in our minds, do we not? Corruption, and decay, pollution and putrefaction all go together. So that not only is a thing becoming corrupt, it is also disintegrating, and moving in the direction of destruction. And that is what the Apostle says about the old man. Put him off, he says, because he is becoming more and more polluted and decaying, and he is advancing rapidly in the direction of destruction. In other words, this is what he says about the life of all those who are not Christian, and I do not hesitate to claim that the history of humanity confirms him to the very hilt. Biographies prove it, history proves it. There is, in both of them, this process of decay and of declension, moving always in the direction of a final destruction.

But let me give you one or two other examples of the same

[129]

kind of statement which are to be found in the Scripture. Listen to the same Apostle putting it to the Galatians in chapter 6, verses 7 and 8: 'Be not deceived; God is not mocked: for whatsoever a man soweth, that shall he also reap. For he that soweth to the flesh shall of the flesh reap corruption.' That is it! Sowing to the flesh always leads to corruption, to the decay that ends in destruction. But on the other hand he says, 'He that soweth to the Spirit shall of the Spirit reap life everlasting.' Or take the Epistle of James, which is really saying the same thing in the first chapter, when, in dealing with temptation and sin, he puts it like this (notice the steps): 'When lust hath conceived, it bringeth forth sin: and sin, when it is finished, bringeth forth death.' Lust begins the process and it brings forth sin; there already is the beginning of the corruption. Then that goes on, and 'Sin, when it is *finished*, bringeth forth death', destruction. The process of corruption ends inevitably in a final destruction. As Paul, again, says in Romans 6:23: 'The wages of sin is death.'

Here, then, the Apostle's argument is that the life of the non-Christian Gentiles is a life which is decaying and putrefying, a life which is on its way to a final destruction. And what an eloquent statement this is of the state of society and of the world today. Are we not witnessing at the present hour this decline, this decaying process? Do we not see it happening in every aspect of the moral realm? I find myself constantly directing attention to it, because the moral declension that we are witnessing today in this country, and in every other country in the world, is the direct outcome of the godlessness and the irreligion and the absence of the Christian spirit in society. It is an absolute proof of what the Apostle says. Put off that old man, he says, he is decaying, and he is going to destruction! And the whole world today is manifesting the truth of the Apostle's diagnosis. The world never improves, *never*!

Now that is a categorical statement which I am ready to substantiate. The world left to itself always gets worse and worse. And if you take a broad, general view of history and come to me and say, But surely, would you not agree that at such and such a time the world did seem to be rising to greater heights? would you not say that there was some evidence of that towards the middle of the last century? I would agree entirely. These cycles certainly occur; there are improvements, then declensions. Yes, but the question is, What is responsible for the improvements? And the answer is always the same – revivals of religion! The greatest and the best periods in the history of the world have, without a single exception, always been those that have followed religious revivals and awakenings. And, therefore, the opposite is still true, that without the influence of the Holy Spirit, the world, because of the decay that is in its constitution, goes from bad to worse.

This is not only true of the world in general, it is true of the individual. Every man who lives, and who passes through middle age to old age, has to fight against cynicism. Very few people carry their youthful idealism with them into middle age and beyond. What is it due to? Ah, to this corruption, this putrefaction, this process of decay! Man left to himself inevitably decays, and he loses the gleam and the vision and the moral resilience and the protest against unworthiness. He protects himself, he lives a life of ease, he does as little as he can, and he says, Why should I be bothered? Anything for a quiet life! That is a part of the corruption. It is not that we start perfect. My point is that, though we are imperfect when we start, we become worse. The old man *is being corrupted*, and is moving in the direction of destruction.

That is the first thing Paul tells us about this old nature that we are to put off. Now, secondly, he tells us something about the influences that are impelling and driving and urging this old man towards destruction. Paul calls them *lusts*: 'which is corrupt according to the *lusts* of deceit'. Lusts! We have already met this term at the beginning of the second chapter, but we must make sure that we are clear in our minds as to what it means. The word itself actually means a strong or an overpowering desire. We remember that our Lord said just before the end, 'With *desire* have I *desired* to eat this passover with you before I suffer.' The word used there is the same word that is used elsewhere for *lust* and *lusts*. It means a vehement desire, whether good or bad. But the very fact that we tend to think instinctively now of something which is bad when we use the word *lust*, tells us a great deal about man and about human nature, does it not? *Lust* by now has come to mean something almost entirely and exclusively bad, and for this good reason, that the overmastering and overpowering desires of the vast majority of people are evil; so *lust* has become synonymous with *evil desire*. And the Apostle says here that these lusts that are within us are corrupting and destroying. 'He that sows to the flesh shall of the flesh reap corruption.' They drive us in the direction of corruption and destruction. Paul actually says, '. . . the old man, which is corrupt according to [as the result of] the lusts of the deceit'. That is the exact translation.

We must attempt a biblical analysis of the expression, and this is where we see the real tragedy of sin. The natural instincts in all of us – for example, hunger, sex, self-defence – are not wrong in themselves, there is nothing wrong with natural instincts. All the instincts that belong to our human nature are, in and of themselves, not only not bad, but good. It is God who has put them into man; it is God who has endowed us with them. They have been given to man for the enjoyment and the preservation of life. God made man perfect, and a part of that perfection appears in the fact that his various instincts and powers and propensities were put in such an order and peculiar arrangement in man that they are all meant to minister to his good and to his enjoyment of life.

The instincts which are mainly in man's body were meant to be under the control of his mind. God gave man both brain and mind, and His will was that they should control these various instincts. But the mind alone is not enough, and God gave man a conscience, which is higher than the mind and gives instructions to the mind. And then, man being made in His own image, the conscience was meant in turn to be controlled by God Himself. Such is man as God made him. Perfect animal, if the term is permissible, with a perfect body. Man has the instincts that the animal has, there is nothing wrong in them. And for a man to say that there is anything wrong in any one of these instincts is to deny the Scripture. Unhappily, there have been foolish people in the church in ages past who have said that sex in and of itself is sinful. That is a lie! And that is why celibacy as advocated by the Roman Church and others is utterly unscriptural.

There is nothing wrong in sex; if there were, it is as much as to say that God has put something evil into man! Away with the thought! At the same time, however, we are all aware that all our instincts must be in their right place, governed and controlled and ordered by the mind and the understanding; and *that*, by the conscience; and *that*, by God himself. Oh! here is the tragedy of man in sin, here is the tragedy of the world: that the order has been reversed, and that mankind is being governed by its instincts, and when the instincts get into control they become lusts. When the thing that is meant to be *under* control takes charge and governs the whole life, there is chaos; and that is exactly what is meant by a lust. It means an affection or an instinct taking charge of us and governing us, silencing the mind and the conscience, and spurning the voice of God. When this happens the state of man is one of chaos and confusion.

The Bible sometimes calls this 'inordinate affection'. There is nothing wrong with the affections as first implanted in man, but the affections must never become inordinate. If they do so, man denies his own being as well as denying God; and that is the trouble, says the Apostle, with the Gentiles who are governed and controlled by their lusts! Put off the old man, he says to the believers, stop being like the Gentiles! You are denying your own human nature, and you are denying the very essence of your being as it came forth from the hands of God! The world's trouble is that lust is in control. It is the one thing that is responsible for all our troubles as individuals, in married relationships, in families, and among relatives, classes in society, groups in industry, nations, big divisions of nations behind certain curtains – it is the whole explanation of everything. Evil desires are in control, while reason and understanding have been thrown overboard. God is not in all their thoughts. There is no doubt that decay and the steady movement to destruction is the result of the dominance, the tyranny, of lusts. What a havoc sin has made of man, and of this world of men! It has turned man upside down, as it were, and has made of him an animal and something even worse, for he was meant to be better; so that when man is governed by his instincts as is an animal, he is worse than a beast.

And that brings us to the third and last thing which the Apostle says on this particular point. You follow his analysis? People talk about psychological analysis. If you are interested in psychology, here it is, at its most brilliant and perfect and wonderful. Man, without God, is moving, says Paul, in the direction of decay. What is taking him there? His lusts! But what is it that controls the lusts? Here is his answer; he says it is *deceit*: 'according to the deceitful lusts'. A better translation, as I have already suggested, is, 'according to the lusts *of deceit*'. In other words the real, ultimate, controlling power is this *deceit*, as he calls it; and what deceit does is to manipulate the lusts. And the lusts in turn manipulate the man; and there he is, the old man, moving rapidly in the direction of destruction. This is a very wonderful way of describing it, is it not? Deceit! I wonder whether we have all realised that the greatest characteristic of the life of the world is deceit? The power at the back of all this trouble is a deceitful power, and this is taught everywhere in the Bible; now let us analyse the position.

Of necessity we start with the devil himself, the one who is ultimately responsible for the fallen state of every individual, and for the fallen state of the whole world. And if there is one thing that is more characteristic of the devil than anything else, it is this element of deceit, his deceitfulness. He has ruined the life of man, he has ruined the world, and he has done it by subtlety and deceit. This is what the Scripture says about him (Genesis 3:1): 'Now the serpent was more *subtle* than any beast of the field.' Note how Paul puts it in 2 Corinthians 11:3: 'For I fear lest by any means, as the serpent beguiled Eve through his *subtlety* ...' That is what he was afraid of with regard to the Corinthian Christians, for indeed the devil had done the same thing in Corinth, and elsewhere. In the early churches as depicted in the New Testament, the devil came in with his deceitfulness and wrought havoc among them. That is his characteristic always. Our Lord says, 'he is a liar from the beginning'; 'a liar, and the father of lies'. The whole trouble with the world is that it does not realise that it is being fooled and deceived by the devil.

But not only is this true of the devil himself, it is true of all his agents. There are some very graphic descriptions of sin in the Bible, and every time it is a picture of deceit. In the book of

[134]

Proverbs, for instance, we see how the harlot is described, with all her deceitfulness of paint and powder, and appearance, and make-believe. Deceit is written over her entire person. Peter puts the matter very clearly in the second chapter of his Second Epistle: 'While they promise them liberty, they themselves are the servants of corruption.' There were people in the early church who said, Look here, we don't say that Peter and Paul and their friends have not preached the gospel; they have preached the gospel, but they have added a kind of legalism to it, they have made it too narrow. And then they went on to say, You need not believe all that they have told you; it is much too strict, it is much too cramped and confined. We have the true gospel, they said, and proceeded to promise the disciples great liberty; you could be a Christian, you could go to heaven, and yet live as you like in this world. Marvellous! wonderful! But listen, says Peter, 'while they promise them liberty, they themselves are the servants of corruption'! 'Wells without water', he tells them, 'spots in your feasts!' The whole of Peter's second chapter is, in fact, an analysis of the deceitfulness of the devil's agents.

But the whole indictment can be summarised in a single word – the word Judas! Judas! – the man who betrayed his Lord and Master. Judas! – the man above all other men characterised by deceitfulness, by subtlety, and by dishonesty. There is nothing more terrible you can say about a man than that he behaved like a Judas. Sin always involves a betrayal, as all parts of Scripture tell us. You will even find Judas mentioned as a betrayer in the Book of Psalms. Sin hardens a man, sin deceives. Beware 'lest any of you be hardened through the deceitfulness of sin', says the writer of the Epistle to the Hebrews. If a man who is a Christian becomes hardened, it is always because of the deceitfulness of sin. People say, You know, I do not feel as I used to do; I seem to have become hard and cold. If so, then somehow or other you are being deceived by sin. Paul has a word for us on the matter in Romans 7: 'For sin, taking occasion by the commandment, deceived me, and by it slew me.' And is not that the whole of his argument in that chapter? Notice how he works it out. He says, Oh! what a terrible, deceitful thing sin is! Sin is so deceitful that it fools a man about the law. The law is good and righteous and holy and just, but you know, he said, I find that the very law that was given to man in order to save him from sin made him sin! The very law that tells him not to do evil creates in him a desire to do it!

It is for this reason that I have often pointed out that all our reliance upon morality teaching is not only unchristian and unscriptural, it is naïve, for it shows a profound ignorance of the psychology of man in sin. 'Unto the pure all things are pure.' Yes! but unto those who are not pure, even that which is pure becomes impure, writes Paul to Titus. The fact is, that because of the deceitful nature of sin within us, being enlightened about the nature of sin may lead us to sin. In telling people not to do certain things, you are stimulating a desire within them to do them. That is why I have always said to young people that, far from advising them to read books on the so-called mastery of sex, and so on, I have told them to avoid them as the very plague. Such books do more harm than good. There is nothing that can deal with this problem but the work of the Holy Spirit within us; anything less than the operation of the Spirit is insufficient for the task.

We need to be fully convinced that sin in ourselves is always deceitful. Jeremiah said this once and for ever: 'The heart is deceitful above all things, and desperately wicked: who can know it?' (17:9) The man himself does not know it; he is a mass of contradictions, he is fooling himself constantly. And that is the terrible thing about sin; it is not so much that it fools other people, it fools the man *himself*. That is Paul's whole agony in Romans 7. What can I do about it? he says: 'Oh wretched man that I am! who shall deliver me from the body of this death?' I cannot deliver myself, because when I try to do so by reading the law, I find it inflames my passions; it arouses certain instincts within me; so the very law cannot help me. What is there, then, that can help me? And there is only one answer. 'I thank God, through Jesus Christ our Lord.'

Thus far I have demonstrated that sin in every respect is deceitful, from the devil downwards – the devil, his agents, sin itself, sin in me, and sin in my members. How does it deceive? How does this element of deceit come out in sin? It does so by coming to

us as a would-be friend. It always flatters us. When the devil in
his subtlety and his deceitfulness came to Eve he flattered her.
He said: God is not fair to you, He has put a prohibition upon
you; He should not have done so; He is afraid that you will
become as He is. In this way he was paying her a subtle compliment. Sin always comes with a smile; it is most ingratiating, it
always pays us compliments; we are very wonderful – if we only
listen! It plays on our pride in some shape or form, our appearance, our good looks, our nature, something about us – wonderful! And so it deceives us by flattering us. It is always attractive,
of course. It is a very ugly thing in itself, but as I have said, it
knows how to use the paint and the powder. That is how the
Bible always describes the harlot. The paint and the powder!
she always pretends to be something she is not. And she knows
that if she does not appear attractive she will not entice. Sin does
that in every realm, it always comes in an attractive form. And
we are fools enough to look on the surface and to judge by outward appearance and not by the reality itself.

And then another thing which sin does – and this is a part of its
whole art of deceit – it always discourages thought, it always
discourages meditation. Sin knows that it has only got one hope
of succeeding, and that is to play upon your feelings and your
desires. If the mind really begins to operate, sin is finished, and
therefore in its subtlety, it plays on the feelings and discourages
mind and thought. We all know something of this. You find
yourself in a temper simply because you did not think what you
were doing. It governed you and controlled you. It makes us
live for the moment only. We fail to think beyond the one present
moment, and then it has got you! If only men and women
thought ahead, how different life would be! But they do not;
sin discourages thought, and this is a part of its strategy of deceit.

And then think of the plausible arguments sin brings forward.
Such and such a thing is quite natural, says sin, it is not as if you
are being asked to do something unnatural; after all you have
been made like this. Why are you being required to crucify your
own powers? That is to deny your personality; you will not be
able to express yourself; surely you are meant to express yourself
and the whole of yourself; it is only natural, says sin. How
plausible its arguments! And, then, in the next place, it is not

only plausible in its arguments, it conceals certain facts and factors. It appears before us decked up, dressed and attractive, and it deliberately keeps in the background the differences between right and wrong; moral categories are not allowed to come in. God, of course not! God's Law, certainly not! They are never mentioned, they never come into the argument. And as for the consequences of a sinful action, does a man stop to think of them, and to work them out? Of course he does not, he must not even think about them. As for the dangers of habit, they never enter into the discussion. No, certainly not, says the man, I'm not proposing to be a drunkard, I am only having one glass of beer, or whatever it is. A drunkard, of course not! He does not realise that the first leads to the second, and the second to the third. The habit grips him. And what a terrible thing a habit is, and how difficult to break! That does not come into the consideration; sin keeps it out of sight, suppresses facts and certain vital factors.

And then the subtlety of sin's appeal, the false motives! Oh, how many a man has gone to destruction because he really thought that he was out to gain some knowledge! A man might say, Of course I don't believe in reading bad books, but after all it is man's business in life to equip himself with knowledge. I am really seeking *theoretical* knowledge and understanding. So on and on he reads! What precisely is your motive and your real reason for reading all the details that are given in the newspapers of divorce cases? Is it that you may be able to discuss certain modern affairs with men and women, and that you may be able to warn the young against certain dangers? Is that your reason? That is probably the reason that sin suggests to us. The plausibility, the deceitfulness of it all! Are we really out for learning, for knowledge, for understanding? Some of the greatest tragedies that I have ever had to deal with in my pastoral experience have arisen in this way. People, quite innocently as they thought, were concerned to help others and to save their souls. They were quite convinced that they had no other motive. Yet it very nearly ended in their own destruction. Were it not that a man can be saved, yet so as by fire, they would have gone to destruction.

But the devil had suggested that the desire to help was good and provided a wonderful opportunity. I sometimes have to address theological students and young ministers on this subject, and I have to warn them to be very careful in every way. It applies to both men and women, it is as dangerous on one side as on the other. People say they want spiritual help, but sometimes it is not spiritual help that they really want, for sin is full of deceit. 'The lusts of deceit'!

Finally, sin offers what it can never give, that is, satisfaction. Sin never satisfies; it never has done, it never will do; it cannot because it is wrong, it is foul. It never satisfies, although it is always offering satisfaction. Indeed, sin working through lusts never really gives anything at all, but simply takes away. Had you ever thought of that? Think of the Prodigal Son who is the classical proof to me of all this. There he is, poor fellow, in the field with the husks and the swine. And this is the pregnant phrase of Scripture: 'No man gave unto him.' But, they had taken a great deal from him, those very people who had emptied his pockets. He had left home with his bit of fortune, and those who became his boon companions. Oh how affable and kind and pleasant they were! How they praised him and toasted his health! He was the finest man in the world! Yet they were robbing him the whole time, they took everything he had got, and in his penury and in his need no man gave unto him. Sin robs us, takes from us, exhausts us mentally, physically, morally, in every respect, and at the end leaves us on the scrap heap, unwanted! It is entirely destructive. It takes away and robs us of character, chastity, purity, honesty, morality, uprightness, delicacy, balance, sensitivity, and everything that is most noble in man. Is it surprising that the Apostle says, 'Put off concerning the former conversation the old man, which is corrupt according to the deceitful lusts'? Avoid sin, I say, as the very plague, get as far away from it as you can, do all you can to destroy it and to mortify it. The New Testament is full of this teaching. Sin is so horrible, so foul, so deceitful! 'Put off, then, concerning the former conversation the old man, that is being corrupted and going in the direction of destruction as the result of the lusts of deceit.'

11

When not to Pray but to Act

'That ye put off concerning the former conversation
the old man, which is corrupt according to the
deceitful lusts; and be renewed in the spirit of your
mind; and that ye put on the new man, which after
God is created in righteousness and true holiness.'

Ephesians 4:22–24

So far, in our consideration of these words of the Apostle, we
have taken them in their *general* aspect. We have seen *why* we are
to put off the old man; and now, the next step is to learn *how* we
put him off. It is not enough just to say, Put off the old man,
put on the new! This is something that has to be done in practice
and in detail and we must know exactly how to do it. Now it may
be that at this point modern evangelicalism shows its greatest
weakness, for this aspect of the Christian life it has sadly neglected.
We have often expressed adverse criticisms of Roman Catholicism,
and we still do so. But we must grant that in this particular matter,
the culture of the spiritual and the devotional life, they have a
great deal to teach us. However we need not go to them. It
was the peculiar teaching of the Puritans of the 17th century.
This kind of pastoral theology, this teaching in detail of how this
fight of faith is to be fought, was the thing in which they excelled.
But all that, I say, has tended to be neglected by us, and to that
extent we are guilty of doing violence to the Scripture. What,
then, is the teaching concerning the putting off of the old man?

The first principle is clear. The 'putting off' is something that the
Christian has to do. It is not something that is done for him.
The exhortation comes to him as a definite command. 'Put off

the old man'! I begin by stating the requirement negatively. Putting off the old man is not something that is to be prayed about. That sounds most unspiritual, does it not? Imagine a preacher in a Christian pulpit telling people that they are not to pray about this matter! But it is essential that we should say that, because there is a tendency on the part of many people, whatever the problem is, to say glibly and immediately, 'We must pray about it! We must take it to the Lord in prayer.' It is quite simple, they say, there is nothing to do but to pray. Is anything worrying you? pray about it! Not at all, says Paul; you do not pray about this, you put off the old man; get on with it! There is something almost violent about this; and I think it needs violence, because there is a great deal of sickly sentimentality and false piety concerning this matter, which leads certain people to live a kind of spiritual life ever in the doldrums. Of course we need to pray about everything, our whole life should be a life of prayer. We should pray without ceasing. What I am saying is that you do not solve this problem by just praying about it. The Apostle does not say to the Christians in Ephesus, With regard to this problem, I want you to pray about it. Far from it. He in fact says, For these reasons that I have given you, put off that old man; you do not pray about this, I am telling you to do it; get on with it and do it.

But what if a believer talks about his lack of strength and power? The answer to that is, that as a regenerate creature, a new-born being, he *has* the power. If in the New Testament we are commanded to do a thing, we may rightly expect to receive from the Lord the power to do it, and therefore there is no excuse at this point. This is a very subtle matter, therefore let me put it in the following way: I suggest that, very often, people, by praying about a matter like this, far from solving their problem are simply increasing it, for they pray in a spirit of fear. They say, I feel myself to be so weak, I can do nothing. And they pray to be delivered from this thing, instead of throwing it off! The way to solve this problem is not to pray; it is to think, and to apply the Apostle's teaching and doctrine, to put off the old man.

Many years ago a lady came to see me about a problem which had been crippling her life for about twenty-two years. It may sound to others a trivial thing, but it was spoiling her life. She had a phobia, a terror, a horror, of thunderstorms. She once had been in a terrible thunderstorm and thought she was going to be killed, and that had fixed on her mind. And in the end it had come to this, that if she were walking to her place of worship on a Sunday morning and happened to see a black cloud, this fear would immediately suggest a coming thunderstorm, and instead of going to church she would go home because of her fear. The phobia had taken many forms: it had prevented her doing many things she had wanted to do, and it had created difficulties in the family; one can imagine the problems that would arise. The lady came to talk to me, purely as the result of something she heard me say as an aside in a sermon, and I listened to her story. Well now, I said, what have you been doing about it? She replied, I have done everything I can; I have talked to all sorts of people. I said, I suppose you have prayed about it? She said, I pray about nothing else, I am always praying about it. I replied, That is probably why the problem has persisted! And I continued, What you need is not to pray, but to think! And then I simply pointed out to her what a bad testimony this was in a Christian person such as she was; had she ever thought of that? Had she ever asked herself the question, Why should I be more afraid of a thunderstorm than anybody else? If all those other people can continue their journey to a place of worship, why should not I? Why is this trouble so peculiar to myself? She had never thought of that. Instead, she had been praying sincerely and honestly, and with great intensity, for twenty-two years to be delivered from the fear of thunderstorms, but the fear remained and was increasing.

There are points, I say in the Name of God and in the name of Scripture, about which you do not need to *pray*, but you do need to *think* and to apply the doctrine. You *put off* the old man! You need not pray for guidance about this! Having realised his character, put him off! This is not a matter of praying, this is a matter of doing. And so we see that the devil in his subtlety and as an angel of light can sometimes encourage us to pray in a blind and unintelligent manner, because he knows that, as long as we are doing that, we will not think and we will not face the scriptural teaching and apply it to ourselves and to this particular problem.

But I must state the force of the Apostle's word in another negative. This is not an experience which you receive or which happens to you. Many Christians are familiar with the teaching which says that the solution of any and every problem in the spiritual life is quite simple; all one has to do is to take it to the Lord and leave it with Him. He will deliver you. Let go and let God! Quite simple! they say, you have simply got to take it to Him; and then you will have this wonderful experience of deliverance. That teaching has been propagated for a number of years now, and there are people who have been trying to practise it. But they have not been delivered from their troubles. They may have had temporary deliverance while they were in meetings, but the trouble comes back again; and they have gone on trying to let go and to let God! But, says the Apostle, that is not what is needed, you must put off the old man *yourself*. You do not ask God to take the old man from you, you put him off!

Surely we must recognise that this 'Let go and let God' teaching is quite unscriptural. If it were true, this whole section of the Epistle to the Ephesians, from verse 17 of the fourth chapter to the end of the Epistle, should never have been written at all. The Apostle should not have written these words, and he should not have gone on to say, Therefore, put away lying; speak truth every man with his neighbour; be ye angry and sin not; neither give place to the devil; let him that stole, steal no more. He would not have said these things; it would have been wrong for him to say them. Instead, he would have said, If any of you believers are tempted to steal, pray about it; let go, and ask the Lord to deliver you from it! But he says nothing of the kind. Instead he says, Those of you who have been given to stealing, stop doing it, steal no more, put off the old man! Thus it is obvious that the teaching which may sound very spiritual can be utterly unscriptural. It not only by-passes the Scripture, it denies the Scripture.

But surely, comes the protest, you receive your sanctification as you receive your justification; you receive your justification by faith, and you must do the same in regard to the old man. But that is where the fallacy comes in. Certainly, justification is entirely by faith, because it is given when a person has no spiritual life, no ability at all. But it is not so with regard to the putting off of the old man. But, says someone, has not Paul said in chapter 2,

[143]

'We are his workmanship, created in Christ Jesus unto good works'? I answer: That is a reference to justification, and regeneration; we are entirely God's work there. But remember that the same Paul who writes, 'We are his workmanship', also says to those who have been saved, 'Work out your own salvation with fear and trembling'! In other words, Put away, put off: then put on. 'We are his workmanship.' Of course! we cannot do anything until He has made us anew. But once He has made us anew, then we are capable of working. So he says, *Work out your own salvation with fear and trembling*. Justification is by faith only. Sanctification is *not* by faith only. The whole of the Christian life is a life of faith, but in sanctification we have to work, and to work out; to put off, and to put on; as the Apostle tells us in all these details which he gives us here. We start, then, by realising that this is something that we *ourselves* have to do. It is not done for us. We do not just wait passively, or relax and expect it to be accomplished for us. Not at all! Put off! Stop doing certain things, says the Apostle. And I say again, what a tragedy it is that men and women should have thought that it was highly spiritual to deny this plain command and exhortation and teaching of the Scripture! That other teaching, as I have often pointed out, really means that the second half of every New Testament epistle should never have been written at all. In the case before us, all the Apostle should have said, either at the beginning of chapter 4 or in verse 17, is just this: In the light of this doctrine, all you have to do is to let go, to abide in Christ, and all will be well; you will be delivered from all your problems; it is quite simple; it is just like lifting up the blinds and letting the sun come in; there is no more to be done. That is all he need have said! But we notice that the New Testament writers give about half of their letters to detailed, practical instructions; they tell people what not to do, they tell them what to do. Clearly, these two teachings are quite incompatible. But the teaching of the Scripture is plainly, *Put off!* It is something that we ourselves have to do. And as I have reminded you, it is useless to say that we have not the strength. We have! If you are a Christian, it is at hand. God never commands a man to do a thing without enabling him to do it. If you and I are born again, the Spirit of God and of Christ is in us, the Holy Spirit is in us, the power is there.

And we have to realise this, and in the strength of divine might and power we act, we do this thing.

Next, how do we do it? There is the principle, and next, the practical application. The first essential is, that we have to remind ourselves of who we are and what we are. The Apostle indeed tells us to do so. He says, Put off the old man because of his sinful character, and put on the new man, which after God is created in righteousness and true holiness. We are no longer what we were, and the first thing we have to do is to tell ourselves just that! The whole art of Christian living is to know how to talk to yourself. If you do not preach to yourself you are not a Christian. A Christian is a preacher, he preaches to himself. You start your day by telling yourself, Now I am the new man, I am no longer the old man; my old man has been crucified with Christ, my old man is dead, finished with, he is non-existent; I am no longer what I was. If any man be in Christ he is a new creature, a new creation; old things have passed away, behold all things are become new. You start the new day by saying that to yourself. It will not be said to you, it will not happen automatically to you. The devil will speak to you the moment you wake up, and he will say a thousand and one things to you to depress you before you are even out of bed. Therefore we have to make a resolution; we are going to get up and to say, I am a new man in Christ. It literally has to be done in detail in this way.

It is not surprising that we fail so much. We do not start the day as we should. We groan, Here are these thoughts again, and here is the problem, another eighteen hours or so before me, what can I do? And before we realise it, we are already defeated. Let us give heed to the Apostle's exhortation – Put off the old man! And if and as you do so, you will realise that Christ has come into your life and has delivered you. So do not hurry out of your bed to get on your knees and pray a prayer of depression. Instead, first of all remind yourself of who you are, for if you pray in a depressed way you are not really praying in the Spirit at all. It is a prayer of unbelief, not of belief. We cannot really pray until we are clear in our doctrine. Let us therefore remind ourselves who we are before we go to God.

[145]

The second essential follows obviously, does it not? We are to remind ourselves again of the nature and the character of the old life. It is depicted here in these terrifying verses 17, 18 and 19; Paul gives his little summary again in verse 22. Notice how concerned the Apostle is that we should do this in detail; he will not let us escape it. He keeps on reminding us of the character of the former life; he bids us hold it before us. And this, I sometimes think, is the whole art of triumphing in the Christian life. I suppose I have to say this more frequently than anything else in my pastoral work. People come about particular problems; they tell me that they have been praying to be delivered, and so on. I say to them, Have you ever really looked this thing in the face? You are frightened of it, you are running away from it, you are cowering, your whole attitude is wrong. But now, wait a moment. Examine this thing, put it up in front of you, analyse it and dissect it, see it for what it is. That is half the battle. And then, says Paul, you will see that the whole thing must be got rid of. Look at it and face it, instead of running away from it. That is the second essential.

And then there is a third point. Impress upon yourself the utter inconsistency of claiming to be a Christian but continuing to live in the old way. So obvious, is it not? And yet how we all fail to do it! You have to look at yourself, you have to look at your old life, and when you do so, you say to yourself: Well now, it is impossible, I am being utterly inconsistent; I say that I have no use for a man who is inconsistent, I have no use for a hypocrite, a man who says one thing and does another. But what am I? how am I living? what do I claim as a Christian, as a member of the Church? Whether I like it or not, and whether I understand it or not, I am making a tremendous claim. As a Christian, as a man who calls himself a Christian, I am saying that I am a partaker of the divine nature, that Christ died to rescue me from this present evil world, that I have been translated from the kingdom of darkness into the kingdom of God's dear Son. That is what I am saying. I am saying that I am a member of the body of Christ, and that by these bands of supply that the Apostle has been talking about, the life of the blessed Head is flowing into me. Is it consistent with that claim to go on living as I have been doing? Is my conduct and my behaviour to be that of the old

realm when I claim to belong to this new realm? The New
Testament is literally full of this kind of argument. Listen to Paul
as he writes to the Philippians: 'Only let your conversation be as
it becometh the gospel of Christ' (1:27). His argument is clear:
Is your behaviour becoming? does it fit in with your profession?
We are all familiar with the argument, the illustration. Do not
have a clash of colours in your clothing, says the Apostle. Do
not dress in a manner that is inappropriate to what you are. Let
your conversation, your conduct, be as becometh the gospel of
Christ. See that your whole life is such that it will suggest to
people that the Son of God left heaven and came into this world,
that He died upon the tree, and that He rose again and sent the
Holy Spirit.

But let me illustrate the teaching by giving you another incident
out of my pastoral experience. Again it sounds simple and almost
trivial, yet I feel it is one of the greatest things that has ever come
within the realm of my experience. It concerns a certain man in
his early fifties, who had lived a very evil and dissolute life. He
was a drunkard, a fighter, gambler, wife-beater, adulterer; there
was nothing, I imagine, short of murder, that the man had not
been guilty of; and indeed, he would have been guilty of murder
in many a drunken brawl if he had not been restrained by his
own friends. He had a fiendish, foul temper, and he became mad
under drink. Eventually he came under the sound of the gospel
and was converted. Now this is where the thing sounds almost
ludicrous, but this is the fact. He was a tall man, athletic, well
built, a fighter. And there was one thing he was particularly
proud of, namely his moustache and its length from tip to tip.
(Is it not extraordinary what people are proud of?) This was his
particular matter of pride. In fact, the cause of most of his
fightings happened to be his moustache, because some other
man would challenge him that his moustache measured more
from tip to tip than his own. And so a quarrel would begin, and
they would end in fighting. But he was not only proud of his
moustache; he also boasted that no man could stand up to him
in his prowess as a fighter. Then the unexpected happened. He
came to the church, and was converted, and we looked on the
event with wonder.

But this is the story. Some six weeks after the man's conversion he came to a week-night meeting, and I noticed immediately as he came in that the moustache had gone. He had not merely cut off the extended ends but he had shaved off the entire moustache. My immediate reaction was one of annoyance; I said to myself, Some busybody in this church has told this man to do that. At the end of the meeting, as he was going out, I stopped him and said I wanted a word with him. Who told you to get rid of that moustache? I said. Nobody! he replied. Now come along, I said; don't shield anybody; this kind of busybody does great harm in a church. I am out to get rid of these self-appointed spiritual detectives, I continued. Tell me the truth. Who told you to get rid of that moustache? He said, Nobody has told me. I still pressed him hard, but he persisted. Well, I said, why have you got rid of it then? I will tell you, he said. I was getting up, actually, this morning and after I had washed, I went to the looking-glass, and I was there, he said, brushing my hair. Suddenly I saw my moustaches – on account of its size he reckoned it as two moustaches – and I said to myself, Them things don't belong to a Christian! So I cut off the ends, he said, and I shaved off the rest.

The man, let me add, could neither read nor write. He had lived such a dissolute, evil life, and had been brought up in such a loose way, that, literally, he could not write, he could not read; and that was his expression, 'Them things don't belong to a Christian!' Illiterate and ignorant, yes, but he had been born again, and the Spirit of God had come into him; and the Spirit of God with His unction and anointing had taught him the lesson, 'Them things don't belong to a Christian!' 'Put off the old man!' And he had put him off in that respect. They belonged to the old life, they had nothing to do with the new life. Very simple, is it not? Ignorant, illiterate man! I would to God that this church were full of such people! I see Christians today, even deliberately, it seems to me, putting on the old man! putting on things that belong to the life of the flesh and the devil and the world. And they have not yet realised that 'Them things don't belong to a Christian'! That is the argument of the Apostle. Work it out for yourselves in detail. The Christian should not even look like the typical man or woman of the world. There are certain things that are incompatible with this new life. Put them off! Get rid of them!

But we must go on to the next step of obedience to the gospel. I quote to you a word written by the Apostle in his next chapter: 'Have no fellowship with the unfruitful works of darkness, but rather reprove them.' The material point here, the operative phrase, is *no fellowship*. In other words he says, Have nothing at all to do with the works of darkness. Be drastic. Have no dealings at all with them. The important principle, it seems to me, is this: Watch the beginning. Have no parleying, have no discussion, have nothing at all to do with sin, if you are a wise man; put off the old man altogether. Have we not all proved this in experience? The moment you even listen to the devil you have practically gone under. If you have a discussion with him, it is certain that you will be defeated. Do not have any talk with the devil; have nothing to do with him at all. Do not speak to him, do not be on speaking terms with him. If you begin to talk to the devil and to listen to him and to say, Well now, why not? I want to understand . . . you are already beaten, he will defeat you every time; he is subtle, he is clever, he is brilliant at the art of repartee; he knows all the arguments. If you begin to have any parleyings with sin, you are done for. Have nothing to do, have no fellowship at all, with the unfruitful works of darkness. Make it a principle, also, that if you are doubtful about a thing, you will not touch it. 'Whatsoever is not of faith is sin.' 'He that eateth and doubteth is damned if he eat', says Paul in Romans 14. If you are in doubt about a thing, say No! Err on that side rather than on the other. Things that are even doubtful should not be touched.

Next we come to another positive injunction which I want to emphasise. And again it is a direct quotation from Scripture. In his Epistle to the Romans the Apostle writes: 'Make not provision for the flesh' (13:14). What a statement! 'Make not (or no) provision for the flesh'! What a tremendous thing it is! These words played their part in the life of St. Augustine. What does Paul mean by saying we should not make provision for the flesh? He means to say, Do not be fool enough to feed that old man that is in you. Do not be fool enough to lead yourself into temptation. Do not make provision for your flesh, the thing that

gets you down! There are certain places that are bad for you –
Stay out of them! To go into such places is making provision
for the flesh! You know beforehand that if you go in, the flesh
will be stimulated. That is making provision for the flesh.
Therefore, never go into such a place. And not only places, but
also people. If there are certain people that always have a bad
influence upon you, avoid them. Put off the old man! You do not
pray about this, you do not argue, you do not need special guidance about this. If experience teaches you that such a person
invariably tends to have a bad influence upon you, avoid such a
person. Make no provision for the flesh.

The same holds good with respect to reading. I have no hesitation in saying that the popular newspapers of this country today
are undoubtedly the worst influence of all as regards the spiritual
life. They are full of suggestion and innuendo. So be discriminat-
ing and careful as you read your newspaper. Avoid that which
tends to harm you and to drag you down. Make no provision
for the flesh! Listen to Job, as he speaks to us in the Old Testament. He was a godly man, and this is what he says: 'I made a
covenant with mine eyes'! (31:1) In verse 7 of that same chapter
he says, 'If my step hath turned out of the way and mine heart
walked after mine eyes . . .' Your heart goes after your eyes!
The eyes are the trouble. You see something, and your heart
goes after it. So, says Job, 'I made a covenant with mine eyes.'
Let me put the matter positively as we find it in Proverbs 4:25:
'Let thine eyes look right on, and let thine eyelids look straight
before thee.' If there is something that is enticing, do not look at
it! That is what is meant by putting off the old man. Make a
covenant with your eyes, look straight on, do not let your eyes
wander, do not let them lust after things, do not let them turn
from the straight path. This is biblical teaching: you do not
merely pray about it; you must just *not look*! Keep your eyes
from things that are likely to entice you or to attract you, whatever they are; make a covenant with your eyes, look straight
onwards, keep stedfast, looking in the direction of God and of
heaven and of holiness. Make no provision for the flesh.

And that brings me to the last principle – I have tried to put the
principles in ascending order – not only must we not make any
provision for the flesh, but we are actually told to mortify the

flesh. 'If ye through the Spirit do mortify the deeds of the body, ye shall live', says Paul to the Roman Christians (8:13). We read a similar command in Colossians 3:5: 'Mortify therefore your members which are upon the earth; fornication, uncleanness, inordinate affection, evil concupiscence, and covetousness, which is idolatry.' *Mortify* your members which are on the earth! *You* have got to do it, and *I* have got to do it; it is not done for us; evil is not all taken out of us in a marvellous, thrilling experience. We have to engage in this work of mortification; we have got to mortify the deeds of the body. And it is to be done through the Spirit! The Spirit is given; we have the Spirit. Therefore, says the Apostle, in His power *mortify*. . . . *Mortify* means *to deaden*, it means *deliberately to attack*, it means *to starve* so that our foes will die of inanition; withhold food from them, make no provision for them, in other words. Another good way of mortifying something is *not to use it.* If you do not use your muscles they will atrophy and they will become weak. So, not to use is a very good way of mortifying. Withhold the food and the sustenance; do not use. And as you do these two things, our enemies will gradually become mortified.

But the Apostle goes even further. We must not merely not feed the flesh and the body in this evil sense; we must not only not exercise the body if we would mortify it. The Apostle goes further in his First Epistle to the Corinthians saying, 'I therefore so run, not as uncertainly; so fight I, not as one that beateth the air, but I keep under my body, and bring it into subjection'! (9:26, 27). At once comes the objection: 'That is legalism, that is a man doing something, falling back on works.' But it is the Apostle who teaches it! And the literal meaning of the term that the Apostle actually used, here translated '*keep under the body*', is *to hit under the eye*; to *buffet*, to disable an antagonist as a pugilist! The Apostle really says, 'I hit myself under the eye.' He virtually says: I am like a boxer, I am not beating the air, I am pummelling myself, I am hitting myself black and blue, I am giving myself black eyes; that this flesh may not get me down. I keep my body under, and bring it into subjection.

Such is the Christian! So we are not to say about our problem, 'Oh, the solution is quite simple; just let up the blinds and the sun comes in, all darkness gone!' But it does not all go! And the people who use these terms know that it does not all go; and there have been people who for years have been trying to lift up the blinds, and they are still defeated by particular sins. Of course they are! They are denying the Scripture. I keep under my body, I buffet it, I hit it under the eye with all my force; I am up against an antagonist, and as a pugilist I am trying to knock him out. That is the scriptural method. So we not only do not make provision for the flesh, we must mortify the flesh, keep it under, keep it down, realising that unless we do so, it will get us down temporarily and we shall be living a contradictory life.

This, then, is the essence of the Apostle's teaching. If you wish to read an expansion of it, and oh, how it was expanded, turn to John Owen's treatise on *The Mortification of the Flesh*; you will find it a very substantial volume. Of course it is, for these things have to be worked out in detail. I have merely given you the basic principles. Let me repeat, then, that whatever it is that troubles you, put it up and look at it in the light of these principles. Do not run away, do not be frightened, do not just say, I must try to pray. Look at the thing and work it out; put it in the light of this context, and then apply the principles and grapple with it in the power of the Holy Spirit. Put off the old man! And do it in detail. The Apostle goes on to details – lying, stealing, corrupt communications. He takes them up one by one, and he says you have to apply the principles with regard to every single item. And thus you will put off the old man that is corrupt and dying and decaying, according to the lusts of deceit.

May God give us honesty! May God open our eyes to the Scripture! May God save us from by-passing the Scripture and eliminating whole sections of it in the interests of a theory! And as He does so, and as we realise that we have the Spirit of God within us, we shall find ourselves being enabled to put off the old man and all that is so horribly true of him, that we may no longer disgrace the fair and glorious name of our blessed Lord and Saviour Jesus Christ.

12

Renewed in the Spirit of the Mind

'And be renewed in the spirit of your mind.'
Ephesians 4:23

Latterly we have been studying two exhortations given by the Apostle Paul to the Ephesian believers, the one to put off the old man which is corrupt according to the deceitful lusts, the other to put on the new man, which after God is created in righteousness and true holiness. But in between these two exhortations comes this verse 23, to which we now turn our attention. It marks the transition in the Apostle's exhortation from the negative to the positive. But before he actually comes to the positive and tells us to put on the new man, he insinuates, he inserts, this particular statement. So the statement is, as I say, the beginning of the positive. But it is much more than that, for it would be very wrong to regard this statement as merely an introduction to what is coming. Indeed I make bold to suggest that this verse which is placed here between the two exhortations, and which, super-ficially viewed, is merely a connecting link, is in reality the key to understanding the secret of being able to put off the old man and to put on the new. Paul chooses to put it in this particular way, for a man will never really put off the old, and he will never put on the new, until he has been renewed in the spirit of his mind. So verse 23 is one of those profound statements of doctrine which abound, we have noticed, not only in the earlier part of this Epistle but even here in this very practical section, where the Apostle is in a sense simply applying his great doctrine and exhorting these Ephesians now to walk, not as other Gentiles walk, but as those who have truly learned Christ. Face to face, then, with such an important statement, we must give it our close attention.

The first thing the Apostle tells us is, 'and *be renewed*' – an interesting expression! It really does literally mean precisely what it says; it means *re-new*, or *being made new again*. It suggests restoration to a previous condition that once obtained. It suggests that there has been a departure from that condition, and that what we need is to be brought back to it. Now I hope to show you the significance of that statement, but that is exactly what the word means. It is important that we should notice that the Authorised Version does not give us the exact tense of the verb here. It is really the continuous present; Paul says that they must *go on being renewed* in this way. It is not something that happens once and for all. We saw earlier that 'putting off' is something that is once and for all; 'putting on' is the same; but this 'being renewed' is something that continues; it is present and must go on and on. Clearly that is a very important point. And the third point about this word is, that it is in the passive; it is not something that the Christian is to do. The 'putting off', as I have been emphasising, is our action; similarly, the 'putting on' is our action; but this is not ours, it is something that happens to us. We go on *being renewed*.

This is indeed the work of God, it is the work of the Holy Spirit. And yet it is obvious, I think, that though we have got to emphasise and to stress this aspect of the matter, the very way in which the Apostle puts it clearly indicates that we can hinder this work. There is no question about that at all. I am not talking about conversion, but about something that is happening to the man who is already born again, for the regenerate are the people to whom the Apostle is writing. It is because they have been born again, he tells them, that he exhorts them in this way. So we do say about the Christian that he can hinder this work, he can quench the Spirit, he can grieve the Spirit. So while the main emphasis is upon the fact that our being renewed is something that is done to us, we must be careful that we do not hinder it or in any way frustrate it, but that we do all we can to promote it and to encourage it. So we may translate the statement in this way: 'that you go on being constantly renewed', for that is what the Apostle is actually saying.

In the next place, we notice that the renewal mentioned is '*in the spirit of your mind*' – a most profound statement, and a most important one for our clear understanding of Christian doctrine. But Paul does not say that we are to be renewed in our mind only, but in the *spirit of the mind*. There has been much discussion about this expression. Some writers say that it means the Holy Spirit, resident in the mind; but it cannot possibly mean that, for this good reason, that the Holy Spirit is never referred to anywhere in Scripture as the Spirit of *our* mind. We are told that the Holy Spirit dwells in us, but He is not *our* Holy Spirit. So *the spirit of the mind* cannot mean the Holy Spirit influencing the mind. The Holy Spirit does influence the mind, but what the Apostle is talking about here is the *spirit of the mind*. In the same way we must indicate that the Apostle is not here referring to our *spirits*.

At this point we must remind ourselves again of the way in which the Bible dissects and analyses the human personality; in other words, we must for a moment glance at *biblical psychology*. And what it tells us about ourselves is this, that in man there is the *mind*, the seat of understanding; there is also the *heart*, the seat of emotions and feelings; there is also the *soul*, which is the seat of the sensations; and then there is the *spirit* in man. There is, of course, a great argument as to whether man is two parts or three. Some say we must only talk about *body* and *soul*, and must not talk *about body, soul* and *spirit*, which is the tri-partite view. This is a subject that can never be finally decided, because we notice that this Apostle himself, in the last chapter of the First Epistle to the Thessalonians, talks about our whole spirit, soul, and body. And we read in the fourth chapter of Hebrews about dividing asunder even the soul and the spirit, and the joints and the marrow. It does not really matter which of the views you take as long as you recognise that, if you say that there is only one organ (as it were) in addition to the body, it is based on the recognition that there are two parts to it – soul and spirit. So it comes to the same thing in the end. There is the soul in man, the seat of the sensations, that by which man has communion with his fellows. But there is something higher, there is the spirit that is in man; and this is undoubtedly the highest thing that is in us and in our constitutions.

In reading your Bibles you must have noticed that these terms

are often used interchangeably; sometimes the word *mind* is used
for the whole person; sometimes the word *heart* is used, not only
for the seat of the affections and the emotions, but again for the
whole personality, including the mind; the *soul* is used in the same
way; and the *spirit* is used in the same way. Someone may then
ask, Can we ever know which meaning is indicated in any
particular context? The answer is, that if you pay careful attention
to the context you will generally be able to ascertain the meaning.
And such is the case in our present study. In our Ephesians text,
Paul talks about the *spirit of the mind*, so *spirit* and *mind* obviously
do not mean the same thing. And indeed he is not even speaking
of *our* spirits; he is speaking in particular of what he calls the
spirit-of-the-mind, and we must search into the meaning of this
word.

I suggest that the word means the interior principle that really
governs and controls and operates the mind itself. By this I mean
that, in addition to our faculties and our powers and our intellectual abilities, there is a sort of spirit of the mind that controls the
whole working of the mind. That is the thing to which the Apostle
is referring here. The word *spirit* means breath, or wind, which
means power. So he is talking here about the power of the mind;
not simply the abilities of the mind, but the power that controls
and directs the abilities. We are obviously dealing with something
very profound here, something to enjoy and to revel in. What a
wonderful book this Bible is! Some people say that to be a
Christian means that you suddenly become soft; you throw your
intellect overboard and just spend your time singing choruses
and being emotional. If there are such Christians they are very
poor Christians. Our New Testament was written to Christians,
two thousand years ago, when they had not got all our educational
facilities. It was written to people most of whom had been slaves;
yet here is Paul analysing the mind into these various categories.
Here is profound thought, profound philosophy, profound
psychology; and you and I are supposed to understand this, to
grapple with it and to understand it, for, as I hope to show you,
'the spirit of the mind' is that which really governs and controls
everything else, that part of yourself that governs and controls
your mind. Being renewed in the spirit of the mind is essential to
Christian progress.

Thus far we have been defining our terms. Now we come to the doctrine. The Apostle here is giving us one of his profoundest definitions of the Christian. Let us watch him as he does it. Here, it seems to me, are the component parts.

First of all, the Apostle indicates what sin and the fall of man have really done to us. This word *re-new* tells us. What the Christian needs, he says, is to be brought back to where he was with respect to his mind. His mind needs to be renovated, renewed, made new again, as it once was, suggesting at once that it had departed from that, which is, of course, exactly what happened when man fell. There is nothing that is more important for us to understand than the doctrine of the Fall, man in sin; it is the key to the whole Bible. I do not see how a man can really understand the doctrine of salvation unless he understands something at least of the doctrine of the Fall. And this explains why the Old Testament is as essential to a Christian as is the New. He cannot understand his New Testament without the Old Testament, because the fact is that God made man perfect, but man fell. And what happened when he fell? The Apostle informs us. When man fell it was not only that he disobeyed God in one particular respect and thereby became a transgressor. At the same time and as a direct result of his fall he began to feel miserable and unhappy. He also found that he had lost a number of benefits that he had previously enjoyed. But, says the Apostle, the most devastating thing that happened was that the spirit of man's mind went wrong.

Here we make contact with the very essence of the Fall. When man listened to the devil, he put himself under the power of the devil, and passed under the *dominion of Satan*, as Paul puts it in his Epistle to the Romans. And the result of that has been that man's mind, the spirit of his mind, has been under an alien domination. The trouble with all of us, as the result of the sin of Adam, is that we are born with a defiled nature. Our essential trouble is not so much that we do things that are wrong – of course that is bad enough – but the real trouble with us all is that, as we are by nature, our whole outlook is wrong. It is the *spirit* of our mind that is wrong; our fundamental way of thinking and of reasoning has become twisted and perverted and vitiated. That is exactly what the Bible says about the whole world in its present position of chaos and of trouble. The world is as it is because men do not know how to think straightly, and the first call of the gospel is for man to think straightly. Be renewed in the spirit of your mind! They cannot do that of themselves, they need the operation of the Holy Spirit, but once regeneration has taken place, they are *exhorted* to take action.

Read how this is put in the Book of Genesis, in chapter 6, at the time just before the Flood. God says, about the world that He was going to judge and to destroy in the Flood: 'Every imagination of the thoughts of man's heart was only evil continually'. What a diagnosis! what a psychological analysis! – every *imagination* of the *thoughts* of his *heart*! In these words we find that 'the spirit of the mind' is analysed still further; the imagination comes in, the feelings come in. It is this principle at the back of the mind that has gone wrong. It is not the mind as an instrument that has gone wrong. We must be perfectly clear about that, because somebody might want to challenge me at this point and say, Are you saying that every man who is not a Christian cannot think at all and has no ability? if that is so, you are obviously wrong. Are there not great scientists who are not Christian? Are there not great philosophers, poets and others who are not Christian? Are you claiming that they have no ability? Of course I am not! This is where it is important to differentiate between the *mind* and the *spirit of the mind*. The trouble with man is not in his mind but in the spirit of his mind. Men have got the faculties, they have got the abilities, they can be geniuses at mathematics, physics, chemistry, philosophy, any one of these things. The mind as an organ, and as a machine that works and reasons and calculates and thinks and so on, produces striking results; but what has gone wrong is the governing power at the back of it all.

Let me use as an illustration what seems to me to be one of the best commentaries on this matter. It is not an exact parallel but it can serve as an illustration. The Apostle Paul, in writing to the Romans, recognises that the matter he is handling is rather a difficult one, so he says, 'I speak after the manner of men because of the infirmity of your flesh' (6:19). In other words, he says,

Because you find it difficult to understand what I am saying, I am going to use an illustration. 'For', he says, 'as you have yielded your members [that is to say, your faculties] servants to uncleanness, and to iniquity unto iniquity; even so now yield your members servants to righteousness unto holiness.' The members that formerly were used in an evil way, the faculties, the powers, were now to be used for good and right purposes. They were the same faculties exactly, but what is changed is the direction, the spirit that controls them.

The Apostle's illustration well serves my present purpose. Here, I say, is the devastating thing that the Fall and sin have done to the human race. The mind of man which was, at the beginning, governed by the spirit is now governed by the flesh. All man's thinking is vitiated to that extent. Man is still able to think and act to advantage as a physicist, a doctor, a philosopher, and so on; although even there at a given point he goes wrong. But the moment you come to the things that really matter – man's whole being and his relationship to God and to time and to eternity – *there* man's thinking fails completely, because the spirit of his mind has gone astray.

If you want to read the essence of this doctrine in the Scripture, turn to the second chapter of the First Epistle to the Corinthians; where we find Paul saying: 'The natural man receiveth not the things of the Spirit of God, for they are foolishness unto him; neither can he know them, because they are spiritually discerned.' Is he saying that the natural man is not a Christian because he has not a brain? He is not! He is saying that his brain is of no use to him because the spirit that controls it prevents his grasping the true doctrine. It is the *spirit* of the mind that is wrong, not the mind as an instrument. If we grasp this we shall never be surprised to find that certain great people are not Christians. Some of them are familiar to us through radio and television and others of them are writers. In consequence, some weak Christians tremble in their shoes, and say – Well, after all, may I be wrong? these great men do not believe in Christ and the Gospel! But they should not be surprised. They are great men; and we grant that they possess greater brains than we have, better instruments as such. But it is not the instrument that matters, it is the spirit of the mind that matters.

We find that Paul gives the same teaching in the second chapter of this Epistle to the Ephesians, where we are told that all men by nature are 'dead in trespasses and sins', and walk 'according to the course of this world, according to the prince of the power of the air, the spirit that now worketh in the children of disobedience'. We find it again in the eighth chapter of the Epistle to the Romans, where we are told that 'to be *carnally* minded is death'. There is nothing wrong with the mind itself, but the spirit of the mind is carnal. 'To be *carnally minded*,' he says, 'is death, but to be *spiritually* minded is life and peace.' To which Paul adds: 'Because the carnal mind is enmity against God: for it is not subject to the law of God, neither indeed can be.' It is the spirit of the mind that is wrong. This, then, is the real trouble with man. It is not merely that he does things that he should not do, and that he does not do what he should do. The tragedy of every man who is not a Christian is plainly this, that in the very citadel, the highest point of his being, in the spirit of his mind, he has gone astray. What can be a greater tragedy than that! Some of the people who live for evil in this world, who make money out of it, and who organise it, have got wonderful brains; they are geniuses at it; they have got great ability, but it is being prostituted, it is being turned and used in an utterly wrong direction. The 'spirit of the mind' has gone astray and therefore needs to be renewed.

But again, we must ask ourselves, What does regeneration do? At this point, of course, the Apostle does not give us an elaborate account of regeneration; he simply places his finger on the essential principle. This is the thing of all things that happens in regeneration. What does man in sin need? Well, obviously, in the light of all I have been saying, he does not need new faculties, because there is nothing wrong with the faculties. A man does not need to have a new brain in order to become a Christian; the same brain will serve him as long as its spirit is changed. My point is that when a man becomes a Christian he does not become one iota an abler man than he was before. He has still got the same brain, the same faculties; whatever they were, they still are. If he was a genius in sin he will be a genius as a preacher;

the Apostle Paul is an illustration of that. He was a persecutor beyond everybody, he beat or imprisoned all the Christians he could find; and then he became a Christian and the greatest preacher of them all. The same intensity! The same zeal!

I have seen people crucifying their faculties, but they were never meant to do that! What you were, you remain; you have the same faculties, and the same powers, but the spirit which controls them is the thing that is changed. So the same natural differences between person and person will still be there. All Christians are not equally able; does that need to be said? I sometimes think it does. All are not called to teach and to preach. Some people seem to think that any man who is a Christian automatically does what other Christians do. It is not so. The abilities are still there, and they have to be considered and taken into consideration. So I say that in regeneration we do not receive new faculties. What we receive is this new spirit that controls, a new disposition is put into us, a new principle of life begins to operate. The new spirit enters into the mind and controls it and directs it; so that whereas formerly it went in a wrong direction, it is now going in a right direction. If it was all out in the one, it is all out in the other. It is the control that matters, it is this life-giving principle. By the renewing, we are to understand that the mind is enlightened. The man's brain *qua* brain is precisely what it was before; but the man, being renewed in the spirit of his mind, and no longer totally disabled by reason of the Fall, becomes capable of receiving the things of the Spirit of God, and the brain that was useless to him before in spiritual matters, now becomes invaluable to him.

The change, then, having come about, what does it lead to? It means that a man who is a Christian not only thinks different things, but still more important, he is a man who is enabled to think in a new way. Listen to the poet speaking about the change that has occurred:

> *Heaven above is softer blue,*
> *Earth around is sweeter green;*
> *Something lives in every hue*
> *Christless eyes have never seen.*

Christless eyes can see, of course. They can see flowers, and so can the Christian eyes, and they are looking at the same flowers. And the non-Christian can tell you the name of the flower as well as the other, perhaps better; he can dissect it, analyse it, he knows all about it, he sees and he can write his report; so can the Christian; they are both looking at the same things, and up to a point the reports are identical. But the Christian sees something the other man does not see. Heaven above is *softer* blue! The non-Christian gives his report. He says, The heavens are blue! He is perfectly right. But he has not seen the softness. The Christian looks up at the heavens, and he sees not only a physical, material something; there is a radiance there that the other man cannot see; it is the glory of God behind it. It is all there in the eighth Psalm. 'When I consider thy heavens, the work of thy fingers, the moon and the stars . . .' The Christian has seen something extra. He not only sees what is there, he sees the fingers of God that have made it. 'The moon and the stars which *thou* hast ordained!' Heaven above is softer blue! Earth around – what about it? Well, it is green, says the non-Christian, and of course he is perfectly right. But, says the Christian, earth around is *sweeter* green! What is happening? In the two men, the brain power is more or less identical; but there is something extra, the spirit of the mind is changed, in the Christian. Something lives in every hue Christless eyes have never seen.

> *Birds with* gladder *songs o'erflow,*
> *Flowers with* deeper *beauties shine,*
> *Since I know, as now I know,*
> *I am His, and He is mine.*

What has happened to this man? The Apostle supplies the answer. The spirit of the mind has been renewed! He has not a greater intellect than he had before, but it is being enabled to function in a new way, he is thinking in a new manner. He not only talks about different things, but he does everything in a different way. 'Old things are passed away, behold! all things are become new.' That is what happens to the Christian. As a 'natural man', perhaps he was a slave to drink, and he could not pass a public house without being tempted, and falling; in he went. But now that he has become a Christian, he passes the same public house, but he does not see it as he saw it before. Physically he sees exactly the same thing, the same building, the same paint, the same colour, the same name over it; there is no change; and yet everything is different, it is not the same place. What has happened? There is no change in the public house, there is no change in his brain *qua* brain. What has changed is the *spirit* of his mind! He is thinking in a different way. Though he looks at, meditates about, cogitates concerning, precisely the same data, he does not see the same thing in the same way. The spirit of his mind is changed. His outlook is completely new.

But someone may ask, What does all this mean in practice? Well, here are some practical deductions. When the Apostle tells us to put off the old man and put on the new man, he is not calling for a mechanical conformity, but asking us to put into practice an intelligent change. That is his reason for speaking of being renewed in the spirit of your mind in between the 'putting off' and the 'putting on'. The Apostle gives these instructions not as a drill sergeant does. The drill sergeant does not appeal to intelligence. He bawls out instructions – Put off! Put on!! That is not what we have here at all. The Christian life is not a mechanical life! Does this need to be emphasised? I have a fear that it does. I see too many Christians doing things in parade ground fashion these days; 'Put off!' 'Put on!' They attend classes of instruction, and are trained how to do this, that and the other. If he says this, you say it too – to be evangelists and to give their personal witness and testimony! There is nothing about that in the New Testament. What the New Testament does is to train the *man*, to set him right, and then he goes on and does the work. It is the spirit of the mind that needs to be changed. The Christian must not do things without knowing why he is doing them. He must not do them blindly just because he has been told to do them. Not at all! Intelligence is essential! The spirit of the mind! If you do not know why you are living the Christian life, you are being a very poor Christian. The Christian is to be able to give a reason for the hope that is in him, with meekness and fear. It is not a mechanical thing; it must be intelligently performed by the spirit of your mind!

Or let me put it like this: the Apostle is not calling only for an outward change of actions and of habits. What he is really calling for is this inward change in the mind, because he knows that if a man's inward mind is changed he will soon deal with the outward actions. In other words, Paul is not asking you to take off one uniform and put on another. You can do that and not be a Christian. Christianity is inevitably something that works from within outwards, never from without inwards. That is the whole principle. Anybody can take off one uniform and put on another. A man who is not regenerate can do that. That is the difference between morality and Christianity. The non-Christian moral man is a man who takes off the bad suit and puts on the good suit, but *he* is still unchanged, and therefore he is not a Christian. To outward appearance he appears to be one, but *the spirit of his mind* is not changed. That is not only the difference between the moral man and the Christian man, it is the difference between the hypocrite and the true Christian. It is the difference between what the Puritans called the *temporary believer*, the *temporary professor*, the *gospel hypocrite*, and the true Christian.

In a sense, this was the curse of the closing years of the Victorian period and the early years of this present century. Christian churches were filled with people who had taken off the old and put on the new, but the spirits of their minds had not been changed. They did not know why they were doing it; it was the tradition; they had been brought up to go to places of worship; not to do this, but to do that. That, without a doubt, was the curse of late Victorianism. Thank God we have come to the end of it! I would rather have the present position than that, because those Victorians who had this form of godliness thought of themselves as true Christians, and yet many of them had never been Christians and had no heart knowledge of the Faith. If this putting off and putting on is not the result of the renewing of the mind, it has no value. We must not only live the new life, but we must want to do so, we must feel that it is inevitable to do so, we must feel that we have no choice. We must understand the logic of the true Christian profession. It is not our actions only that Christianity is concerned about, it is much more concerned about *us*. That is why the Bible tells us that in the final outcome Jacob and not Esau, was God's man. Esau was much more of a gentleman than his brother and a much nicer man, but he was not godly, he was 'a profane person', as we are clearly told in the Epistle to the Hebrews. Jacob, with all his rottenness, was God's man. It is not our actions alone that matter; it is we ourselves, and the spirit of the mind.

But we move on to my third and my last practical principle. We now recognise that becoming a Christian does not mean that you simply change your moral suit or your outward behaviour. Nor does it merely mean that you change your opinions, or change your mind. But it most certainly means changing the *spirit* of your mind. What a distinction! In other words, Christianity is not something that you and I take up intellectually; it is something that takes us up, and captivates us, and governs us, and controls us. But I must sound a note of alarm! I have known people – God forbid that I should be guilty of judging! – but I have known people who, having come to live in evangelical circles, begin to use evangelical phrases. They hear them so frequently that they adopt them, and begin to use them. And if you are a superficial observer you might say, these people are now truly Christian, can you not hear them? they are talking now as evangelical believers! But a parrot can do as much as that. It can repeat evangelical phrases and clichés; if it only hears them often enough it will repeat them. And it is possible for man to do the same. You may say to me, But how do you know this about such people? In the following way! If you suddenly confront them with a question or a problem where they cannot supply a pat answer, you will find that they do not know how to think spiritually. The spirit of their minds is not changed at all; it is the old mind which is repeating phrases, using the language, but they betray – how tragically! – that really they have never started thinking in a Christian way at all. They say things now and again that shock and amaze you, and you say, I thought so-and-so had really seen the truth; and he betrays at once that he has never really seen it. Such people are repeating borrowed phrases, nothing more! Any person of average intelligence, hearing a thing frequently, ought to be able to do so! But the Christian is tested, not simply by what he says, not simply by the opinions he puts forward, but by the spirit of his mind!

We must take Paul's message to heart. If the spirit of our mind is changed and is renewed, we shall be thinking in such a way that we shall put off the old man, and will put on the new man. And we shall do it properly and in the right way. The terrible thing is that it is possible for us to appear to be right in almost every respect, and yet in ourselves to be wrong the whole time. We can put Christianity on as clothing, or as a mask. Do you not know people like this? You feel that everything is right about them except themselves! In other words, everything seems to have changed except the vital thing, the spirit of the mind. And here, says the Apostle, is something that must never cease. Obviously, at the time when we are converted we see the one great truth, but we need to be taught much more, do we not? We need to be taught how to think. You may hear young Christians saying things that are quite appalling from the standpoint of a mature Christian. In a sense they cannot help it; they are babes, the spirit of their mind has to be renewed; they have to start learning to think in this new way; the whole outlook, the whole attitude, the very spirit of their thinking has got to be entirely renovated. And then, as time goes on, you will begin to see them working the matter out and applying it. And it is one of the most glorious and fascinating things that happens in life. I am speaking as a pastor. I know of nothing more thrilling, more entrancing, than just to watch some of my friends, undergoing this very process of having the spirit of their minds renewed. It is wonderful! It is not simply that they stop doing what they used to do, or that they have begun to do things that they did not formerly do, and are speaking in a new way. Much more fascinating and charming is it to see that the very spirit of the mind is different! The whole outlook, the very method of thinking, has now become Christian! We need to be Christianised in the whole of our being; and obviously, first and foremost in the mind itself, for 'as a man thinketh in his heart, so is he!'

So 'Be renewed in the spirit of your mind'.

13
The New Man and his Origin

'And that ye put on the new man, which after God
is created in righteousness and true holiness.'

Ephesians 4:24

Our text is a statement that really should not be taken on its own.
It belongs to the section beginning at verse 22: 'That ye put off
concerning the former conversation the old man, which is corrupt
according to the deceitful lusts; and be renewed in the spirit of
your mind; and that ye put on the new man, which after God is
created in righteousness and true holiness.'

We are now looking at the last statement, in verse 24. It is the
positive injunction which corresponds to the negative injunction
which we have already considered in verse 22. We realise also that
there is the vital connecting link in verse 23. In other words, we
are not capable of putting off the old man nor of putting on the
new man unless we are constantly being renewed in the spirit of
our minds. We must also remember as we look at this positive
side of the Apostle's injunction that these two things must always
be taken together, the putting off of the old, the putting on of the
new; we have to differentiate between them, as the Apostle does,
in thought and in understanding, and indeed they are separate
actions, but at the same time we must understand that the two
things must always be going on at the same time. Nature abhors
a vacuum, and the spiritual life is exactly the same. There is never
a condition in which a man has merely put off the old man. You put
off the old man, you put on the new man, at exactly the same time.

Very often in the history of the Church men and women have
failed to realise this as they ought, and have brought upon themselves various types of trouble. There are those, for instance, who

[167]

have put the whole of their emphasis upon putting off the old man. Now this is one of the dangers of what is called Mysticism. If you are familiar with the teaching of the mystics and the way of mysticism you will find that it always starts with a negative phase, the way of negation. You have to go through what they call the dark night of the soul, by which is meant the process of putting off the old man – self-examination, seeing your sinfulness, and dealing with it. This is certainly essential, but if you stop at that, you fall into some of the excesses and real dangers of mysticism. You will go back to the level of works again, quite unconsciously, and there you may find yourself in a state of misery and of desolation.

But this evil is not confined to mysticism. The same error, namely, of looking only at the negative and concentrating solely upon putting off the old man, is undoubtedly the direct cause of some of the less pleasing aspects of what is called Puritanism. The danger of Puritanism always is to lapse into legalism. And there is no question at all that some of the Puritans quite unconsciously became legalistic, because they gave more attention to putting off the old man than to putting on the new. They were for ever examining themselves, dwelling upon their sins, trying to get rid of them, imposing disciplines upon themselves, and thus, undoubtedly, some of them became morbid, introspective, and depressed. Because of this they gave a picture of the Christian life which is not balanced and which is therefore not true; quite unconsciously they became legalistic. Furthermore, if we put the whole of our emphasis upon the negative aspect – the putting off of the old man – it will undoubtedly lead to spiritual depression; and this can be a most serious thing. But above all, it is a very false representation of the Christian life. Paul's writings show the balanced life which the Christian is to maintain. We have an excellent illustration of this at the beginning of chapters 4 and 5 of 2 Corinthians. As you read, notice his parallels as he sets the positive against the negative: 'Cast down, but not destroyed' and so on. He is not going to continue lying on the ground; he is having a terrible time, yes, but he always stresses the counterpart, which is the putting on of the new. His phrases are perfectly balanced. And Christianity means a balanced life; we must beware of concentrating wholly on the negative.

But in the same way we must be very careful not to put the whole of our emphasis upon the positive only – the putting on the new man – and not troubling to put off the old man at all. Many have been guilty of this error also. It is the high road to what is called Antinomianism, in which people say, Well, of course I have put on the new man; it does not matter much about the old man; I just ignore that. If things happen to go wrong, it is not I, it is the flesh in me. There were people of this kind in the early Church, and there have been such people ever since. Ah, they say, the one thing is to concentrate on the fact that you are born again, and that you must be bright and cheerful! But their lives are seen to be studded with sins and faults and failures, and their testimony to the truth of the Christian faith is nullified. And it is all due to the fact that instead of putting off the old as well as putting on the new, they have chosen only to put on the new.

There is a sense in which this second danger, while it is a possibility, really cannot go on for very long, because a man cannot truly put on the new unless he puts off the old. He may put on the appearance, but he cannot really put on the new. As the Apostle again demonstrates so abundantly in the sixth chapter of his Second Epistle to the Corinthians, the thing is finally impossible, and for this reason, that there cannot be communion between light and darkness, or concord between Christ and Belial. What part hath he that believeth with an infidel? What agreement hath the temple of God with idols? The great principle, therefore, is perfectly clear. The negative and the positive are always to be done simultaneously, and a man who has truly experienced the renewal of the spirit of his mind will always do this; he will want to get rid of the old, but he will also want the new.

Against this background, therefore, we set ourselves to consider the putting on of the new man, and as it is the exact opposite of putting off the old man we can adopt precisely the same procedure in our investigation of it as we adopted in the case of the negative. The Apostle writes: 'And that ye put on the new man, which after God is created in righteousness and true holiness.' The figure is again that of putting on an article of clothing. We have divested ourselves, we have put off; now we clothe ourselves, we put on. But what exactly does Paul mean by telling us to put on this new man? Here again we must be extremely careful, for there have been many who have interpreted this quite wrongly by regarding it as an exhortation to people to become Christian. They think that to put on the new man means that by doing so you become Christian. But that is a sheer misunderstanding of the text and its context. The Apostle is addressing his exhortation to those who are already Christians. He has reminded them of this abundantly in his first chapter; he has continued to remind them of it in the second and third chapters, and here again in this chapter. Indeed, the whole section we are dealing with starts with the words: 'This I say therefore, and testify in the Lord, that ye henceforth walk not as other Gentiles walk'. You no longer go on walking in that way. In other words, they are already Christians. So this exhortation is only addressed to believing Christians. It has nothing to say to people who are not Christians, because they cannot put off the old man, they cannot put on the new man, they are still in their old state, they are unregenerate.

The exhortation is addressed to those who are already regenerate, in whom the new man is already existing; and what the Apostle is really exhorting them to do is to live in a manner that is consistent with the new man that is in them. I cannot do anything better therefore than to repeat what I said negatively in terms of putting off the old man. I said that when the Apostle tells us to put off the old man, he means, Stop being what you are not! and I used an illustration. We say to a man, Don't be a baby! You are now an adult man, well then, do not behave as if you were a baby! Stop being what you are not! That is putting off the old man. Putting on the new man is the opposite of this. It is, Be what you are! The trouble with us all is that we are not what we are. I am not trying to be paradoxical; this is Christianity! Be what you are! But let me explain my meaning.

Look at the problem in the light of what this same Apostle says in his Epistle to the Philippians. If you read superficially you may think he is contradicting himself: 'Wherefore, my beloved, as ye have always obeyed, not as in my presence only, but now much more in my absence, *work out your own salvation with fear and trembling. For it is God that worketh in you both to will and to do of his good pleasure* (2:12, 13). On the one hand he tells us to work a thing out ourselves: then he says that it is God who is doing it. How do you reconcile the two things? It is quite simple. *We* are to work out our own salvation with fear and trembling, *because* it is God that works in us. It is because of what God has done in us that we are able to do it, and we must do it because God has done it in us. Because He has worked it in, we are to work it out. There is no contradiction. We are to realise what we are, and to live accordingly. It is because you are a new man that you are to put on the new man. It is a picturesque but helpful way of putting it.

We do this very thing in common practice constantly. We tell our children to remember who they are. The school tells its members to remember the school to which they belong. Indeed, the whole of life is really being governed by this kind of appeal. You are not to let down your side. You *put on* the side, as it were, you pull yourself together, you remind yourself who you are. It is because you are this or that, that you have got to live as you are. There must be no contradiction between what you are and what you are doing. *Be* what you are! Be it in every respect in the whole of your conduct and the whole of your behaviour. That is exactly the meaning of this exhortation. It is idle, therefore, to address this exhortation to a man who is not born again, to a man who is still in his sins, to a man who is not yet a new man. The man who has not got the new man cannot put on the new man! It is because the new man is in us that we are to put him on.

In the next place, let us consider the reasons why we should do so. And the first reason is one that I have been hinting at already, even in what I have been saying. The first and chiefest reason for putting on the new man is because of the nature and the character of the new man. We saw negatively that the chief reason for putting off the old man was not only that we were no longer the old man, but still more because of the character of the old man: he is 'corrupt according to the lusts of deceit'. And we could see that if we only understood the true nature and character of that kind of life, we would hate it and want to get rid of it. But the exact opposite works here. We are to put on the new man because of the nature and the character of the new man, who, after God, is created in righteousness and true holiness. We see the whole of Christianity in this statement. It reaches to the very heart and centre of Christianity. And the test of our profession of the Christian faith is our apprehension of what is meant by *the new man*. Do we know what the new man is? Is the new man in you? Is it your chiefest joy and boast that the new man is *in* you? The very terms, of course, tell us much about it. The *old* and the *new*! We are lifting up our heads; here we have got something – the new man! This is essential Christianity. People who are merely moral, they know nothing about the new man; people who think that just to be good is to be Christian, know nothing about the new man. They are not interested; in fact, very often they object to the very term.

I remember a lady once complaining to me about a friend of hers who had been converted, and she said, 'You know, she keeps on talking about being born again; I don't understand this, she seems to me to be going astray; she was a nice, decent and good woman before; she always went to church; but now she is always talking about this new birth!' It seemed to her something very terrible and wrong, something tinged with fanaticism. She feared that her friend was going astray, perhaps even in her mind. And yet she was a good, moral, religious woman. But obviously she knew nothing about the new man, even though it is the very centre and nerve of the Christian faith.

What is this newness? It does not primarily refer to time, although time is not excluded. But it especially means new in quality, something of a different quality and order, something that is essentially and in every respect different from the old. The matter is well illustrated by the case of Nicodemus. 'Rabbi,' he said to Christ, 'thou art a teacher come from God, for no man can do these miracles that thou doest except God be with him.' Here is a good, godly, religious man, a teacher in Israel; he comes to Christ and says, What is this you have got that I have not got? what must I do in order to get it? Our Lord replies, 'Verily, verily, I say unto thee, except a man be *born again* he cannot *see* the kingdom of God.' You must be born again! Such was Christ's teaching. He is not just another of the religious teachers; He is not just the last of the prophets; He is not just a great super-politician; He is the One who comes to talk about this new birth, this new man, this new life, this regeneration. This being so, says Paul, if you have learned Christ truly, if you really have laid hold of the truth as it is in Jesus, this is what you have learned! It is the very centre of the Christian message. But let us take it as it is split up by the Apostle himself.

The first thing about the new man, says the Apostle, is that he is *created*. Notice the complete antithesis to the old man. What he tells us about the old is that he is *corrupt*, which we found meant that he was being corrupted more and more. What is character-istic of the new man? He is 'created'! In the one case there is a process of death and decay, in the other of creation! The word 'creation' in itself suggests to us something new, a complete con-trast with the old. Then, too, we saw that the corruption of the old resulted in destruction. But creation is the beginning of *life*. The old is linked with all that is fading and waning and decaying, whereas the new is the exact opposite of everything that suggests corruption and decay.

But still more important in this word '*created*' is the idea that something is brought into being out of nothing. When God created the heavens and the earth and all things, He created them out of *nothing*. It was the word of His fiat. He said, 'Let there be', and thus He brought them into existence. Creation is making something out of nothing. Similarly, the new man, says Paul, is something that is *created*. In other words, the new man is not something that evolves by a gradual process out of the old man. It is not a slow, almost imperceptible process of renovation. It is not an improvement of the old man. It is a creation, a new work. God puts into us something that was not there at all before. That is what it means to become a Christian. And if we are not clear about this, our notion of Christianity is entirely wrong. The Christian is not the 'old man' improved. The Christian is not a man who is trying to be better than he once was. Not at all! Something absolutely new is put in at the centre – '*created*'! That is the whole meaning of regeneration, of being born again. That is what our Lord was telling Nicodemus – 'that which is born of the flesh is flesh; that which is born of the Spirit is spirit'. Here we see the contrast – the Christian is entirely different! absolutely new!

[173]

We are to understand, then, that God has done in our souls the same thing as He did when He created the world and when He created man. The 'new man' is indeed a new creation! The Apostle has already been giving us this teaching in this very Epistle; for example, he says that 'We are his workmanship, created in Christ Jesus unto good works, which God hath before ordained that we should walk in them' (2:10). A new principle of life is put into us by God through the Holy Spirit, and this is the principle of the life of Jesus Christ Himself. So that we find the Apostle Peter saying that 'we are partakers of the divine *nature*'. The truth is so staggering that we can scarcely receive it. And is not the Christian Church in the state she is today because we do not realise what we are and who we are? Are we people who are merely trying to live a little better than the majority depicted in the newspapers? Are we just moral, decent folk. . .? We are that, but we are infinitely more; God has put something of His own nature within us: we are 'partakers of the divine nature'! That is what it means to be a Christian.

Listen to the Apostle saying it again in 2 Corinthians 5:17: 'If any man be in Christ he is a new creature (a new creation); old things are passed away, behold, all things are become new.' A new principle of life has been put into the Christian. He has a new disposition – the life of God in the soul of man! That is Christianity! And I am emphasising it for this good reason; the realisation of it is the high road not only to a true understanding, but to the true enjoyment of the Christian life. Indeed, I will go further. This is the high road to revival! Let us never forget that two hundred years ago the book (Scripture apart) that influenced George Whitefield and John Wesley more than any other was 'The Life of God in the Soul of Man', written by a Scotsman, Henry Scougal. And it was as they read Scougal's book that the conviction came alike to both of them: I have not got this; I am a good man, I am a moral man, I am a religious man; but I have not got this; this is something different, this is something apart from me as it were, this is something that God must impart to me! And they went to their New Testaments and they found the same truth was there! They learned that the Creator, the One who made man at the beginning, comes and, as it were, re-makes him, and puts into him this principle of life. It is His action; believers are His workmanship; the work is not something we painfully do, it is something He does. And because He has done this to us, let us live accordingly. That is what it means to put on the new man, because the new man is in you.

But that does not exhaust the doctrine. The new man, says Paul, is created; but he introduces the additional phrase *'after God'*, another very vital term! He does not say *'by* God'. He does not only mean that God has done it, although God *has* done it. This is something additional. Literally it means that the new man has been created by God after God's own image; that what God has created and implanted in us is something that partakes of His own likeness. This is not my theory, scholars are all agreed that that is the only way of interpreting the expression 'after God'. These words take us back to the first chapter of Genesis where we find God saying, 'Let us make man in our image, after our likeness; and let them have dominion over the fish of the sea, and over the fowl of the air, and over the cattle, and over all the earth, and over every creeping thing that creepeth upon the earth. So God created man in his own image'; and then, in order that we may never forget it, the word is repeated, 'in the image of God created he him; male and female created he them' (verses 26–27). Notice the repetition of *image* and *likeness*, for 'image' and 'likeness' mean essentially the same thing.

Would that the whole human race realised the truth here revealed! Is man the kind of being that he is depicted in films and newspapers and gossip, and as you see him on the streets of our cities? That is a travesty, an insult to the name of man! It is the decay that we have been talking about under 'the old man'; that is what is going to destruction, 'the lust of the flesh, and the lust of the eyes, and the pride of life'. That is not man! It is a foul travesty. What is man? Man is a creature created 'after God', in the image and likeness of God! Obviously, man was not an exact likeness of God. That is only true of the Lord Jesus Christ Himself, of whom we are told in the Epistle to the Hebrews, that He is the 'express image of his [God's] Person'. Man is not God, he has been made in the likeness, in the image of God; he is a created copy, of something that is essential in God. When God

[175]

said, 'Let us make man in our image, after our likeness', that is what He meant. Man is not made a god, but God puts into him something that is a reproduction of that which is God Himself.

Jonathan Edwards of Northampton, Massachusetts, can help us at this point. He was that mighty American, who died two hundred years ago, on 22nd March, 1758. Read about him, and read his works, now republished, as much as you can. Get hold of them, and devour them. Edwards said that the image of God in man can be divided into two parts, the natural and the spiritual. 'The natural image consists very much in that by which God in His creation distinguished man from the beasts, namely, in those faculties and principles of nature whereby he is capable of moral agency.' That is one part of the image. Man is a moral agent; an animal is not a moral agent. So that the natural part of the image means all those faculties in man that distinguish him from the animal. But there is also a spiritual side to the image. 'The spiritual and moral image,' says Edwards, 'consists in the moral excellency with which God has endowed man.' Similarly, John Calvin taught that 'the image of God extends to everything in which the nature of man surpasses that of the animals'. What does it mean then?

Man's spirituality is a part of God's image in him, for God is Spirit. Man is a spiritual being; no animal is a spiritual being. So that, in making man in His own image, God put in us this element of spirituality. And that is something that those who are not Christians know nothing about and never display. They live like animals. Where is the spirit? It is gone! Again, God is immortal, He made man immortal. Man would never have died were it not for sin. But death has come in as the result of sin, and as the result of sin only. The psychical powers of man, man's rational faculties and his moral faculties, are a part of the image of God in man. The intellect! The will! Our self-consciousness! There is no evidence to show that an animal is self-conscious. An animal cannot contemplate itself and look at itself objectively and think about itself. Man can do so; God can do so. Self-consciousness, the power to reason and to think, and self-contemplation, are a part of the image of God in man. And once again, notice man's dominion and lordship over the earth, as mentioned in Genesis. God is the Lord of all; He made man in His own image and He made him the lord of creation; He made him king and prince over all the animals and everything that is in earth. God put into man something of that which characterises Himself. Man's very body supplies evidence of this. God made man upright. The animals are not upright. God made man upright, to show that he had this dignity, this regal quality about him. Man does not go on all fours, he stands erect; the very uprightness of a man's body is a part of the image of God in him. Still more important is the fact that God made man, originally, righteous. He gave him a moral and an intellectual integrity. Man, as he was made by God, was righteous and holy and true. There was no sin in him, there was no defect, he stood before God a morally righteous creature, fit for communion with God, and one who enjoyed communion with God.

Why is the world as it is? you say. The answer is that man fell. And when man fell the image of God in man was defaced. I do not say that the image was destroyed or altogether lost, because when man sinned and fell he did not cease to be man, he did not become a beast, he was still man. And that is the tragedy of man, that he still bears *some* of the marks of the image of God. He can still think; he can still reason; he still stands erect and upright; he still has psychic powers in that he can reason about himself and contemplate himself. These traces remain. But what was really the crowning gift of the image – the righteousness, the uprightness, the holiness, the truth – was lost, and man was driven out from the presence of God and became a stranger to Him.

What, then, is the new creation? What is the new man? What is this new thing that God creates and puts into us? Scripture tells us that believers have been created again after the image of God, and that they receive back the righteousness, holiness and truth which were lost through sin and the Fall. Can anything be more important than that we should realise what it is to be born again and to have the life of God in our souls? If only every true Christian in the world today realised that this new creation, this new man, this new being, was within him, the whole Church

[177]

would be revolutionised! All our failures, all our sins, are ultimately to be traced to the fact that we do not realise as we should what God has done to us, and the character and the nature of the new man, the new life, that He has put within us. It is only as we understand this fully that we are in any way capable of putting on the new man. Do you know that the life of God is in your soul? That is the question.

14

Righteousness, Holiness and Truth

'And that ye put on the new man, which after God is created in righteousness and true holiness.'

Ephesians 4:24

We continue our consideration of the Apostle's message with respect to the new man and the creation of the new man in the very image of God; and as we have seen, we can think of this in terms of regeneration.

We must, however, remember that this is the second half of this great Epistle, where Paul is applying the teaching, and is concerned about the behaviour and the conduct of these Christians. So here he does not give an exhaustive treatment of this whole question of the image, nor even of regeneration; because he has this practical concern in his mind, and he is naturally, therefore, out to emphasise in a very special way the ethical and practical aspects of this tremendous thing that God does to us in regeneration, and thus restores in us the image of Himself. So let us now look into this.

This process, this act of regeneration, this renewal of the image, this thing which happens to us in the re-birth, this new creation, is, as the Apostle John puts it, like the implanting within us of a divine seed. Peter says that we become partakers of the divine nature; John tells us that this seed abides in us. At this point Paul is concerned to emphasise that there are two special characteristics of the seed, this divine life, this new principle that has been put into us, and we are told that they are the exact opposite of the characteristics of the old man which are described as lusts. The opposite of lusts, says Paul, is righteousness and holiness: 'the new man, which after God is created in *righteousness* and true *holiness*'.

How important it is that we should have a right conception of such terms as these! *Righteousness* means *essential rectitude*, the love of that which is right and true. And perhaps still more important, *a just and right relationship among the powers of the soul.* In the old man the powers of the soul are not in the right balance or proportion. He is eccentric and unbalanced. Instead of being governed by his mind and his understanding, still more by the spirit of his mind, he is governed by his desires. The desires may not be sinful in and of themselves, but if they control, if they are in the supreme position instead of being in the subordinate position, then the balance is lost, and things are not in their right and due proportion. Righteousness, I repeat, means that state in which there is a just and a right relationship among the powers of the soul. Man again becomes as he was at the beginning, with everything in the right position in his make-up. He is no longer governed by his body but by the higher things, by the spirit and by the mind. The new man loves that which is right, and therefore does that which is right in all his relationships in life.

There are some who would say that the difference between righteousness and holiness is the difference between a man's relationship to man and his relationship to God. Well, that is true in a sense, but I do not accept it as showing the real difference between these two things. Righteousness gives the impression of this right ordering, and right understanding, and therefore right living. It indicates a rectitude, an uprightness, which is restored to man by the creative act of God when He regenerates a being. Holiness suggests something which is entirely separate from evil, something which is put on one side and which separates itself. It not only separates itself from evil, but it hates evil! It means *essential purity of nature and of being.* In other words the difference between the two things is intended to emphasise this positive element of purity which governs the whole. It is no longer a matter of the right balance and proportion; it is the very nature of the things in themselves which is balanced. Furthermore, holiness in the new man is a reflection of this essential characteristic or attribute of God – holiness! purity! something ineffable! something which we cannot describe because of the inadequacy of our language, but something which is eternally different from sin and evil in its essence and in all its manifestations. The Holiness of God! God is holy!

[180]

These, then, are the two characteristics which the Apostle tells us are most prominent in the new nature, this new life, this new principle, this seed, that has been put into the new man. But we notice that he adds something even to that. Unfortunately the Authorised Version is not quite as good as it might be. It reads: 'which after God is created in righteousness and *true holiness*'. But it is generally agreed that it should read: 'which after God is created in righteousness and *holiness of the truth*'. It is important for us to note this difference in translation in order that the contrast intended by the Apostle may be brought out. In verse 22 as it appears in the Authorised Version we read of the deceitful lusts, and we agreed that it should read *lusts of deceit*. The entire life of the ungodly, the unbeliever, the unregenerate, is governed by a lie, by deceit, by something which is false – the whole characteristic of the devil. But here, says the Apostle, is the complete antithesis to that: the righteousness and the holiness are *of the truth*! The entire life of the new man is something which is characterised by truth. And here surely is something which is quite foundational and fundamental. We see the difference between these two lives – the horrible character of the life of deceit! the truth and the beauty and the wonder of the life of righteousness and of holiness! We see why we should hasten to put off the old man and to put on the new man. In the Epistle to the Colossians we find an exact parallel to the Apostle's statement in Ephesians: [Believers] 'have put on the new man, which is renewed in knowledge after the image of him that created him' (3:10). In other words, the Apostle is saying that this new life is entirely governed by truth; the righteousness and the holiness are really produced by truth; they are stimulated by truth, and are encouraged to grow by truth.

It seems to me that this is a very fruitful way of looking at the Christian life, and it is something which is frequently emphasised in the New Testament. For example, in the eighth chapter of John's Gospel, where it is recorded that our Lord had been preaching about His relationship to the Father, we are told that it so amazed the people listening, that many of them believed on Him; and further on we are told: 'Then said Jesus to those Jews which believed on him, If ye continue in my word, then are ye my disciples indeed, and ye shall know the *truth*, and the truth shall make you *free*.' The *truth*! Continue, He says, in this word of Mine that you have heard, and then 'ye shall be my disciples indeed; and you shall know the truth, and the truth shall make you free'!

We find another illustration of the same thing in our Lord's high-priestly prayer, in chapter 17 of John's Gospel, where we read His petition for His people: 'Sanctify them through thy truth; thy word is truth.' It is truth, we note, that sanctifies, so He prays that His Father may sanctify them through the *truth*. There is a sense, therefore, in which we can say that the object of salvation, as well as its essential method, and its ultimate end, is to bring us to a knowledge of the truth. Notice how the Apostle Paul puts it in the second chapter of his First Epistle to Timothy: '[God our Saviour] . . . will have all men to be saved, and to come unto the knowledge of the truth' (2:3, 4). How important is the place that is given to *truth*!

But why is it that the kind of exhortation that we have here about putting off the old man and putting on the new is ever necessary? Why is it that as Christian people we are not all perfect? Why is it that the Christian Church appears as she does at the present time? What is the matter, what is the real explanation? I suggest that it is partly and chiefly because our fundamental conception of salvation is wrong. We do not think of it in terms of *truth*. Too often we think of it in terms of feeling, or experience only. Perhaps we have been miserable and unhappy after being defeated by something; then we have been delivered, and we tend to think, Everything is all right now, I am happy, whereas before I was miserable; I have now got a joy which I did not have before, and I have got victory where formerly I was defeated. And we stop at that! It is natural, but it is altogether wrong. Experience is a vital part of our Christian life, but it is not the whole of it. And it is because we tend to stop at these particular points and junctures, instead of going on and conceiving of our experiences in terms of *truth*, that we find ourselves in these constant difficulties and troubles. The Apostle writes his Epistle to get Christian people to realise that man is as he is, in sin, because he has believed a lie, because he has become a stranger to the truth; and what man needs above everything else is to be brought back to a knowledge of the truth! Of course he needs to be delivered from his particular sins; of course he needs to be given joy and many other things; but the real trouble with man is that he believed the word of the devil, he believed a lie, he followed the father of lies, the one who was a liar from the beginning; and he has lived a life of deceit, and been under the dominion of deceit ever since. What man needs above everything else is to be brought back to a knowledge of the truth.

There is only one way in which that can happen; and that is that man must be given a new principle of life. He cannot see truth without it. 'The natural man receiveth not the things of the Spirit of God'; he is incapable of it, he is at enmity against God, his whole life is opposed to God. So it is not enough to give him instruction. If it is put before him, he will not see it. But when a man is created anew after the image of God, and given this new life, he has the capacity to see truth and to believe truth and to enjoy truth, and to grow in grace and the knowledge of this truth. And that is the thing that happens to us in regeneration. We receive the capacity of truth which we literally had not got before, and this, in turn, makes it all the more important that we should have the right view of salvation. We must always look at it as a whole, we must never stop at particular points.

To some people, salvation just seems to be a matter of forgiveness. They were in trouble, they were accused by their conscience, they felt and heard the thunderings of the law of God, they felt as if they were at the foot of Mount Sinai; they saw the lightning flashing and heard the thunder rolling and the awesome voice, and they trembled and they quaked, and became eager to know whether there was a way of forgiveness. And they find there is! But, alas! the tragedy of so many is that they stop at that point; and the result is that their lives are unworthy, they fall repeatedly into sin. Ah, they say, the blood of Christ covers me. . . ! That is perfectly true, but they go on at that level, they never rise, they never grow. And it is to them that Paul says, Put off the old man, put on the new; it is because you have not seen the truth that you are living at that low level. They have only taken a little section of it; they have stopped at forgiveness, or at some other experience. Some stop at justification only, and do not hesitate to say

[183]

that they can take their justification, as it were, in isolation, from Christ and then later they may take their sanctification. But that is the error. You cannot divide Christ; you cannot divide truth. All parts of salvation result from a knowledge of the truth! And the truth is, that 'of God, Christ Jesus is made unto us wisdom, and righteousness, and sanctification, and redemption'. You cannot divide it up and take parts of it. It is a whole. The thing, therefore, that the Apostle would have these Ephesians understand is that the righteous and holy principle that is within them enables them to comprehend, to lay hold upon, and to enjoy and practise the truth. It seems to me that Paul puts the matter in one verse in his Epistle to the Romans; 'God be thanked,' he says, 'that ye *were* the servants of sin; but' – now! – 'ye have obeyed from the heart that form of doctrine which was delivered you' (6:17). Why did they obey it from their hearts? Because they had seen it and had believed it; the mind had been rendered capable of taking it; and as a consequence it had moved them to action. So the intellect and the heart and the will are involved; truth takes up the whole man, and moves the entire being. The man has been created anew in righteousness and holiness of the truth!

This brings us to the greatest and most important of all questions. What is this truth that leads to righteousness and holiness? The answer is that it is the truth about GOD, the Father, which is the great message of the Bible from beginning to end. It does not end even at the Lord Jesus Christ. He is not the terminus; He brings us to GOD! It is because we forget this that we are in trouble on the ethical and moral level. There is only one way to ensure that men and women shall live a righteous and a holy life, and that is that they know GOD. Look at the theme in the Old Testament. God revealed His holiness to men at the very beginning. He went on doing so. It stands out pre-eminently in certain places, in the giving of the law, in the terms and the character of the law and the commandments. It is found throughout the teaching of a mighty succession of prophets. Their burden and message was the holiness of God set over against the folly of God's own people, the people He had made for Himself, in forgetting the holiness of God!

[184]

But still more, of course, is this truth taught and revealed in the Person of our blessed Lord and Saviour. 'The law was given by Moses, but grace and *truth* came by Jesus Christ.' He did not hesitate to stand up and say, 'I am the way, the *truth*, and the life; no man cometh unto the Father but by me.' He had come to declare God; 'No man hath seen God at any time; the only begotten Son, which is in the bosom of the Father, he hath declared him'! At the end of His life He tells Pilate that He is come into the world 'to bear witness unto the *truth*'! He had come to save us, but do not put that first; He had come to bear witness to the *truth*, and it is only as He brings us to a knowledge of the truth that He saves us. Everything is in terms of the truth, and it is truth about God!

The whole purpose of the gospel, the object of the whole of salvation, is to bring us to this knowledge of God. Not to give us certain experiences and feelings only! Thank God, we get these, as it were, in passing, but if I have not got this salvation, experiences and feelings may be spurious and false; they may be of the devil and his counterfeits; for the cults can make people happy and give them various kinds of deliverance, even healing their bodies at times. No, it is not that, it is to know God, and to come to the knowledge of the truth, and the truth is – the holiness of God. It is there in the sixth chapter of Isaiah: 'Holy, holy, holy, is the Lord of hosts. The whole earth is full of his glory'! But do we really believe this? Do we see it and know it as we walk about the world? Is this the thing that dominates all our thinking and our understanding and all our conversation? But, you may say, that is Old Testament! Of course it is, because it is the same God everywhere, and the whole object of the Old and New Testaments alike is to show us the holiness of God. The law alone could not do it. Christ has done it! And we must not stop at any point short of this truth, that God is Light, and that in Him is no darkness at all; that God is the Father of lights with whom is no variableness, neither shadow of turning. When His only begotten, beloved Son who had come from His eternal bosom was here as true man in this world, when He prayed to Him He addressed Him, not as *dear* Father but as *holy* Father! That is the truth. 'Our Father, which art in heaven, *hallowed* be thy name.' The characteristic of spirituality is not glibness, it is reverence, it is a holy awe. The characteristic of spirituality is to *know God*, and if we know Him we know Him to be the *holy Father*, whose name is *hallowed*.

The truth also teaches us God's utter hatred and abhorrence of sin. Holiness is not an experience that we receive in a meeting. It is to understand that the holy God *hates* sin, the deceitful thing that governs men and gives them these lusts and passions and makes them creatures of such evil desires. He *hates* it. And it is only the man who really knows that, who will hasten to put off the old man and to put on the new man that after God is created in righteousness and in holiness. So read the Ten Commandments! Listen to Him speaking in Habakkuk where He declares that He is of such pure eyes that He cannot even *look* upon sin. He hates, He abominates it. That is how the Bible preaches holiness! 'Sanctify them through thy truth'!

Remember also God's revealed determination to punish sin. That is what I learn in the truth. He had made man in His own image and likeness, but when that same man rebelled against Him and disobeyed and listened to the voice of the devil, He drove him out of the garden of Eden, and set the cherubim and the flaming sword to prevent his return. That is how God dealt with the man that He Himself had made, after His own image and likeness. God punishes sin because He hates it and it is an intrusion into His holy universe. Read also about the Flood, how He destroyed the whole earth apart from one family of eight. Go on and read about Sodom and Gomorrha. Go on and read about His treatment of the children of Israel, the nation that He had made for Himself and fashioned for His own delight. Though they are His own people He drives them away to the captivity of Babylon, He sends them into Assyria, He raises up heathen nations to destroy them and to chastise them; He is punishing sin.

Next read the teaching of the Son of God Himself, the Lord Jesus Christ, and you will find that He exhorts people to flee from the wrath to come. He talks about the place where their worm dieth not and the fire is not quenched, where an eternal gulf is fixed, where the evil and the impenitent spend their eternity in suffering. Go on to the Book of Revelation and you will find that nothing unclean or vile will be allowed to enter through the gates into that holy city. Without are dogs and sorcerers, and all that work iniquity; not inside, but ever out, driven out and kept out, and remaining out. God has revealed this; this is a part of the truth! You do not wait for an experience, you read the Word of God and study it. You have got a nature now that enables you to do so and to receive it and to take it. Put on the new man! He is created in righteousness and holiness of the truth!

And then go on to realise that this communion with God is only possible on certain conditions. Take Psalm 15: 'Lord,' says this man, 'who shall abide in thy tabernacle? who shall dwell in thy holy hill?' He answers, 'He that walketh uprightly, and that worketh righteousness, and speaketh the truth in his heart.' And listen to him again in Psalm 24. 'Who shall ascend into the hill of the Lord? or who shall stand in his holy place? He that hath clean hands, and a pure heart; who hath not lifted up his soul unto vanity, nor sworn deceitfully. He shall receive the blessing from the Lord, and righteousness from the God of his salvation. This is the generation of them that seek him, that seek thy face, O Jacob.' 'Holiness, without which no man shall see the Lord.' Who shall dwell with the burning, devouring Fire? Who among us shall dwell with everlasting burnings? But you say, You are quoting the Old Testament, you are taking us back to the Psalms and to Isaiah. What about the blood of Christ? has not this made everything different? can I not now run into the presence of God as my Father? Well, listen to the author of the Epistle to the Hebrews. Though you come with holy boldness by the blood of Christ into the Holiest of all, you still come with 'reverence and godly fear', 'for our God is a consuming fire'! Without holiness no man shall see the Lord, without holiness no man can have communion with Him, no man can truly pray to Him.

And then finally let us realise what our sin and rebellion must mean to such a Being! Have we any conception of what man's first disobedience meant to this holy God? Have you seen the insult involved in sin, and the enormity of sin? Now, says Paul, put on the new man, realise these things, this righteousness, this holiness; it is not merely that you have done something wrong that makes you miserable and unhappy afterwards – oh! try to think of it as it appears in the sight of this holy, august Being whom

[187]

you have wronged and whom you have insulted. It is the know-ledge of the truth that leads to sanctification. It is through the truth that we are to be sanctified, and that we come to realise the nature of sin and to hate the lusts that are born of deceit.

Let us realise more and more that the ultimate purpose of redemption is to enable us to glorify God, and to enjoy Him for ever. We are so subjective and so man-centred nowadays, that we even view the origin of salvation in a wrong way. Do you know why God sent His Son into this world and to the cross on Calvary? Why did He do it? Ah! you say, that we might be saved! As I said before, that is not the first thing. And we must never put it first. What God Himself has said is this, 'Not for your sakes, but for my holy Name's sake'! The first object of salvation and redemption is to vindicate the character and the being of God. God in Christ is vindicating Himself as He recon-ciles the world unto Himself. So your first objective and mine, our chiefest desire, should not be that we may have this or that, or even become this or that, but that we may ever be well-pleasing in His sight and that we may ever live to the praise of the glory of His grace. In this way we put off the old man and we put on the new man, which after God is created in righteousness and holiness of the truth.

15

Be Up and Doing!

'And that ye put on the new man, which after God is created in righteousness and true holiness.'

Ephesians 4:24

So far we have been looking at some of the reasons why we should put on the new man. There remains one further thing for us to consider, and a most important one it is – How do we put on the new man? If we avoid this question, or evade it, we are in a very dangerous position. There is nothing, I suppose, that is finally so dangerous as to look at a great truth like this merely in a theoretical manner. Nothing can be more dangerous to the soul than to have a form of godliness but to deny the power thereof. Our Lord Himself said, If ye know these things, happy are ye if ye do them. It can be devastating, as history proves abundantly, for men to look at this exalted and glorious doctrine of the new man in a purely objective, academic and theoretical manner, as a wonderful concept. But the Apostle here, and in this whole section of his Epistle, is concerned to be intensely practical. We shall find him going on to say: 'Wherefore, putting away lying, speak every man truth with his neighbour', and so on. But before we come to the actual details we shall look at this question of how to put on the new man in a general manner.

There are certain principles which we must bear in mind, and the first, of course, is that this is something which we ourselves have to do. I indicated this as we were dealing with the practical part of putting off the old man. And it seems to me to be essential to emphasise it again as we begin to consider the activities required of the new man. The key verse with regard to the whole matter is found in the second chapter of the Epistle to the Philippians where the Apostle says to believers: I am exhorting you 'not as in my presence only, but now much more in my absence, work out your own salvation with fear and trembling. For it is God which worketh in you both to will and to do of his good pleasure.' Paul is not asking natural people to do this; of course they cannot; he is asking people in whom God is working mightily by His Spirit to work it out. It is no use saying, I have not got the power: you do have the power, and what you are exhorted to do is to realise that the power is in you and that, as you exercise yourself, you will discover that the power is there. That is the mystery of God's way of sanctification. You do not wait to have the power; in the rebirth the power is there, and as you exercise it, you will find you have got it, and as you exercise it you will have more of it. It is exactly the same as with our muscles; you will never know your muscular power until you begin to use your muscles, and as you use them you will often be surprised at the strength and power you have got. God gives us the power; what we are called upon to do is to use it and to exercise it.

Again, take a similar statement in chapter 8 of the Epistle to the Romans: 'If ye through the Spirit do mortify the deeds of the body, ye shall live.' 'Through the Spirit'! The Spirit provides the power, and the Spirit is in us. So, that being the case, we are exhorted to put off the old man and to put on the new man.

In the second place, the putting on of the new man is something that must be done completely, it must always be done as a whole, and it must apply to the whole of our life continuously. In other words, we must never do the work in compartments; we must put on the new man not only in certain parts of our lives, it must be in the whole of our life. We must not put on the new man only at certain times or when we are in certain company, or when we are in certain places. That would be to deny the whole principle. The new man must be the reigning and the governing principle of the whole of our life; having been born again we have been moved from the world into the Kingdom of God; and therefore the whole of our life and of our conduct will and must be entirely different from our life and conduct in the past. But it is possible for the Apostle's expression 'put on' to be misused. The term 'put on', as we have already seen, makes us think of putting on a cloak or a gown or some other article of dress. It is a good term to use as long as we do not abuse it. But, alas! we are all very prone, I fear, to do just that! In the Victorian era, people would, as it were, put on their religious cloak on Sundays and go to a place of worship; and after they had gone home on Sunday night they put it off again, and lived as hard-headed business men of the world for the rest of the week, so that you would never suspect that some of them were Christians at all. In our own day we may see a group of people talking together. We look at them and think that their whole demeanour and deportment, their whole appearance and mannerisms, are typical of the people of the world. We are much surprised therefore when we discover that they have met together for the purpose of worship, for their behaviour did not suggest the putting on of 'the new man'. Hypocrisy, that is, putting on a mask, is the exact opposite of what the Apostle means. 'The new man' is not something that you put on now and again, when you suddenly become serious; it is a governing principle in the centre of a man's life, that controls everything he does, wherever he is, whatever the company. Putting on the new man means that the new man is at the centre and directing all my activities, in every conceivable situation.

In a sense it should never be necessary for the Christian to pull himself up and remind himself that he is a Christian. If you really put on the new man, you will always remember that you are a Christian! There are people, of course, who are so much afraid of being humbugs as Christians, and so much afraid of being hypocrites, that they never put on the new man at all; nobody knows that they are Christians for they just appear as men and women of the world. And that is equally foolish and equally bad. We must bear in mind that the Apostle is simply using a picture to impress upon us that always, in everything, and in all places, we are to live the life of the new man in Christ Jesus.

The whole matter of putting on the new man is in essence the application of truth to ourselves. It is the most important thing that one can ever discover in the Christian life. The real secret of Christian living is to discover the art of talking to yourself. We must talk to ourselves, we must preach to ourselves, and we must take truth and apply it to ourselves, and keep on doing so. That is the putting on of the new man. We have to hammer away at ourselves until we have really convinced ourselves. In other words, this is not something that you wait for passively. If you wait until you feel like the new man it will probably never happen. We must be active in this. There is no greater snare in the Christian life than to entertain the idea of waiting until we feel better, and of then putting on the new man. On the contrary, we have got to go on telling ourselves the new man is already in us. In his Epistle to the Romans the Apostle Paul says, 'Reckon yourselves to be dead indeed unto sin, and alive unto God' (6:11). Reckon yourselves! Say it to yourself! Persuade yourself, argue, say it to yourself, announce it to yourself. The moment you wake up in the morning say to yourself, I am the new man in Christ Jesus, I am not the old man, I do not belong to the world, I belong to God, I belong to Christ. That is the truth about you whatever your feelings may be. You see the analogy; in the physical sense, you may not feel like getting up in the morning, but you get up. You may not feel like dressing, you prefer to lie in bed, but you get up and put your clothes on. You must do the same in the spiritual sense, says the Apostle. The devil will be there governing your feelings, and he will suggest his thoughts, his innuendos and insinuations, the moment you wake up. Evil thoughts may come, and a thousand and one things. Then is the time to stand up and say, No! I am the new man in Christ, and I am not going to live my day like that, I am going to live as the man I am! That is putting on the new man. You say it to yourself, whatever your feelings may be, because you know it is true.

And let this principle of activity apply to my third general point. Use everything that you know of that reminds you of the new man and that feeds and helps to build up the new man. This is the exact opposite of what you have to do in putting off the old man, regarding whom the Apostle says, 'Make no provision for the flesh', do not feed him! If you know that reading a certain type of literature gets you down, stop reading it! Starve the old man, strangle him, be violent with him, *mortify*, says the Apostle. And mortify means mortify; you hit him, you pummel him, you throttle him, in order to get rid of him! But as for the new man, feed him, give him the sustenance that is likely to help him and to make him grow; and do this diligently and constantly. How do you do that?

Well, first of all, you read your Bible. If the essence of putting on the new man is the application of truth to yourself, what can be better than to familiarise yourself with the truth? Ah, but you say, I do not always feel like reading the Scriptures. I know you do not; so you make yourself read the Scriptures. This is not a question of feeling, this is something that is essential to your life and well-being and health. Therefore do it, rouse yourself to do it. It can be done, it has got to be done. We can shake ourselves physically, and we can shake ourselves spiritually. 'Stir up the gift that is in thee,' says Paul to Timothy, and he says the same thing to us. You may say, I do not feel like it; how can I over-come that difficulty? In various ways! Sometimes it is quite a good thing to prepare yourself for the reading of the Scripture by reading something about the Scripture, by reading some biblical exposition or by reading a portion of a biography or some state-ment of experience. In the days when people used pumps to get their water supply, they would sometimes find that when they tried to use the pump nothing happened. What was to be done? They took a little can already filled with water, and poured it into the pump, and then, when they resumed pumping, out came the water. This procedure illustrates a great principle in the spiritual life. You have got to prime the pump, and that frequently! You have got to understand yourself. You must know how to handle yourself. And there are many things which one has to do in order to bring oneself into the right state and attitude and condition. It is fatal just to sit down and wait until you feel like reading Scripture. Rouse yourself! Stimulate yourself! And then when you come to the Scriptures, do not read as it were mechanically, and end by saying, My Scripture portion for today is so-and-so, and I have done it, and off I go! You might as well not have done it; there is no value in such superficial reading. When you come to do it, see that your mind is on it; concentrate, read intelligently, look for truth. Merely to read through the Bible once a year is doubtless a good thing, but, done as a cold duty, it may be of little value spiritually. We have to learn to read with a spiritual

[193]

mind and understanding. Ask questions; say, What is this saying? what is it saying to me? what is the point here? what kind of person is the writer addressing? This done, it becomes not only interesting, it becomes absorbing. And as you are doing it, you are feeding the new man, and thereby putting him on. So we rouse ourselves in various ways to read the Scriptures.

Then, too, we must pray. We should never attempt to read the Scriptures without praying God to bless them to us and to enlighten us by the Spirit. Oh, what a difference it makes! And we are to pray about every aspect of our lives. We are God's children; well, go to Him as your Father, tell Him about your difficulties and your weaknesses, ask Him to give you wisdom and understanding. The more you pray, the more you thank God for what He has done for you and to you in Christ and by the Spirit, the more you are putting on the new man, and the more his life will be manifest in your activities. So prayer – solitary, isolated, lonely prayer, and also prayer with others – is a second way of putting on the new man.

Again, we must seek fellowship with like-minded people. The saints have always found it most strengthening to meet together, to talk together about these things, to pray together. 'Iron sharpeneth iron'; like attracts like; birds of a feather flock together, inevitably. The new man is there and it talks to the other, who recognises its presence. And as you see the same nature in another you are strengthened. That is the value of a church; and that is why your radio, and your television, and all the rest of such things put together, will never be a substitute for the church. Impossible! They cannot be! the church is where two or three are gathered together! And not only is He there, but we recognise one another, and that stimulates the life of each one. So the church is essential. The author of the Epistle to the Hebrews gives the warning, 'Neglect not the assembling of yourselves together, as the manner of some is' – the 'some' doubtless including the people who went astray. Fellowship with other believers belongs to the divine pattern. When the saints come together and the Spirit is present, *then* God acts; He works still through the church; the church is His own creation.

There, then, are certain obvious general principles. They will cover all the details and all the particularities of our actions. But at the same time let me give you some of the truths about which we have to remind ourselves in particular. Put on the new man! Very well, what do I remind myself of? The first is this, that I really have no choice at all in this matter of putting off the old man and putting on the new man. Why? Because I am not mine own. There is no need to argue about these things, says Paul: flee fornication – why? – because you are not your own, you have been bought with a price! The Christian is not a free man, the Christian is the bond-slave of Jesus Christ. That is why I always feel it is very wrong to appeal to people to do these things; we need to be exhorted, not appealed to. I do not like that preaching of sanctification which says, Now do this and you will be marvellously happy and you will have victory, and so on. That is the wrong way to put it. You are not your own, you have been bought with a price: you have no right to do anything else, you are a rebel if you attempt it. We have been bought and purchased by the precious blood of Christ, as of a lamb without blemish and without spot; He gave Himself, and all that that involved, that you and I might be new men. Remind yourself of that. Remind yourself of that first thing in the morning, remind yourself of that constantly throughout the day. You are not your own, you have been bought with a price.

And that in turn leads to this, does it not: the privilege and the dignity of our position. 'Created', he says, 'after God' in this righteousness and holiness of the truth. You know, if you and I only remembered who we are and the dignity of our calling and our position, there would be very little problem left in our lives. But we have got to remind ourselves of this; we have got to tell ourselves who we are and what we are. Listen to Paul putting it to the Thessalonians: he says, You are not children of the night, you are children of the day, you are children of light! 'We are not of the night, nor of darkness. Therefore let us not sleep, as do others; but let us watch and be sober.' '. . . now are ye light in the Lord', he says to the Ephesians. 'Walk as children of light'! Did you notice how he put it there in writing to the Romans: 'The night is far spent' – we have finished with all that; for us it is no longer 'chambering and wantonness' – that mighty word came, you remember, to Augustine and was the word of life and of God and of regeneration to him. 'The night is far spent, the day is at hand. . . .' Let us not any longer, therefore, walk in that way, '. . . but put ye on the Lord Jesus Christ, and make not provision for the flesh'. We are the children of God, the children of light, the children of the day; and what we mean by putting on the new man is that we remind ourselves of that, and, remembering that, we walk as such, and our whole demeanour and deportment, our very stance, our entire attitude, is the complete antithesis of those who belong to the night and the darkness and who hide behind doors and who are ashamed of the light and the sunshine. 'Children of the heavenly King, as ye journey, sweetly sing'! 'Only let your conversation be as it becometh the gospel of Christ', says Paul in Philippians 1:27. Well there it is, let us remember these things.

And that in turn leads us to remember this. Let us ever remind ourselves of the family that we belong to and the family that we therefore represent. We are indeed the children of God. 'Beloved', says John, 'now are we the sons of God' – now! already! And this is such a startling and staggering conception of the Christian life that a man who once realises it finds himself inevitably putting on the new man. We are, now, the children of God! That is the whole trouble with the Christian Church today, she does not realise that. The Church is regarded as just another institution, and our assemblies are so like political gatherings. We are the children of God! And we are altogether different from the world – this is the thing that we need to recapture, and that it is our privilege to represent the family in this world of time. We are strangers and pilgrims in this world. As Christians we really no longer belong to it; we are still in it, but our citizenship is in heaven, and we are visitors, we are strangers, we are here for a while; and we must live as such; we do not conform to this, we belong to that, and the whole glory and dignity of the family depends upon us and is in so many senses in our hands.

And that, you see, in turn leads to this, that we put on this new man and he governs the whole of our activity because, being strangers in a strange land, we are being observed, and people are looking at us; and they say, Who are these people? – Well, comes the answer, they are Christians. Oh, they say, this is Christianity, is it? And they are going to judge Christianity and they are going to judge God, and they are going to judge the whole of the Gospel, by what they see in us. Of course, they are quite wrong in doing so, but they do and you have got to take people as they are, and you cannot blame them for doing it. You and I therefore should remember that. Putting on the new man means being always conscious of our responsibility. Listen to Peter saying this. Look it up in 1 Peter 2:11–12. 'Dearly beloved,' he says, 'abstain from fleshly lusts, which war against the soul; having your conversation honest among the Gentiles: that whereas they speak evil against you as evildoers, they may by your good works, which they shall behold, glorify God in the day of visitation.' Now there it is in a nutshell. You are strangers and pilgrims, says Peter, you do not belong here; well now, these Gentiles are watching you and are looking at you, they are speaking against you, they say you are mad, they say you are fools, they say you are hypocrites; they are saying things like that, but, says Peter, so live as to convince them and to silence them, and to bring them into such a position that they shall praise and glorify God in the day of visitation. You will find the same injunction everywhere, running right through the whole of the Scripture. Now, putting on the new man just means that. And if we really do believe these things and that Christ has died to make us such and to make these things possible for us, I say it needs no pressing; our very sense of honour is involved, and we shall feel that we are cads if in any way we let Him down or misrepresent His wondrous grace and love with respect to us.

And that brings me to my last point, which is this: our destiny! All these things follow in a logical sequence. Is there anything which is more powerful as an argument than this? Having reminded yourself that you are but a stranger in this world, well then, go on to remind yourself of where you are going! 'And that, knowing the time, that now it is high time to awake out of sleep: for now is our salvation nearer than when we believed'! We are moving on. Every day takes us nearer. Nearer what? To what is coming – the night is far spent, the day is at hand. What day? The day of Christ, the day of the Lord, the day of His coming back, the day of the Last Judgment, the day when all men will have to appear before Him, the final end of history. 'The night is far spent, the day is at hand'! Or listen to John putting it in his way. 'He that hath this hope in him . . .' – what is it? Well, he says it is this, 'We know not yet what we shall be', but we do know this, 'that we shall see Him as He is, and we shall be like Him'; our very bodies glorified, we shall be perfect and spotless, without any vestige of sin remaining; we shall be like Him! That is what we are going to. Now if we really believe the Gospel, if we have truly learned Christ, we have learned that all He has done is to prepare us for that day. It follows, if we believe that, we must rouse ourselves, put on the new man; the night is far spent, the day is at hand; let us no longer sleep, let us prepare for the crowning day that is coming, for the beatific vision, for our final glorification, for our entry into the eternal city, for the joy and the bliss and the glory of sharing the life of God throughout eternity. That is putting on the new man, reminding yourself of this truth.

And then finally remember this (and I believe this is the climax, the mightiest argument of all). If we are Christians it means, as the Apostle has already told us in his third chapter, that Christ dwells in ou hearts by faith. Or listen again: 'Know ye not that your body', your very body, 'is the temple of the Holy Ghost which is in you?' What is it to put on the new man? It is to remind yourself that Christ is dwelling in your heart by faith, that the Holy Spirit of God that dwelt in Him dwells in us. If only every Christian in the world today lived in this world as remembering that the Holy Spirit dwells within him or her, what a revolution it would create! The whole Church would be transformed! People would not recognise themselves! And the world would look on astonished and amazed! That is what it means to put on the new man, to realise that He is in you, and that anything unworthy or sinful grieves the Holy Spirit that dwells within us.

Let us therefore start our day by reminding ourselves of these things – I am a child of God; I am born again; I am a partaker of the divine Nature; Christ is dwelling in my heart by faith; wherever I go, whatever I do, the Holy Spirit is in me and in my very body, so that my every action is known to Him, the *Holy Spirit*! And as you live your day remembering that, it will obviously change everything. And that is to put on the new man, which after God is created in righteousness and holiness of the truth.

16

How and Why the Christian Puts on the New Man

'Wherefore, putting away lying, speak every man truth with his neighbour: for we are members one of another.'

Ephesians 4:25

We come now to what is in a sense a fresh subsidiary section in this great Epistle. You remember that the whole Epistle is loosely divided into two great sections: the exposition of doctrine; and now, here, the application of that doctrine; but the Apostle has not gone very far before he is back again with the great and fundamental doctrine concerning the nature of the Church. He deals with that until the sixteenth verse in this fourth chapter, and then, he really does come to this practical section, which begins at verse 17, 'This I say, therefore, and testify in the Lord, that ye henceforth walk not as other Gentiles walk.' There again we found that this involved him in a very necessary description in detail of the kind of life that was lived by the Gentiles, in order that he might say to them: You cannot possibly continue living that kind of life, if you really have learned Christ, and if you really do know the truth as it is in Jesus. Very well then, he says, winding it all up and summing it all up again, I exhort you therefore to 'put off concerning the former conversation the old man, which is corrupt according to the deceitful lusts; and be renewed in the spirit of your mind; and that ye put on the new man, which after God is created in righteousness and holiness of the truth'. Here then, having said that, he now proceeds with the word *wherefore*. And here he is introducing us to the really practical aspect of this whole teaching. The general governing principle is

[199]

that we put off the old man and that we put on the new man. But the Apostle cannot leave it in that general form, he feels it is necessary for him to apply it in detail and to take up particular questions, particular aspects of conduct and of behaviour. And that is what he begins to do here in verse 25; and we shall find in a sense that he continues to do this right until the end of the Epistle. But, as I have pointed out before, he keeps on interspersing it with doctrine, and that for a reason which I hope to deal with now.

This, then, is his argument. You are no longer what you once were, indeed you have become something that is entirely different; now then, put off in every way everything that is suggestive of what you once were, put on everything that really does belong to, and is true of, this new man that you are in Christ Jesus. He wants them now to see how this is to be done. As we therefore approach this section, which is a long section, it seemed to me that nothing surely could be more helpful or advantageous than that we should look at the teaching as a whole first of all; because there are certain principles with respect to it which govern every one of the single detailed applications. And therefore I would invite your consideration of these general principles, these common lessons, which seem to me to stand out clearly and prominently in this entire section. Now here are some of them.

The first is that truth must always be applied. 'Wherefore', says the Apostle. Truth is not merely a thing to be regarded objectively and to be enjoyed intellectually: truth is to be applied. I remember once an occasion when a man preaching with great eloquence, said a very striking thing. As a result certain people in the congregation spontaneously broke out in applause. They clapped their hands, and the good preacher, man of God as he was, pulled them up and said, 'The truth is not to be applauded, it is to be applied!' How true that is! We do violence to truth unless we realise that it is to be applied. The purpose of all doctrine, and of all knowledge, is to lead us to a life that is in conformity to the truth that we believe. I need not stay with this, our Lord has put it once and for ever in a memorable phrase, 'If ye know these things, happy are ye if ye do them.' It is a terrible thing to stop at knowledge only. Knowledge is absolutely essential, that is why the Apostle has devoted the whole of the first three chapters, and indeed most of this fourth chapter to it. Knowledge is absolutely essential, we can do nothing without it; but to stop at knowledge – theoretical, academic knowledge – is quite as bad, if not worse, than to be ignorant.

In the second place, I would say that a real and a true understanding of the truth always does lead to application. So that if a man does not apply the truth, his real trouble is that he has not understood it. For if a man is gripped by a truth and sees what it means and what it implies, of necessity he must apply it. That is why the Apostle introduces these sections generally with words like *therefore*, and *wherefore*.

Thirdly the Christian faith and teaching apply to and affect the whole of life in its every detail. Paul tells us not to lie but to speak the truth; not to steal; not to talk foolishly; he goes into details concerning parents and children, husbands and wives; every conceivable thing is touched upon, every aspect and walk and department of life. The Christian truth and faith apply to them all. There are no compartments in the spiritual life, and there is nothing so fatal as to divide our lives up into compartments. The characteristic jibe of this present century against our Victorian grandfathers is that they were very religious on Sunday but that they forgot Christianity during the rest of the week. There may be some truth in the accusation, and there may be substance in it as it applies to us also. It may indeed be one of the reasons why the vast bulk of the people are outside the Christian church today. It must be emphasised that Christianity covers the whole of life: we are to be religious not on Sundays only, but always! Our conduct should be the same everywhere, in the church, in the mart, wherever we are. Or, to put it another way, our Christian faith must be manifested and put into practice, not only in our public or our professional conduct, but in every part of our conduct. There is a type of man who is very scrupulous in his public conduct, but who does not apply the same canons when he comes to his private behaviour. There are men, in business, who would not dream of telling a lie or doing anything dishonest, men who observe their *professional code* with the utmost fidelity; but their standards in their private conduct in their homes and in the bosom of their families is something strangely and strikingly different. Paul shows us, here, that such variations are entirely wrong. The Christian teaching, the Christian principle, covers and governs the whole of our life, in every single detail. In a sense, the supreme glory of the Christian life is that it gives us this wholeness, and delivers us from the dichotomies and the divisions which are ever characteristic of sin, not only as between man and man but even within the man himself.

There are certain characteristics which stand out as we view the Apostle's method of teaching his ethics and his morality. And this is his pattern: he first of all puts a negative, telling us what we must not do; he then puts a positive, in which he tells us what we should do; and thirdly he gives us the reason for the required action. Take note of it in verse 25: 'Wherefore, putting away lying [the negative], speak every man truth with his neighbour [the positive] for we are members one of another [the reason for the action].' I do trust that you are all as fascinated by the method as I am. You can analyse these Epistles as you can analyse the sonatas or symphonies of Beethoven; there are these definite steps; the teaching is not thrown out anyhow; there is a definite scheme here – negative, positive, reason.

A vital principle is involved in the Apostle's method here. These people had been brought up in heathendom and had been living the life that was so characteristic of that type of life at that time – it was a life of lying and fraud and stealing and deceit and all the rest of it; well, they have become Christians, but it does not mean that automatically all is well with them; no, they are in the fight of faith now, and they are troubled by these old tendencies. What does the Apostle tell them to do? You notice at once that his advice and his exhortation are not simply that they should pray to God to take these things out of their lives. Over this question of lying, he does not say, Pray to God to deliver you from the tendency to lying. What he actually says is, Stop lying! see to it that you always speak the truth! and for this reason. Now I think you will agree that this is a very important principle. There is the type of teaching which would always tell us that whatever the problem or the difficulty, there is only one thing to do and that is to take it to the Lord in prayer, ask Him to deliver you from it, to take it out of you; and you just stand by and watch the victory. No, says the Apostle, 'Wherefore, *put away* lying, *speak truth* every man with his neighbour.' This is something that you and I have got to do. 'Let no corrupt communication proceed out of your mouth.' 'Let all bitterness, and wrath, and anger, and clamour, and evil speaking, be put away from you.' 'Let him that stole' – not pray that he may be delivered from the tendency to steal, but – 'Let him steal no more'! 'But let him rather labour, working with his hands the thing which is good, that he may have to give to him that needeth.' You and I are called upon to do these things – to apply in actual practice the teaching that we claim to believe, and always to *know* why we are behaving thus, and to be able to give a reason for our conduct.

We must know each time why we have stopped doing something, why we have started doing something else, and we can tell other people why. When they come to us and say, 'Why have you stopped doing the things you used to do with us? and why are you behaving differently?' we do not just stand and say, 'We do not know; we have now joined a company in which these things are not done and in which other things *are* done', and no more. We must be ready not only always to give a reason for the *hope* that is in us, we must be able to give a reason for our conduct and our mode of behaviour.

The Apostle really implies all this by using the word *wherefore*. In other words, the reason for Christian behaviour is found in the teaching which he has already been giving them. But he does not leave it merely at *wherefore*. He every time provides us with the *particular* reason. 'Wherefore,' he says, 'putting away lying, speak every man truth with his neighbour.' Why? Because 'we are members one of another'. That is why we stop lying, that is why we begin to speak the truth. It is a special and unique reason.

Why is this point about the uniqueness or the special character of the reason so important? It is of vital importance because there are other forms of moral and ethical teaching and behaviour. Christianity has not a monopoly of ethical and moral teaching. There are pagan moralities. There are so-called humanistic moralities, and ethical and cultural systems, and they are very evident in this modern world in which we find ourselves. As believers we must be able to draw a clear distinction between *Christian* morality, ethics and culture, and every other form of morality, ethics and culture. Otherwise we shall be unable to state the Christian truth plainly and clearly. Let me put this into its historical setting to make it more plain and clear.

Last century in particular, a type of teaching came in, sponsored and started very largely by Thomas Arnold, the famous headmaster of Rugby. He and others began to teach and to propagate a new teaching which they still called Christianity, but which really was nothing but a moral and an ethical teaching. It had practically nothing to say about the supernatural or about the miraculous; it said very little about the spiritual element; there was no redemption in it whatsoever, and not a word about regeneration. Arnold's whole idea was that Christianity was a way of living, and that you became a Christian as you heard or read the teaching of our Lord in particular and applied it to your daily life. That was the teaching. It was almost exclusively a matter of conduct and behaviour, ethical and moral practice. And it became tremendously popular. It has sometimes been called *public school religion*. There are those who would even call it today *B.B.C. religion*. That is the kind of teaching to which I am referring, and many still believe that that is Christianity, and that we make ourselves Christian by not doing certain things and by doing other things, by conforming to a moral, ethical pattern, or to a certain type of culture.

I have no hesitation, however, in saying that Arnold's teaching denies utterly what the Apostle is teaching in this Ephesian Epistle. There is nothing finally that is more opposed to the Christian message than just that type of teaching. And therefore it does seem to me to be tremendously important that before we come to consider in detail such matters as lying, and being angry and subject to wrath, and stealing, and using corrupt communications, we should be clear in our minds that the Christian message has nothing in common with pagan and humanistic, moral and ethical teaching and ideas with respect to life.

If we are not clear about this we shall take away the uniqueness of the Christian message. Our claim is that Christianity is absolutely unique, that there is nothing like it, and never has been, and never will be. But if we adopt this other teaching, we have entirely taken away the uniqueness of Christianity. It becomes a mere collection of moral and ethical principles, exactly as we find in the writings of many of the Greek pagan philosophers who lived and taught and died before the Lord Jesus Christ ever came into this world; the uniqueness of Christianity has gone, it is just one of a number of great moral systems. But still more serious, it takes away the uniqueness of our Lord Himself, it makes of Him just one of a number of other great teachers with respect to life. And as you read the writings of the people who belong to that other school (and there are many of them still, and they often write in religious books and periodicals), you notice that they habitually give their whole case away by compiling lists of those whom they name as great ethical, moral teachers – Moses, Isaiah, Jeremiah, Jesus, Paul, Mohammed, Buddha, and so on and so forth. Our Lord is put into a category, He is just one person amongst a number of great teachers, He no longer stands alone and in a category apart. He is just a great teacher, *one* of the great teachers, one of the great religious geniuses that the world has thrown up, He just belongs to a series. And so He is deprived of His uniqueness and His essential glory. Some of the most difficult people to preach to and to get hold of at the present time are the cultured pagans, for they feel that they have no need of Christianity. They do not lie, they do not steal, they do not commit adultery, they do not use these corrupt communications. And therefore Christianity is represented as nothing other than a moral, ethical system that tells us not to do certain things and to do others, they react by saying, 'I am already living that sort of life; that is what I already believe; I practise that kind of thing, and I really do not see any need to come to your churches on Sunday, I can live my life quite as well out in the country; indeed, I am helped by the glory and the beauty of nature. Why the Christian church? why do you separate yourselves from others? why do you say that you have got something separate and different?

This is a matter, therefore, that involves the very heart and core of the Christian position; and so I want to suggest some of the essential differences between Christianity and any and every form of pagan culture or a collection of pagan virtues.

The first important difference is to be found in the reasons that non-Christians give for living their own type of life. They invariably isolate their conduct and behaviour as something in and of itself. They isolate certain virtues, or list a series of abstract virtues, which, they say, are the things that men must put into practice – their approach is essentially theoretical and abstract; they pick out such virtues as appeal to them and urge us all to apply them. And so they make their appeal to us in terms of the country or the school or the family or class to which we belong. They say, We never do that, 'it is not done' – *we* always do this; *this* is the 'done thing'. The virtue they isolate and urge us to apply is always something impersonal and abstract. But the Christian reason is always essentially different. The reason why the Christian does not do certain things, but does other things is always in terms of the Lord Jesus Christ! He reasons that, because Christ has come into the world and died for him and has risen again, and has given him a new life, *therefore*. . . .! Notice the beautiful phrase used in verse 27 of the first chapter of the Epistle to the Philippians: 'Only let your conversation be as it becometh the gospel of Christ': not your country; not the 'done thing'; but 'as it becometh the gospel of Christ'! Our reason is always personal, it always refers back to the Lord, who He is, what He has done, how He has done it, and why He has done it. The reasons are diametrically opposed and different.

In the second place, these pagan systems (I call them pagan even though they may use Christian terminology) always presume natural ability; obviously, because they come to us and tell us to pull ourselves together, to conform to the pattern. They are presuming that we have the ability and the power to do so. Because of that, it is generally a kind of teaching that only appeals to a certain type of person. In ancient times it only appealed to the cultured, the able and educated; so that when our Lord was exercising His ministry, and John the Baptist sent his two emissaries to Him to ask the question, 'Art thou he that should come, or do we look for another?' the reply He sent back was this: 'Go and tell John again the things that you have seen and heard; the blind receive their sight, the lame walk, the lepers are cleansed, the deaf are made to hear, the dead are raised, and – a terrible anticlimax? – 'the gospel is preached to the poor'. That is his climax, even after mention of the raising of the dead – 'the gospel is preached to the *poor*'. Why does He say that? Because pagan systems, pagan ethics and moralities, had nothing to say to the poor. You have to be a cultured man before you can apply pagan culture and humanistic morals and ethics. It presumes it in you, and if you have not got it, it has nothing to say to you. That is why the masses of the people have never been touched by such a teaching, and are not being touched by it today. In other words non-Christian teaching has nothing to offer to failures. If a man is unable to respond to it they just denounce him and leave him, they cannot understand him; they say he is unintelligent, a fool, and there they leave him, and have nothing to give him. Christianity, on the other hand, presumes one thing only, and that is that we are given new life, that we are regenerated. *Wherefore*, says Paul, you must not walk any longer as other Gentiles walk and as you once walked; for you have been born again, you have got the new man in you, you have got an ability given by God. Nothing of that other, it is all natural and human; this is divine, this is of God, this is miraculous, this is supernatural; it presumes the dwelling of the Holy Spirit within us. What a difference! How can they ever have been confused?

But we come to a third difference. Moralities and ethics, divorced from the Christian faith, for the reasons I have been giving, minister to self-satisfaction and to pride. Obviously a man preens himself on the fact that he is not a liar, his word is his bond; I am a man of my word! my word is my bond! I have got a code! And he is very pleased with himself! The Apostle Paul was very pleased with himself before he became a Christian. A person who holds to any kind of moralities and ethics apart from Christianity is always pleased with himself and his achievements! 'Concerning the righteousness which is of the law, blameless!' I exceed all my fellow-countrymen in my efforts and endeavours. Certainly I am doing very well, I am already living this cultured, ethical, moral life! Self-satisfaction and pride! Christianity always keeps us humble, always makes us conscious of what we are not, and what we are failing to do. And as we

[207]

look at Him, we all feel that we are worms. And when we are addressed in the words, 'Let this mind be in you that was also in Christ Jesus', we feel that we are down in the dust. The two systems are obviously exact opposites, all along the line.

We thus establish a fourth principle: non-Christian systems really leave the old man and the old nature quite untouched. They merely whitewash the surface a little and conceal the foulness that is within. Scratch that surface and you will soon discover what is still there. Offend or cross the people who seem so moral and ethical and you find that their morality is only skin deep. It leaves the old man exactly where he was and what he was, but it puts a veneer on the surface, it whitewashes him, it gives an appearance, but it does no more. Christianity, on the other hand, creates a new man, a new nature, a new creation, a new heart, a new outlook. Or, to quote again the principle which stands out in this series, it is all the difference between something being done on the outside and something being done within. The worldly systems simply spend their time in pouring chemicals into the polluted stream. Christianity goes back to the source of the stream and makes that pure; it goes down to the very depths, it produces a new creation, a new man comes into being.

In the fifth place, I suggest that worldly moral systems simply hinder and put a brake upon great outbreaks of vice and the coarse manifestations of vice; they do not really deal with vice itself. A man who follows these systems will never be guilty of anything gross or obviously foul. He believes in being respectable. He embraces nothing openly coarse or foul or ugly – he would not dream of it! – but in principle and in essence the evil is there in his own life! Christianity, on the other hand, deals with the whole problem. We see it perfectly illustrated in the Sermon on the Mount. For example, the Pharisees taught that as long as you had not actually committed adultery all was well, and you were perfect as regards that commandment. Not at all, says Christ; if it is in your mind and heart and thought and imagination, and if you have played with it, you are guilty of it! His words go right down to the roots and to the depths. They concern not only coarse manifestations, but all kinds of manifestations. Non-Christian systems are only concerned, I repeat, with *public* behaviour, and private behaviour is often so different. I use a modern illustration to illustrate my meaning. Look at the lists of certain gentlemen who are speaking so busily at the present time in the name of morality against the use of hydrogen bombs and other such horrors. They have a sense of moral indignation. In the name of humanity, they say, this is an impossible thing, we must denounce it, we must stop it! Their moral conscience, their sense of righteousness, is roused! But go into their life history and story; is there the same keen edge to their moral conscience as regards their fidelity to their wives? A public morality that does not apply itself in the most tender and noble relationships of life is a fraud. I am not interested in the moral indignation of men who have not the same moral indignation in *all* the realms and departments of life. It is an appearance only, it is not genuine.

In the sixth place, the non-Christian systems really deal with nothing but repression. They know nothing about expression. They are negative, they lack freedom. But Christianity has both. You stop doing one thing, you do the other. You not only stop lying, you speak truth. But the contrasted system is always negative and purely repressive; it knows nothing about the glorious liberty of the children of God. The fact is that pagan and similar cultures are always manufactured, they always lack life, and they always lack spontaneity. They are a kind of standardised product, the result being that they always produce the same type of mind and outlook; they all look the same and they all do the same things in the same way. They violate personality because they press all personalities into a single mould. But Christianity never does that. In Christianity there is always variety in the unity. We who are Christians do the same things, but we are not all the same. Thank God there is variation and variety among us, a diversity in unity. We do not conform to a standard pattern. If you happen to find Christians who do always the same thing in the same way, suspect them! there is something wrong in their teaching. As there were differences in the Apostles, so there are differences in all Christians. No two preachers who are Christian should preach in exactly the same way; one may be quiet, the other may be vehement. Let them be so, God has made them such. But in these other systems they clamp down upon your very personality, and they produce a standard type like peas in a row, or like a series of postage stamps. This indicates the falsity of the non-Christian systems; they are the antithesis of the true which is the Christian.

Lastly, the non-Christian systems are always cold. It is the coldness of artificiality. It is all the difference between a rose blooming on a branch in your garden and an artificial rose. They look very much alike at first, do they not? but oh! that artificial thing! – it is cold, it is dead, it is hard, there is no warmth about it, there is nothing that really attracts when you get near it. And that is true of all the merely moral, ethical systems. You cannot really get near people who are merely moral and ethical, there is a coldness about them; they are self-content, they are very perfect, but you do not get sympathy out of them, there is no warmth, they do not encourage you, they do not sympathise with you. But when you come to the Christian, what a contrast! He is warm, he is human, he is sympathetic, he is approachable, he is encouraging, he is not for ever standing on his dignity, he can forget himself, he can enthuse, he is governed by a principle of love, which is found at the centre of his life and radiates from him. He is not always watching and observing himself on the outside; there is this spontaneity, this principle, this blessed principle of life. He is what he is by the grace of God, and because the grace of God has been able to do this for him, he makes you feel that grace can do it for you also!

I close by telling the story of the conversion of a man aged seventy-seven; it happened about twenty years ago. He was a terrible character, a drunkard, a wife-beater, a gambler, everything a man should not be. But that man became a Christian, and in this way. Drinking his mug of beer one afternoon, he happened to hear two other men talking about the gospel, and as he listened he heard one saying to the other, 'You know, I felt that there was hope for me there.' And something hit this old man; he said, 'If there is hope for him, there is hope for me.' But the impact made upon others by the merely ethical people is very different. They never make you feel there is any hope at all.

You probably say to yourself, It is very wonderful, but who am I? I cannot do it, I am made differently. So they condemn you and they leave you out in the cold. Not so the Gospel of Christ! There is warmth, life, radiance, a dynamic quality. You look at a man and you say, He is what he is by the grace of God! If grace did it to him, it can do it to me!

I am reminded of another similar instance. Some thirty years ago I stayed overnight with a doctor, who was then an old man, and he told me his life story after the evening service. He said, You know, I have been in trouble about my life right from its start; it started even when I was at home. My father was a member of an Anglican church; my mother was a member of a Unitarian church. And this, he said, was my problem. My father, while he was a very nice and good man, simply could not go to the local market every Friday and come home sober. My mother, as far as I was aware, never did anything wrong at all. She was highly moral, as Unitarians generally are. But you know, he said, I could not get away from it, there was something about my father, despite his big failing, that helped me and appealed to me more than the perfect correctness of my mother. I could go to my father when I had done wrong, but I never felt that I could go to my mother, there was this coldness. He then said that, when he later became a medical student his old problem was perpetuated. I used to go on Sunday mornings, he said, to listen to the great Unitarian preacher, Dr James Martineau, who preached great ethical discourses; and I admired the language and the diction, and the division of the matter, and the thought, and the logic. And then, he said, I used to go on Sunday nights to the Salvation Army, where there was no formal service and no eloquence and many things that really were offensive to me as a man of culture; but yet, he said, my heart was warmed there; I used to feel there was something that would help me in my personal failures and my personal problems. In the morning service I sat and I admired, in coldness and intellectual detachment, but I was not helped with my personal, moral problems, and my heart was not warmed. But in the evening, what a difference!

We all need to learn the lesson that these stories convey. As we stop lying and begin to speak the truth, as we stop using corrupt communications, as we stop stealing, and all else that is evil, we must do it in such a way that the drunkard, the hopeless man who has lost his very will-power, meeting us and coming into contact with us, will feel that there is a hope for him. We must always do these things in such a way as to make people look to Christ and to know that we are what we are solely by the grace of God in Christ Jesus.

17

'Putting away Lying'

'Wherefore, putting away lying, speak every man truth with his neighbour, for we are members one of another.'

Ephesians 4:25

The Gospel of Jesus Christ is intensely practical, and it is practical, as we have seen, for its own special reasons, which are far removed and remote from the reasons which the world gives for its culture, its moralities, and its codes of honour and of behaviour; the reasons found in the Epistles of the New Testament are always peculiarly Christian.

Let us now look at the first detailed injunction that the Apostle gives to the Ephesian believers. We have remarked on his method before: first of all the negative injunction, 'putting away lying'; then the positive injunction, 'speak every man truth with his neighbour'; and then the reason for doing both, 'for we are members one of another'. The first thing, then, that Paul includes in his list is this lying or falsehood, falsehood in general, for as we all know, alas! you can lie without saying a word. You can lie sometimes by not speaking, by allowing something to be said which you know to be wrong, you can lie with a look. So that the term *lying* really does cover falsehood in general. But why does Paul start with falsehood and lying? Doubtless for many reasons, but he gives us one which in a sense sums them all up, here in this verse. But we shall divide the verse up, the better to show how the Apostle was in a sense driven to put this in the first place.

One reason seems to be almost a mechanical one. We have noted what he has been saying in the previous verse, correctly translated: 'that ye put on the new man, which after God is created in righteousness and holiness *of the truth*'. We are thus reminded that the most essential characteristic of the Christian life is truth, *the Truth*. This is the thing that makes the Christian life such a complete contrast to the non-Christian life, to the life of the world. Also, in describing the old man, the Apostle has been speaking about corruption and the lusts *of deceit*, which are the greatest characteristic of the sinful life. Nothing is so characteristic of the Christian life as the fact that it belongs to the whole realm of truth. We describe what has happened to a man who has become a Christian by saying that he has *seen the truth*, or he has *seen the light*. That is what we claim, is it not, for the Gospel and for the Bible? This, we say, is truth! and nothing else is truth! All other views of life and of man and of existence and of the purpose of life and what lies beyond, are lies! We thank God that we have been delivered out of the realm of the lie by which the world is governed. But we have been brought into the realm of truth, and we glory in it. 'God our Saviour,' says Paul in writing to Timothy, 'will have all men to be saved, and to come to the knowledge of the truth' [1 Timothy 2:4]. John in his First Epistle argues repeatedly that the Christian is in the realm of truth; the darkness is past, the light has come. Clearly, therefore everything about us should be indicative of the fact that, having arrived at a knowledge of the truth, we are now living in the truth, and are seeing the whole of life in a true manner. So naturally, having ended with the word truth, Paul takes it up again. And this therefore is the thing that comes first, 'Therefore, putting away lying . . .'; it is utterly incompatible with the realm to which you now belong.

This, of course, leads us of necessity to other aspects of this matter. Is there anything that ultimately is so vital and so essential a part of the character of God as truth? The Bible is full of this teaching. Have you noticed the extraordinary statement that the Apostle makes at the beginning of his letter to Titus: 'God who cannot lie . . .' God cannot lie! That is God! God is the 'Father of lights, with whom is no variableness, neither shadow of turning'. What a tremendous statement! There is one thing that God can never do, God can never lie. It would be an essential contradiction in His very nature and being. God is light, and in Him is no darkness at all. He cannot be tempted with sin, neither can He tempt anyone. God is the essential, everlasting, and eternal Truth. And to be a Christian means that we have been brought into fellowship with such a God!

When the Apostle says that we must put away lying, he is not interested in it as the moralists and the humanists are; he does not merely say that lying is a terrible thing, it can do a lot of harm, etc. etc. Of course, it *is* a terrible thing, but, as Christians, we have better reasons for putting it away. We have been reconciled to God, we say that we know God, we say that we are in fellowship with God and in communion with Him. The Apostle John stresses the fact that if a man says 'I know him', but does not keep His commandments, 'he is a liar'. It is impossible, he says, at one and the same time to walk in the light and in the darkness; and to know God and to have fellowship with God means, of necessity, truth and truthfulness. David understood this, even with the lesser light of the old dispensation. It was the thing that troubled David after his most terrible sin; so he cries out of the agony of his heart, in Psalm 51, 'Behold, thou desirest truth in the inward parts'. He knew that no pretence, no sham, no lie can avail in the presence of God. He says, It is no use pretending, it is no use trying to hide anything, 'Thou desirest truth in the inward parts'! And if I am not open here, he seems to say, and absolutely, utterly truthful, it is of no value at all. Men can deceive their fellows, but God is all-seeing. He demands, insists upon, this honesty, this truth in the inward parts. So naturally, at the very top of the list, you must have this with which the Apostle starts: 'putting away lying, speak every man truth with his neighbour'.

But we move on to the next words of the Apostle. As it is true to say that there is nothing that so represents God as truth and truthfulness, it is equally true to say that the devil is a liar, and that that is of the very essence of his nature and of his being. The Lord Jesus tells us so in the eighth chapter of John's Gospel. To those Jews who were arguing and wrangling with Him, and objecting to the truth because it condemned them and searched them, He says, 'You are of your father, the devil, and the lusts of your father you will do. He was a murderer from the beginning and abode not in the truth, because there is no truth in him. When he speaketh a lie he speaketh of his own, for he is a liar and the father of it.' This is how the New Testament deals with speaking the truth and refraining from lying. It requires the Christian to see what it means and what it involves, not merely for the sake of being a gentleman and a man of his word, and being truthful. The world can do all that, but it is not Christianity. We Christians are required to see the lie in all its evil character, and you can only do that as you put it into the Christian context. So that all the moralising that passes in the name of Christianity is finally the greatest denial of Christianity. It does away with its uniqueness, which is its central glory.

Take the terrible case of Ananias and Sapphira as an illustration of the vast difference between the lie and the truth. It had been agreed amongst the early Christians that they should sell their goods and their possessions and bring the proceeds to the common pool. It was quite voluntary, there was no compulsion, and a number of people had done this, and among them Ananias and Sapphira. They had come to the apostles and said, We have done what we promised to do and here are the proceeds. But they had kept back some of the money; and the Lord moved Peter to say to Ananias: 'Ananias, why hath Satan filled thine heart to lie to the Holy Ghost?' Satan had filled the man's heart! It was not just a question of telling a lie! When you are a Christian the sin does not stop at that, it goes beyond it. 'Satan hath filled thine heart to lie to the Holy Ghost'; and in order to show what a terrible thing it was, he was struck dead at that very moment, that God might there call the attention of the early Church and of all Christian people in all places to the very end of time, to the terrible character of this particular sin. From our standpoint as Christians, to lie is to indicate that we have an affinity with the devil. And a liar, an habitual liar, belongs to the kingdom of the devil, whose whole being is a lie. He is the father of lies, there is no truth in him. He is the embodiment of evil, and to lie is what he teaches others to do.

So, says the Apostle in his Epistle to these believers, As new men and women, put on the new man that is in you; and in this respect, first and foremost, stop lying, and speak every man truth with his neighbour; because if you do not, you are conveying the suggestion that you are still in the grip of the devil and that you belong to his kingdom. But that is not true of us as Christians! As again the Apostle John puts it in his First Epistle: 'We know that we are of God, and the whole world *lieth* in the wicked one.' In this, and in similar scriptures, the Apostles take us back to the very foundations of our faith. I keep on saying this because it will help us not only with this first injunction but with all of them. We have got to learn to look at these things in a Christian way, and the moment we do this, no matter what the subject is, we are taken back to the very foundations of our faith. So when you tell a man in the Christian Church to stop lying, you are doing something that is altogether different from the way it is normally done in the world, which is simply concerned about a façade and an appearance; for you cannot do it in a Christian way without going back to your doctrine of God, back to your doctrine of the devil.

The next thing we come to is this. We must stop lying because the very first sin of man was the result of a lie. In other words, the world is as it is because of a lie. Here again, we are back to a fundamental, foundational truth. Why is the world as it is? The Apostle Paul, writing his second letter to the Corinthians, puts it in these words, 'As the serpent beguiled Eve through his subtlety' (11:3). The cause of that first sin was the lie that the devil whispered to Eve. It was a lie about the character and being of God. 'Hath God said?' God pretends that He is good to you and that He loves you and that He is out for your best interests, says the devil; but the actual truth is, said the liar and the father of lies, that He is against you and that He is keeping you down for His own interests, because He knows that on the day in which you eat of the forbidden fruit you will become as gods yourselves, and you will be equal with Him, and then you will really have your rights; He is against you! Such was the devil's lie! That was the whole cause of the trouble. It was the thing that led to the Fall, and that began the process that has led to the whole of human history as we know it. That is the thing that accounts for the state of the world today. The original sin was produced by a lie. We have got to realise that here we are looking at something

[217]

that is a full representation of that which led to the rebellion of the devil himself and then through him to the rebellion of man. This is the thing that has brought the world down from being a paradise to being the world in which you and I live at this moment. And it is as we thus look at it in this doctrinal way and see its fundamental nature and character that we can truly deal with it in a radical manner.

I would say, in the next place, that lying is the most prominent and the most common characteristic of the life of sin. Consider the sequence of events. You commit a sin; you do not want to be found out, and you do not want anybody to know it, so you tell a lie. Because you have told that lie you have to tell another one to cover it; and on and on it goes, by a horrible process of geometric progression. It multiplies and multiplies until the whole life becomes a lie and a sham. Is there anything which is more characteristic of the non-Christian, sinful life than this element of lying? Deceit and lying, sham and pretence, are more obvious in the life of the world than anything else. Have you ever tried to analyse life from this angle? Think of a company of people on what is meant by the world to be some happy occasion, some reception, some party. Look at the affability and the friendliness. But then just watch the glances, just listen to the whispering! Ah! the camaraderies, the friendship and the affability, how delighted we are to meet . . ., and oh! how fond they are of one another! – and yet they are muttering beneath their breath. Is not that the life of society? What if people really spoke the truth to one another and told one another what they really think of one another and what they really believe? I can safely say that the whole life of society, in any realm or at any level – no matter how polite it is, no matter how exalted it is – is run on this principle of deceit and of lying. And we all know it to be so. But the pretence, the sham, and the play-acting goes on. This is, without doubt, the most characteristic thing about the life of sin.

In the same way, is not the addiction to lying one of the chief causes of the complications of life? Why does life become so involved and complicated and so difficult? The answer is because of this element of lying, because the moment we depart from the truth, as I say, that in itself has got to be covered by another lie, and that by another, and so the whole life becomes such a complex and complicated tissue of lies. Sometimes we see this very plainly in an occasional criminal prosecution that is reported in the press. A man starts by making one mistake, perhaps a very trivial one, but it does not matter how small the thing was, it was wrong and he should not have done it; but because he has done the wrong he feels that he has got to cover it, and the whole thing develops and snowballs, as we say, until the poor man finds himself in a court with a tremendous charge against him. Due to the original lie his life becomes involved and complicated; he has to cater for this and to cover that, to manipulate this thing and to be careful at that point, and so the whole of his life which was meant to be, and had been, comparatively simple, becomes involved, and he is juggling; he has got to keep it going some-how, and all his difficulties are due to a lie.

Is there anything, any single thing, I wonder, that causes so much unhappiness and misery in this world as lying? Again, we simply need to know life and the facts of life to know this. Lying, and pretence, and dissimulation, and shamming – oh, the unhappiness they cause, the suspicions they arouse, the lack of ease and repose and quiet, and the lack of trust! If only lying could be entirely banished, what loads would be lifted off minds and hearts! Oh, the havoc that is caused by lying, the heartbreak, the sadness, the unhappiness, the suffering to innocent people that is caused by this lying. It is no wonder that the Apostle tells us to put it away at once as the first thing we deal with!

Can we not also say that there is nothing which shows us the real nature and character of sin as lying does? What is the real essence of sin? what is at the back of it all? what is the cause of it? There can be no doubt about the answer to that question! Self! Self is the ultimate cause of sin. And it manifests itself in self-regard, self-centredness, and selfishness. Well, you say, what has all that got to do with lying? I can tell you. We express ourselves most profoundly in our speech, we express ourselves more in our speech than in anything else. It is the one thing perhaps of all things that differentiates man from the animal. The animal can express its nature in its behaviour; you can have a

[219]

quiet dog or a fierce, angry dog; and so with all other animals. But man has this unique capacity of speech, and it is in a sense his glory. There is nothing through which a person expresses his or her personality more profoundly than in speech. This gift of speech and communication, linked with fallen man's self-regard and self-centredness and selfishness, leads to a desire to be highly thought of, to be praised, to impress people, to be important. We want everybody to think well of us. We want everybody to praise us. We want to be important, to cut a figure. And how is this to be done? In the world that is found in the wicked one, it is often accomplished by the lie, enabling you to build up the personality that you think you are and that you want to be, and that you want other people to think you are. You have got to be important, so sometimes you make deliberate mis-statements, you invent 'facts'. The anatomy of sin, the anatomy of lying! At the moment I am engaged in dissecting it, and is it not an ugly thing that we have uncovered? I am doing it in order that we may so see it that we shall put it away once and for ever, as the Apostle is exhorting us to do.

So we make our deliberate mis-statements and inventions, or again we may lie by saying nothing. We just conceal the truth by withholding it. And then another very common way – exaggerations! You have got a story to tell, and it is quite a good story, but you rather feel that if you embellish it a little it will be still more wonderful, it will make *you* still more wonderful, so you exaggerate. And every time we tell the story it grows with the telling. We told it the first time and it produced a good response; ah! we thought, that is good! We add a little to it, still better response! And on and on it goes. In the end, what we are now saying has really never happened at all; it has been so exaggerated that it is nothing but a lie. Why does mankind do this? Why exaggerate? why add to things? why withhold? why fabricate? why invent? Trace it out, pick it up at any point in yourself or anybody else, and you will always find that its purpose is to minister to this self and this self-importance. It is our aim to win the good opinion of others, and to be praised and to be highly thought of; so we pursue a course of lying and building up the façade, putting on the camouflage, appearing to be something that in reality we are not. There is nothing that finally shows the real, foul character of sin so much as lying, because speech is ultimately the supreme way of manifesting our personality.

But to go further, nothing shows more clearly the utterly despicable character of sin and the nature of sin as lying. If you were to canvass the opinion of any group of people you may happen to meet, if you were to ask them, What do you think of a man who is a liar? they would be unanimous! There is nothing that human nature, even in sin, so despises in its judgments as a liar. We will excuse a man many things, but we have no use for a man who is a liar. The whole of mankind, fallen and debased in sin as it is, agrees that a liar is the most despicable kind of man. And yet, though we may all agree about that in theory, lying is the commonest, the most universal of all sins. Some are guilty of certain sins, some commit others, but here is something that is common to all men. Though we hate it and despise it and denounce it, we are guilty of it. It reveals the radical nature of sin, because it is not merely a matter of acts on the surface, but an expression of that which is the essential being and personality of man since the Fall. And it all revolves around this self.

What a terribly deep and subtle thing sin is! And at this point I must again denounce superficial moralists who treat a lie as if it belonged to the surface of life, and say that it should not be regarded too seriously. On the contrary, a lie is a thing that comes out of the depths of a man's being. What a hateful, foul thing it is! There is nothing that shows more clearly what a terrible hold sin has upon human nature, it does not matter how refined, it does not matter how cultured. Visit the highest circles, visit the most base, you will find it everywhere. Of course, the way in which it is done differs. You can lie, as it were, with the horny hands of the sons of toil, and you can lie softly with kid gloves. The way it is done is not the thing that matters. As it becomes more refined it becomes more subtle, and to me more hateful because it becomes much more hypocritical. There is almost something to be said for the barefaced liar rather than for the one who so cleverly and cunningly hides it, perhaps with an innocent expression. And thus, I say, lying shows more clearly perhaps than anything else the depth of sin, the hold and the power of sin. Though with our minds we despise the thing, we do it! And thereby we show that sin has introduced a dualism and a false dichotomy into us. It demonstrates that we are slaves and serfs.

Lastly, I would underline the thing that the Apostle picks out here, namely, that there is nothing which is so opposed and so inimical to the doctrine of the church as lying. As we have seen, the first section of this fourth chapter of the Ephesian Epistle is entirely devoted to the doctrine of the church – one Lord, one faith, one baptism; one body, one Spirit, we are called in one hope of our calling. The church is like a body fitly joined and compacted together, all members joined to the Head and receiving the same blood supply. Indeed, the body is one! Is there anything that is so destructive of this truth as lying? Lie not one to another, says the Apostle, but 'speak every man truth with his neighbour, for we are members one of another'! And I believe he was thinking particularly here about the church. There are those who suggest he was thinking in a more general manner, but I am not persuaded of that. Certainly it is true in the general aspect, but it is particularly true of the church, and here Paul is dealing with the whole thing in the context of the life of the church. We are all members one of another! If you tell a lie to another member, you are really damaging yourself; in a sense you are lying to yourself. There is no such thing as an independent existence. 'No man liveth unto himself, no man dieth unto himself,' says the Apostle to the Romans. So that to lie to another member of the same body of Christ is to be lying to yourself. You are doing harm to yourself because you are doing harm to the body to which you belong. You can say, 'I can cut my finger without doing any damage to myself.' But the fact is that you cannot! If you cut your finger, *you* will suffer. It is not your finger only that suffers, *you* suffer, the whole suffers. We are members one of another.

Think of it like this: How can there be fellowship if there is lying? It is the exact opposite to true fellowship, is it not? What makes fellowship possible is trust, mutual trust, mutual reliance, a feeling that you can trust one another, and therefore you can speak, and speak freely and openly, one to another. But the moment the element of lying comes in, fellowship is destroyed: you are no longer free; you do not know how much you can believe, or what you can believe; you do not know how much you can trust the other person. And if fellowship is broken, you are in a kind of police state in which everybody is spying on everybody else. You say, I wonder whether so-and-so really means that; I wonder whether that is really true. In this way fellowship is destroyed. Lying is destructive of fellowship. And what happens to us as Christians is not so much and not only that we are saved individually; we are all saved and made members together of the body of Christ; we are like a building that is being constructed as a habitation of God; we are all individual stones in that wonderful building; but it is the *unity* of the building that matters. Lying makes unity impossible, for it cuts at the very root of the whole doctrine of the Christian church at its most essential point. If you like you can add to that a more general statement. A lawyer once came to our Lord and said, 'Master, which is the great commandment in the law?' And the Lord replied, 'Thou shalt love the Lord thy God with all thy heart, and with all thy soul, and with all thy mind; this is the first and great commandment. And the second is like unto it, Thou shalt love thy neighbour as thyself' [Matthew 22:36–39]. Love thy neighbour as thyself! You do not believe in fooling yourself, do you? Well then, do not fool your neighbour! If you love him as yourself, you cannot; you will stop lying to him; you do not believe in lying to yourself, then do not lie to him. Love thy neighbour as thyself!

So much for the general aspect; but, as in the Epistle, our chief attention must be devoted to the realm of the Church and the redeemed. When we say that we were once under 'the power of darkness' but have been delivered and translated into the kingdom of God's dear Son by the washing of regeneration and renewing of the Holy Ghost, what course is open to us but to put away lying, and speak every man truth to his neighbour? Let it be known and obvious to everybody that we are no longer children of the devil; we are no longer children of darkness and of night; and of the sham and pretence that is so characteristic of the world with its diplomacy and its affability that nobody believes in! I suppose that nothing does such great harm to the relationship between nations as the expression of this very thing that I am talking about. Statesmen write their memoirs after a war comes to an end; during the war we read about their meetings and how wonderfully well they are getting on together; later their memoirs appear and give quotations from their diaries, in which they tell us the things they were saying about one another secretly. How can you have trust while that sort of thing goes on? How can there be confidence when the whole thing is pretence and sham and acting, and is based upon lies and dissimulations? It is wrong in the whole of life, it is what makes the world what it is today. But among Christian people such conduct should be unthinkable. We are the children of God, the children of light, we belong to the truth, we are the children of One of whom it is written, 'God, who cannot lie', and we are to be like our Father and to tell forth His praises, to manifest His virtues and His glories; and we do so by putting away lying and speaking truth one to another, thereby proving that we are indeed new men and women, that we are brethren, and children together of the living God.

'Wherefore putting away lying, speak every man truth with his neighbour, for we are members one of another.'

18

Sinful Anger and Righteous Anger

'Be ye angry, and sin not: let not the sun go down
upon your wrath: neither give place to the devil.'

Ephesians 4:26–27

In these words the Apostle continues the series of particular
injunctions that he is giving to the Ephesian Christians in order
to illustrate and to make quite plain to them what exactly is
meant by putting off the old man and what is meant by putting
on the new man. In particular he is concerned with the doctrine
of the church, the unity of the church, the church as the body of
Christ and our being members together and in particular in and
of the same body. So that what he is really saying in effect is
that we must put off that old life of sin and put on this new life
of holiness because sin is not only something that is wrong in
and of itself and indicative of the old life – sin always breaks
fellowship; and that is his immediate practical concern at this
particular point. Sin breaks fellowship: holiness on the other
hand always promotes fellowship, and as he deals with these
particular examples and illustrations he obviously keeps that in
his mind the whole time. As we come to Paul's second injunction
we find him dealing with something else besides lying, which
not only breaks the fellowship amongst Christians but again
violates the whole fundamental basis and foundation of the
Christian life. So he takes up the question of anger, a very common source of sin and disruption in the life of the Christian
Church. I have no doubt that he put these things in the order in
which we find them because it undoubtedly represents the degree
of their frequency. And here again we see that he does not merely
deal with this problem from the standpoint of morality, or of

pagan philosophy, but in his own specifically Christian way. And that is, as we have seen, the only way in which we as Christians should face every single problem that confronts us in the Christian life. Our way of tackling these problems should be totally unlike that of the world. Very well then, what exactly does he say? What is the meaning of this statement, 'Be ye angry, and sin not'?

There are some people who think that it means that if you cannot get rid of anger altogether, the best thing to do is to suppress it, and to hold it down as much as you can. And that, I suggest, is quite wrong. The Scripture knows nothing of such teaching. That is what the world does, and the result is that ever and again when men are taken unawares, the trap door suddenly opens and the whole thing reappears, as violent as it ever was before. No, suppression is certainly not the Christian way of dealing with anger and its problems. What then does the Apostle mean? Clearly and obviously this is a positive command. It is not some concession that is made to a weakness. He says that it is our duty to be angry in certain respects, but that we must never be angry in a sinful manner, never in a temper.

There are times when we are meant to be angry – 'Be ye angry'! But never in a way that becomes sinful, and never in a way that opens the door of opportunity to the devil. How are these things to be reconciled? how do we work it out? We can do nothing better, it seems to me, than to take the Apostle's statements as he puts them, starting with 'Be ye angry'. In other words, there is a right kind of anger. In and of itself anger is not sinful. It is a capacity which is innate in every one of us, and clearly put into us by God. We can really call it one of the natural instincts. The capacity for anger against that which is evil and wrong is something which is essentially right and good; and it is because the non-Christian moralists so frequently forget this, that those who follow them find themselves in a false position. The pagan idea always is that you are to crucify your instincts, no matter what they are. But that is a false asceticism. The Bible never teaches us to crucify a natural instinct. What we are to do with them is to control them, not to get rid of them altogether. The Stoics believed in getting rid of them; they tried to kill them;

the Epicureans just regarded them with disdain, and both were wrong. According to the Christian teaching, the instincts are to to be governed, to be controlled and to be rightly used. Anger is something which is placed in us by God; it is a capacity within man which results in his being roused by the sight of certain things. And the result is that it is a priceless and precious thing.

To prove that anger is not sinful, and indeed something which is altogether right in and of itself, I simply need to draw attention to a statement which is made in the Gospel according to St. Mark about our Lord Himself: 'And when he had looked round about on them (the Pharisees) with *anger*, being grieved for the hardness of their hearts . . .' (3:5). A similar statement is found in Luke's Gospel: 'The Lord then answered him and said, Thou hypocrite'! (13:15) One of these lawyers, Pharisees, teachers of the law, was trying to trap Him and to trip Him, and our Lord turned upon him and said, 'Thou hypocrite'! He spoke with anger! Again, read the account, in John chapter 2, of the Lord's anger with those men trading in the Temple: 'When he had made a scourge of small cords, he drove them all out of the temple, and the sheep, and the oxen; and poured out the changers' money, and over-threw the tables' (2:15). Here was our Lord in righteous anger and indignation, making a scourge of small cords and literally driving the traders out, and cleansing the temple.

Furthermore, no-one who is at all familiar with the Bible can have failed to observe a term which is used constantly in the Old Testament and the New about God Himself – the wrath of God! For example, the Apostle Paul, writing to the Romans, says: 'I am not ashamed of the gospel of Christ: for it is the power of God unto salvation to everyone that believeth; to the Jew first and also to the Greek. For therein is the righteousness of God revealed from faith to faith; as it is written, The just shall live by faith' (1:16–17). Why is Paul so pleased about this? why is he so anxious to preach it and to proclaim it in Rome and everywhere else? He gives the answer in verse 18: 'For the *wrath of God* is revealed from heaven against all ungodliness and unrighteousness of men, who hold down the truth in unrighteous-ness.' The wrath of God! Both John the Baptist and our Lord preached and exhorted people to 'flee from the wrath to come'. The Apostle John in the Book of Revelation, speaking about the end of the world and of time and history, and about the judgment that will be ushered in by the Lord Jesus Christ, says graphically 'for the great day of His wrath is come' (6:17). So we realise that this is something that we must not dismiss.

And again the Apostle Paul, in writing to the Corinthians in the Second Epistle, makes this thing quite explicit and shows how at a given point we should feel anger and a righteous indignation, with ourselves. He is talking about godly sorrow, and says, 'Godly sorrow worketh repentance to salvation, not to be repented of; but the sorrow of the world worketh death. For behold this selfsame thing, that ye sorrowed after a godly sort, what carefulness it wrought in you, yea, what clearing of yourselves, yea, what *indignation*, yea, what fear, yea, what vehement desire, yea, what zeal, yea, what revenge!' (7:10–11) Indignation! Anger! They were angry with themselves and the cause of the trouble, with the man who had sinned and with their own failure to recognise the sin, and with their failure to react to it as they should have done. The lesson for us is that we should always be angry against and about sin and evil. 'Be ye angry', says the Apostle! In a sense he is just putting in New Testament language what one of the Psalms puts like this: 'Ye that love the Lord, hate evil'! (97:10) The two things go together: if you really love the Lord you must hate evil; evil and sin are definitely to be hated.

It is not at all surprising that the Apostle should give this exhortation to the Ephesian believers, these Gentiles, whose manner of life before their conversion he describes in the words: 'having the understanding darkened, being alienated from the life of God through the ignorance that is in them, because of the blindness of their heart: who being past feeling have given themselves over unto lasciviousness, to work all uncleanness with greediness' (4:18–19). We have earlier seen that '*past feeling*' meant that their consciences had become calloused and hardened, their sensibilities had become dull and blunted, they could not react to anything; they were 'past feeling', they were so steeped in sin that nothing any longer could move them or shock them. They were past feeling! – they had become morally indifferent, they had become supine. This is always characteristic of godlessness and irreligion. It is one of the terrible aspects of paganism, that men and women become so steeped in sin that they are not aware of the fact that they are sinning, they cannot react at all, they never feel any sense of indignation or horror; they never become angry at all; they are past feeling. In the second half of the first chapter of his Epistle to the Romans, Paul tells us all about it. Men and women had forgotten God, and were worshipping birds and four-footed beasts and insects; they were also worshipping one another. And not only had they become immoral, they had almost lost a sense of morality; they were guilty of the most foul and repulsive perversions. The whole world had become a sink of iniquity.

Paul therefore says to the Christians, You have to get right away from the world's sins; you have got to learn to be angry about them; you must be roused; you must not be complacent and say that sin does not matter! Such an attitude belonged to their past, he said, but they must not be like that any longer. A failure to react with indignation and anger against sin and evil is always a sign of moral decadence and of godlessness and irreligion. I remind you of a word that I quoted earlier from the prophet Jeremiah, chapter 8, which describes sin at its acme. Let me give you the climax to the whole statement because it is such a great one. Listen to this. He says, 'Were they ashamed when they had committed abomination? No, they were not at all ashamed, neither could they blush.' What a terrible state to get into! You are not quite hopeless while you can still blush, it means that there is still something in you that makes you feel a sense of indignation and of shame and of anger. But certain people had become so sunk in sin that the prophet says 'Neither could they blush'. And what we need if we are in that condition is this exhortation of the Apostle: Be angry! rouse yourselves! do not allow yourself to be governed by that old mentality! put off that old man, put on the new man! We must learn, says Paul, to be really angry against iniquity and sin. God made us in such a way that that should be our natural reaction; it was the natural reaction of the Lord Himself; it is God's reaction to sin.

[229]

And how greatly this exhortation to anger is needed in the world today! Is not one of the greatest tragedies in the world at this hour the failure to feel moral indignation and wrath because of things that are happening? Is not there a fatal tendency to be complacent and to explain everything away, and to remain indifferent? Even though we hear people 'on the air' and on public platforms deliberately teaching 'Evil, be thou my good', still there seems to be no protest. We seem to have lost the capacity to be roused morally by a sense of indignation. This is, to me, one of the major problems in the world today. There has been a steady decline in morals, not only in behaviour but in outlook and in reaction. We merely shrug our shoulders and allow sin to go unrebuked. I believe this was true of the attitude of the world to Hitler before the Second World War. This attitude would have been unthinkable fifty years before. There would have been protests, and Hitler would have been stopped. But not so in the world decadence of the thirties! We could not be bothered, we wanted to go on enjoying ourselves and having our good time, and we somehow hoped that world troubles would not affect us and all would be well. And so the whole sorry process was allowed to start and to continue.

But this is not only evident in our attitude towards international affairs – as, for example, towards the rise of dictators and the toleration of things in nations, which should never be tolerated – but it seems to me that it is also creeping into the whole of life. I myself cannot be but appalled at the reaction to such a document as the Wolfenden Report, with its idea that you can regard certain perversions as natural. The plain fact faces us that the whole category of sin is rapidly disappearing. Indeed, many are claiming that there is no such thing as sin. No – the man was born like that, he has just got that tendency in him, and it is very strong in him, not so strong in another! Evil is explained away; there is no protest, there is no moral indignation. And it is into such a situation as this that the word of the Apostle, the word of God, comes: 'Be ye angry!' Learn to react against these things! Feel a sense of indignation! There are certain things that should rouse us and should be denounced. An absence of a sense of shame and of anger and of righteous indignation is always the hallmark of deep degradation and sinfulness, and of a loss of the sense of God. Our Lord was angry when He observed manifestations of sin. And what measures our approximation to Him is that we manifest a similar reaction when confronted by similar things. It is our duty to be angry at certain points and with respect to certain matters.

But we move on to a second point, for the Apostle adds to 'Be ye angry', 'Do not sin'! that is, do not be angry in a sinful manner. We have been looking at the right kind of anger, we must now look at the wrong kind of anger. Notice that we are walking on a kind of knife edge. In other words, we can swing from one extreme to the other, and in consequence we have to be very careful. We have already seen other examples of this. The Apostle has already told us to speak the *truth in love*. Some people put the whole emphasis on truth, while others put it on love; the first set of people have no love, the second set of people have no truth; but they are both wrong, for we must speak the truth in love! Similarly here – 'Be angry, but do not sin!'

There is a wrong way of being angry. And what is this? What must we never be guilty of? First, we must never be bad-tempered people. That is entirely and utterly wrong. To be bad-tempered, to be irritable or irascible, is something which is sinful and is condemned everywhere in the Scripture. So it is no use saying, 'Ah! but I happen to have been born like that.' If you are a Christian, you have been born again, so you must not use that argument. It is wrong at any time and on any showing. We are not to explain what we are and what we do in terms of the balance of the various ductless glands, for that would be to do away with sin. We have to know ourselves and we have to deal with ourselves; and we are forbidden to be bad-tempered, irritable, irascible people. But we do not stop at that; there is another thing which we must not be. We must not be easily provoked. In the thirteenth chapter of the First Epistle to the Corinthians the Apostle says that one of the most glorious things about love is that it is not easily provoked. A man who is easily provoked is bound to fall into sin very frequently. We must not be fiery. But let me put the case positively, in terms of the way James in his Epistle describes the wisdom that is from above:

'The wisdom that is from above is first pure, then peaceable, gentle, and easy to be entreated, full of mercy' (3:17). We must not be easily provoked. Yet how easily provoked some of us are, by all sorts of things! Now here is the test. Are you easily put off or put out by anything? It does not matter what it is. And can it upset you and disturb you and keep your mind on it and prevent your concentrating on something else? Christians often express to me their irritation at hymns or tunes and such-like things, and I get the impression sometimes that they have been so put out and so put off that they cannot settle down and listen to the sermon. Easily provoked! That is sinful. We should not be easily provoked. We must seek after the love which enables us to bear all things, and which is easy to be entreated.

But we must go further. Any anger or expression of anger that is excessive, violent, uncontrollable, out of control, is a wrong sort of anger. We talk about a man being in a towering rage. That is definitely, utterly sinful. We talk about people seething with anger, shaking with anger. Oh! that is sinning in anger – the white face, the very body trembling, the eyes blazing. . . . You have seen it, have you not? Now that is altogether wrong and sinful. It is lack of control, and such a man is being angry and sinning; he is being angry in a sinful manner.

The next step is the one that the Apostle himself gives us, in the words, 'Let not the sun go down upon your wrath.' In the original the word *wrath* is not the same word as *anger*; hence it is a pity that the Revised Standard Version has put *anger* in both places. The second word, 'wrath', is a stronger word than 'anger'. It means exasperation, it means anger roused and nursed and nourished until it becomes a settled condition; it means hatred, bitterness of spirit, vindictiveness. It means that you are determined to get your own back, to seek vengeance and absolutely determined to get it. It is a settled condition of anger; it has become part and parcel of you; it is a mood; it is a condition which is permanent; and it is bitter and hateful and determined to get its own back. That is wrath as the Apostle uses the word here, but that is not the wrath of God, there is nothing of that in God's wrath. What the Apostle is condemning is the wrong sort

[232]

of anger. The anger that we are to feel as Christians must never be felt by us just because we happen to be the sort of person that easily becomes 'heated'. That is always wrong. In the same way our anger must never be personal, but rather against the principle of iniquity and sin. My anger must never be the result of my being the sort of man who is rather peppery, as we say, and testy, and a bit on edge always, easily provoked and ready to explode. That is the thing that we are required to put off. In other words, the anger about which the Apostle is speaking is an anger that should always be aroused against evil and sin – those things that caused the anger and the indignation seen in our blessed Lord Himself.

This brings us to our third big principle. How are we to deal with this sinful anger, this sinful tendency to lose control of ourselves and yield to the wrong type of anger? We are to note that the Apostle bids us remember that such loss of control over ourselves belongs to the old man, the old life, and we are to put that off. In the second place, such loss of control always gives the devil his greatest opportunity. Paul adds verse 27 to verse 26: 'neither give place to the devil'! What he means by that is, Never open the door to the devil. When you lose your temper you open it wide; it could not be wider. Nothing opens the door more widely than anger, and for this good reason. The moment you are controlled by your temper you are no longer able to reason, you are no longer able to think, you can no longer give a balanced judgment, for you are altogether biased on one side and against the other side. In other words, the power to reason and to think and to equate and evaluate – all that makes man man – is gone; for the time being he is like a beast, the creature of his own passion and of an instinctive kind of power. And of course that is just the very situation in which the devil sees his most glorious kind of opportunity! It was when he persuaded Eve and Adam to be angry against God that he very easily had them in his hands. He aroused in them bitterness and enmity against God, and made them believe that God was against them; and so immediately the devil could do as he liked. And think of the matter as you know it in life. Is there anything that leads to more trouble than

[233]

anger? Things said in anger and in a bitter moment! – you would almost cut your tongue off, if you could, to get them back; and sometimes, though forgiven, they leave permanent wounds and scars. What havoc is wrought in the world by sinful anger!

And then a sinful anger leads to the nursing of grievances, to a desire for revenge and to have our own back; it leads us to despise people and to treat them with contempt. Sinful anger! The moment it has taken over the devil enters in. He will keep it going and insinuate thoughts and ideas and implant them. Indeed, the whole of life can be ruined just because of anger. Anger is always a cause of confusion, not only in the life of the individual but in the lives of all those who are involved in the business of living with such an individual. Nothing, I maintain, so constantly gives the devil an opportunity as loss of control in anger.

But let us note a still more important principle. Vindictiveness, or the wrath that the Apostle condemns, is a denial of the whole Christian gospel. Without doubt the Apostle had this in his mind. If you become vindictive, if you get this settled wrath, if you have a desire for vengeance in you, you are denying the whole foundation of the gospel as laid down in the Epistle's earlier chapters, namely, that God forgives us in spite of our being what we are. We are Christians entirely and solely by the grace of God. It is all due to God's mercy. It is in spite of our being what we are, in spite of our being hateful and hating one another, in spite of our being ungrateful, in spite of our being rebellious, that God sent His own Son, and He took our sins upon Him. He died for us while we were sinners, while we were enemies. Our salvation is all of the free grace of God. As a Christian you say that you believe this gospel. But if you are in a condition of settled wrath against another person, how do you reconcile it with your Christianity? Come, let me ask a more practical question. How can you say the Lord's Prayer every night and morning? 'Forgive us our trespasses *as* we forgive them that trespass against us'! You pray that prayer, and you are denying it in your life and in your practice.

Listen to what our Lord said in the parable that he spoke on this subject, as found in Matthew's Gospel, 'Likewise shall my heavenly Father do also unto you, if ye from your hearts forgive not every one his brother their trespasses' (18:35). The parable is not difficult to remember. A servant owed a great sum of money to his lord who was about to put him in prison; but the servant said, Have mercy upon me, give me time and I will pay you everything. Very well, said the lord, certainly I will. And then the servant was very thankful and very pleased. But he happened to meet a fellow servant who owed him a hundred pence, a mere triviality, and he said, Pay me what you owe me. The man said, I'm sorry, I have not got it. He therefore took him by the throat and said, You have got to pay me every farthing. The man then said, Have mercy, give me time. No, said the servant, I will not give you time, you must pay at once, up to the last farthing. And he threw him into prison! The lord called that man to him and said, You wicked servant! why did you not deal with your fellow servant as I dealt with you? And our Lord Jesus Christ, applying his parable, said: 'Likewise shall my heavenly Father do also unto you, if you from your hearts forgive not every one his brother their trespasses.' If you cannot forgive your brother, I tell you in the Name of God you are not forgiven yourself. You cannot play fast and loose in God's moral universe. Listen to John stating the truth in his First Epistle: 'If a man say, I love God, and hateth his brother, he is a liar: for he that loveth not his brother whom he hath seen, how can he love God whom he hath not seen?' Evil behaviour is a denial of the very foundation of the gospel. The new man, Paul tells us, who, after God, is created in righteousness and true holiness, is created in the image of God! So if I claim to be a Christian, I believe I am renewed in the image of God, and therefore I must do to others what God has done to me. He has forgiven me in spite of my being what I was. I must forgive another in spite of his being what he is. That is the logic! It is a foundation truth of the gospel.

Again, I as a Christian claim that I have received the Holy Spirit. 'And the fruit of the Spirit is love, joy, peace, longsuffering, gentleness, goodness, faith, meekness, temperance.' And therefore, not to forgive, but to be in a towering rage, losing control, shows an absence of the fruit of the Spirit.

Furthermore, believers are members of the same body of Christ

[235]

and we need one another, and we are interdependent upon one another. Therefore, if you think about harming your brother, you are harming a part of yourself, a part of your own life and of the body to which you belong. It is a denial of the whole doctrine of the church. Sinful wrath and the seeking of vengeance is a usurpation of God's right of judgment. The Apostle tells us so in his Roman Epistle. 'Dearly beloved, avenge not yourselves, but rather give place unto wrath': – that is, the wrath of God – 'for it is written, Vengeance is mine; I will repay, saith the Lord. Therefore if thine enemy hunger, feed him; if he thirst, give him drink, for in so doing thou shalt heap coals of fire on his head. Be not overcome of evil, but overcome evil with good' (12:19–21). 'Vengeance is mine, I will repay, saith the Lord'! I know this or that thing is terribly wrong, says the Christian, but I am not the judge, I leave it all to God. That is the Christian way! Put off the old man! Put on the new man!

Finally, if this is the way in which we are to deal with a false, sinful anger and wrath, my final question is this: When am I to do this? when am I to deal with it? And the Apostle supplies us with one of the most glorious answers in the whole Bible: 'Let not the sun go down upon your wrath'! Do it at once! Do not go to bed, do not give yourself to sleep, with this in your mind or your heart. Clear it at once. Never go to sleep without settling your moral accounts. Never leave a thing like that on your books. Get rid of it! Erase it! Paint the blood of Christ on it! Get rid of the thing! Let not the sun go down upon your wrath. Never go to sleep with a bitter, hateful, angry thought in your heart. Do not let these things have a lodging place. If you have had some terrible provocation during the day – and such things do happen – and you really have felt a righteous anger and indignation, do not let it *settle* there to become a bitter, malignant hatred.

Let me remind you of what our Lord Himself said about this matter in the Sermon on the Mount. He is talking about a man going to the temple to take his offering, his gift, to God. But He says, If you find yourself even at the very altar and suddenly you remember that a brother of yours has something against you, 'leave there thy gift before the altar', before you have given it, 'and go thy way; first be reconciled to thy brother, and then come and offer thy gift' (Matthew 5:23–24). That is very strong, is it not? Imagine it! Here you are! you are actually in the temple, you have actually advanced to the altar, you are going to put your gift upon the altar. But you suddenly remember! Leave your gift there! go away, settle it with your brother, put matters right with him first. 'First be reconciled to thy brother, and then', and only then, are you fit to 'come and offer thy gift' unto God.

I sum up the whole position like this. Hate sin, always; hate sin in the sinner, always: but never hate the sinner. Both sides of the truth are absolutely essential. Sin must never be condoned. Sin must never be excused. Sin must always be condemned. There are people who are sinners who do not like that! Ah! they say. but where is your principle of grace and of love and of mercy and of compassion? The sinner should never speak in that way. He should feel that he deserves all he is getting and infinitely more. He should never defend himself; he should feel indignation against himself; he should be angry with himself; he should hate himself. Sin is to rouse a holy anger in us, every time it occurs, and in every form. But the sinner is to be forgiven; the sinner is to be loved. The sinner is to be helped to forsake his sin and to rise up. This blessed balance of the Scripture! – hatred of sin, but never hatred of the sinner: anger, but never in a sinful way. And above all, I repeat, always make sure that you never put your head down on your pillow to rest and sleep for the night with any spirit of bitterness or hatred or lack of forgiveness in your heart or mind or soul. 'Let not the sun go down upon your wrath'! You may have a great struggle with yourself, but do not go to rest until you have settled it. You may have to argue it backwards and forwards; go on, I say, until you have realised the love of God in Christ to you, until you have seen Christ bleeding and dying on the cross that you might be forgiven; dwell on it until He has melted your heart and broken you down and made you sorry for the one who has offended you, and until you forgive freely. Then, but not until then, get into your bed and put your head down on the pillow, and sleep the sleep of the just and the righteous and the holy, because you have a right to do so; you will be doing it as the Son of God Himself did it;

you will have acted in your life and domain as God Himself has acted with respect to you.

'Be ye angry, and sin not; let not the sun go down upon your wrath: neither give place to the devil.'

19

Not Stealing but Labouring and Giving

'Let him that stole [*or* the stealer] steal no more; but rather let him labour, working with his hands the thing which is good, that he may have to give to him that needeth.'

Ephesians 4:28

Here we come to the question of stealing and we cannot help noticing that in every one of his practical exhortations the Apostle is selecting things which really are of vital and pivotal importance. There are many statements in the New Testament to the effect that people who habitually continue to practise certain things are simply not Christians. Now let me show you this same Apostle, who is sometimes described as the Apostle of faith, making just such a statement. 'Know ye not', he says, 'that the unrighteous shall not inherit the kingdom of God? Be not deceived: neither fornicators, nor idolaters, nor adulterers, nor effeminate, nor abusers of themselves with mankind, nor thieves, nor covetous, nor drunkards, nor revilers, nor extortioners, shall inherit the kingdom of God' (1 Corinthians 6:9–10). And you notice that in this list from 1 Corinthians there is mention of thieves. So again, you see, Paul is reminding us that if a man persists in stealing, he is thereby proving that he is not a Christian. You will notice that I say if he *persists* in stealing, that is, if there is no change in him in that respect. He does not say that a Christian may not fall into temptation once, or perhaps more than once, but what he does say is what the New Testament says everywhere, that a man who persists in stealing is thereby proclaiming, whatever may be his doctrinal beliefs, that he is not a Christian.

Here the Apostle uses the same method as before. First of all he tells us what not to do; then he tells us what we ought to do; then he gives us the reason for not doing the one and for doing the other. 'Let him that stole steal no more', is the negative; 'rather let him labour, working with his hands the thing which is good', is the positive; the reason for it all, 'that he may have to give to him that needeth'. Very well, as we look at this important injunction there are surely certain things that stand out at once as messages, as principles, as teaching. And the first is this one. We all ought again to rejoice at this great and glorious and wonderful Gospel. The Gospel is the power of God unto salvation, and it can save men from any kind of sin. That is what makes these lists that we are given here and there in the Scriptures so wonderful. The Gospel of Jesus Christ is not for good people, it is for sinners; it was while we were yet sinners and without strength Christ died for us. It is for people who are guilty of all those terrible, horrible things in that list in 1 Corinthians 6; it is for such that Christ has died, yes, for thieves and robbers, for those who were stealers. That is, I say, the central glory of the Gospel, there is nothing beyond its power, nothing beyond its scope. There is no man who is hopeless when he is face to face with the Gospel, there is no particular sin that excludes a man in that way. This Gospel is a power. And in going through these different items that the Apostle gives us here we ought to be reminded that when this power enters into a man's life, whatever it was that held him captive, he can be set free. There is our first proposition, and it is one, I say, in which we should rejoice.

Then I come to a second one, which is sometimes misunderstood but which is clearly of central importance. The Gospel saves from all kinds of sins; yes, but it is important that we should observe the way in which it does so. Here we have an injunction that has often surprised many people. They say, Does the gospel really tell a number of Christian people that they must give up stealing? I thought, says someone, that you have been emphasising that these people were regenerate, that they have been born again, that they have been created after God in this new pattern, that the image of God has been restored upon them; and now are you telling us that the Apostle has to say to those selfsame people, 'Let the stealer steal no more'? Yes, that is precisely what the Apostle does say. And it is something at which we should not be surprised. If we are surprised it is undoubtedly due to the fact that we are wrong in our view of the doctrine of regeneration, the new birth, and as to what that means. There is considerable misunderstanding about this. Take for instance Paul's statement to the Corinthians: 'If any man be in Christ he is a new creature; old things are passed away, behold, all things are become new' (2 Corinthians 5:17). These words are often misinterpreted to mean that when a man is regenerate, when he is in Christ and becomes a new creature, everything that was true about him previously has ended; none of it remains whatsoever, and he is an entirely new man in every detail and every single respect. But obviously that is entirely wrong. It is a complete misinterpretation of Paul's words, because if that were true the Apostle would never have had to write to Ephesian believers to tell them to put away lying, to be angry without sinning, to stop stealing, and these various other things that we are considering in detail. In other words, it would be entirely wrong to interpret regeneration in a kind of magical sense. The world does so, however. It says that we Christians claim to be born again and therefore that we ought to be absolutely perfect. If, therefore, it finds a Christian falling into sin, it says, So much for your Christianity! I thought it delivered a man from all sin and made him perfect at once! But the world has ever proved itself unable to receive and understand the principles of Christianity, and not least the doctrine of regeneration.

How are Christians to meet the world's sneer? and how are they to interpret regeneration? This is important not only in Britain, it is even more important in a sense on the foreign mission field, where people are suddenly saved out of heathendom and all that belongs to it; and if this doctrine of regeneration is misinterpreted it is bound to become a stumbling-block to the faith of many inside the Church, and to many who are seeking, outside. The answer is this, that sometimes in regeneration a man is delivered completely from certain particular sins without making any effort at all. But that is not a universal rule. Another man can be truly regenerate and still need this detailed instruction and still find a certain element of struggle in his life. We may not understand this; it is something within the sovereignty of God.

But what we are absolutely certain of is that in regeneration we are not automatically delivered from all our sins and rendered immune to every conceivable temptation. To assert that we are immune is patently not true; the Pauline teaching and experience alike prove it. But God in His infinite wisdom employs different methods in different cases.

I well remember two men who were members of the same church, and who in their pre-conversion days were drunkards. Listening to the Gospel the two were converted, saved, regenerated; but it was most interesting to notice the difference in their experience. In the case of the one man the very taste for drink was taken away immediately; he literally never had another moment's trouble with it. But the second man, who equally had given it up and was no longer a slave to it and no longer subject to it in any sense, did not find deliverance from it in a moment as did the first man; he knew what it was to struggle, and to feel a terrible temptation at times. And yet the two men were equally regenerate. So we learn that the exhortations we find in the Epistle are necessary. We are born as babes in Christ and we do not know everything at once; we do not see everything clearly at once; we need instruction, we need to be taught, and to grow in grace and in the knowledge of the Lord Jesus Christ. That is why these letters were written.

This is a most interesting and fascinating thing. We all must know something about it in experience, how at first, although as it were we had seen everything in a new way, yet we had not seen *particular* things in the new way. We really had undergone this mighty transformation, and yet it had not occurred to us that certain things would have to be dealt with. We had to receive instruction about them. And unless we, as Christians, are becoming more sensitive in this respect from year to year, it means that we are not growing, and that there is something wrong with us. At first one sees the big central things, then one has to learn about these other things. Such was the position of believers in Ephesus. There was nothing that was more characteristic of heathendom than stealing. It is always one of the leading characteristics of a godless and irreligious society. They had been steeped in it, they had been brought up in it, and it had become such a matter of habit, of custom and of practice, that at first they did not realise that there was anything wrong in it, and they needed to be enlightened and instructed in the way that the Apostle is here instructing them. And this is as true today as it was then. The babe in Christ does not see everything, he needs and he is given particular detailed instruction. Occasionally, as I say, the besetting sin is taken right away at once; very often, indeed I would say generally, it is not, but the man is given the new attitude, the new outlook, and so he is enabled to overcome it. Being born again, there is a new principle in him; the Holy Spirit is in him; he has got a new power in him, so that with the instruction and the power he is enabled to deal with it. And this is the New Testament method of sanctification.

But we must look further into the matter. Why must stealing be forsaken? why does the Apostle say, 'Let him that stole steal no more'? This is a very relevant subject, and alas! it has a very urgent practical reference. The newspapers are telling us about an appalling increase in petty theft and pilfering, and even large-scale robbery. Increasingly it is becoming an urgent problem, in a sociological sense, in this country. So let us look at it. What does stealing mean? Obviously the Apostle was thinking primarily of actually laying hold with your hands of something that does not belong to you. He puts an emphasis upon the hands; that was the commonest form of stealing then, as it is still one of the commonest forms of stealing. But it does not stop at that. Stealing does not always apply to things in the material realm. Stealing really means taking possession of and using as your own something that does not belong to you, appropriating something that is not yours, to serve your own ends and your own gratification. So it applies to many things besides actual material things. We can steal money; yes, but we can steal time also; we can steal almost anything, we can steal thoughts, we can steal ideas, the offence that we call plagiarism, the taking of another man's ideas and giving them out as your own. You may write an article but it is what you have got from somebody else and you do not acknowledge it – that is theft. You may preach another man's sermon, and that is theft, robbery, stealing. You preach it as your own, but it is not your own. Stealing is to take possession of anything that belongs to another and that is not really yours, and to possess it and to regard it as yours, and to give the impression that it is yours.

I sometimes am given a real shock in this way. I receive a letter from the secretary of a Christian Union, say in a business firm or in the Civil Service, a bank or some such organisation; and to my utter amazement and astonishment the invitation to me to speak at the meeting of the Christians belonging to the Christian Union in that firm or business is written on the official notepaper of the firm or Civil Service or the bank. I regard that as stealing. Christian people have no right to use official notepaper to serve their own personal, private ends and objects, even though it may be a Christian Union. Now let me give you another illustration of stealing. Lest we should think that the Apostle was just writing to a handful of pagans and that we, never having been pagans in this sense, do not need this exhortation, consider the question of time. If I happen to be paid by a firm to do a given piece of work, for me to spend a part of that time in trying to evangelise a fellow worker is stealing. I have no right to use my employer's time even to evangelise another soul. I am paid money to use a certain space of time in doing what the firm has told me to do, and though it may be an excellent thing to tell another soul about Christ and salvation, I have no right to do it in the time that does not belong to me, but is my employer's time.

Thus we are to understand that the exhortation to stop stealing has a very wide and a very practical relevance, and we must be careful to take it in this large way. Anything that belongs to another, or to the State, must not be appropriated by us and used for our own personal ends and objects, however exalted they may be. Stealing also includes a failure to pay to another that which is his due. To keep back from another that which is his due, whether you keep it back from the State in the form of customs duty or income tax or whatever else it is, is stealing. If it belongs by law and by right to another, and we withhold it we are guilty of stealing. Not to pay that which we should pay is stealing, as well as actually appropriating that which does not belong to us.

'Let the stealer steal no more.' This is the Apostle's exhortation. There is nothing, perhaps, that shows what a despicable and

degrading thing sin is more than stealing. And according to the
New Testament the way to overcome sin is to see it for what it is,
to despise it, to hate it, and to say, That is impossible for a man
who is a Christian! Is there not something which is inherently
and essentially shameful about stealing? It involves stealth,
concealment, furtiveness, looking out for your opportunity
when you are not being watched, doing it after dark, doing it
when nobody is around. Oh! is there not something utterly
despicable about it! There is an inherent and an essential shame
and treachery about this very act. All that is involved in it, all
that is indicated by it, is full of this horrible characteristic. And
then another element enters into it: stealing always involves the
misuse of an ability which is given to us. The Apostle is thinking,
I have said, in terms of hands. Look at that man, he has seen
something that he covets; it belongs to another, and he uses the
hands that God has given him to lay hold upon it and to possess
it. What a misuse of these wonderful instruments! The hands!
given us by God! amazing instruments! and look at the use to
which the thief puts them!

But it does not apply only to one's hands, it applies in all the
other respects that I have been outlining. Look at the way in
which thieves misuse the power of thought, the power of reason,
the power of logic, the power to foretell and to plan. Look at the
sheer ingenuity, the mastery from the standpoint of the brain,
that goes into very much illicit trade and business and all that is
involved in the great comprehensive term thieving! The acute-
ness, the ability that men display in evading and avoiding, and in
pursuing their quest. What a prostitution of some of the mightiest,
noblest gifts that God has given to man! Think too of the perverted pleasure that the thief obtains in this misusing of his
gifts. He actually thinks that he has been clever when he steals!
Oh, what a perversion! Is that the standard of ability, is that the
way in which we measure capacity? It is an utter insult to human
nature and to the most wonderful things that God has given to
us as men, that a man could pride himself on having done such a
thing and on his ability to do it. Is there anything more repre-
hensible!

What is really at the back of stealing? The answer is, of course, selfishness. It is one of the central manifestations of self. The desire to have, and to possess what I want. It is just one of these horrible manifestations of self showing itself in the desire to have and to possess and to hold, that it may build up in various ways the one who steals. That is really at the root of it. But it also needs to be emphasised that stealing is really the desire to have without effort. There is not only the desire that self may possess and have, but there is this additional factor, the desire to have without working for it, without labouring for it, as the Apostle puts it here. So that ultimately the trouble with the thief, the stealer, is that he dislikes work. He is the sort of man who really despises honest work and labour. His idea is to have the maximum and do the minimum. He is not particular as to how he does it, how he gets it, as long as he gets it. He exalts possessing it to the supreme position. He eventually comes to the point of thinking that if a thing can be obtained by theft, a man who works like a slave and who sweats and half-kills himself in order to get it in possession, is no better than a fool. And he is rather proud of himself as a consequence. *He* has not half-killed himself. His phrase is 'easy money', is it not? So simple! why work when it can be obtained like this! In this way he is displaying his utter degradation.

Surely we are witnessing something of this mentality at the present time. There is a certain modern philosophy which despises work, which puts pleasure and enjoyment in the supreme position, and which regards work as just a nuisance, something that is essential in order that I may have enough money to enjoy myself! The end of such logic is to get the money and the enjoyment without the work. The moment you begin to regard work as something degrading, you are on the slippery slope. The moment you fail to see the dignity of work and the essential rightness of work, the moment you begin to think in terms of 'having' rather than truly and honestly earning, you are beginning to open the door that will lead to some form of dishonesty. Possession should never be in the supreme position. The mere having, the mere gaining, the mere enjoying, is never to be the supreme thing. A society a country,, a world, which begins to despise labour and effort is proclaiming that it is godless. Any failure to realise the dignity of work proclaims the same thing. The whole notion of obtaining the maximum and giving or doing the minimum is utterly irreligious, it is profoundly unchristian; but who can deny that it is something that is affecting every stratum of society in Britain today? There are drones and parasites in every class of society; but it matters not what class it is; any man who thinks in terms of what he may have that he may enjoy with the minimum of effort, is a drone, is a parasite, is a denier of the very essence of the Christian teaching. The problem is not a political but a spiritual one.

Again, the man who steals persuades himself that he has a right to anything that he likes or desires. He sees the object of his desire. He does not stop to ask if it is his or not, or somebody else's; all he says is, Now I like that, I wish I had it, I would be very happy if I did have it, I could do wonderful things with it, therefore I take it. That is the reasoning, that is the mentality, and it shows a complete and entire lack of respect for others and their possessions. And that is the worst thing of all, perhaps, about thieving and robbery. It is a lack of respect for others. I am only thinking of myself and what is good for me and what I want and what I can enjoy. If I began to think in the same way about the other man, I would never take what was his because I would respect his rights to it. But I exclude him, I violate his personality, I alone matter, nobody else counts. That is the philosophy at the back of the mind of the thief.

We see, therefore, why the Apostle was pressing the matter so much upon the Ephesians. The outlook of the thief makes fellowship impossible. And he is writing to members of Churches, he has just been telling them that they are all together members of the body of Christ and that the body is one. But how can there be unity and fellowship if each man is appropriating the possession of another and each man is out for himself? The hand says, I am not interested in the foot, I take everything I can from it! The result is chaos, monstrosity; there is no fellowship possible where there is not trust. Therefore, says the Apostle, let the stealer steal no more! To steal is lawlessness, it is anarchy, it is every man for himself, it is out-and-out selfishness. That is why the Apostle says, 'Let him that stole steal no more'!

[247]

How should the Christian, then, regard and deal with this whole problem and temptation to steal? Again I must point out that the Apostle does not just say, Pray about it, ask God to take it out of your life, and He will do it for you! You need not do anything yourself, let Him do it all, He will do it all, just look to Him, He will take it out of your life if you ask Him! The Apostle does not say that! Instead, he gives a positive injunction. Stop doing it! says Paul. Let him that stole *steal no more*! Stop doing it! But how do you stop doing it? First of all, take a good look at the thing. Analyse the thing, and have a good look at it and say, Is this it? am I guilty of that? it is impossible! And you stop thieving. But you do not stop at that. You then make your positive approach to the problem. And what is the positive approach? The Apostle leaves us in no doubt – Let him (the thief) steal no more – 'but *rather* let him labour, working with his hands the thing which is good'. This is truly a great word: let him labour, let him work!

Now the word *labour* in the original is a very strong word; it means working to the point of fatigue. Not just working; you must labour, says the Apostle. Here again I want to emphasise this great Christian principle of the dignity of work, the dignity of toil and labour, the dignity of producing something. It is only Christianity that teaches a thing like this. Do you remember the words of Paul when he was saying farewell to the elders of the church at Ephesus? 'Yea', he says 'you yourselves know, that these hands have ministered unto my necessities, and to them that were with me. I have showed you all things, how that so labouring ye ought to support the weak, and to remember the words of the Lord Jesus, how he said, It is more blessed to give than to receive' (Acts 20:34, 35). Obviously, he was able to claim that he was giving them an example and a pattern of work. Christianity has always stood for the dignity of work, for the dignity of labour, as can be proved historically. Heathendom and godlessness are always characterised by slackness and indolence and laziness. As this country becomes more and more godless and irreligious it becomes more and more lazy in every stratum of society. It always happens. But on the other hand, every revival of true religion exalts the dignity of work, because it brings a man to see that God has given him his body and all his faculties and he is meant to use them. Man was not made just to sit back and to enjoy himself and to get every boon for nothing. That is enervating, that is insulting, it does not develop a man's faculties and powers. But the moment you see yourself as a Christian, as a man made in the image of God, you want to use your faculties.

What you find historically is that the Elizabethan period, which stands out as a very great era in the history of this country, as the time when this country began to lay the basis of her great prosperity and success, was a period that followed the Protestant Reformation. Of course! The moment people were awakened to the truth of the Gospel and saw themselves subject to God and to His will they began to work. The Puritan Era led to the same thing, and still more strikingly. However much we advanced in the Elizabethan period, we advanced much more in the Crom-wellian period. And what made that period really great was again the selfsame thing, this dignity of work. Some people have been troubled by this. They are troubled by the fact that the Quakers and people like them have become very wealthy people. It is no problem at all. The explanation is clear. When men are truly converted, first of all they see how wrong sin is and they cease to squander their money on useless trifles. At the same time they take up with this positive principle, the dignity of work, so they are diligent and they work. They do not begin the Christian life by saying, How best can I shorten my working day, do as little as I can and get as much as I can? Not at all! They *enjoy* the work, they are creating something, they are making something, they are doing something, they are labouring. And of course it is quite inevitable, their diligence leads to success, and in many cases they become wealthy. If you work hard and do not squander your money you are bound to accumulate wealth, you cannot avoid it, you cannot evade it. And that is the real explanation of this position.

The Apostle, then, tells us to work and to labour with our hands, and it may be that, as Christians in a generation such as this, we are perhaps called to teach people this above everything else, and so testify to Christ and to His grace. We are to show that the supreme object in our lives is not enjoyment and pleasure, is not to have a life of ease, and then to set up committees to know how to employ our leisure time, the problem of how to handle the leisure hours! Far from it! We must be doing something, we must be working, we must be labouring, and doing it with all our might, indulging in a little honest sweat and knowing what it is to go to bed tired out, feeling that we have lived like a man and not as a sluggard, not as a parasite, building ourselves up on somebody else's capital and taking of the sustenance and strength of another. 'Labour', says the Apostle, 'working with your own hands that which is good.'

Is it not amazing to notice how slow we always are to learn the great lessons of life and of history? Surely we all have observed that it is rather a dangerous thing for people to inherit wealth. I am not saying that the situation need always go wrong, but I am saying that it is always dangerous. I am rather sorry for young people who inherit wealth, because they are in a very dangerous position; it is not surprising that they often go wrong. How often has it happened that a father has worked hard and laboured as Scripture tells us; he has built up a great business and laid a good foundation; his son comes along, inherits it all, and squanders it all. Poor boy! I am sorry for him. He received wealth without working for it, without labouring for it; he has got the wrong attitude towards life and living, and it is not surprising that he misuses it. It is a dangerous thing to have wealth and possessions without having earned them in some shape or form, and a society that experiences much of this kind of thing is asking for trouble.

'Let him labour, working with his hands the thing which is good, that he may have to give to him that needeth.' Our next step is to note the essentials of the principle of stewardship. Why do I possess things? Oh, not like the stealer, the thief, looks at it, not merely for myself and what I may get out of it! Not at all! I am a steward, I just hold these things, they are not really mine. They are not an end in themselves, they were never designed for personal gratification only. I just hold them for the Giver, because God is the Giver of every good and every perfect gift, and I am appointed by Him to be the guardian, the custodian, the steward. They are not mine, I simply have them for the time being.

And, finally, we are to be concerned for others and their need. 'Labour, working with your own hands,' says the Apostle, 'the thing which is good, in order that you may have to give to him that needeth.' Work because work is a good thing! If you make money at it, then hold it as a custodian, and give to those who are in need in any shape or form; exercise any good that you can do. 'It is more blessed to give than to receive', says the Lord Jesus Christ. That is one of His sayings that is not recorded in the Gospels, but the Apostle had been told it. He says, Do you remember how the Lord Jesus said that it is more blessed to give than to receive? Then be like that, says Paul. And indeed, this is really what he is saying in this exhortation. He is simply telling us to be like the Lord Jesus Christ. What was He like? The Apostle answers the question as he writes his second chapter to the Philippians: 'Look not every man on his own things, but every man also on the things of others. Let this mind be in you which was also in Christ Jesus: who, being in the form of God, thought it not robbery to be equal with God: but made himself of no reputation, and took upon him the form of a servant, and was made in the likeness of men: and being found in fashion as a man, he humbled himself, and became obedient unto death, even the death of the cross.' And again, in writing to the Corinthians, he says, 'Ye know the grace of our Lord Jesus Christ, that, though he was rich, yet for your sakes he became poor.'

Not only did Christ not steal that which did not belong to Him, He did not even hold on to that which was His, the everlasting riches, and for our sakes He became poor. And He lived in this world as One of the poor; He had no house of His own, He had no home of His own – 'The Son of man', He said, 'hath not where to lay his head'. We read that 'every man went unto his own house; Jesus went unto the mount of Olives'!

What a different realm this is from the realm of stealing! It is the difference between Christianity and paganism. Paganism, godlessness, irreligion, is a sphere where every man is out for himself, where every man is trying to get as much as he can for nothing that he may enjoy it. Christianity stands for consideration for others, self-denial, self-abnegation, self-abasement, seeing the needs of others, and giving. 'Let this mind be in you which was also in Christ Jesus.' Moral teaching stops at saying, Do not

[251]

steal! do not touch it! And oh! what a poor thing morality is! But Christianity bids us 'Labour, working with our own hands that which is good, that we may have to give to him that needeth.' 'Let this mind be in you which was also in Christ Jesus.' Giving! Others! Seeing need! Sacrificing! It is the exact antithesis of the other! Because we are new men, let us put off the old man, and let us walk in the footsteps of our blessed Lord and Master, who said, 'It is more blessed to give than to receive.'

20

How to Communicate with our Fellows

'Let no corrupt communication proceed out of your
mouth, but that which is good to the use of edifying,
that it may minister grace unto the hearers.'

Ephesians 4:29

Our text brings us to problems concerning our conversation, our
speech one to the other, our communication with one another, in
this particular form. We cannot help noticing that in these
particular injunctions the Apostle seems to bear in his mind most
of the time the great importance of speech. His first injunction
was, 'Wherefore, put away *lying*, speak every man truth with his
neighbour'. Now that is a question of speech, and later in the
chapter he comes back to it: 'Let all bitterness, and wrath, and
anger, and clamour, and *evil speaking*, be put away from you, with
all malice' (verse 31). And again he will take it up in the third
verse of chapter 5, where he says: 'But fornication, and all
uncleanness, or covetousness, let it not be once named among
you, as becometh saints: neither filthiness, nor foolish talking,
nor jesting, which are not convenient: but rather giving of
thanks.' Obviously, therefore, in the opinion and estimation of
the Apostle this whole question of speech is a vital one and of
necessity should receive great prominence as we are dealing with
and considering the application of the truth to the details of our
lives. And this is not surprising because, as I have already
reminded you in regard to the question of lying, speech is, after
all, the distinguishing and differentiating factor in man's life.
When you come to compare and contrast man and the animals
there are many differences, but this is probably the most prominent and most important; the thing that makes man man is
the gift of speech and of expression. In this ability to express

himself, we see the image of God in which man was originally created coming out most clearly. Man can think and reason and look at himself objectively and consider himself; the animals cannot do that.

But our text goes even further: man can speak, he can express himself, he can put thoughts into words and into language. It is in many ways God's greatest gift to mankind, and this being so, it is not surprising that it is the thing which is most misused. In the spiritual realm the devil centres his attack upon that which is most precious in man. And the devastating thing about sin is that it always destroys first that which is best in us. The higher centres are always the first to be affected by sin. It is not surprising, therefore, that considerable attention is paid by the Apostle to this whole question of speech, as it is so expressive of the very essence of man's being and personality. In the third chapter of his Epistle, James makes exactly the same point. Man's tongue is there compared to the rudder of a ship, also to the bit, the bridle, that is put into a horse's mouth: in both cases a very little thing, but what an important thing it is! It changes the course of a great Atlantic liner; it is the thing that keeps within bounds and controls the horse, with all his vigour and power. Therefore, says James, as Christians you have got to realise the vital importance of guarding the tongue and the lips. What havoc, he says, is wrought by the misuse of the tongue! It is a very world of iniquity, it is something that can kindle a flame and a fire that is terribly destructive.

This is the scriptural way of reminding us that in our life lived in this world there is nothing which is of greater importance than the power of speech, because after all we express what we really are by what we say. The words of our Lord Himself – 'Out of the abundance of the heart the mouth speaketh' – tell us the same thing. As we speak, we are really expressing what is in our heart. Sometimes our friends remind us that we 'give ourselves away' by our speech. But our Lord has a further truth to tell us: 'A good man out of the good treasure of the heart bringeth forth good things: and an evil man out of the evil treasure bringeth forth evil things. But I say unto you, That every idle word that men shall speak, they shall give account thereof in the day of judgment. For by thy words thou shalt be justified, and by thy words thou shalt be condemned.' We are all slow to realise the importance of speech. We talk so freely, so glibly, so loosely; and yet, says our Lord, 'By thy *words* thou shalt be justified and by thy *words* thou shalt be condemned.' He assures us that in the day of judgment a man 'shall give an account of every idle word that he has spoken'. He means that it is when we are off our guard, as it were, that we really express what we are. Morality can put a certain control upon us. But you really discover the weakness of the non-Christian, moral man in his unguarded moments, when suddenly something happens to him and he expresses himself; then he really shows what he is; and that is one of the ways of differentiating between the merely moral man and the Christian man. The Christian man is not a man who is always repressing himself; there is something different at the centre, for out of the *abundance* of the heart the mouth speaketh; it is what slips out that really tells us the truth about one another.

It is not surprising, then, that the Apostle pays great attention to this question of speech. You Ephesians, he says, were once pagans and you were typically pagan in your conversation and your speech. But now, he says, you are new men, you have put off the old man, you have put on the new man, and there is no respect in which you can show this so plainly and clearly as in your conversation, in the kind of thing you talk about, and in the way you speak. And we notice once again that he adopts the same formula that he has adopted in all the other cases: first of all, negative injunction, then positive injunction, and thirdly explanation. 'Let no corrupt communication proceed out of your mouth'; there is the negative. But what are you to do? 'Speak that which is good, to the use of edifying'; there is the positive. But why should you do this, what is the reason? The reason is, 'that it may minister grace unto the hearers'. We adopt the Apostle's own classification, for we cannot improve upon it.

The negative injunction runs: 'Let no corrupt communication proceed out of your mouth', that is to say, the Christian should be altogether different in this matter of speech from the non-

Christian. We must therefore ask ourselves what it is that characterises the speech, the conversation, of the unregenerate and the
godless, and it is suggested by the very terms used by the Apostle,
which we find elaborated elsewhere in Scripture. One characteristic of the speech of the ungodly is excess, and lack of control.
Ungodly people talk too much; they talk without thinking, they
are always talking. If you travel in buses or by train, or if you sit
in a public room, you will find that there is this constant chatter-
ing; it is always characteristic of the ungodly. Probably we have
not all realised that Christian people do not talk as much as
non-Christian people.

Another characteristic of the conversation of the non-Christian
and the thing that really makes it what it is, is that it is just an
expression of self. The life of the unregenerate man is always
selfish and a self-centred life, and his conversation and speech is
turned to an opportunity for self-display. This explains why
such persons, when together, all endeavour to talk at the same
time. The one cannot wait for the other to finish, they want to
get their word in. There is evermore present the desire to be
interesting and entertaining and to be admired, with people
saying, How wonderful! They all want to hold the floor, they
all crave for self-expression and to obtain something for the self.

If you analyse speech and conversation with all these things in
mind – the excess, the failure to speak in turn, and the cutting in
on one another – you are bound to conclude that they are nothing
but a sheer manifestation of self and self-importance, the desire
for admiration and for praise. These characteristics abound in
the conversation of the ungodly.

Then, too, the Apostle introduces something that surely has a
new urgency, alas! in the present day, namely, the lack of delicacy.
He refers to that which is corrupt, worthless, ugly, unbecoming,
rotten and foul. These are alternative translations of the word he
uses. Of course, we have got polite terms for this evil thing; we
speak of piquancy, adding a little spice to the conversation,
suggestiveness, vulgarity, uncleanness, coarseness, obscenity.
This is always the characteristic of the conversation of pagan
society, even at its best. I say even at its best! It is perhaps one
of the greatest manifestations of the Fall and of the polluting
effect of sin, that even men belonging to learned professions and

societies, when they meet together at their dinners and parties, always spend some of their time in telling stories, as they call it, to one another, repeating stories, collecting them, taking the trouble to remember them. They do it because they know that they will be admired for it, and become a centre of attraction. And the more daring the more wonderful! Able and intelligent men, high in their professions, literally spend their time in doing that kind of thing. It is plain evidence of the coarseness that sin introduces into human life and into men's hearts; yet it is considered clever, entertaining. 'Have you heard this?' they say, and everybody listens! Men of intelligence, yes, and men of integrity, are capable of spending their time in this way, an awful manifestation of the polluting effect of sin!

I could very easily digress at this point to call your attention to the obvious increase of this kind of thing in the life of our own and other countries. A coarseness, a looseness is creeping into conversation. People use terms in public, that no one would have dreamt of using forty years ago. Have you not noticed it coming into articles and journals, not only newspapers? Is it not happening in general? This curious tendency to be daring – indeed it has become so customary that it is no longer daring or shocking. And it is becoming appallingly common. Even in journals of repute one cannot but notice the curious, sad decline that is so evidently taking place. And often the godless world turns into a joke, and regards as amusing, that which is really tragic. Why should a married man's unfaithfulness to his wife be regarded as funny? Why should there be constant jokes about this sort of thing? Nothing causes greater unhappiness to men, women and children than just this very thing, and yet it is regarded as a theme for joking. Acts of infidelity become the subjects of laughter and merriment! Corrupt communication, corrupt conversation, is a mark of the unregenerate. Have nothing to do with it, says the Apostle. It is corrupt in itself and it corrupts others. And this was the thing that was uppermost in the Apostle's mind here, as it is in all these separate injunctions. He wants believers to consider the influence of their words upon others, so he says, Do not let any corrupt communication proceed out of *your* mouth; a bystander may hear it and it may do harm to him.

What influence can words have? James reminds us that they

inflame, with a passion of hell! Many a man has gone wrong in life by merely listening to conversation that stimulates, and inflames and arouses everything that is unworthy. The Apostle Paul in writing to the Corinthians, warns them that 'Evil communications corrupt good manners.' Therefore, he says, for the sake of others, let none of this come out of your mouth. To put it quite simply and plainly, what he is really saying is, Stop doing that sort of thing! But notice particularly a further word he uses: 'Let no corrupt communication *proceed* out of your mouth.' In other words, if it even enters your mind, if it is beginning to form on your lips and your tongue, stop! If it has even arrived in your mouth, do not let it come out! Crucify it, kill it, murder it, stop it! If you yourself are guilty of evil thoughts, if the devil suggests them to you – you cannot stop him, he will hurl his fiery darts at you, he will insinuate them into your very minds, subtle innuendos – even so, says the Apostle, what I am telling you is this, Never let corrupt words proceed out of your mouth, let them die upon your lips, for the sake of others. Such is his negative injunction before he urges the positive.

What should proceed out of your mouth? 'that which is good, to the use of edifying'. I must again emphasise that a part of the central glory of our Christian faith and life is just this, that it is never merely negative. This is not morality, this is Christianity. Your moral man can put the curbs and the brakes on, and he may be not guilty of certain things, but at that point he stops. But Paul sounds a positive note. The gospel of Christ brings us a life, a new life, and it is full of positive activity and of exertion; and this is always the Christian way. Notice the Apostle's expression – 'that which is good to the use of edifying'. Unfortunately our Authorised Version is really not good at this point, for it puts it the wrong way round. It says, 'that which is good to the use of edifying'; but Paul actually says, 'that which is good for the edification of the need'. The Revised Version supplies the better translation: 'such as is good for edifying as the need may be'. But the Revised Standard Version is better still: 'only such as is good for edifying, as fits the occasion'. What, then, are the principles that are to govern my talk and conversation with others? First of all we shall look at the general principles.

The first is obviously that our conversation must always be under our control. In our former unregenerate state – and, alas, we lapse into it sometimes, even as Christians – we have all been guilty of becoming drunk in conversation. Watch people in conversation, and especially at conferences. The conversation starts rather quietly; the pitch rises; in the end people are shouting; there is much clamour; it is sheer intoxication; they have become drunk on conversation, all controls have gone. One says a thing, another wants to cap it, and a third wants to be yet more daring, and the control has entirely gone. The Christian's tongue should never be out of control. We must never become so excited that we are really not responsible for what we are saying. There must always be thought behind Christian speech and conversation, because, as I said earlier, our speech and conversation is an expression of our total personality. And that which differentiates the Christian from the non-Christian is just this very thing, no longer excess, but control, discipline, order. The chaos is gone. The God who commanded the light to shine out of the darkness at the creation has shined in our hearts to give the light of the knowledge of the glory of God in the face of Jesus Christ. He has brought order, there is control, and everything is in position. And of course, our conversation is controlled by the truth which we believe.

The second obvious thing about Christian speech is that it is no longer selfish or self-centred. The believer should never set out just to be admired or to be important or to be thought wonderful in conversation. Never! That is the old man. Put it off! stop it! says Paul. Have nothing to do with it, you have been brought out of that; never put yourself forward or seek an opportunity for *self*-display. That which should characterise the speech of the Christian is a concern for other people. Paul has been saying this in every one of these particular injunctions. He has said 'Let every man speak truth with his neighbour', for the sake of the *neighbour*! 'Be ye angry and sin not; let not the sun go down upon your wrath' – do not go to sleep thinking evil about your *neighbour*! 'Let him that stole steal no more, but let him rather labour, working with his hands the thing which is good, that he may have to give to *him that needeth*'! In each command the neighbour is prominent, and it is still the neighbour in this matter of speech and talk and conversation. You are not just to display yourself, and to show off, as we say, for the Christian is a man who all along does not merely think of his own things but also of the things of another. He is like the Lord Himself, and His is the mind that must be in us. He did not consider Himself; for the sake of others and for our sakes, He humbled Himself.

These, then, are to be the general principles in our speech and in our conversation. But what are the particular principles? First of all, says the Apostle, our conversation must be 'good', not corrupt. And to 'good' he adds 'edifying'. There must be some purpose in it, some point in it, some value in it. We are not just to chatter away the time and talk about nothing. Oh! the hours we have all wasted in life in sheer idle talk and chatter and gossip, and all to no value! The Christian must turn from this. He need not always of necessity be talking religion, but whenever he speaks there must always be some point and some value in it. It must always be good, it must always be clean, it must always in some sense or another be edifying, so that people say at the end, It was a good thing to have spent some time with that man or with that woman, I feel better for having done so. I am almost tempted to say that one of the main differences between pagan and Christian conversation is that Christian conversation is always intelligent and the other is not.

But the command goes further. It includes mention of the need, the edification of the need, or as the Revised Standard Version puts it, 'as fits the occasion', or, as the need may be. This is particularly important. And it is just here that some of us who are Christian – and this perhaps applies particularly to evangelicals – so frequently fall into error and into a snare. Here I am in conversation with another, or with a number of other people. I must not do certain things; I must consider others; my speech must be good and edifying. Yes, but go further, says the Apostle, Your talk must be 'as fits the occasion'. A difficult thing, but a vital one!

'As fits the occasion' means that I must consider the people to whom I am speaking; I must make an assessment of them, and my speech and conversation must be appropriate for them. But many Christian people do not do this; what they do is to deliver a sermon; they address an individual as if he or she were a public meeting; they sermonise; they give a little address or sermonette; they make very good statements about the gospel and the way of salvation, but sometimes it is not at all appropriate and does not fit the occasion. They act in this way because they are thinking about themselves only, and are not estimating the other. They say to themselves, Now that I am a Christian and must engage in good and godly conversation, I must always be giving my testimony or preaching the gospel or getting in a little word somewhere or other. No, says the Apostle, that is a wrong approach. If you approach it in that way, you are more concerned about yourself and about doing your duty than you are about manifesting the true Christian attitude in this matter. The Christian's word of edification should always fit the occasion! So we are not to repeat phrases in parrot fashion and feel that we have done well and performed our duty. Not at all! Instead, we are to discover, first of all, what is the exact position of other people. My business is to speak to them in such a way as to help them exactly where they are; 'cast not your pearls before swine', says our Lord. Do not hurl chunks, as it were, of good red meat at a babe who can only take milk! These are the Scriptural terms, are they not? 'I could not speak unto you', says Paul to the Corinthians, 'as unto spiritual, but as unto carnal, even as unto babes.' 'I have fed you with milk and not with meat.' The fact was that they 'were not yet able to bear it'!

The author of the Epistle to the Hebrews bemoans the same fact. He says to his readers, I want you to go on to perfection, but I am held back in my teaching, for you are not willing to receive more than the *first* principles of the gospel of Christ. Yes, but what wise teachers men of this type were! Recognising that their readers were not yet in a fit condition to take the more advanced teaching, they gave them the teaching that was appropriate to their condition, 'as fits the occasion'! Clearly, this is the way in which all Christians must speak. We do not just talk and talk and talk; we do not merely make our correct statements. We have to learn to understand other people and their needs. And we should be so anxious to help them that we take time, we meditate, we think, we feel our way, we see the position and then we apply the necessary and the appropriate word. It demands great wisdom, great understanding, great patience. Do not be unfair to people, do not expect them to be what they are not. Our business is to take people as they are and to try to bring them from that one position to another. So let us be careful that our word, our good word of edification, shall always fit the occasion and be appropriate for whatever circumstances apply in each individual case.

The object of our 'communication' is 'that it may minister grace unto the hearers', that is, that it may impart grace to them in some shape or form. Never forget, says the Apostle in effect, that the man or woman or company of people to whom you are speaking, possess immortal souls; that their life does not end in this world, they go on to eternity. And if we keep that in mind it will surely govern and control our whole conversation. Minister grace to them! Some with whom you talk will be unconverted; let there be something about you and your whole manner of speaking, and about what you say, that will arrest them and call attention to the truth. Do not preach, but let your conversation in general be such that some aspect of grace becomes evident to them. And if on the other hand they are children of God, help them to build up their little stock of grace and of knowledge and of understanding; they are exhorted, as you are, to grow in grace and in the knowledge of the Lord. Let contact with you help that process, and let your conversation with them be conducive to their edification.

I can sum up the Apostle's teaching by pointing out that what he is really doing here is to ask us to behave like our Lord Himself. How did He behave? We have a description of Him written by the prophet Isaiah in one of his great Messianic passages. In his fiftieth chapter he looks forward and sees Him, and tells us the Messiah is speaking the following words: 'The Lord God hath given me the tongue of the learned, that I should know how to speak a word in season to him that is weary.' My dear Christian people, there are weary people round and about us, weary of sin, weary in sin, weary of life. There are Christian people round us carrying burdens, carrying loads, suffering illness and sickness, disappointment, the treachery of friends, some fond hope suddenly gone, dashed and vanished illusions; there are men and women round and about us who are weary! And as we meet them and speak to them, let us forget ourselves, let us not regard the meeting as an occasion when we can display how wonderful we are. God forbid! Let us pray that we may have this tongue of the learned that we may be enabled to speak a word in season to some poor, weary soul. Our Lord came from heaven to do that; and of Him it was written, and He verified it in His life, 'A bruised reed shall he not break, and the smoking flax shall he not quench.' That is the way for us also. As we travel through this journey of life we are to help men and women by a word, a word of encouragement, a word of cheer, perhaps a word of rebuke, but a word that will remind them that they are under God, and that if they are in Christ they are precious to Him. Let us go out, therefore, to succour the weary and help the infirm. Let us indeed help one another in the whole of our life and conversation, but above all in our speech. Let no corrupt communication proceed out of our mouth, but that which is good for the edification of others, the improvement of the need, that which fits the occasion, that we may ever administer grace to the hearers. Thank God for the *Christian* life, in which everything is changed, and all we are and do and say is so different from that which characterised the old unregenerate life. Blessed be the Name of God, who has had mercy upon us and sent His Son not only to die for us and deliver us from hell and its corruption, but who has given us this new nature, and who has fashioned anew our lives after His own image.

21

'Grieve not the Holy Spirit of God'

'And grieve not the holy Spirit of God, whereby ye
are sealed unto the day of redemption.'

Ephesians 4:30

We come in our systematic study of the fourth chapter of this
Ephesian Epistle, to the arresting and amazing statement which
the Apostle here, as it were, hurls into the midst of a series of
practical injunctions and exhortations. And surely as we find
ourselves confronted by this thirtieth verse, there must be many
things which come immediately into our minds. The first is that
there is nothing, perhaps, which is quite so characteristic of the
method of this great man of God, the Apostle Paul, as the way
in which he does the very thing which we are considering here.
Though he has an obvious division of his matter in this Epistle,
as in every other, dealing with his doctrines in the first half and
then going on to their practical application, he is never a slave to
method. And thus you find him in the practical section, while
actually dealing with specific, particular matters in a thoroughly
practical and pastoral manner, suddenly hurling in a mighty
statement like this, which again brings us face to face with the
great central, pivotal doctrines of our Christian faith and profession. And in doing so, the Apostle really does show us not
only his own method but certain profound truths about the
whole of our Christian life and deportment.

The first thing we must consider is the question of the connection
of this particular statement. And here there is disagreement
among commentators, not serious of course, because in the last

analysis it does not really matter. There are those who say that the statement really comes as a kind of climax to what Paul has already been saying; that having told us not to lie and not to be angry in a wrong sense, and having told us not to steal any more, and not to allow any corrupt communication to proceed out of our mouth, he says in effect, Be sure not to fall into these sins, because to do so is to grieve the holy Spirit of God. And, of course, this is perfectly true. But I think it is equally true to say that when the Apostle penned these words he also had in mind what was to follow: 'Let all bitterness, and wrath, and anger, and clamour, and evil speaking, be put away from you, with all malice; and be ye kind one to another, tenderhearted, forgiving one another, even as God for Christ's sake hath forgiven you.' In the analysis which I put before you when we were dealing with verse 17, I suggested that this thirtieth verse is an introduction to that which is to come, rather than a summing up and enforcing of that which has gone before. I say all this merely for the sake of orderliness and the tidiness of our minds and our thinking. The more tidy our minds are as we read the Scriptures the better Christians we shall be. But undoubtedly, as I say, this statement covers both the preceding exhortations and injunctions and also those which follow. It comes here as a kind of centre, a focus, of all that is said in regard to the particulars.

In the second place, in this verse we have what may very well be described as the *differentia* of Christian ethics; that is to say, we have here what really makes Christian ethics what it is and differentiates it from every other kinds of moral or ethical system. All the others will tell you not to lie, they will tell you always to speak the truth, tell you not to lose your temper but always to be controlled and disciplined; they will tell you not to steal, they will tell you not to use bad language or any kind of corrupt communication, and to be kind and good, helpful and philanthropic; they do all that, but never in their systems do you find the command, 'and grieve not the holy Spirit of God'; never! This is, I say, the peculiar thing, the *differentia*, the thing that marks it off, separates it, from everything else. And that is important, of course, in this way, that unless our conception of the Christian life and of Christian living and of conduct and of behaviour includes such a command and is based upon it, and is

[265]

always leading us in this direction, it is not truly Christian. Good conduct is not of necessity Christian. And it is a tragic fact in the life and history of the Church, that so often morality, a morality which may even use Christian terminology, is taken for Christianity. But this is the test: Is the whole of our life centred in a truth like this? is this at the very heart of our whole outlook upon conduct and behaviour and at the very heart of our practice?

Furthermore, in this verse and statement, we have what we may well describe as the very heart and nerve and centre of the biblical doctrine of Sanctification. It is an appeal, yes, but notice the kind and the type of appeal that it is. Notice the nature of the Apostle's appeal. Negatively he is not appealing to them to conform to a law or to a moral code or a code of ethics. He mentions no such thing. His appeal is not on a legal level, it is not that Christians should keep up to a certain standard. Standards are good in their place, but that is not the peculiarly Christian thing. Still more important is it to observe that Paul does not appeal to believers to refrain from certain things for their own benefit. In this his argument is quite opposed to certain popular schools of thought and of teaching which invariably teach sanctification in terms of ourselves. They come to us and say, Are you having any trouble in your life? are you being got at by a particular sin? are you being constantly defeated? If so, come to us, and to our clinic, and we will help you to deal with the particular sin that is getting you down. Not a word of that here, for it is not the biblical way of presenting sanctification. It does not start with ourselves, it is not in terms of ourselves. It does not say to us, If you want to live a victorious life and to be really happy and to have great enjoyment and wonderful experiences, stop doing this and that. Not at all! Of course, evil things are bad for me, and of course, as I am about to show, they will affect my experience, but that is not the first thing. If we lack understanding of biblical doctrine we shall betray the fact by the things we put *first*; it is the thing a man puts first that really tells you where he stands and what is his foundation.

Here he shows us what it should be. It is His glory! That is why I must not do certain things. 'Grieve not the holy Spirit of GOD, whereby ye are sealed unto the day of redemption.' Here is the Christian way, here is the biblical way of looking at this whole matter of sanctification. Not for ourselves, but for His sake! Our sanctification, our life, our conduct, is ever to be the realisation and the outcome and the outworking of what He has done for us, and of our sense of His glory and our desire to live to the praise of the glory of His grace.

The doctrine taught by the Apostle is that wrong living in any sense, or in any shape or form, grieves the holy Spirit of God, in whom believers are sealed until the day of redemption. The order of words in the Greek original gives further emphasis to the statement: 'Grieve not the Spirit, the holy Spirit of God'! That is how the Apostle put it: 'the Spirit, yea, the holy Spirit of God, in whom ye are sealed unto the day of redemption'!

The first thing, obviously, that we are taught here pertains to the Holy Spirit in the life of the believer. It reminds us that in the first chapter the Apostle puts it in this same interesting and extraordinary manner in terms of sealing. And here in his fourth chapter we are told that the seal that God gives us of the fact that we are among the redeemed is the Holy Spirit Himself. It is not a statement regarding what the Holy Spirit does to us, but that God seals us *with* the Holy Spirit. The Holy Spirit himself is the seal. And He seals unto us the gift of salvation and all its concomitants, as the Apostle assures us in the first chapter, where he says; 'in whom, after that ye believed, ye were sealed with that holy Spirit of promise, which is the earnest of our inheritance until the redemption of the purchased possession'. And here in this fourth chapter, the Apostle, taking it for granted that they are mindful of what he has already told them, now simply makes use of that argument in order to enforce and to apply this series of particular injunctions with regard to their ethical conduct and behaviour.

The important thing for us to hold in our minds at this particular stage is that the Holy Spirit has been given to us and that He dwells within us. No man is a Christian unless the Holy Spirit is in him. 'If a man have not the Spirit of Christ', says Paul to the Roman Christians, 'he is none of his' (8:9). This is a doctrine that runs right through the New Testament. We need not go into it here in particular. In chapter 3 of the First Epistle to the Corinthians the Apostle reminds us that the Holy Spirit dwells within the *church* as a body; at the end of chapter 6 in that same Epistle the Apostle puts it like this, 'What? know ye not' – and he is now talking about the individual, not about the church as a body – 'know ye not that your body is the temple of the Holy Ghost which is in you, which ye have of God, and ye are not your own? for ye are bought with a price; therefore glorify God in your *body*, and in your spirit, which are God's' (verses 19–20). The thing which the Apostle surely has in the forefront of his mind in this thirtieth verse of the fourth chapter of the Epistle to the Ephesians is, that the Holy Spirit dwells within us, that our bodies are the temple in which the Holy Spirit dwells. Now we shall see how he applies that argument and works it out.

The second thing which the Apostle tells us is that the Holy Spirit can be grieved. Now this, I say, is a most wonderful and astounding statement, and it sheds a flood of light upon the whole Christian doctrine of redemption. Christians are always to remember that God is eternal, Father, Son and Holy Spirit. God *is*! He is independent of everything, He exists in Himself, existed before time, before the world was, and He has no need of anything. There is a great theological term which I must use at this point because it helps to express the idea which here faces us – God is *impassible*; by which is meant just this, that God is not only not dependent upon us, or upon the world, or upon all the things that happen in it, but in an ultimate sense is not affected by them at all. You and I are creatures who are constantly being affected by the things that happen round and about us, and that is why we give place to anger and to wrath and the various other things with which we have been dealing; we are subject to them and we are affected by them. But God in and of Himself is outside it all. And yet we are told here by the Apostle, 'Grieve not the holy Spirit of God'!

Now how are these two things reconciled? That is the question. In an ultimate sense we cannot reconcile them, it is a great mystery that is beyond our understanding; but we are entitled to say this, that because of the way of salvation and redemption, and as a very part of these mercies, God as it were has stooped to our level. We see it in the incarnation of the Son; He took on human nature, and therefore He knows our ignorance and our weakness and our frailty; He knew by experience what it was to hunger and to thirst and to be tired; He brought Himself within that possibility. And here we are told the same thing about the Holy Spirit, that for the purposes of redemption and of salvation, because He has come to reside and to dwell in us, it is possible for us to grieve Him. Now this is a kind of temporary condition, but it is a true one. In salvation He has put Himself into a relationship to us in which it is possible for us to hurt Him, to grieve Him, to disappoint Him.

The analogy that we must bear in our minds is obviously this, that our relationship to the Holy Spirit is a relationship of love. And this is the very essence of the Christian doctrine of salvation. We have finished with law, we are no longer under law; but we are under grace, and we must never think of ourselves in those old legal terms. When a Christian sins, what he should be most conscious of is not so much that he has done that which is wrong, or even that he has broken God's law; what should really trouble him is this, that he has offended against *love*. The very term *grieve* establishes that. Our relationship is now a personal one. And it is because we forget this personal relationship that we get most of our troubles and problems in our Christian lives and experiences. We will persist in regarding the Holy Spirit as no more than an influence or as a kind of power. But we must realise that He is a Person! You cannot grieve an influence, you can only grieve a person. You cannot hurt a power, you can only hurt a person. He can be disappointed in us. A principle cannot be disappointed, it is only a person who can be disappointed. And here, I say, is one of the most vital and important things for us ever to grasp, that we are in this relationship to the Holy Spirit; if we are Christians He is in us, He dwells within us! Wherever we are, He is! And let us never forget His tenderness. Is He not represented in the Scriptures as a dove? He descended upon our Lord at the baptism in the Jordan in semblance of a dove! And that is the Spirit who dwells within us. He is in us, our bodies are His very temple.

Now obviously all this is only true of those who are believers;

[269]

it cannot apply to a non-Christian. An unbeliever can resist the Holy Spirit, but he cannot grieve Him. The only person who can grieve Him is one who belongs to the family, and is in this personal relationship. It is in this way that I, as a Christian, must look at sanctification; not simply in terms of particular actions or happenings or experiences. I must forget all that, as it were, and realise that the Spirit is in me and is always with me. My every action is known to Him, and it is possible for me to grieve Him, to disappoint Him, to sadden Him. That is the meaning of this term *grieve*.

Our next point follows in logical sequence. How then do we, or may we, grieve the Holy Spirit of God? And the answer is plain before us. Anything that we do which is not holy is grieving to Him. 'Grieve not the Spirit, the *holy* Spirit of God!' And this must be interpreted in its fullest sense. Obviously the things that the Apostle has been detailing grieve the Spirit. Anything which belongs to the flesh grieves the Spirit. Take the list given in Galatians 5: 'Now the works of the flesh are manifest, which are these: adultery, fornication, uncleanness, lasciviousness, idolatry, witchcraft, hatred, variance, emulations, wrath, strife, seditions, heresies, envyings, murders, drunkenness, revellings, and such like.' All works of the flesh, and they grieve the Holy Spirit of God. But let us remember that we grieve Him not only in actual deeds or practices. We have been reminded already that we can grieve Him with our words. He is always with us, He hears everything we say, 'Let no corrupt communication proceed out of your mouth', therefore. He is grieved by it: and by other things that Paul goes on to mention. But we must go a step further. You can grieve Him by your thoughts. He is in you! He is within you! How often has the devil tripped us all at this point? You say, But I don't do such and such a thing. No, I know you do not *do* it, and you may not have done it because you are a coward, but you thought it, and you enjoyed it, and you played with it in your imagination, and you thought all was well because you had not done it. Not at all! you have grieved Him! An unworthy or an impure thought, a thought of anger, jealousy, or envy, grieves Him, hurts Him, as much as does the

[270]

action. Everything is known to Him; He knows the innermost recesses of your mind and heart and being, and He is as much grieved by unworthy thoughts as by unworthy words and unworthy actions.

But these are not the only ways in which we grieve Him. There is something which I think is even worse, namely, our failure to realise His presence within us, our failure to honour Him as we ought, our failure to realise that He is always with us. Is there anything more insulting than that? Can another person insult you or hurt you more grievously than by just going on as if you were not there? by behaving and conducting himself or herself as if you were not in the room? Is there anything more humiliating? As Christians then, we are never to forget that the Holy Spirit of God is in us and with us. Do we honour Him? To fail to do so is to grieve Him!

And then another way in which we grieve the Spirit lies in our failure to respond to His promptings and His leadings and His influences, and all that He does in us and to us and upon us in order to further the work of sanctification within us. The Holy Spirit has been given to apply the redemption that has been purchased and worked out for us by the blessed Son of God. It is He that works in us both to will and to do, says Paul, of His good pleasure. And we then work out what the Holy Spirit works in us constantly, as He dwells within us. 'The flesh lusteth against the Spirit, and the Spirit against the flesh'! He is within us in order to do that. It is He who prompts us, who leads us, who creates desires within us. You suddenly find yourself desiring to read the Word: the Spirit is at work! He suddenly will stimulate you perhaps to prayer, or to meditation. He will tell you to leave something, and to do something; it is all the Spirit, it is all a part of His great work of sanctification. Not to respond, or to postpone, or to say, Well, I cannot do that now, I am doing something else; or to fail to give yourself and to be led by Him – oh! these are the ways in which we grieve Him. 'As many as are led by the Spirit of God', says Paul to the Christians in Rome, 'they are the sons of God.' If you do not follow His leadings, or if you try to thwart them, or if you try to postpone them, it is to grieve Him. Fall back upon the human analogy – the parent and the child – and you will see how the Spirit can be grieved by any disinclination on our part, by any tendency to say, I will do it later on, putting Him off, as it were; how grieving to the Spirit that we should not immediately respond and recognise His working and be grateful to Him for condescending to dwell within us and to be concerned about our sanctification!

So you see these are some of the ways in which we do and can grieve the Spirit. *Why* should we not grieve the Spirit? Why must we pay heed to this exhortation of the Apostle: 'Grieve not the holy Spirit of God, whereby ye are sealed unto the day of redemption'? The words are an appeal both to our hearts and to our understanding. It is not only the understanding, it is, as I have been emphasising, very much the heart and the sensibilities. Why should we not grieve Him? In a sense I have already been answering the question. We must not grieve Him because He is who and what He is. And that ought to be enough! He is the third Person in the blessed, holy Trinity, and He is dwelling as a guest within us, in our very bodies, 'a gracious, willing Guest'. The very greatness of His Person ought to be enough for us. We all know what this is in practice, do we not? There are certain things that we may normally do, but if we happen to have some distinguished guest staying in the house we refrain from doing them; we feel instinctively we should be on our best behaviour when we have got some honourable person with us. If there are little children in the house they are told to keep quiet, not to make too much noise in the morning, or at any other time, because so-and-so is staying here. Quite right! It is a mark of respect and of honour. People take great trouble to read books of etiquette in order that they may behave properly in certain high social circles. Think of the punctiliousness with which people study the rules if they should have the privilege of being presented to the Queen. How careful we would be of our speech in Buckingham Palace! We should be infinitely more careful of our speech wherever we are, because of the Guest who dwells within us. Our thoughts, our imaginations – He is there, He knows about them! It is comparable to swearing in the presence of a saint, or using unworthy language in the presence of some holy person. This is Christian sanctification – a realisation that He is within us! Not, how can I get rid of this sin or that? Instead, we must think of HIM; that is incentive enough. We do not need some magical experience, we must just realise the truth which is given to us in the Word of God! If we but realised that He is always within us, our whole conduct and deportment would be entirely different.

Again, think of the base ingratitude that we are guilty of when we grieve Him in any way. Think of all that has been done for us; think of the planning of God in eternity; think of the subordination of the Son to the Father, and of the Spirit to the Son and the Father. Think of the Spirit as co-equal, co-eternal, the third Person in the blessed, holy Trinity, and yet for our redemption He subordinated Himself, and He has even condescended to dwell within us. It is base ingratitude not to realise the Person and not always to do everything that is well pleasing in His sight. To grieve Him is to be a cad, it is to be guilty of a base ingratitude for all He has done for us.

Another thing that grieves the Spirit, as the Apostle reminds us here, is a complete failure on our part to understand the final object of salvation. What is the final object of salvation? that my sins may be forgiven? that I may be happy all the day? that I may get rid of all the problems in my life? Not at all! These are incidentals. What is the end and object in view? It is the day of redemption! 'Grieve not the holy Spirit of God, whereby ye are sealed *until* . . .' – that is the end! Oh, these lesser things, thank God for them, while we are passing through this world of time; but they are the temporaries. The grand end lies ahead. What is it? It is the day of the Lord that is coming, it is the day when Christ will come back and judge the world in righteousness, and destroy His every enemy, and when He will remove every vestige of evil out of the whole cosmos, and usher in His everlasting kingdom. And we, as believers, shall be in it, in glorified bodies, perfect, without spot or wrinkle or any such thing, a part of this glorious Church, the bride of Christ, with everything which is unworthy and evil removed. *That* is the end, the day of redemption, the coming in of the full and final and perfect salvation!

The Apostle has really said it all in the fourth verse of the first chapter: 'according as he hath chosen us in him before the foundation of the world, that we should be holy and without blame before him in love'. The end of redemption and salvation is not so much the particular things that may be true of us here and now in *this* world, but that 'we should be holy and without blame before him in love' – in this world, yes, but especially at that great day, the day of redemption! A man, therefore, who grieves the Spirit does not understand as he ought the whole object and purpose of redemption. Why did Christ die on the cross? Was it simply that you might not go to hell? No! Answer the question positively – that you might go to glory! Do not always look at the negative; do not say, I am delivered from this, that, and the other; of course you are, but you are delivered *for*, prepared *for*! It is that which matters. Is it not tragic when people preach sanctification in subjective, personal terms, instead of holding before us the vision of the day of redemption, the glory that awaits us, the perfection for which we are being prepared? That is the object of it all! Peter, putting in his own style and words the thing which Paul says here, tells us, 'He that lacketh these things is blind, and cannot see afar off, and hath forgotten that he was purged from his old sins.' 'Add to your faith virtue, and to virtue knowledge', and so on, says Peter, in his Second Epistle, for if you do these things you will have 'an abundant entrance' into that final state of the kingdom of God. The trouble, alas, in our lives is that we either do not know, or do not believe, or do not apply these Christian doctrines. And to display a final kind of ignorance at the very centre about the whole object of redemption, is to grieve the Spirit.

Thus I have given you the great things, and they ought to be enough, but in order to encourage and to help, let me become personal and, indeed, subjective. For *your own sake*, do not grieve the Spirit, because if you grieve Him it will inevitably lead to a loss of the gracious manifestations of His presence. Grieve Him and He will withdraw Himself. I mean by that, He will withdraw the manifestations of Himself. If you grieve the Spirit, you will not have a sense of God's love to you, you will not have the joy of salvation, you will have no assurance, you will not have certainty, you will not have peace, you will not be able to say, The Spirit bears witness with my spirit that I *am* a child of God. All that is implied in the sealing; and if you grieve the Spirit the evidences of your sealing will become faint, and indeed, may altogether disappear. Do not misunderstand me, I am not saying you are lost, but I am saying that you will miss and lose the comforts! The Christian is a man who is meant to know the joy of the Lord. 'Rejoice in the Lord alway, and again I say, Rejoice', says Paul to the Philippians. He is also saying it here to the Ephesians. The Christian is not a man who trudges his weary way through this world, moaning and bemoaning. When he looks within he sees nothing but sin, and he does moan; but he must not merely look inward, he must look *out*, and as he sees himself in Christ, he should be filled with joy unspeakable and full of glory; he should go singing as he marches to Zion. 'Children of the heavenly King, as ye journey sweetly sing; sing your Saviour's worthy praise, glorious in His works and ways.' But you will not be able to do so, if you grieve the Spirit! All the tender visitations of His love, and the intimations of His rejoicing in you, will be withdrawn, and you will be left to yourself, and you will lose all the wonderful experiences of the times when He comes and embraces you and enfolds you in the arms of His love and lets you know that you belong to Him. So for your own sake grieve not the Spirit.

But then let me add to that. If you grieve the Spirit and He withdraws His gracious influences, it means that He leaves you to the supremacy of the flesh; that is to say, you will be left with all the power of the flesh within you, and the devil making use of it to attack you. He will assault you, he will insinuate vile, foul, ugly thoughts and desires into your mind and heart. You will feel that you are living in hell and that hell is within you. And it is all because the Spirit, in order to teach you a lesson, is no longer, as it were, striving against the flesh. You have grieved Him. So if you are being subjected to most terrible temptations, examine yourself; it may be that you are being delivered over to Satan, to correct you and to bring you to your senses, and to lead you not to grieve the Spirit, the Holy Spirit of God.

Finally, if we grieve the Spirit and He withdraws His manifestations, this does not mean that He will abandon us. He will come back; He is there the whole time, He has just withdrawn His gracious manifestations, and He will convict us, He will thunder out the law again, He will make us feel we were never saved, that we are lost, that we are damned and reprobate; He will do it in order to bring us back again to where we ought to be. And if you do not want to know these mighty strivings and convictions of the Spirit within you, do not grieve Him. Let us be clear about this doctrine. The Spirit never abandons the child of God; the seal is a seal, and a seal is no seal which can be broken at any moment and then put back again and then broken again. You do not go in and out of salvation; you are not saved today and lost tomorrow and then saved again. That is not biblical teaching. A seal is a seal, it is *God's* seal, and no man can break it. So that when I say the Spirit withdraws Himself, I do not mean He goes out of you; He still stays there, but the gracious manifestations are withdrawn. And then because He is still in you He will convict you, He will strike you down, He will prostrate you, He will make you feel helpless and hopeless. And then, when you feel that you are abandoned by Him, He will again reveal the Lord Jesus Christ to you as your Saviour who died for you and who still loves you, and He will wash away your sin again and He will smile upon you once more, and He will restore unto you the joy of salvation. Grieve not the Holy Spirit of God. He is in you and He will have you, and He will bring you to that glory of perfection; and if you will not be led by Him, be sure that He will chastise you! 'He which hath begun a good work in you will perform it until the day of Jesus Christ.' Do not grieve Him, I warn you, do not grieve Him! For if you do you will bring upon yourself grievous experiences and agonies of soul that you need never have had.

What then are we to do? Simply this! – remember that the Spirit is always in you. Start your day by saying, I am a child of God, and therefore the Holy Spirit of God dwells within me. Wherever I may be, whatever I may have to do, whatever may happen to me, He will be with me; my every thought, word and deed will be in His sight and in His presence. Oh, how I thank God for the privilege! how careful I should be in nothing to grieve Him or to disappoint Him! Grieve not the Holy Spirit of God, whereby ye are *sealed* until the day of redemption. Remember Him, remember what He is doing in you, think of the glory for which He is preparing you, and the things that grieve Him will become unthinkable.

22

Forgiven and Forgiving

'Let all bitterness, and wrath, and anger, and clamour,
and evil speaking, be put away from you, with all
malice: and be ye kind one to another, tenderhearted,
forgiving one another, even as God for Christ's sake
hath forgiven you.'

Ephesians 4:31–32

In the last two verses in this fourth chapter, the Apostle is
continuing the list of particular injunctions that he is giving the
Ephesians in order to teach them how exactly and in practice to
put off the old man and to put on the new man. That is the over-
ruling principle, that is the doctrine which is to cover everything.
The Apostle is not interested in conduct as such, he is interested
in conduct as it is an expression and a reflection of the new life
which they had received as the result of regeneration. In verse
31 we come to exhortations which in general remind us of the
exhortations found in verses 25 to 29. There were references
there to speech, and to anger, and so on, and some may therefore
wonder whether the Apostle is not here repeating his injunctions.
But he is not doing so. Though the terms are the same in certain
respects, there is an essential difference; and the difference has
been brought in by the thirtieth verse, in which we are told not
to grieve 'the holy Spirit of God, whereby ye are sealed unto the
day of redemption'. The difference is that in verses 25 to 29
Paul is looking at conduct in general, giving a very general and
broad description of conduct, whereas after verse 30 he becomes
much more personal and intimate, and is much more concerned
about the state of our spirits. We can therefore regard these two
verses as being a kind of practical exposition of what we are to

avoid if we are anxious not to grieve the Holy Spirit who dwells within us.

Notice, in the first place, that the Apostle adopts the same formula as before; he puts his negative first, and then his positive, and then he supplies us with a reason or a motive or an argument. We have seen him doing this in every one of these particular injunctions, so that we have nothing to do but to follow the Apostle's own division and classification. In verse 31, therefore, he brings us first of all to the negative: 'Let all bitterness, and wrath, and anger, and clamour, and evil speaking, be put away from you, with all malice.' And as we read these horrible words we are again given a picture of the mentality and the outlook and the inner life of those who are not Christian. The Apostle has given us several descriptions of the unconverted world in this Epistle; and, of course, what he wants is that these people should see that old life as it really is, so that seeing it they shall so hate it as to renounce it and turn their backs on it for ever. Put it away from you, says Paul, have nothing more to do with its evils, discard them; these things must never be true of you in any sense. But, obviously, he again feels the importance of particularising. And we too have to do this. It is not enough to confess sin in general, we must confess particular sins. It is rather a dangerous thing to confess sin in general. We bring these things home to ourselves by confessing them in particular. And the Apostle teaches us to do so by giving us these lists.

He starts with the word *bitterness*, 'Let all *bitterness* be put away.' Bitterness is a state of the spirit. It denotes a sort of persistent sourness and an absence of amiability. It is an unloving condition. Indeed, it is a condition which never sees any good in anything, but always contrives to see something wrong, or some defect and deficiency. The proverb tells us that 'All seems yellow to the jaundiced eye', and the same is true about bitterness of spirit. It puts into everything it looks at some unworthy element. Because the person himself is jaundiced and bitter, everything he looks at is tinged by the same thing; it is like looking through coloured spectacles. The Apostle brings this out in many places, as for example in the third chapter of his letter to Titus, 'For we ourselves also were sometimes foolish, disobedient, deceived, serving divers lusts and pleasures, living in malice and envy, hateful, and hating one another.' We need not stay with this. I would remind you that we have already had ample opportunity for seeing the sham, and the pretence and the veneer which the world puts on. It gives a wonderful expression of affability, while the fact is that behind the paint and the powder there is nothing but bitterness, the result of brooding upon wrongs, either real or imaginary. We are all bitter by nature when in an unregenerate state; for which reason, as Christians, we have to put it away from us. I grant that there may be genuine grievances; but what makes us bitter is that we ponder them and meditate upon them and stay with them; in other words, *we nurse our grievances*, we dwell on them, we pay great attention to them, and if we are tending to forget them we deliberately bring them back and allow them to work us up again into a state of bitterness. But, of course, this happens not only with real grievances; many grievances are purely imaginary, and have no real substance at all, but because we have become bitter we see them where they really are not, and we nurse them, and, in turn, become more and more bitter.

Bitterness, then, describes the kind of life which has become sour; it is not ready to believe good of anybody or anything, but always ready to believe evil; it is always somewhat cynical, takes the glory out of everything, tries to spoil everything. When it is shown something beautiful, it does not praise the ninety-nine per cent that is beautiful but always points to the one per cent of defect. We all know the kind of individual who is always pointing out the troubles and the defects and the faults and the blemishes. There are many such people. Every preacher, I am sure, could name them. There are some people who never write and thank you for sermons, but if you should by a mere slip of the tongue say something wrong they write to you about it. It is the only time they do write. The bitter spirit sees the faults and the blemishes but never seems to see the good. I do not want to stop with this.

There are, of course, many people who feel that they have had good cause for being bitter; there were many people in the two World Wars who lost a husband or an only son. It is very easy to understand how they have become bitter with regard to the whole of life; but it does not excuse it, it is wrong, they should never have allowed themselves to become bitter. They have been dealt certain hard blows by life, but that is no justification for bitterness or for sourness or for becoming cynical. Even if life is described to them at its best, their very expression lets you know that they are not really disposed to allow themselves to enjoy anything. The saddest people I know in this world are these bitter people; they make themselves miserable and for the time being they make everybody else miserable. It is a terrible thing to be nursing a grievance, real or imaginary. Put it away from you, says Paul, put it away from you; that is the old man, that is the pagan, that is the unregenerate world, it should never appear in the Christian.

But let us move on to the second word. Bitterness is something that always expresses itself in speech and in action. So after naming it, the Apostle mentions *wrath* and *anger*, as the forces frequently behind behaviour. We have already considered the terms, so I only remind you that *wrath* means violent excitement or agitation of the mind, a kind of boiling over; whereas *anger* is a more settled and regular state and condition of the mind. Anger is never at the same white heat as wrath; it is a more settled condition of the mind and of the spirit.

In turn, wrath and anger tend to express themselves in speech. Here again Paul uses two terms, and the first is *clamour*.

Clamour means a kind of brawling; it includes shouting and violence. We all know, alas! what it means; men and women in a state of rage or of wrath do not speak to one another, they shout at one another, they lift up their voices. What a terrible thing sin is! and what an anatomy of sin we have in this chapter, what a dissection! But it is true! This is life! And this is something with which we are all, alas, familiar, this brawling, this shouting, in an uncontrolled way. It is something that should never be present in the life of the Christian, either in an individual sense or a corporate sense.

But there is something that is even worse than brawling or clamour, namely, *evil speaking*. And *evil speaking* means the cool, deliberate saying of things that are harmful to others; it includes the enjoyment linked with slandering others, deliberately saying or repeating things about others that are calculated to do them harm. Evil speaking! What a description of modern life! What a description of the world today! and as it has always been! It is an evil that makes so utterly fatuous all the nonsensical talk we hear about development and evolution and progress. The unconverted world was like that two thousand years ago; it is exactly like that today. No change at all! Think of the evil speaking in which the world indulges, and the harm that is done to character, and the harm that is done to life, in this way.

And then, as if all this were not enough, the Apostle adds the word *malice*. Malice means wicked desires with respect to others, a determination to harm others, again a kind of settled spirit which so hates others that it thinks of ways of harming them, plots such ways, gloats over them, and then proceeds to put them into practice; it is a kind of malignity. Evil, malicious gossip and slander also form a part of this malice that he tells us all to put far from us.

The Apostle says that all these evils must be put away from us once and for ever as something loathsome and blasphemous. Actually the term *evil speaking* is really our word *blasphemy*, and therefore the teaching is that we not only blaspheme when we say things that are wrong about God but we can really be guilty of blasphemy when we say evil things about one another. After all, man is made in the image of God, and to speak evil of another person is a form of blasphemy, for you are speaking evil of someone who has been made in the image of God. So the Apostle says that all this kind of thing is totally incompatible with the new man.

But again I must remind you that the Apostle is exhorting the Ephesians to put away all this evil. He does not say that because they have become Christian it has automatically dropped off. So any kind of evangelistic preaching that gives the impression that the moment you become a Christian all your problems are left behind is just not true, and the Apostle realised that the Ephesians were still subject to this kind of thing. And again we notice that he does not merely tell them to pray that these sins may be taken out of their lives. Pray by all means, but do not forget that Paul tells the Ephesians to put them off, to put them far from them, and we must do the same. It is not pleasant. It is not at all pleasant even to preach on these things; it is very unpleasant for us to face them, and to see if there is within our hearts any bitterness of spirit, or any malice or hatred or wrath or anger; but, says the Apostle, we must do it, and if we find any vestige or trace of these things within us, we must take hold of it and hurl it away from us, trample upon it, and bolt the door upon it, and never allow it to come back. We must do just that! Let it, he says, be put away from you! Put it away once and for ever, and realise that it is a denial, a complete denial of everything that you claim to be and to have as newborn people in the Lord Jesus Christ, in whom the Holy Spirit of God has come to take up His blessed residence. If these things are in us the Holy Spirit is grieved, for the fruit of the Spirit is love, joy, peace, longsuffering, gentleness, goodness, faith, meekness and temperance. All that is contrary to this fruit must be put away, says Paul. But, thank God, he does not leave it at that! He goes on to his positive injunction. Be kind one to another, tenderhearted, forgiving one another.

Thank God, I say, that the Apostle does not stop at the negative but brings us on to the positive. Indeed, as I have already said, you cannot truly deal with the negative unless you are at the same time doing the positive. The way to get rid of the defects is to cultivate the virtues. To use a well-known phrase of Thomas Chalmers, what we need is to apply *the expulsive power of a new affection*. I use a simple illustration. The way the dead leaves of winter are removed from some trees is not that people go around plucking them off; no, it is the new life, the shoot that comes and pushes off the dead in order to make room for itself. In the same way the Christian gets rid of all such things as bitterness and wrath and anger and clamour and evil speaking and all malice. The new qualities develop and the others simply have no room; they are pushed out and they are pushed off.

We must watch very carefully the precise way in which the Apostle gives his instruction. We read '*Be ye kind*', but what he really wrote was '*Become kind*'. Not simply *be* kind, but *become* kind. In other words he is suggesting here a process of cultivation. We are quite deliberately to cultivate this type of personality and of attitude towards life, and as we do so, our lives will be filled with these positive qualities and there will be no room for those of a contrary kind. Remember again our Lord's own illustration at this point. It is no use just getting rid of the devils that are in the house and sweeping it and garnishing it; if the Holy Spirit does not come in, the spirit you have driven out will come back and bring others with him much worse than himself. Now that is the principle here. That is where, in the last analysis, morality in and of itself never succeeds. And you and I, alas! in the second half of the Twentieth Century are living in an era which is just a visible proof of the breakdown of mere morality. For the last hundred years people have been turning their back upon Christianity, saying that miracles, the new birth, and much else that is supernatural, are not necessary. But of course, they say, there is good moral and ethical teaching in the Bible, so we hold on to such things as the Sermon on the Mount, for example, but we shed the rest; we want the morality, and we will teach the morality only. And what is the result? The present immoral, and even non-moral, state of society! No, you cannot do these things without the positive. *Become*, says the Apostle; cultivate it, go in for it, give time and attention to it. In other words, you see that the word used indicates that this does not happen automatically. You do not receive it as one critical experience. Instead, become! go on! You cannot suddenly get rid of the bitterness and become kind in a flash; far from it! This is again a settled condition, a process of cultivation, which results from the application of the truth which we have seen and believed.

At this point the Apostle introduces his great positives. Having got rid of all the horrible things detailed, what have we to become? He tells us in great and glorious Christian terms! And what wonderful terms they are, and how different from the things we have just been looking at! Kind, tenderhearted, forgiving! You will never find these great Christian terms anywhere else. Let us look at them again. What is the meaning of the term *kind* in 'Be ye *kind* one to another'? It is certainly the opposite of being bitter, but beyond that, the real meaning of the term in its origin is *to be useful* to, and *to be helpful* to others. So that it is not merely a condition or a state, but it is a condition and a state leading to a desire; the kind man is a man who is useful and helpful to others. The bitter man, of course, stands apart and looks, and in his sour way he is never helpful, is never useful. Bitterness, as we have seen, always takes from, it detracts, but kindness is that which gives, it is useful, it is helpful, it is always valuable. It means being benevolent towards others.

Paul, in his First Epistle to the Corinthians, chapter 13, tells us: 'Charity suffereth long, and is *kind*'. Be kind one to another! Have and cultivate this benevolence of spirit and of attitude; instead of always being on the look-out for something you can find fault with, be always on the look-out for something you can praise. Help others. Life can be hard, difficult, and very trying, and in consequence certain people do become sour and bitter. Do not add to that bitterness, but try to help them – help them over the stiles, help them to carry their burdens and to solve their problems and bear their difficulties. That is what is meant by kindness. Be always on the look-out for an opportunity of showing benevolence and of giving assistance and aid.

Next, the Apostle introduces another wonderful term – *tenderhearted*, which scarcely needs exposition. Remember how he had told us that these same people, before their conversion, were '*past feeling*'; and that meant that their hearts had become hard, in a kind of calloused condition. The lining of the heart, which is meant to be smooth and soft, becomes hard and like leather; it becomes stiff, and it not only does not move and bend itself, it prevents the heart that is inside it from responding and beating and moving as it should. And the Apostle tells us that as Christians we are to be the exact opposite of that; we are to become tender-hearted, or according to what is probably a better translation, *having strong bowels of compassion*. It is an appeal for us to become understanding and compassionate and loving. The ancients invariably put the seat of the affections in the bowels. They regarded the bowels, the abdominal organs at any rate in general, as the seat of the emotions. We find Jeremiah crying out, 'My bowels, my bowels!' He means that he is suffering anguish in his spirit and in his feelings.

If we are to understand certain expressions in the New Testament it is essential that we should bear this in mind. For instance, Paul says to the Philippians: 'God is my record, how greatly I long after you all in the bowels of Jesus Christ' (1:8), by which he means, 'I long after you all with the affection and feeling and the sentiment of Jesus Christ Himself'. And then again later: 'If there be therefore any consolation in Christ, if any comfort of love, if any fellowship of the Spirit, if any bowels and mercies . . .' (2:1). Once more he is talking about sympathy and compassion and understanding and a loving nature. The Apostle Peter uses exactly the same term in his First Epistle: 'Finally, be ye all of one mind, having compassion one of another, love as brethren, be *pitiful*' (3:8); where to be 'pitiful' means to be tenderhearted; it means that you are not in the calloused condition in which nothing that has happened to anybody else makes the slightest difference to you. It means that you have not come to the sorry conclusion that life is a hard and a terrible business, that it is every man for himself, that you are going to live for yourself, and that you really cannot give your time and energy to others and their problems. Now that is the attitude that you have got to put away. And the opposite of that is to become tenderhearted. This means that you are concerned about other people and that you can feel for others, that you are sympathetic towards others, and that you have got a great heart of compassion towards them; that indeed you can see so much the troubles of others that you forget your own troubles.

Is there any word that is needed so much in this modern world of ours as just this? There is nothing to me that is so appalling about life today as the hardness that has entered into it. I am constantly hearing from people who have this sort of complaint against our National Health Service. Not a few doctors and nurses are good Christian people, and what I am saying does not apply to them, I know, but it does apply to many others. The patient is regarded as a number. It is to me almost beyond comprehension that anybody treating a sick man should never talk to him or explain to him what is the matter with him, or what is happening to him, or give him a word of comfort and of cheer. He is not just a test tube! But, alas! one is given to understand that much of that kind of thing is coming in, and the tenderheartedness and feeling for another is ebbing away. That patients can be regarded impersonally in this way passes comprehension. But it is true, unfortunately. Life has become hard. Professions become a means of making money so that men can enjoy themselves in various ways, and the former wonderful personal touch and sympathy is going out of life. And this is happening all around us in all kinds of ways. Are not many problems being avoided and evaded? I know that there are great difficulties in life today, and that many changes have taken place; even so, I find it very difficult to understand people who somehow seem to be so self-centred that they can avoid plain human responsibilities and can harden themselves against the need of others. That is pagan; the pagan does not care for others; he is out for himself and his own enjoyment. Against all this, we need to give heed to Paul's word – 'become tenderhearted'!

And then the Apostle goes on to say, *forgiving*! – the opposite of malice. 'Forgiving one another', he says. It means that we must realise that men and women are what they are because of sin. Paul does not say, as so many foolish people, who, misunderstanding Christianity, are saying today, that they refuse to see any wrong in people at all. That is not Christianity; that is make-believe. Christianity is always realistic. Certain people, says Paul, have done wrong to you! Forgive them! He does not say, Pretend that they have done nothing; that is not forgiveness. Forgiveness is realising to the full the wrong they have done, and then forgiving them. It means forgetting also, and we are to forgive and to forget readily and freely. And it is only the Christian who can do this, for he has become able to look at the offender now with a new eye. Before, he saw him as a person who was doing him harm; now he sees him as a victim of sin, a pawn and a dupe of the devil; and he says, Yes, he is like that and I was like that, and there are relics and remnants of that in me still; who am I to say I will not forgive that man? He reasons it out in terms of his doctrine and his theology, and begins to feel sorry for the man. The result is that he forgives him. The fact is that his heart has already become tender towards him, he is already kind in his outlook, and quite inevitably the result is that he forgives him.

[287]

But we move on to the last section, which supplies the reason why we should do this, or how we are to do this, the grand motive for it all. Listen to the Apostle. 'Be ye kind one to another, tender-hearted, forgiving one another, even as God for Christ's sake hath forgiven you'. Look at this *even as*. It means that if you forgive and are kind and are tenderhearted towards others you become like God. Our Lord put the same teaching in the following words: 'Love ye your enemies, and do good and lend, hoping for nothing again; and your reward shall be great, and ye shall be the children of the Highest, for he is kind unto the unthankful and to the evil' (Luke 6:35). Be kind, says Paul, become kind, and as you become kind you become like God, for God 'is kind to the unthankful and to the evil'. Do we not want to be like God? That is the exhortation! Read Psalm 103, find the same teaching there: 'Who forgiveth all thine iniquities; who healeth all thy diseases'. Read that Psalm and become like that. But we need not go back as far as that, for the Apostle himself has said it all in this Epistle. In chapter 2 we read, 'But God' – who is so different from man by nature and from man in sin – 'who is rich in mercy, for his great love wherewith He loved us ... and hath raised us up together ... in Christ Jesus: that in the ages to come He might show the exceeding riches of His grace in His *kindness* towards us. ...' So that, as the Apostle exhorts us to become kind, he is exhorting us to become the children of our Father which is in heaven, to become children of the Highest, to be perfect, even as God is perfect.

But a second argument is used by the Apostle. He tells us to forgive others in this way because God has forgiven us. Notice that he does not say, Forgive one another because God is *going to forgive* you. Not at all! He says, 'even as God for Christ's sake *hath forgiven* you'. It has happened. This is most important, for the only people who will carry out this exhortation of the Apostle are those who know that God has forgiven them. Nobody else! But those who do know that He has done it, will forgive others. The vital question therefore is: Do you know that your sins are forgiven? How can I know, says someone, that my sins are forgiven? I will give you a very good test. If you want to know whether your sins are forgiven or not, here is my test. Are you forgiving others? Are you ready to forgive others who have harmed you and sinned against you? Or look at it in another way: Does this argument of the Apostle appeal to you? As I read out these words, 'Be ye kind one to another, tenderhearted, forgiving one another, even as God for Christ's sake hath forgiven you', are you softened in your feelings? do you feel melted? are you ready to forgive at this moment? If you are, I do not hesitate to say you are a Christian. But if bitterness is still rankling there, and if you are saying in spite of these glorious words, 'But after all, I did nothing and I don't deserve such treatment', you had better go back and examine your foundations. I find it very difficult to see how such a person can be a Christian at all.

This is the Lord's argument in a parable found in chapter 18 of Matthew's Gospel. I made reference to it in an earlier chapter. A servant owed his master ten thousand talents; he could not pay, he pleaded for time, and his master said, Very well, my good man, go and take time. But when he went out from his master, he met a servant who owed him a hundred pence, a mere fraction of what he himself owed; he took him by the throat and said, Pay me what you owe me. Have mercy, have compassion, give me a little time and I will pay it, replied the other. Not a bit of it, he said, you owe me this and you must pay it at once. What was our Lord's comment on such behaviour? He said, If you behave in that way you have no right to think that God has forgiven you. The teaching of that parable is not that God forgives us because we first forgive. That is the wrong way round. But the teaching is very definitely this, that the man who realises what forgiveness is, forgives! The man who realises the mercy and the kindness and the compassion that has cancelled his own great debt, says, 'I cannot refuse.' His heart is melted, he has a sense of compassion. 'Even as God for Christ's sake *hath* forgiven you'! Has He done it for you? Then what God has done for you, you cannot refuse to another.

Last of all, consider the *way* in which God has done it. In Christ! That is the only way in which even God can forgive. Let nobody tell me that he is relying upon the love of God only for the forgiveness of his sins. God forgives sins in Christ, for Christ's sake. He forgives sins in spite of us; it is not because of any goodness in us, or anything we have done or ever shall do, that God forgives us. 'While we were yet without strength, in due time Christ died for the ungodly'. It is for sinners that Christ died, it was, 'while we were enemies we were reconciled to God by the death of his Son'. We are forgiven in spite of ourselves, not because of any merit or any goodness in us. God does it entirely of His own free grace; it is all of God; it is all of His grace; it is a pure gift; we were enemies, without strength, ungodly and vile and sinners. But God forgave us freely. And you and I must do that to others who are vile and ungodly and enemies and hateful.

Above all, remember how He did it. 'Even as God *for Christ's sake*' – in Christ – 'hath forgiven you'. God, who owed us nothing, because of His kindness, His tenderheartedness, His love, His grace, His mercy, His compassion, not only sent His only begotten, beloved Son into this world of sin and shame, but even to the cross on Calvary's hill that we might be forgiven. 'He hath laid on him the iniquity of us all'. He has taken our sins and put them on Him and punished them in Him, that we might be forgiven. That is how God has forgiven you; He bore the suffering Himself in His own Son. If He has done that for us, can we possibly refuse forgiveness to another? It is inconceivable. If you want to know whether you are a Christian or not, here is the test. As I remind you again of how God has forgiven you in Christ, and by His death and by His shed blood upon the cross, and His burial in the grave, I ask you, Is your heart tender? Are you bearing malice at this moment to any individual? Can you refuse forgiveness to any, even though they may have hurt you to the very depths of your being? are you ready now to forgive them? If you are, believe me, you are a Christian. I am certain of it. In the Name of God I tell you that your own sins are forgiven; I loose you from your sins. But if you are still hard and unforgiving, I have nothing more to say to you except this; while you remain like that I have no evidence, and you have no evidence, that you have been forgiven. A man who knows forgiveness has got a broken heart; he realises he is a vile wretch to whom God owes nothing, but for whom God sent His only Son, and the Son has borne all his sin and iniquity; and salvation has been given as a free gift entirely and altogether and only in Christ.

'Become kind, tenderhearted, forgiving one another, even as God for Christ's sake hath forgiven you.'

[290]

23

'Imitators of God'

'Be ye therefore followers of God, as dear children;
and walk in love, as Christ also hath loved us, and
hath given himself for us an offering and a sacrifice
to God for a sweetsmelling savour.'

Ephesians 5:1 and 2

Here in this new chapter we come to what is perhaps Paul's
supreme argument, to the highest level of all in doctrine and in
practice, to the ultimate ideal. There is nothing possible beyond
this. This is the highest statement of Christian doctrine that
one can conceive of or even imagine. It is really staggering, it is
almost incredible; but here it is. 'Be ye followers of God'! It
would be interesting, from the mere standpoint of mechanics,
to know whether this injunction belongs to the previous section
of the Epistle or to the one that follows. Frankly, I cannot make
up my mind, I really believe it belongs to both. It is partly
suggested, I think, by what Paul said at the end of chapter 4:
'Be ye kind one to another, tender-hearted, forgiving one
another, even as God for Christ's sake hath forgiven you. Be ye
therefore followers of God.' And yet the good men who divided
up this letter into chapters ended chapter 4 and started this new
section in chapter 5, and I believe there is a great deal to be said
for that also; for here Paul seems to me to be laying down what
is after all a principle that governs everything; he is gathering
up his message as it were; and then he will proceed to draw his
practical deductions in verses 3 to 5. But the point is that the
Apostle is here reminding us of something that we must never
forget in the whole of our lives, all our thinking, all our conduct
and practice and behaviour. 'Be ye followers of God, as dear
children'! Now then, what does this mean?

Well, you notice first of all that again he is introducing us to a principle of doctrine. In this most practical section where he is dealing with the most ordinary things in life, suddenly he throws in this. That is why these Epistles are so romantic if you study them properly. You may say to yourself, Oh well, I have finished with my doctrine at the end of chapter 3, I can then go on to something else! But you cannot! You have not finished with doctrine. He cannot talk about anything except in terms of the truth, and so suddenly, you see, when he is dealing with the most practical things in life, he suddenly hurls this upon us and we stand before the most staggering and astonishing statement that we can ever face. What is it? Well, let us look at it.

'Be ye therefore followers of God'. A better translation is desirable, for the word *followers* does not bring out the meaning as it should. The Apostle really says: 'Become *imitators* of God', indeed 'Become *mimics* of God'. Our word *mimic* comes from the very word the Apostle used. We are to mimic God, we are to imitate God. Is this possible? Is not this gross exaggeration? Has not the Apostle run away with himself, and allowed his eloquence to dazzle him? Is he seriously asking men and women like ourselves, living in a world like this, surrounded by temptations, harassed by the devil, with sin and evil and unworthiness within us, to be 'imitators of God'? Is it possible? A question like this must have an answer, and I suggest we approach it in this way. We must look at God and consider His being and nature. If I am to imitate God I must know something about Him. And, thank God, He has been graciously pleased to reveal Himself to us. He does it in His Word. We see it in the Lord Jesus Christ. And we are entitled, therefore, to say that there are certain attributes of God which can be divided into two groups. There are attributes of God that are not communicable, certain things that pertain to God that are true only of Him, and we cannot imitate Him in those respects. For instance, His Glory! We cannot imitate the glory of God! His eternity! He is from eternity, to eternity; He is everlasting. That is an attribute of God. We cannot imitate that. His majesty! Who would be so foolish as to try to imitate the majesty of God! Add to these His omnipotence, His omnipresence, His omniscience. They are attributes of God, yes, but they are incommunicable, they belong to God alone, and they make God God. They are in God because He is God, and we are never called upon anywhere to imitate the incommunicable attributes!

But there are other attributes in God which *are* communicable. They are communicable because they are moral in their nature. These are the ones that we must understand if we are truly to follow our text. What are they? Holiness! 'Be ye holy', says God, 'for I am holy'; that is to say, 'Be ye holy *because* I am holy'. This is communicable, this is something that I am to imitate. As God is holy, I am to be holy. Righteousness! God is righteous – and believers are to be righteous. His justice! His goodness! His love! His mercy! His compassion! His tenderness! His longsuffering! His lovingkindness! His faithfulness! His forgiveness! All these are communicable attributes of God, and we are expected to manifest them, we are to have them, we are to show them, they are to be parts of our life and living.

'Be ye therefore imitators of God', says the Apostle. Become imitators, mimics, of God. In what respect? In respect of these communicable attributes! We are not just to be good people, we are to be imitators of God! 'Be ye imitators of God'! Here is the appeal; and we only realise its greatness, and value, and its staggering character as we realise the biblical teaching about the being and the nature of God, and these two types of attributes.

But *why* are we to be imitators of God? Why are we in these respects to be in our daily lives *as God is*? It is first and foremost because we are God's children. 'Be ye therefore imitators . . . as dear children'. Here once more we enter into a realm that is altogether different from what the world knows, and again the Apostle's argument compels me to repeat what I have often emphasised; I mean the essential difference between Christianity and mere morality. Some of the most unchristian people in the world today are men and women who are living upright and moral lives and are satisfied with themselves and think that that is the acme. That, I say, is the opposite of Christianity, it is goodness for the sake of goodness. They are very good people, I know, but the Apostle's teaching is a thing about which they know nothing at all. It is because we are children of God that we are to refrain from some things and to do others. The Apostle, of course, has already been reminding us of this; it is not a new idea that he suddenly introduces here. We saw it at the very beginning of the Epistle: 'Blessed be the God and Father of our Lord Jesus Christ, who hath blessed us with all spiritual blessings in heavenly places in Christ: according as he hath chosen us in him before the foundation of the world, that we should be holy and without blame before him in love: having predestinated us' – to what? – 'unto the *adoption of children* by Jesus Christ to himself, according to the good pleasure of his will'. This is echoed in the second chapter where we read: 'Now therefore ye are no more strangers and foreigners, but fellowcitizens with the saints, and of the household of God' – children of God! adopted into the household and family of God, belonging to God, related to God!

If we do not understand this we are missing the whole point of the Christian message and we will never understand this appeal for conduct and behaviour. As Christians we are not merely believers; we *are* believers; you cannot be Christians without believing; but the Christian is not merely one who has believed a certain body of doctrine. Nor, as Christians, are we merely forgiven. We *are* forgiven, thank God; there would be no hope for us if we were not forgiven. But Christianity is more than forgiveness. Neither does being a Christian stop at the rebirth, glorious though that is. We must go beyond that, for what does our rebirth mean? It means rebirth after the pattern and the image of the Lord Jesus Christ Himself. We have already been looking at this in chapter 4: 'Put on the new man', Paul says, 'which *after God* is created in righteousness and holiness of the truth'. The Christian is a child of God. He has been adopted into God's family. He is a partaker of the divine nature. He is born from above, he is born of the Spirit! And, of course, the trouble with those who object to living the Christian life is that they have no conception of such a blessing as this; they have never seen it at all, they are quite unaware of it, they think of Christianity as a moral code imposed upon them, and they resent it. Poor things! They are just ignorant of Christianity! Here is the reason for living the Christian life. We are to be imitators of God because we are children of God! God's people! That is what Christianity means.

But not only are we His children, we are His *dear* children! or
– a better translation – children beloved. The Apostle assures us
that we are not only children of God in the sense that we are in
that actual legal relationship; we are children beloved, He has
shown His love toward us and He goes on doing so, He shows
His care for us, His solicitude for us. Do you know, that if you
are a true Christian you are dear to God? I have the authority
of the Lord Jesus Christ for saying this. The very hairs of your
head are all numbered! God knows His children one by one, He
is interested in us; the analogy is a human one, but we can multiply
it by infinity. God's interest in and concern for His children is
infinitely greater than the greatest and the noblest natural parent's
interest in his or her child. God is lovingly concerned about us.
He watches us just as the natural parent watches his little child
beginning to walk for the first time, or as the child goes out to
school for the first time. He stands at the gate and watches him
as he goes round the corner and out of sight; that is an expression
of loving interest. It is not a mechanical relationship; children
are dear, children are beloved! And, says Paul, that is God's
relationship to us; He has looked down upon us, and He loves
us; He is interested in us, we are dear to His heart, He is taking
an intense personal interest in us.

What, then, is to be our response to God's love? Quite inevitably,
if I believe and realise something of this truth, the greatest desire
of my life should be to show my love to Him, and to please Him
in everything. Nothing gives God greater joy – I say it on the
authority of my text, and on all the parallel texts in the Scriptures
– than to see His children living in a manner that is worthy of
Him. So if we are children worthy of the name, our supreme
desire in life should be to please Him and to give Him joy. We
are told that there is joy among the angels of God over one sinner
that repenteth, and that joy is also in the heart of God as His
children live in a manner that is worthy of Him. 'Become imitators of God, as children beloved'!

Again, if we realise the truth of this relationship, our greatest
desire in life will be to be like God. Look at a little boy who loves
his father and knows his father's love to him; his great desire is

to be like his father; He likes to sit in his father's chair; likes to take his father's place; tries to walk like his father; tries to speak like his father! He is imitating his father the whole time. He wants to grow up to be a man like his father! That is human nature, is it not? That is ordinary human love at its best. Again, I say, cleanse it, multiply it by infinity, and you discover what the Apostle is telling us to do. 'Become imitators of God' – why? – because He is your Father!

And then another deduction. The honour of the family is in our hands. That is true of us always as children in a family. We are representatives of the family, and as people look at us they not only judge us, they judge our families. That is why we are all so careful to tell our children to behave themselves when they go out to a little party. We know that it is not the children who are going to be criticised, but the parents. The child is the representative of the family, and therefore he should not be thinking of himself so much as of the family. 'No man liveth unto himself', says Paul to the Roman believers, 'no man dieth unto himself'. To his Lord every man stands. And we, if we are Christians, cannot divorce ourselves from our relationship to God. We cannot say, I want to be saved, I don't want to go to hell, I want to be forgiven, but I don't want this Christian life; I want to have a good time in such-and-such a place, and I want to go into this, that and the other. But you must not argue like that if you are a Christian; if you are a child of God you are a member of the family, and what matters is the honour of the family, not what *you* want and like. These things operate as principles in human relationships, how much more so here – 'Becomes imitators of God'!

Surely, the privilege of belonging to such a family even while we are yet in this world as it is, round and about us, with all its sin and its shame and its muddle and its agony, should move and animate us. Is there a greater privilege than being a Christian? Can you mention to me anything in this world that is comparable to the fact that we are children of *God*, that we belong to His family, the household of *God*? We are not at home in this world; our citizenship is in heaven; we belong there; He leaves us in this world of time for a while, and the world is antagonistic, it is hateful and sinful. But we have been called out of its darkness, we have been taken out of the kingdom of Satan, translated into the kingdom of God's dear Son, adopted into the heavenly family and put into this royal household. Is there any honour in the world that is comparable to that?

If you realise the honour, you will be careful about your behaviour. As you walk down the street you will say to yourself, I am a child of God, I belong to the royal family of heaven, and people are looking at me and watching me, and they are perfectly right in doing so; they will be judging God, they will be judging Christ by what they see in me. So, Paul says, 'Be imitators of God', walk down the street, if I may so put it, as God's representative. Live in such a way that everybody knowing you will be made to think of God, because you are a child of God. Our Lord Himself put it so clearly: 'A new commandment', He says, 'I give unto you, that ye love one another; by this *shall all men know that ye are my disciples.*' By looking at you and seeing you loving one another they will say, What is this? we have never seen anything like this before, this cannot happen among ordinary men. And they will be driven to the only adequate explanation: By this shall all men know that ye are my disciples'. Or again, as our Lord put it in the Sermon on the Mount: 'Let your light so shine before men, that they may see your good works, and glorify your Father which is in heaven.' In other words, the conduct of the Christian makes people think of his heavenly Father; they cannot look at the child in his walk and behaviour, without thinking of the Father. 'Become imitators of God, as children beloved'!

One final question – how are we to imitate God? The Apostle answers us. He tells us that we are to do it by walking in love – 'and walk in love'! He means that the whole of our conduct and conversation must be carried on in the realm and in the sphere of love, for God is love. He has already hinted at it in the last verse of the previous chapter: 'Be ye kind one to another, tenderhearted, forgiving one another, *even as* God for Christ's sake hath forgiven you'. And as our Lord Himself said in His Sermon on the Mount: 'Be ye therefore perfect, even as your Father which is in heaven is perfect' (Matthew 5:48). He says you should live in this way, 'that ye may be the children of your Father which is in heaven'. And how does He behave? 'He maketh His sun to rise on the evil and on the good, and sendeth rain on the just and on the unjust.' That is how God behaves! He does not confine His blessings to the good and the just. Not at all! He gives them to the evil and the unjust also. What then am I to do? Our Lord Himself supplies the answer: 'Love your enemies, bless them that curse you; do good to them that hate you, and pray for them which despitefully use you and persecute you'. In other words, we must apply to others what God has done to us. Even if people are our enemies and treat us in a very cruel and most unjustifiable manner, we are to deal with them as God deals with His enemies, with the unjust and the vile and the evil. We are called upon, as God's children beloved, to imitate God, and this means that we will not live an ordinary sort of life. Our life will be absolutely different.

'If', says our Lord, 'you love them which love you, what reward have ye? Do not even the publicans the same?' Publicans love those who love them; there is nothing clever or extraordinary about that. And then He says, 'If ye salute your *brethren* only, what do ye more than others? Do not even the publicans so?' There is nothing wonderful in that! It is the world's morality. 'What do ye more than others?' says our Lord; which really means, 'What is there special about that?' Our life, you see, is to be a very special one. You cannot be a child of God without being a very special person! There is nothing ordinary about the Christian; he is extra-ordinary, in every single respect, because he is a child of God, and he does things that nobody else can do – the 'publicans' cannot, the non-Christians cannot, he alone can! Our whole life is to be special, because we are children of God.

And so we put it finally, 'Be ye therefore perfect, even as your Father which is in heaven is perfect.' Ah! but, you say, He is in heaven, and I am on earth, can it be done on earth? It can, says Paul; 'walk in love, as Christ also hath loved us and hath given himself for us an offering and a sacrifice to God for a sweet-smelling savour'. We shall look at it in greater detail later. It is one of the most glorious statements in the whole Bible. But here it is, lest somebody might feel, Ah! that is all right, it is all very well to say 'Be ye perfect, as your Father which is in heaven is perfect', but I am walking the streets of this sinful world. It is all right, you have got a Brother, who has been in it, and He has walked the streets of this world, and this is how He walked – in love! He *gave* Himself, for us, an offering and a sacrifice. He gave His life, His body to be broken, His blood to be shed, for His enemies, for sinners vile. And it went up to God as a sweet-smelling savour. And as you and I imitate God and imitate the Lord Jesus Christ, who is the firstborn amongst many brethren, our lives and our activities will go up into the presence of God as a sweetsmelling savour; God will enjoy it, God's father-heart will swell with love and satisfaction as He sees His children imitating Him in the sight of men.

Be, become, therefore, imitators of God, as children beloved.

24

The Atoning Work of Christ

'And walk in love, as Christ also hath loved us, and
hath given himself for us an offering and a sacrifice
to God for a sweetsmelling savour.'

Ephesians 5:2

In verses 1 and 2 of this chapter the Apostle is making the highest
conceivable appeal to Christian people for conduct and behaviour
worthy of their high calling in Christ Jesus. After urging them
to become imitators of God as children beloved, he next says,
'Walk in love, as Christ also hath loved us'. In other words, the
Apostle teaches us that the whole of our Christian life is to be
ordered in the realm of love. This is the ultimate test of our
Christian profession. All our professions and claims and activities
must be measured by this yardstick of love. 'Though I speak with
the tongues of men and of angels, and have not love, I am become
as sounding brass, or a tinkling cymbal'. Though I have wonderful
understanding and enlightenment in doctrine, and faith so that I
could remove mountains, and have not love, it profits me
nothing. Though I give my body to be burned – not only am
very active in church or religious or Christian work, but even
give my body to be burned – and have not love, there is nothing
in it, it is of no value at all. Love is the test; everything in the
Christian life is designed to bring us to this condition. We are
to be like God, as the children of God. God is love, and therefore
the greatest characteristic of our lives, as the Apostle puts it, is
to be love! to walk in love! The Apostle is very anxious that we
should know what that means; he has already put it to us partly,
at the end of chapter 4, in terms of what God has done for us,
where he says, 'Be ye kind one to another, tenderhearted, forgiving one another, even as God for Christ's sake hath forgiven

[300]

you.' And here he goes on to show that the highest manifestation of God's love is that which we see in our Lord and Saviour Jesus Christ and in His work on our behalf. 'Walk in love', he says, '*even as* Christ also hath loved us.' And then he goes on to show us how our Lord has shown that love to us.

Now once more I cannot proceed without turning aside to point out that we are here confronted by one of these amazing things in the style and characteristic of this great man of God as a writer. Here in this most practical section of his Epistle, when he is talking about our behaviour towards others, our speech, and our conduct, down to the minutest detail, suddenly in the midst of it all he introduces this tremendous statement of the doctrine of the Atonement. He cannot leave it alone, because in the Christian life, doctrine and behaviour are indissolubly linked together and they must never be separated. It is no use talking about conduct and behaviour in a Christian sense without doctrine. And when people neglect doctrine you will always see it in their lives. But on the other hand doctrine alone is of no value. The two things must and will go together. And here, you see, suddenly, as I say, unexpectedly in the midst of this most practical section, he holds before us one of his own greatest and mightiest statements of the doctrine of the Atonement. I do not know what you feel, but I always feel that there is nothing more exciting than to read this man's epistles. You never know what is coming; and if you still feel that, when you have finished the first three chapters of the Epistle to the Ephesians, you have finished with doctrine, you will see that you are making a big mistake. Suddenly it comes out when you are least expecting it, it does not matter where he is nor what he is handling – these great central truths, they are always in his mind and in his heart, and he suddenly throws them out without any warning whatsoever.

Here therefore, it seems to me, the Apostle tells us two main things, and we must look at them. First, of course, he gives us this objective statement of the doctrine of the Atonement clearly defined and stated. But then secondly he shows us how that doctrine is to influence us and to become our example as Christian people. The two things are here. And then as we look at them it behoves us obviously to keep certain points in our mind. The first thing is this.

The Scriptures are never satisfied with a mere general statement about the love of God. In fact it seems to me that the fundamental trouble, speaking generally, in the Christian Church today is that the love of God is thought of and conceived of in purely general terms; the love of God is being put up *against* the doctrines, and that is why it is not being understood nor appreciated as it should be. The Bible never leaves the love of God as something vague and general. People sometimes say: Of course, I am not interested in doctrines and theology, I am interested in love, and what we want is to get everyone loving one another, and we must be manifesting this love. But they do not tell you what the love is; they do not understand the love of God, they do not know what it means; all they have is some sickly, sentimental notion as to God's love; but the Bible never leaves it at that, it knows us so well that it knows that it must define exactly the use of its own terms. We must know what this love is, and so Paul gives us this doctrinal exposition of it.

And the second point is that our conduct, as I say, is always determined by our doctrine. 'As a man thinks, so he is' (Proverbs 23:7). It is true in every realm. All of us by our conduct and behaviour are proclaiming our views, our philosophy of life. It is inevitable. Our behaviour is determined by our thinking; even if it is lack of thinking it comes out in our conduct. 'As a man thinks, so he is'. Very well, as a Christian thinks, and he thinks in terms of his doctrines, so he behaves. Inevitably our conduct is determined by our doctrine.

Before we look at the doctrinal background to the Apostle's statement, and then at its practical application, I would remind you that our realisation of the love of God and the love of the Lord Jesus Christ is to be measured by the extent to which we are manifesting this love in our lives. Isaac Watts is perfectly right when he says, 'Love so amazing, so divine, demands' – *demands*! Some people think they are being ultra-pious by changing *demands* into *shall have*. But that is quite wrong. If you feel that you have come to the end of the demand, you have not understood it; there is no end to it. 'Love so amazing, so divine *demands*' – and goes on demanding; Isaac Watts was right – '*demands* my soul, my life, my all.' You prove that He shall have it in your conduct, not as you sing, but as you behave in your home, at the bench, in the shop, or in the profession. It is much easier to sing it, than to practise it, but it is the practice alone that proves that you are really doing it.

We turn now to the statement of the doctrine. Notice the actual terms that the Apostle employs. 'Walk in love', he says, 'as Christ also hath loved us'. The first thing we shall consider is that Christ has loved us. The Apostle is saying that the whole of our Lord's activity was produced and determined solely and entirely by His love. He does not say that the measure of His love is that He loves His heavenly Father. The measure of Christ's love is that He loved *us*! You will never know the love of Christ truly until you have grasped the Christian doctrine of sin, until you realise the truth about *yourself*. If you feel yourself to be a very good person, who has lived a good life and done much good and has never done anybody any harm, well, of course, it would have been strange if He had not loved you, would it not? And that does not tell you very much about His love. But when you realise that the truth about us is what Paul is telling us in the fifth chapter of the Epistle to the Romans, it is then that you begin to see something of the love of God. What are we? We are not only without strength, we are ungodly, we are sinners, we are enemies of God, we are vile. 'In me', says Paul again, '(that is, in my flesh,) dwelleth no good thing'. But 'Christ hath loved *us*'! There is the measure! We cannot have a true conception of the love of the Lord Jesus Christ apart from the full teaching of the gospel. It is no use talking vaguely about love. You must have some standard by which to measure it. And this statement supplies it, 'He hath loved *us*'. Entirely of His own love He has loved us. There was nothing in us to recommend us to Him, nothing to draw His love, nothing to attract it. Ugly, vile, foul – those are the terms that are used; 'hateful, and hating one another', says Paul to Titus; that is what we were. And it is only to the extent that we realise what horrible creatures we are by nature and as the result of sin, and as the result of our inheritance from Adam, that we begin to understand the meaning of the love of God and the love of the Lord Jesus Christ. 'Hath loved *us*'! Paul has been describing us in our unregenerate state in the previous chapter – Gentiles who 'walk in the vanity of their mind, having the understanding darkened, being alienated from the life of God through the ignorance that is in them, because of the blindness of their heart: who being past feeling have given themselves over unto lasciviousness, to work all uncleanness with greediness'. That is the sort of people He has loved – loved *us*! That is the first statement.

The next thing Paul says is this: 'hath loved us, and given himself for us'. A better translation would be, 'hath given himself up for us'! He did not merely allow things to happen to Him. 'He hath *given himself* up.' He was active in this work. Clearly, the Apostle is anxious that this should be emphasised. Also he is emphasising the fact that He did not merely give up His *possessions*. Certainly, He did give up many possessions, as we are told, for example, in the exposition which the Apostle gives of this very phrase in the second chapter of the Epistle to the Philippians: 'who, being in the form of God, thought it not robbery to be equal with God': which really means, 'did not regard it as a prize to be held on to, to be clutched at'. He did not hold on to His prerogatives, the prerogatives of His eternal deity, but He laid them aside, He emptied Himself, He divested Himself of these signs and insignia of His everlasting glory, and 'made himself of no reputation'. Here is a theme to occupy us for all eternity! He gave up things which He possessed, and possessed as a right! He did not clutch on to this right of His, the prerogatives of Godhead there with the Father, and all their signs and accompaniments; no, He deliberately laid them aside. Or, as the Apostle puts it in writing the second Epistle to the Corinthians, 'though he was rich, yet for your sakes he became poor'.

In these statements there is an indication of the possessions which Christ laid aside; He gave up His possessions, He put them into the background, as it were, and not only took on human nature but came in the form of a servant; He humbled Himself, not only to become a man but to become a servant, an artisan. Consider all that was involved in 'laying aside'. But the Apostle's point is that He did not merely give up all those things, but He gave *Himself. Himself*! His life! His very Self! He gave it all up, as a sacrifice. Not the things which He could command and lay aside, but His very Self! Submitted Himself; sacrificed Himself utterly, absolutely! And, as I say again, we must emphasise the activity involved here, the positive nature of what He did. 'He gave up *himself* for us'. In chapter 10 of John's Gospel, our Lord puts it like this: 'Therefore doth my Father love me, because *I lay down my life, that I might take it again.* No man taketh it from me, but I lay it down of myself. I have power to lay it down, and I have power to take it again. This commandment have I received of my Father.' This corresponds with what the Apostle Paul is saying here. It adds to the measure of the love. It was not a passive submission. It was active, deliberate, and positive. He said towards the end that He *must* go to Jerusalem; 'the Son of man *must* be lifted up'. The disciples tried to dissuade Him, but He said, No, I *must* go. When they tried to defend Him, even Peter with a sword, He says, Put it back into its scabbard. Do you not know that I could command more than twelve legions of angels and could be carried to heaven without going through this? I have come to do it, I must, 'the hour is come'! We must emphasise the activity, the deliberate character of it all. *He gave Himself* up!

And then we come to these two great terms, 'an *offering*, and a *sacrifice*'. An offering is a gift that is presented, something that is offered to another. And what the Apostle here says is that Christ gave up Himself as an *offering* to God. But the word *offering* is not sufficient in itself to convey the whole of the Apostle's meaning. A second term is needed – 'a *sacrifice*'! To discover the meaning of sacrifice, we must go back to the Old Testament. The Apostle was a Pharisee, well versed in his Old Testament Scriptures; when he preached he always argued out his case from the Old Testament. The New Testament is a fulfilment of the Old; the Old points forward to the New and what the New means by *sacrifice* is what the Old means by *sacrifice*. The Holy Spirit guided the early Church, which was mainly Gentile in character, to preserve the Old Testament as absolutely essential; and a Christian who thinks he can do without the Old Testament is merely displaying his ignorance. You do not understand the New without the Old. Take a great Epistle like the Epistle to the Hebrews; you do not begin to understand it unless you know

[305]

the Old Testament teaching about sacrifices, and offerings, and shedding of blood, and so on.

A sacrifice was something which was offered by a priest upon an altar. In the Book of Leviticus in particular and in other Books as well, God gave full instructions to His servant Moses as to how all these various sacrifices should be defined and how they should be presented and offered. God was indicating to Moses by means of these types and symbols the only way whereby, finally, men could be reconciled to Him; they were all pointing forward to the Lord Jesus Christ, who is *the* Sacrifice. Under the old dispensation, an animal was taken and it had to be a perfect animal. It had to be free from all blemish. The high priest, representing the people, put his hands upon the head of the animal, thereby symbolically transferring the sins of the people to the animal. The animal was then slain; its life was taken and its blood was poured out and collected in a bowl. The animal was slain because it now received the punishment due to the guilt of the sins of the people, whose sins had been transferred to it. Next, the high priest took the blood and presented it to God in the innermost sanctuary of the temple, there before the ark; he sprinkled it on the ark and before the ark. Then the body of the animal was placed upon the altar in the temple's outer court, where they burned it, and the smell ascended up into the presence of God. That is what is meant by the term *sacrifice*! And the Apostle is here telling us that that is what was happening when the Lord Jesus Christ died upon the cross on Calvary's hill, when His body was broken and His blood was shed, an offering and a sacrifice to God!

But one more term needs explanation – 'an offering and a sacrifice to God for a *sweetsmelling savour*', or the '*savour of a sweet smell*'. What does that mean? Perhaps the simplest way of understanding it is to read two verses from the eighth chapter of the Book of Genesis, where we are told that, after the Flood, 'Noah builded an altar unto the Lord; and took of every clean beast, and of every clean fowl, and offered burnt offerings on the altar. And the Lord *smelled a sweet savour*; and the Lord said in his heart, I will not again curse the ground any more for man's sake. . . .' Here is this man whom God had chosen, this man who had pleased God and who was saved with his family in the ark; he comes out of the ark, and one of the first things he does is to build an altar, to show his gratitude to God. He takes clean animals, and offers them upon the altar, and he burns them, and the smell ascends, and it is pleasing to God.

This is an anthropomorphism, of course, but it gives us some conception of the pleasure and satisfaction that this sacrifice gave to God. It regards God as if He were a man, and He smells this smell ascending from the offering and the sacrifice, and it pleases Him. It was a sweet smell, it was satisfactory to God, God liked it, God enjoyed it. He smelled a sweet savour and then, because it pleased Him, He said in His heart, 'I will not again curse the ground any more for man's sake'. And here in Ephesians the Apostle is teaching us that the offering and the sacrifice of the Son of God upon the cross came up into the presence of God as something that pleased Him, that satisfied Him, something that gave Him joy and pleasure. Yes, but more, it means that God was indeed fully satisfied with what had been done. His law made certain demands upon sinners; and Christ's offering on behalf of sinners came up before God as a sweetsmelling savour, a savour of a sweet smell; God is perfectly satisfied. Our Lord said, 'It is finished'; and I believe the Father said, Yes, it is finished, it is enough, I require no more. The sacrifice offered on Calvary had ascended into the presence of God as 'a savour of a sweet smell'. God and His holy law are fully satisfied and pleased, and man is reconciled to God and can be forgiven.

But I must bring one further expression to your notice. 'He hath loved us, and hath given Himself an offering and a sacrifice to God for a sweetsmelling savour *for us*' – *for us*! What does this mean? It means, *in our stead, in our room, in our place*. Now the term itself, the word 'for', can be, but is not always, translated like that – I am not basing the whole of my doctrine on the word *for*: I am basing it on the word *for*, plus the use of the term *sacrifice* and the whole context. And taking them all together, it is certain that the *for* here means *in our stead*. It is vicarious, it is substitutionary; the word plus the context, I say, makes that inevitable. In a sense, the word *for* is neutral; we always have to interpret it in the light of its surrounding context, and as we do so here we are driven to the inevitable conclusion, that the Lord performed His sacrificial work in our stead, in our place, on our behalf.

[307]

Having looked at the terms, we are now able to draw our conclusions. What was it that was happening there on the cross? What is the meaning of the death of the Lord Jesus Christ? Is it just a case of passive resistance? Is *that* what we have got there? Is our Lord and Saviour Jesus Christ the supreme Pacifist? Is it just the case of a good and noble Person whose teaching was much too good for mankind? a Person centuries ahead of His time, who taught this wonderful ethic and who practised it in His life, though misunderstood and maligned? There He is, with His cruel enemies condemning Him to an unjust death; but instead of fighting, instead of raising an army, instead of even battling His case in court, He just does nothing – passive resistance! pacifism! He wants to conquer by love.

In view of what we have been saying, you must realise that that is impossible as an explanation. He gave Himself up. He was active! This is not a passive action! So the death of our Lord is not just a manifestation of the cruelty of men. In this transaction we must not put our emphasis upon men. Peter, preaching on the day of Pentecost at Jerusalem, said that what had happened was 'according to the predeterminate counsel and foreknowledge of God'! He repeats it again in his speech in the fourth chapter of the Book of the Acts of the Apostles where he says that it was God who had caused Herod and Pontius Pilate to do what they did to Him; God had already determined it. Therefore, do not look at men. Our Lord is not just submitting passively to the cruel actions of men; that is not what is happening at all! He came *in order* to go to Calvary. He could have avoided it, He could have escaped, but He set His face stedfastly to go to Jerusalem. He could have commanded more than twelve legions af angels to come to His aid, but He did not; He said, If I do that, how shall I fulfil all righteousness? The cup is there, and He had come to drain it; He says, 'Shall I say, Father, save me from this hour?' No! 'For this cause came I unto this hour' (John 12:27). All along the line it is the intense activity that is being emphasised. So that as we look at His death upon the cross we must not think of it as our Lord merely putting up with what men have done to Him in their cruelty and in their malignity. It is not even our Lord just going on being obedient to His Father's will, even though it includes suffering thus at the hands of men. In itself, that is not enough;

[308]

that is not sacrificing, it does not bring in the content of that great word with all the Old Testament parallels.

I say again that the great thing is the activity and the voluntary character of what was happening; 'No man taketh my life from me, I lay it down of myself'! said our Lord. He gave Himself up, He offered Himself as a sacrifice. He became, I say again, the Victim on whose head our sins were laid. That is the Old Testament imagery, that is what God taught Moses to teach the people. The sins must be transferred to the victim that is to be offered. And Christ Jesus made Himself a victim for us. And it was as One who had become Victim for us that He was smitten, that He was killed, that His blood was shed and His body broken. As a spotless lamb became the substitute for the sins of the people under the old dispensation, so did the Lord Jesus Christ become our Substitute. John the Baptist saw it at the very beginning, and pointing to Him, said, 'Behold the Lamb of God' – the Lamb that God Himself had provided – 'the Lamb of God, that taketh away the sins of the world!' A Sacrifice! The One to whom the sins and guilt are transferred, and who then is smitten and slain! God 'hath made him to be sin for us, who knew no sin; that we might be made the righteousness of God in him' (2 Corinthians 5:21). 'Who his own self bare our sins in his own body on the tree, that we, being dead to sins, should live unto righteousness: by whose stripes ye were healed' (1 Peter 2:24).

I can tell you why the Christian Church is as she is. She has been evacuating the biblical doctrine of the cross from the death of the cross, and has been describing it as some vague manifestation of love. Then she has been weeping in sorrow and in sympathy for Him. But He said to the women of Jerusalem, 'Weep not for me, but weep for yourselves'; do not be sorry for Me, He said, I have come to do this. 'I am the good Shepherd. The good Shepherd *giveth* his life for the sheep.' All the Scriptures, from beginning to end, emphasise the same thing, that it is in Christ's sacrificial work that we see the love of God; that God sent, and gave Him up even to the death of the cross, and laid upon Him, His only begotten Son, the sins of men. 'God so loved the world that he gave' – to the shame, the agony, the suffering, the separation between His Son and Himself when He was made sin – 'He gave his only begotten Son, that whosoever believeth in him should not perish, but have everlasting life'. That is the measure of the love!

And the Son gave Himself willingly and voluntarily. The Apostle writing to the Galatians says: 'Christ hath redeemed us from the curse of the law, being *made a curse* for us: for it is written, Cursed is everyone that hangeth on a tree.' His death was not mere passive resistance, it was not even the death of a martyr, but something infinitely greater. He was *made a curse!* He was made of a woman, made *under the law*, 'that he might redeem them that are under the law'. Made of a woman, made under the law, that He might receive the *curse* of the law! The law says, 'Cursed is every one that hangeth on a tree.' He was made a curse *for* us! Nothing less than that! He bore our sins. He took upon Him voluntarily our position. He had already indicated this at the beginning of His public ministry, when He went to John the Baptist to be baptised. John could not understand it, but He insisted upon John baptising Him, because He was identifying Himself with our sins! He did not need to be baptised – John was right in saying so – but as the Messiah, the Deliverer, He puts Himself in our position, our sins come upon Him, He takes the burden. He says, 'Suffer it to be so now, for thus it becometh us to fulfil all righteousness.' From the beginning to the end of His earthly ministry there was the same emphasis.

It is, therefore, quite fitting to say that no-one really begins to understand the love of God and the love of the Lord Jesus Christ who does not believe the substitutionary and penal doctrine of the Atonement. Think it out. Where do you see the love of God, if God's Son is simply suffering the cruelty and all that men are doing to Him, in a useless manner? What is the point of it? If it achieves nothing, if it is not substitutionary, if it is not penal, if He is not really *dealing* with sins, it is useless suffering. It is pointless, it is sheer cruelty, there is no love there. Oh, the tragedy, that men should think that they are exalting the love of God in that way, whereas in reality they are evacuating it of its real essence and of its endless and eternal profundities! Here is where you see the love of God, that 'God spared not his own Son, but delivered him up for us all'! He did not spare Him anything; He poured upon Him the vials of His wrath against sin. He did not spare Him *anything*. And it was *for us*, and because of His love for us! Not what *men* did to Him, but what *God* did to Him as the Judge of all the world, the righteous Judge eternal, the Holy Father – *that* is the supreme issue in the 'death of the cross'! And the Son *gave* Himself willingly, there was no compulsion. He set His face stedfastly. His one desire was to do His Father's will and thus to bring about our salvation. And it is only as you see Him as the innocent Victim, the Substitute, who has voluntarily put Himself in *our* place to receive *our* punishment, that you even begin to understand and to measure the eternal love of God in Jesus Christ our Lord. And the Apostle Paul confirms all that we read elsewhere in Scripture – 'as Christ also hath loved us and hath given himself for us an offering and a sacrifice to God for a sweetsmelling savour'.

What is the lesson for us? 'Walk in love *as* Christ also hath loved us.' The precept is obvious. Our love must flow from and correspond to that of our Lord Himself. He did not consider Himself. 'Let this mind be in your which was also in Christ Jesus.' 'Look not every man on his own things, but every man also on the things of others', says the Apostle in his Philippian Epistle. That is what our Lord did. 'Let *this* mind. . . .': what was His mind? He did not consider Himself, He did not demand His rights, He did not consider His innocence, He did not consider His feelings, He did not consider His comforts, He did not consider His *ease*; He did not consider Himself at all. He *gave* Himself *up*! 'Walk in love, as Christ also hath loved us, and hath given himself for us.'

Finally, I repeat what I said earlier, that our Lord accomplished His work for us *in spite of us*. As He argues at the end of the fifth chapter of Matthew's Gospel, in the Sermon on the Mount, there is no merit in loving those who love you; the Gentiles do that. There is nothing wonderful in being kind to those who are kind to you; the worst man in the world does that! But what makes us Christians and proves that we are such, is that we do to others what He has done for us. We are ungodly, sinners, enemies, vile, we have nothing to recommend us; and He gave Himself up for us as an offering and a sacrifice to God. So that when you

[311]

and I meet difficult people, people who have nothing to recommend them at all, people who are as vile and as objectionable and as foul as they can be, who attack us and persecute us and deal with us spitefully and malign us, we are to deal with them as our Lord dealt with us. Walk in love! Pray for them! Bring yourself to feel sorry for them; so sorry, that you will have a burning desire within you that they may be delivered; so sorry that you will get on your knees and feel deep heart concern for them because they are the victims of sin and of Satan. Love your enemies! Bless them that curse you! Pray for them that persecute you and use you spitefully and malign you. Walk in love, as Christ also hath loved us, and hath given Himself up for us an offering and a sacrifice to God as a sweetsmelling savour.

Is there anything in the world which is comparable to the privilege of being a Christian? We are asked and invited and called upon to live as Christ lived; and we are the only people in the world who can live as Christ lived. A man who is not a Christian cannot live like that. He needs to be born again, he must have a new nature and a new life. He must have his eyes opened to the blessed truth of the Gospel. Nothing but *that* can ever enable men and persuade men to walk in love even as Christ did. What a privilege, what an honour, what a high calling, to be imitators of God and of the Lord Jesus Christ!

25

The Distinct Functions of Church and State

'But fornication, and all uncleanness, or covetousness, let it not be once named among you, as becometh saints; neither filthiness, nor foolish talking,
nor jesting, which are not convenient: but rather
giving of thanks. For this ye know, that no whoremonger, nor unclean person, nor covetous man,
who is an idolater, hath any inheritance in the kingdom of Christ and of God.'

Ephesians 5:3-5

To begin with, I propose to consider these three striking verses in
a general manner only, feeling, as I hope to show, that before we
come to study them in detail it is vitally important that we should
look at them as a whole and gather one great lesson at least which
is taught here so clearly and which is needed very badly at this
present hour. First of all, however, I must remark on the Apostle's
use of the word *'but'*: 'But fornication, and all uncleanness', and
so on. Paul is about to contrast these various evil things with
that which we have been considering in the first two verses of
this fifth chapter: 'Be ye therefore imitators of God, as children
beloved; and walk in love, as Christ also hath loved us, and hath
given himself for us an offering and a sacrifice to God for a
sweetsmelling savour. *But*' – and at once you feel you have moved
into a different atmosphere.

As I contemplated this statement I confess that I came in a way
to understand the feelings of the Apostle Peter on the Mount of
Transfiguration in a way that I had never understood them before.
Our Lord took Peter and James and John up a certain mountain.

There He was transfigured before them and spoke with Moses and Elias. Peter was enjoying the whole situation so much that he said, 'Lord, let us make here three tabernacles, one for thee, and one for Moses, and one for Elias.' In other words, he wanted to stay there! He had never experienced anything like this before, neither had James and John. Seeing the Lord thus in His glory was heaven to Peter. What could be better than to put up tents and to stay there and remain in the wonderful enjoyment of it all? But he was not allowed to do so. Why not? Well, the answer is this. There they were up on the mountain in this rarefied, glorious atmosphere; yes, but the world was still there at the foot of the mount; indeed, at that very moment a poor man with a lunatic son had come in desperation to the rest of the apostles asking if they could help. So our Lord does not allow them to stay in the enjoyment there on the mountain-top, He leads them down, and there they find a great disputation going on, wrangling and arguing, everything as it were at cross purposes. Instead of staying on top of the mount putting up tents as Peter proposed, they have to come down to the plains and back again to the stark and ugly realities of life in this world as the result of sin. And that is exactly what we are told by this little word *but*.

Speaking for myself, I must confess that nothing would be more excellent and delightful than to continue with verses 1 and 2, looking at God and our relationship to Him, realising His love to us, that we are not only His children but dearly beloved children, and contemplating the Lord Jesus Christ and all He has done for us in His sacrificial atoning work on our behalf. How wonderful to go on for ever in such an atmosphere! 'But' we must not do that; we must follow the Scriptures and we must take the Scriptures as a whole. There is nothing more dangerous to the life of the soul than always to be reading our favourite passages and it is not only dangerous to the soul, it is an abuse of Scripture. We must follow the Scriptures wherever they may lead us or take us. There are many people today who say, I do not like this negative aspect of the truth, why can we not keep to the positive always? I say to them, very well, you keep to it, and you will soon discover why the negative is necessary. We must take the Scripture as it is, not simply take what pleases us. We must submit ourselves to it utterly and absolutely, and follow it every step of the way. In other words, Christianity is something which is very practical, and if we do not realise that, we have completely misunderstood the Scriptures. We are, of course, the children of God – thank God for all we have been learning in verses 1 and 2; and we are to be like Christ, to walk as He walked in love; yes, and the Scripture is so anxious that we should walk in a manner worthy of our Father in heaven and of Jesus Christ who has identified Himself with us, that it takes great pains to instruct us in the details of our walk, both negatively and positively. So far in this chapter we have had the positive, we are now coming to the negative.

And the message is this, that there are certain things which we as the children of God must *never* do. We must realise that there are certain things which are utterly incompatible with our life as the dear children of God and as those who are joined to the Lord Jesus Christ. People do not like negatives, but the fact is, that the extent to which you do not like negatives is the measure of your lack of spirituality. The whole object here is to show the importance of the *negative*.

But is it not enough just to contemplate our glorious position? Will not that solve all our problems? The answer is, No! The negative is painfully essential for several reasons. The first is that unfortunately we constantly need to be reminded, that the one grand end and object of Christianity and of salvation is to make us *holy*. Notice how the Apostle puts it in the first chapter of this Epistle: 'Blessed be the God and Father of our Lord Jesus Christ, who hath blessed us with all spiritual blessings in heavenly places in Christ; according as he hath chosen us in him before the foundation of the world', – what for? – 'that we should be *holy* and without blame before him in love.' That is the end and object of the Christian gospel, the Christian faith. But we are all so subjective; we have got troubles, so we want guidance; we want things to happen miraculously to us; we think that Christianity is there to do this, that and the other to us and for us. It is not, primarily. Thank God, it includes that, but we must never lose sight of the fact that the primary object of Christianity is to make us holy and unblameable in the presence of God. The

Apostle says it again in the second chapter of his Epistle to Titus, where he says that Christ 'gave himself for us', – what for? – 'that he might purify unto himself a peculiar people, zealous of good works'. He came in order to do precisely that, not simply to save us from hell and to give us forgiveness, but to purify unto Himself this people for His own peculiar possession; and it is their characteristic, that they deny ungodliness and unrighteousness and are zealous of good works. We always need to be reminded of that because, unfortunately, as a result of the Fall and the sin that remains in us, we are always reducing the ultimate end and objective of the Christian faith. We must, therefore, ever be reminded of it, so the negative becomes essential.

A second reason for the negative is that we are always in danger of not applying the Christian faith to ourselves, but of being content to enjoy it in a theoretical manner. That can be done very easily. What is there more enjoyable than a great exposition of truth such as we have in this Epistle by the Apostle? It is a great intellectual treat. But what is easier than just to take it in general and to say, How marvellous! how wonderful! and never apply it to ourselves at all. We have all done it, we are all guilty of it. And because of that we need to be brought right down to earth; we need the negatives.

Again, there is always the danger of Antinomianism, and in the following way. We have just been reading that our Lord Jesus Christ gave Himself for us, an offering and a sacrifice to God for a sweetsmelling savour. Therefore, we say, we are saved, and we are safe; if He has done that for us He will never let us go. But at this point we are liable to say to ourselves, Well, it does not matter very much, therefore, what I do. If my ultimate salvation is certain and assured, I can live as I like. That is Antinomianism! Some of the first Christians fell into that snare; Christians are always liable to fall into it. It is the particular danger of men and women who have the greatest understanding of the truth. A man who believes in justification by works is never in danger of Antinomianism. It is the peculiar danger of the man who understands doctrine and is interested in it, and who sees this glorious aspect especially of our being chosen and elected, and our assurance, and our final safety; the devil tempts him along the lines of Antinomianism. The Apostle knows that, so having given the positive, he says, '*But*', and begins to supply details in the negative.

A fourth reason is this. We ever need to be reminded that our Christianity and our profession of the Christian faith is something that is meant to show itself in every single detail of our life. Christianity is not something to be enjoyed only in a place of worship or when we are reading about it in the Bible or in other books; it must show itself in the most ordinary details of life, in *everything* that we do. That is why Paul again goes into details, and even mentions our ordinary conversation, for he knew perfectly well that it is quite possible to listen to an exposition of truth in a church gathering and then to go out and immediately start talking in a frivolous and flippant manner, and perhaps even worse. So he tells us not to do that, and shows us that it is a very poor grasp of Christian truth which only operates when we are listening to it and does not manifest and reveal itself everywhere, always, wherever we are and whatever the company, and whatever we may chance to be doing. Our Christianity must show itself *everywhere* in our lives.

I would also give this as a final reason. We always need to be reminded that the Christian life is the *fight* of faith. The Apostle Paul is very concerned about this. In the last chapter of the Epistle we are exhorted to 'put on the whole armour of God', Christian people! Why? Because 'we wrestle not against flesh and blood, but against principalities, against powers, against the rulers of the darkness of this world, against spiritual wickedness in high places'. We must not regard the Christian life as something which is received in one great experience and that thereafter problems and temptations never recur, for the believer is absolutely perfect. Not at all! It is the *fight* of faith and we need the whole armour of God; we have got to watch, and pray; we have got to realise that we are surrounded by enemies and foes seen and unseen, some of them within us, and during all our days we have to be on guard. And the Apostle illustrates his point by taking up these particular things that are dangerous to the soul and showing us, negatively, their utter incompatibility with the Christian life and profession.

This, then, is one's first general reaction to the Apostle's *but*, and his recourse to the use of negatives. Oh! I am no longer on the Mount of Transfiguration, but I am looking at the lunatic boy; I am down in the dull plains of life, I am back to the hard reality of life and living, I wish I could stay up there but I cannot; that experience awaits me in glory; I have to live in this world first; I must get on and see it through.

Again, one cannot but take note of the Apostle's method of dealing with these moral questions. As is his invariable custom, he deals with these problems of fornication, uncleanness, covetousness, filthiness, foolish talking, jesting, and all the rest of them, entirely in terms of his Christian doctrine. Notice the terms he uses – 'as becometh saints'; 'which are not convenient' – by which he means that these evil things are not becoming to, do not fit, do not suit, believers in Christ. And then specifically: 'This you know, that no whoremonger, nor unclean person, nor covetous man, who is an idolater, hath any inheritance in the kingdom of Christ and of God.' It is because of *that* kingdom, not the kingdoms of this earth, that Paul is concerned about these things. His concern is doctrinal – saints! becoming! convenient! kingdom of Christ and of God! In other words you will never find in the New Testament any appeal to people to be moral on the grounds which are so familiar to us. Maybe when you left home for the first time you promised your father and your mother that you would not do certain things; soon you begin to waver, and the moralist comes and says to you, Do not break your promise, remember what you promised your parents. But you will never find that kind of plea in the Bible; it belongs to the world; it is not a part of Christianity. The Apostle's exhortation is – because we are saints, because we are in the kingdom of Christ and of God, because of the things that are becoming in that realm. The New Testament is interested in morality, not because of the honour of the school, or the honour of the country, or the good of mankind; not a bit! Saints! Citizens of the Kingdom of Christ and of God! And again, it is not interested in morality in and of itself, it is not interested in morality as an idea, it is not interested in sins in and of themselves, and because they are bad, and because of their evil consequences and nefarious results. Not at all! There is nothing at all about them in those respects. Paul con-

[318]

centrates on the incompatibility of sin with who and what we are! His words apply to Christian people only, nobody else. If we do not understand these principles, we shall be misinterpreting the Scriptures.

Let us be intensely practical. Notice that the Apostle does not go into these sins in detail and then denounce them. He does not analyse them and expose them and give statistics, proving that people who take to drink or give way to various kinds of sin, suffer accordingly. Here, say certain reformers, are the results, and here are the statistics! I put the matter in this way for the following reason. There are many societies in the world today that are concerned about the moral situation, and they always put it in terms of statistics. They say, 'Now look here, so much is spent on drink and on tobacco every year, and yet people are complaining that so little is spent on the National Health Service', and so on. Or they look at the matter from the standpoint of the diseases contracted by the people who are guilty of these things – look at the consequences! All perfectly true! But the Apostle does not do that at all! It simply is not here. Nor is it to be found anywhere in the Bible. He does not just denounce these things in and of themselves and lash at them.

I am calling attention to this because it does seem to me to be urgently important that we should become clear in our minds as to the relationship of the Christian Church to moral problems and moral organisations in the world. There are, as I say, morality councils. I received a letter recently from a high Church dignitary asking me to attend a meeting of The Morality Council, to advertise it, and so on. I believe that I owe it to my friends to tell them why, as a minister of the gospel, I keep clear of such things, why I do not have a Temperance Sunday, then a Moral Sunday, and all these various other Sundays, and why I do not take part in these organisations and activities. You are aware of the morality councils, temperance societies, and various other societies to look after this interest and that. They are all involved in improving the moral situation. And indeed, we must be concerned about the moral situation, but to me it is very urgent that we should be clear as to *how* we should be concerned and what part we are to play in all this. Very recently an important series of meetings has been held; the Magistrates' Association meetings have been held in London, and they have been addressed by various people. And in the reports of these meetings, I notice a marked element of confusion. For instance, take statements about juvenile delinquency made by a distinguished statesman who, I am told, is a practising Christian. He said: 'The prevention of crime calls for understanding and action by society as a whole.' He then referred to the 'insolence and apparent disregard for justice which is prevalent among our young people of a certain age today. . . .' 'We are dependent', he continued, 'on the courts, and the police, and all the other different agencies, to work with us in free synthesis, and thus to strive to work for and defend liberty. Any attempt to change that system would, I am sure, be an inroad on liberty. . . . My appeal is to a wider audience, to the churches, to parents, and to teachers, to do their part in dealing with the problems of juvenile crime; without them we are all powerless.' In these words, I suggest, is seen a characteristic confusion, that is not confined to statesmen alone, but, alas, is also found in the Church herself. And it is in order to indicate the danger which results from this confusion, that I am calling attention to this subject. The Apostle compels me to do so, for his way of approaching the situation is not the one that I have just been representing to you. How, then, do I justify my contention that the Church is not to be interested in the manner indicated, and that this appeal from a statesman to 'the churches and the teachers and the parents' is a complete misunderstanding of the Scriptures?

I begin by asking a question. What have all these movements and organisations really achieved? They have multiplied from the days of the Victorians onwards. We have never had so many. What have they achieved in the matter of temperance or in the matter of morality? Look at the facts! Why are men so concerned about these problems? Why is the Society of Magistrates informed that 'There are five thousand people now sleeping three in a cell in our prisons, the highest figure on record'? And this, in spite of these societies and these special Sundays and appeals, and the money that is given to them! Is it not about time that we asked, What do these moral efforts really achieve?

Before we give our time and energy, and our Sundays which

are meant for the preaching of the Gospel, to such activities, we are entitled to ask, What does all this lead to? I would have thought that the moral state of this country today shows that there is a sense in which *all* such activities are futile. You cannot persuade people in this way, for the very good reason that the New Testament doctrine of sin shows the thing to be impossible. I like many of the men who belong to and support Societies of this kind. I know they are honest and sincere men, but I never speak on their platforms, not even that of the Lord's Day Observance Society, because you cannot make a man observe the Lord's Day by Act of Parliament; that is not the way to do it.

I would also state it as my firm conviction that such activities are not a part of the Church's business as such. And here I feel the confusion comes in as between the realm of the Church and the realm of the State. The Church is appointed and ordained of God; so is the State, says the Apostle in Romans 13 and elsewhere. They are both appointed by God. God is working in this world today in these two realms, the realm of the Church, the realm of the State. God appointed the State, the powers that be, the rulers, judges and magistrates. The two realms are both meant to work in their appointed ways, and there should never be any confusion between them. And as I see the position today, this is largely the trouble, that the people who ought to be preaching the gospel are preaching politics and morality, and those whose business it is to handle politics and morality are trying to preach. As a result there is utter confusion and both realms are failing to carry out the thing for which God has ordained them.

The Christian Church is not a moral agency. What is she then? She is a regenerating agency! She is *not* a moral agency; there are many other moral agencies; the Church is not, she is supernatural, she is divine, she is filled with the Spirit; she converts men, she regenerates men; I say *she* does it, she is used of God to do it. That is her realm. Furthermore, the Church does not exist to produce good men. The Church exists to produce new men! And a new man is infinitely greater than a good man; you can be a good man without being a Christian at all. I repeat the word; the Church exists not to produce moral men, but to produce those who, in Scripture, are called *saints*. If you do not see that

[321]

distinction, you do not know what Christianity is! Certainly a Christian is a good man and a moral man, but if you simply describe him in those terms you are insulting him; you are not describing him. The Christian is a *saint*! He is a regenerate man! He is a child of God! He belongs to Christ, he is 'in Christ'! We are not in the realm of morality and goodness, we are in the realm of sainthood and of the Spirit! And therefore I argue that the acceptance of a moral-agency role by the Church means that the Church is misrepresenting her own message. It is for this reason that I cannot pay any attention to the appeals of the distinguished statesman whom I quoted earlier. It is insulting to the Christian Church to appeal to her as you appeal to school teachers and parents and various other people who have to try to deal with the problem of juvenile delinquency; it is failing to understand what she is and what she is meant to do.

Let us be clear about this. The Church is not a Department of State. And it seems to me that while there is union between Church and State this confusion is bound to persist. But we must reject it with the whole of our being; it is a serious misunderstanding of the nature of the Church; she is not merely a moral agency. Erastianism is in a sense a denial of the Christian message. The State is not above the Church. The Church is not just *one* of the activities of the State. The Church does not belong to the same realm as the State; it is the Kingdom of Christ and of God! And we must ever fight for this distinction.

The business of Christian preaching is not merely to restrain and to prevent sin. But when the Church preaches morality and links herself with such movements as I have been mentioning, she puts herself into that negative position. I know of nothing that is doing more harm to the Christian Church and to the gospel today than the impression that is given that the Church's business is always to be protesting about this or that. Is it not a common complaint of the unconverted that if they go to Church they will simply have to listen to preachers denouncing atomic bombs, or talking about the race question, or denouncing drink and tobacco, or some other disputed thing; and, they say, the Church is negative; it is always prohibiting things and holding you down. And the result is they will not even listen to the gospel. It is a complete misrepresentation of the Church and her message!

If we remain on the moral level only, or give the impression that the Church is one of the agencies that the State proposes to use in order to deal with such problems as, for instance, juvenile delinquency, then, I say, the Church is leaving out the greatest thing of all, namely, our relationship to God! Statesmen, indeed all servants of the State, doubtless desire to have good moral conditions, and to keep men from open sin; that is perfectly right in their sphere. But the gospel is at work in a very different way. A man may not be guilty of any one of these delinquencies, and yet the New Testament says that, as far as his relationship to God is concerned, he is as bad as the man who lives in the gutter. And as I am never tired of asserting, I am not at all sure but that, from the standpoint of the gospel, the most dangerous people today are the good, moral men, the good pagans! They feel they do not need the gospel, they are self-sufficient, they do not give way to intemperance in any shape or form, they are paragons of all the virtues; yes, but the New Testament says they are as much damned as the drunkard and the wife-beater and the adulterer. The fact is that the Christian Church is concerned about a man's relationship to God, and says that if that is not right, all these other things do not matter. If the Church remains at that moral-agency level only, she is leaving out of her message the most glorious and vital thing of all, which is the dynamic of the gospel. 'I am not ashamed of the gospel of Christ', says Paul to the Roman believers. Because it has got great moral uplift value? Not at all! – 'because it is the *power of God* unto salvation to everyone that believeth'. When it comes to a man, it does not merely address a moral appeal to him, it lays hold upon him, it puts new life into him, it changes him, it makes a new man of him. It is dynamic! But if we simply talk about goodness as such, and the importance of observing laws and being moral, and not doing this and that, the dynamic is missing, and salvation is not preached.

I would also emphasise that if and when the Church is spending her time in preaching on the negative aspect, she is neglecting the positive message which alone *can* deal, and *does* deal, with the very problem that the unconverted are facing, and this to me is of the utmost importance. I maintain that if I spent my Sundays preaching on these different *days* that are appointed, and supporting these good causes and societies and so on, I would be wasting my time and the time of the church. For this reason, that while I am doing that, I cannot be preaching this positive message of salvation and deliverance. And I would go further, and say that there is nothing in the end that can deal with this problem but the dynamic, the spiritual power, of the gospel. It is the power of God unto salvation!

To illustrate what I mean, I mention the early part of the eighteenth century. The moral conditions in England then were even worse than they are today. Read *England: Before and After Wesley*, by J. Wesley Bready. Read of the conditions in London and elsewhere in this country. There were efforts being made then to deal with the problem but they accomplished nothing. Suddenly came the evangelical awakening with the gospel preached as the power of God unto salvation and the Holy Spirit poured out in revival. What happened? The moral conditions were changed! – not entirely, but the change is almost incredible! That is how it happened then. It had already happened at the time of the Reformation. It had happened in a sense in much the same way in the 17th century as the result of the Puritans. It happened also to a great extent in the 19th century. When the church preaches the gospel as the power of God, as spiritual dynamic that can operate in men and change them, it is *then* that she deals with the social problem; not when she is talking about the social problem, and giving statistics and making moral appeals. *That* is a waste of time, and we must reject it as a temptation from the devil! I do not hesitate to say so. The devil is perfectly satisfied as long as the church is just reading, Sunday by Sunday, little moral essays, trying to give a little moral uplift, and making an appeal to people to be decent. I am certain that at such times the devil rejoices, because he knows that his kingdom will not be affected.

What, then, is the relationship of the church to this moral situation? I suggest that, in the first place, the Church deals directly with the moral situation in the preaching of a gospel that can convert and change men. Secondly, by producing Christians in number, it also affects the life of the State for good. In any case, Christians cannot get desirable improvements by Acts of Parliament today, for the Christian vote is so small! Christians are but a small proportion of the community. And the powers that be know perfectly well that they can ignore the Christian church, and they do ignore the Christian church. They are interested in votes, they are interested in majorities, they keep their eyes on election results; it is true of all the parties, and they pay scant attention to us, for we do not count. But last century, as the result of the great awakening and revival in the 18th century, and then the revivals of 1858 and 1859, there were so many Christians in this country that statesmen had to pay attention to the Christian vote, to the so-called Nonconformist vote! It was so powerful that Charles Stewart Parnell was really driven out of public life by the Nonconformist Vote! There were, in fact, so many Christian voters that the State had to listen to their voice. Therefore, if Christians want to help the State, the best way of doing it is by preaching a gospel which will produce so many Christians that the State will have to pay attention to what we say. But, as long as nothing more than morality is preached, not only does the State not listen, but Christians are not being produced. Traditions that come down from grandfather to father and to son are gradually dying out, people are no longer influenced by such things; the churches are empty, and the Christian view does not count at all. So if I want to help the State, this is my way: try to fill the State with Christian believers, new men and women in Christ Jesus. That is the way to help the State. I say that everything else is the business of the State, it is the sphere of the State, appointed by God to do a certain work. But the two tasks, as we must see, are very different. At the same time, I agree that Christian men and women should play their part in the State. Let Christian men and women become members of Councils, let them go into Parliament, let them do everything they can to influence the enactments of the State. Wilberforce and Shaftesbury in the 19th century set an example to others. It is not ministers occupying pulpits who should be preaching political sermons. Let them preach the gospel to the Wilberforces and the Shaftesburys, to encourage them, to build them up in the faith,

[325]

to give them confidence. Then those who are called to such a work can go into Parliament, to speak and act and to organise movements. It is the laymen who are to do this, not the church!

But what is the State to do? The Apostle makes this quite clear in the thirteenth chapter of Romans. It is the business of the State to deal with certain matters by laws and enactments. It exists to prevent crime, to control crime as far as possible by every legitimate method. And not only so, but it is the business of the State to *punish* crime. 'The magistrate beareth not the *sword* in vain'! Yet some moderns are prepared to say that punishments should be abolished. They tell us that if we are only kind and speak in a kindly way to thugs, to cowardly persons who attack children and old women, we will gradually make better men of them. That is a complete misunderstanding of the doctrine of sin and the biblical doctrine of the State. It is the duty of the State to *punish*. People are to be kept under *law* until they come under grace. It is as idle and as futile to talk in a sweetly reasonable manner and to make moral appeals to a man who is governed by evil and lust and vice as it was for the late Mr. Neville Chamberlain to go and do a similar thing with a man like Hitler. The State is not to be preaching; the State is to use the sword; it is to govern; it is to pass Acts of Parliament; it is to *punish*, and to teach men that if they will not respond to a right view of life they merit punishment and will certainly receive it. Under law until you come under grace! Grace and law cannot be mixed, they do not belong to the same realm.

But some people say, Surely you are going too far, you are going to extremes; why should the church be opposed to these movements that are doing so much good? I reply that if you make doing good the end, then you must go into everything. I have got to admit that Christian Science does a great deal of good, I have known people stop drinking as the result of Christian Science, I have known people who are desperate worriers cease to worry: am I therefore to preach and to support Christian Science? Of course I am not? We are interested in truth, we are not concerned simply about things that do good. What we desire is that men should be brought into this new Christian relation-

[326]

ship; they must become *saints, children of God*! That is our business; the other is the realm of the State. Let the State continue with its activities. But let there be no confusion of thought, otherwise there will be failure in both realms. And I cannot but feel that it is because the State for twenty to thirty years has been thinking of itself as a reforming institution that there has been a substantial increase in crime of late. The State bears the sword and it is to punish. It is to teach people by that method if they will not listen to any other. Let the State exercise its proper function, let it cease to try to preach; and let the church continue to perform her function.

What is the function of the church? At the very outset there must be a realisation of the problem of sin; and the moment it is realised how deep-seated and violent sin is, it will also be realised that moral suasion never can work and never has worked to overcome it. It is because of the nature of sin that the Son of God had to leave heaven and go to the cross. Realising this, our business is to go on preaching the gospel in all its fulness. What else? Oh! this, I think, is the most important thing of all today: we are to pray for *revival*! We are but few voices; we are but a small company; what do we need? We need an authentication of our message which will arrest the attention of the world. We need a repetition of that which happened in the 18th century and other centuries. And when the church is experiencing revival, men and women will be changed and converted in large numbers, there will be more Christians, and they will influence the whole life of the State. Read your history and you will find that this is true. After a great revival in the church the whole moral life of a nation is elevated for a number of years. Then the influence of the revival wanes; down goes the moral condition. There is another revival and again there is this impact upon the whole life of the community – *invariably* it happens. So we must pray for revival, preach the full gospel, and plead with God to visit us and give us power. And in the meantime let individual Christians play their parts as citizens, as members of the State. Let *them* do it, not the Church; let them do it as citizens, exert their influence, do all they can. I am not criticising such efforts; it is the confusing

[327]

of the realms of Church and State that I am criticising. And if we can but get men and women again to realise how separate the two realms are and how different their functions and their objectives, I believe that in God's good time we shall see this modern, terrible problem of juvenile delinquency and general immorality, in all classes and in all ages, dealt with in the manner that God has used throughout the ages and the centuries. Oh! may God give us grace to think these things through, to have a clear understanding of them, that we may function as God intends us to function, to His glory.

26

Evils not even to be Named among Saints

'But fornication, and all uncleanness, or covetousness, let it not be once named among you, as becometh saints; neither filthiness, nor foolish talking,
nor jesting, which are not convenient: but rather
giving of thanks. For this ye know, that no whoremonger, nor unclean person, nor covetous man,
who is an idolater, hath any inheritance in the kingdom of Christ and of God.'

Ephesians 5:3-5

Thus far, we have considered these solemn words in a general
sense. We must now look at them in more detail. As the Apostle
himself follows this procedure we must also do so, however
painful a process it may be. While the Christian must never be
content merely with grasping principles, yet he must start with
principles. Much of the trouble in the Church today is undeniably
due to the fact that people do not grasp principles; they miss the
wood because of the trees. On the other hand, it is equally
dangerous to be concerned with principles only. We are meant
first to grasp the principles, and then we are meant to apply
them in detail to every action and aspect of our Christian life and
living. Notice how the Apostle comes down to details and covers
the whole of life.

We must never lose sight of the fact that the ultimate object of
Christianity is that we should be holy, and that we should walk
before God blameless, in love. That is the end and the object of
the Christian faith, it is to prepare us to walk before God in this
world and to spend our eternity in the *presence* of God. And if we

lose sight of that, well then, our Christianity so-called is utterly and entirely in vain. And what the Apostle is doing in this great section is to show these people how they are to become holy and to walk before God in love, in holiness and in purity.

There are certain things which as Christians we are to avoid and to renounce completely; we are to have nothing to do with them. What are they? Read again this terrible list, and remember that the Apostle was not trying to reform the world; he was writing to Christians. These words are addressed to members of the church at Ephesus, and other churches. They are not general, moral advice to the world outside, but words addressed to Christians; and therefore we deduce that Christians *need* such words to be addressed to them. And God knows that this is still the case. So this is not, I say, the church's general moral programme in which she can join with the world and the State in trying to clean up society. Not a bit of it! This is addressed to the church. And these are the things which we are told that Christians must renounce and avoid completely and entirely. Most of the Apostle's words explain themselves, but some of them need a little comment. First and foremost, 'fornication, and *all* uncleanness'. Every form, every type, every suggestion of it is to be avoided – '*uncleanness*'. We are to have nothing to do with it. Not only the specific thing itself but *all* uncleanness. We must work that out for ourselves. How prone we are at times to think that things done in the mind are not as bad as things done in actual practice; but *all* uncleanness, every form and type of it, is to be banished out of our lives.

Then we come to the next, which is *covetousness*. This means, of course, avarice, love of money; love of money as money; love of money partly for itself and partly because of what it can do for us, the things we can buy with money, the things we can procure with money, the things we can do if we have got money – in fact the love of all that money can do and achieve – that is what Paul is condemning under the word *covetousness*. We are to have nothing to do with it, we are to leave it alone; it belongs, he says, to the old life, but has nothing to do with the Christian life. Covetousness!

The next word is *filthiness*. This includes *obscenity*, anything that is obscene in speech. But it does not stop at that, it includes everything that is vile or disgusting in conduct also. And it is a good word that the Authorised translators have used here. How expressive it is! – filthiness! We are to have nothing to do with anything that is shameless and ugly and polluted – *filthiness*! It does not belong at all, says the Apostle, to the Christian life.

Then we come to *foolish talking*. This means empty, frivolous, senseless, thoughtless, foolish and sinful talk and speech. It is interesting to notice that Paul lists this with other things that are foul and revolting; he puts them into the same list. Empty, thoughtless chatter, babbling, he says, does not belong to the Christian life either. The Christian's talk must never be empty, senseless, frivolous; a Christian man should never be a frivolous person, nor should he speak in a frivolous, light, vapid, empty manner. It is typical of the life of the world, but it has got nothing to do with the Christian life. I must emphasise here the aspect of taking *thought*. The life of the Christian should be characterised by this element of thoughtfulness. And this not only applies to our speaking but even to our singing. 'Holy, holy, holy, Lord God Almighty'. We do not jig, we do not rush, such words as that. The difference between Christian and non-Christian singing, in a sense, is the element of thoughtfulness. We do not sing tunes, we sing the words! Let Christian singing be bright, certainly, but never breezy, never jaunty! And then the Apostle introduces the word *jesting*, that is to say, clever, polished, witty talk which has a harmful and sinful tendency. The original word has got the idea of *turning* in it – the turning of a phrase, the clever, sophisticated, witty, polished shafts which such people throw out, or any double meaning, any suggestiveness, anything which is ribald or scurrilous, in any sense. And that again, he says, should have no place in the Christian life, but must be banished altogether – '*foolish talking* and *jesting*, which are not convenient'. And again, in the fifth verse we find another terrible collection of words: *whoremonger, unclean person*, with a second mention of covetousness.

It is no part of the business of Christian preaching to spend too much time upon them; it surely should be enough for Christian people to mention them and to make certain that they are clear in their minds as to what they mean and represent, and what they stand for. The Apostle really is saying that these are the things that characterise non-Christian society and this is only too accurate a description of the life of pagans in the time of the Apostle. But these Ephesian Christians had been brought out of that sort of life; they had been translated from the kingdom of darkness into the kingdom of God's dear Son, and Paul is virtually saying to them, You cannot bring these evil things into Christ's kingdom; His kingdom is altogether different; He died to 'purify unto himself a peculiar people, zealous of good works.' Have nothing to do with these evil things any longer, they belong to the kind of life that is lived where the Gospel and its teaching are not in control.

But is it necessary for me to point out that the evils listed in our Epistle are becoming increasingly evident in the life of our country today? They are becoming more and more evident and prominent in the life of non-Christian people in every class, in the professions, in all circles of society. I remember as a young man being shocked at the kind of thing that could happen among learned men even in professional circles; the type of story that was told; one did not expect it from such people, but one got it! And it is still taking place! And I am sorry to add that foolish talking and jesting seem to be coming more and more into Christian work. Why should it be regarded as an excellent bit of technique for a speaker on a Christian platform to start with a joke? But this is the sort of thing that is coming in increasingly. And very often a story is told which has not the remotest connection with the Gospel, but it is told simply (as we are told) to make contact with the congregation! I once took part in an anniversary service in a certain part of this country. There were about eighteen hundred people present, and I had to sit and listen to the first speaker who – and I do not exaggerate – for a quarter of an hour simply told the people a number of stories. I could not see the remotest Christian application in any one of them, and indeed he did not even try to apply them. And the people were roaring with laughter, greatly enjoying themselves. But entertainment has got nothing to do with the Christian life or with the activities of the Christian church. *Foolish talking* and *jesting* have no place in the Christian life, and in Christian conduct, and among Christian people. They do not belong to Christianity. Even if you left out that which was grossly offensive, you would still be using the same terminology, the same kind of technique. Christians do not tell stories to one another; they have something much better to say to one another. That is what the Apostle is saying.

How then are we to avoid these evil things? The Apostle tells us. First of all he plainly tells us that we are not to do them. But he does not stop at that; he says, 'Let it not be once *named* among you'. You must not even *mention* it! You must not *hint* at it. You must not come anywhere near to approaching it. Not only must you not do these things, says the Apostle, do not talk about them, do not mention them, they are unmentionable, they should not come in at all in any shape or form, either in your speech or even in your thought.

Again, we have got to work this out in terms of our own modern position. The Apostle was writing in an age when they did not have daily newspapers or radio, or films, television and all the rest of it. In those days men were confined to speech in this matter of propagating unworthy ideas, and those ideas which lead to sinful action in practice. So Paul puts it in these terms, 'Let it not be once *named* among you', do not mention it! never introduce it in any shape or form! But now we have got to work this out in a greatly different context. And if it was difficult for Christian people in the first century of our era, what is it like now? There is a sense in which it is true to say that it was never more difficult to live the Christian life in its fulness than it is today. I do not mean that people are now more sinful, for they were committing all these sins long ago, but what I mean is, that the Christian is *surrounded* by incitements to engage in sin in a multiplicity of ways, whereas in days of old speech alone was chiefly involved.

The principle laid down by the Apostle is that we are to avoid in every shape and form *anything* that in any way is likely to draw us to do any one of these things – fornication, uncleanness, and all the rest of them. The whole art, the whole strategy, of Christian living is to keep watch against temptation at the beginning. If you allow temptation to get the slightest foothold in your mind, you will soon be overcome. It is the preliminary onslaught that must be met; that is why Paul says, 'Let it not be once *named* among you'. If you want to stop doing these things, he says, stop talking about them. If you watch the beginning, then you will not have so much trouble. We are to keep clear of everything and anything that in any way does us harm and tends to incline us in the direction of things that do not belong to the Christian life. And in these modern times we shall be fighting all along the line, from the moment we get up in the morning until we go to sleep at night; for the whole world is shouting these things at us. It does so in its newspapers. And you start with your newspaper in the morning, perhaps at the breakfast table. 'Let it not be once named among you', says Paul; yes, but it will be named, on the front page probably. It is essential to read your newspaper with discrimination, and to leave certain things unread. You wish to be abreast of the news, and to be an intelligent citizen; you also read your newspaper so that you can vote intelligently. But as you read, you must avoid, avert, keep yourself to the things that matter and avoid *all* others. Magazines likewise! You look at a railway bookstall, and you will see them! and you note their suggestiveness! You watch people buying them, magazines that by their very title tell you what they are. *For Men Only*! Why for men only? Obviously there is something wrong there. Then, the photographs and the advertisements! Avoid them, says Paul, have nothing to do with them, turn your eyes away. Plays! Films! Things that come over on the radio and television! the foolish talking, the jesting, the cleverness, the suggestion, the innuendo!

Do you want to make the fight more difficult for yourself? Do you think you really can stand up to the devil and to the lusts that are within you? Is it not better for you to do what the Apostle commands at the end of the thirteenth chapter of his Epistle to the Romans: 'Make no provision for the flesh'? If you look at things and read things that you know to be evil, you are making provision for the flesh. Do not be surprised, therefore, if you fall. Have nothing to do with them. Let them not be so much as once *named* among you! Nip them in the bud, stop at the beginning, do not have any interest at all in them. And what of the books, the novels, and even the biographies? Biographies are being increasingly published one after another, in which revolting details are being revealed which are of no value and of no uplift to anybody at all. There is a delight at the present time in pornography, and people are attracted to the unsavoury and unseemly. What the Apostle is really urging is the turning away from evil *in toto*. If there is a suspicion of a lack of cleanliness in a book or article, do not read it, you can do without the knowledge and the information. Oh! you say, but I am a student of sociology, I am interested in this and that. Then give up your interest, I say. To the pure all things are pure, but if you are not pure even good things can become bad. The whole emphasis of the Apostle is that we must have nothing to do with evil things, let them not even be *named* once among you, as becometh saints; keep as far away as you can from them all.

The Apostle next proceeds to tell us how to do this positively; he is not content to give us the negative only. He says, 'Let it not be once named among you; neither filthiness, nor foolish talking, nor jesting, which are not convenient, but rather' – here is the positive, what we are to do – 'giving of thanks'. This he elaborates later in the chapter (in verses 19 and 20), where he says, 'Speaking to yourselves in psalms and hymns and spiritual songs, singing and making melody in your heart to the Lord; giving thanks always for all things unto God and the Father in the name of our Lord Jesus Christ'. We shall look at these verses later. Meanwhile I remind you again that the Apostle is here dealing with what should prevail among Christian people in Christian circles. He is not telling us here how we are to talk and conduct ourselves with non-Christians, but in the church of God. And he stresses that we are to give thanks, even as he does in his Epistle to the Thessalonians – 'In everything give thanks: for this is the will of God in Christ Jesus concerning you' (1 Thessalonians 5:18).

The command has a wide application. The Christian is not to be dull! And if you draw the conclusion from what I have already been saying that I am advocating a kind of dull, mechanical life, you are very much mistaken. The Christian is not to be a dull and a morbid and an uninteresting person, not for a moment!

He is never to be guilty of jesting and smartness and cleverness, but that does not mean that he has got to be dull or pompous or uninteresting. Not at all! The Christian is a person who is to be giving thanks! He is to express joy and happiness in his life, for he is one who has got a profound sense of gratitude to God and to the Lord Jesus Christ within him, and is a man who *wants* to be giving thanks! So we must get rid of all notions of dulness. That is where a false Puritanism has so frequently done harm. There are people who have interpreted this kind of injunction in an entirely negative manner; their lives are negative; they avoid doing wrong things, it is true, but they are useless, they are of no value to anybody; they repel people from the Christian faith. The true Christian life is never a dull life. Giving thanks! says Paul. Joy is to be evident in the life of the Christian. It should show itself in his conversation, in his speech, and in all his deportment.

But, you may say, How are we to do this? Here again I must start with a negative. There are people who immediately interpret what I have just been saying by putting on a breeziness and a brightness. God forbid that we should ever do that! It is as bad as the dulness of your false Puritan. We must never put on anything. A joyful deportment must express itself in us because we are Christians. It is not to put on an inane grin and to be a bright and breezy and cheerful, backslapping kind of person. I cannot imagine the Apostle Paul doing a thing like that. Neither, let us remember, does it mean that we use glib catch phrases and clichés. There is a type of person who, in conversation, keeps on interjecting the words, Praise the Lord! Praise the Lord! thinking that by so doing, he is obeying the injunction: 'But rather giving of thanks'. But that is not what is meant by giving of thanks! Not catch phrases, not clichés, not the expressions which come lightly off the lips! It is rather something profound that is in the mind of the Apostle here, something that expresses the depth of being and of personality. And a man is not conscious of it, he does not do it by rote, or mechanically! It is the result of a change of heart, it is the new nature expressing itself, it is an evidence of life 'more abundant'.

The Apostle, it seems to me, interprets this statement of his own very perfectly in the last chapter of his Epistle to the Colossians, where he says: 'Let your speech be alway with grace, seasoned with salt, that ye may know how ye ought to answer every man' (4:6). A Christian's speech is to be always with grace; and it is seasoned with salt that keeps the polluting element out of it. The speech of the non-Christian is characterised by thoughtlessness, like a bubble, but the Christian's speech is thoughtful and profitable to others. People should always feel somewhat better from having spoken to us. They should have gathered something: not only positive instruction, but the coming into contact with us ought to do them good, and to make them feel better. There is something solid about the Christian in his conversation and in the whole of his life and activity.

I will go further. I find nothing here which excludes even an element of humour in the conversation of the Christian. But it is always, of course, a humour that is under control. It is never foolish talking, it is never jesting. The humour of the Christian is that which is natural, which is inevitable in the man. The Christian is never a man who tries to be funny; that is the thing that must go right out. He never does it simply in order to impress us, to call attention to himself, to cut a figure, or to be the centre of interest in a conversation, never! Nor does he monopolise the conversation. The better the Christian the better he is as a listener. If God has given him a gift of humour, let him use it, let it come out naturally; but it will always be controlled, it will never be ribald, never be scurrilous, it will never do harm to anybody; there will be a kind of beauty about it which will be of value and uplifting.

Thus the Christian is a man who is always to be giving thanks, in appearance, demeanour, deportment, conversation, speech; he always remembers who he is and what he is; he always realises that he is what he is by the grace of God; he is always conscious that he has been delivered from his old evil, foolish life, the life of the world with its glamour and its emptiness, and he thanks God he has been taken out of it. He does not want anything more to do with it. His new life is not the old life with a few bad things left out of it. I regret to have to say it, but whenever I hear certain Christians speak in public or in private I am still made to think that in their old lives they would have made excellent comedians. And I feel that that should never be true of a Christian. The same

[337]

kind of thing, the same sort of phrase, the same sort of attitude! They have cut out certain parts of it, but the main thing is still there! It should not be so with the Christian; he is a new man, and he knows that he has been delivered from 'the old man' at the cost of the death of the Son of God; he owes all to God and to Christ, and this should dominate the whole of his life and come out in all he says and does. We are all failures, we are all miserable sinners in these matters, are we not? But realise what we should be, says the Apostle. Let the things of the Spirit of God characterise our lives, so that as people come and talk to us they find something attractive about us, something clean and pure, something uplifting, intelligent, thoughtful and profitable; let them feel that there is an element of praise in your whole life, which causes them to say, What do they find to praise God about? where do they find it in a world like this? would that I were like that!

In the next place, notice that the Apostle is very much concerned about the question of covetousness, for he mentions it twice; and the Christian is to deal with this positively also. The love of money, Paul tells Timothy later, is the *root* of all evil. But the term 'covetousness' includes more than money; it also includes what money can achieve and produce, and if a man loves money in that way, it is not surprising if he makes shipwreck of his life. It is the root of *all* evil. The way to avoid this particular snare and danger is to put your money to right use! Give thanks to God through your money; show your gratitude to Him by supporting everything that belongs to Him and His Kingdom. If you feel that this thing is worrying you, kill it by giving the money in a right cause. I am not saying that a man should give away all his money, the New Testament does not say that. But it tells us that we are stewards of our possessions. A steward is not a man who gives everything away, but a man who uses it in the right way and does not put it to a wrong use. Were he to give it *all* away, he would not be a steward, for there would be nothing left to look after. The way to kill covetousness is to use our possessions to the glory of God as an expression of our thanksgiving and praise to God for all that He has done to us, for His sending of His dear Son to die for us and to deliver us out of that old life that was so foul and so evil, so superficial, so useless, the life of the world.

Furthermore, notice how the Apostle introduces the word '*saints*' into his appeal. 'Fornication, and all uncleanness, or covetousness, let it not be once named among you, as becometh *saints*'! Christians are *saints*! There is nothing that the Roman Catholic Church has done which is worse than her misuse of the word *saint*; according to that view, only certain Christians are saints. The Roman Church canonises them, and a man or woman then becomes Saint So-and-so. It is quite false. Every Christian is a saint. The Epistles are addressed to 'the *saints* at Corinth', *saints* in all the churches. 'As becometh *saints*', says Paul to all the members of the church at Ephesus. Everyone of us is a saint, so let us denounce and deny that Roman Catholic error. But what is a saint? He is a *holy person*, one that has been set on one side by God for His own pleasure and for His own use. We find the same word in the Old Testament. In Exodus and Leviticus and elsewhere we read about the vessels that were to be placed in the tabernacle and on the altar; they were called *holy vessels*, that is to say, they were not to be used for ordinary cooking or ordinary eating and drinking, but were set apart for a particular purpose and for God's own use. And the same thing is true of Christians. That is what a saint is, and you and I are saints. We have seen already that Christians are dearly beloved children of God, yes, and saints for that reason, God's own peculiar possession, those whom He has set apart for Himself, for His own delight and pleasure. And every true Christian is a saint! Remember who you are, says the Apostle. Remind yourself of it the first thing in the morning, say it as you are travelling to your office or your work in your car, or in the 'tube', or on the bus. If you are walking or cycling, say to yourself, I am a saint, I am a separated person, I am in the world but I am not of it, and there are certain things, therefore, which I must never do or even dream of doing.

Still further stress is supplied by the two expressions – 'as *becometh* saints', and 'which are *not convenient*'. Paul is saying that certain things do not become the saint, they are not befitting, they are not seemly. And here again the figure that is in his mind is one that is perfectly familiar to us all. There are some people who do not dress in a manner that is appropriate to their age or condition. If you saw a very old lady dressed as if she were twenty, you would say, It is not becoming! Certain things go together, certain things do not – Does that match the other thing? Is there a clash in those colours? Does the attire fit the occasion? 'As becometh'! Paul is using an illustration from the world of dress, and he says, We all know that some things do not become the Christian, they do not fit in with his profession, they are 'not convenient', they are not suitable. The man of the world watches a Christian going into a place he should not enter, and he says, Do you see what that Christian man is doing? And even the man of the world is shocked and amazed. Even the man of the world recognises the hypocrite, he knows that a certain kind of conduct does not fit with a true Christian profession. Let us all take note! As *becometh* saints!

And then the Apostle proceeds to condemn covetousness because it is *idolatry*. And there is no more terrible sin than idolatry. It means that you make a god of something, and you worship it. But *covetousness* is idolatry. The New Testament tells us so time and again. It does not matter what it is, anything that you and I tend to set up as the big thing, the central thing, in our lives, the thing about which we think and dream, the thing that engages our imagination, the thing that we *live* for, the thing that gives us the biggest thrill; if it is *anything* other than GOD, it is idolatry. And it is for every one of us to examine ourselves. Some people worship money, what it can do and what it can bring and get; some people worship status and position; others, their own brains and ability; still others, their own good looks. It is idolatry. And it is the ultimate sin. We are meant to worship GOD and to worship Him alone. There is but one God and He recognises *none* other. God forbid that any one of us should be worshipping or giving ourselves to *anybody* or *anything* save the only true and living GOD!

Let us ever remember that we are *saints*, set apart for God, meant to live to Him and His glory, to worship and to praise Him alone; and remembering it, let us realise that certain things are incompatible with Christianity, that we are to renounce them for ever, avoid them and evade them in every way conceivable, and positively live a life which is a constant expression of thanksgiving unto God, who has had mercy upon us and who, while we were yet sinners and enemies, ungodly and vile, gave His only begotten Son even unto the death of the cross, that we might be rescued and redeemed and have a share in His own eternal inheritance.

27

The Kingdom of Christ and of God

'For this ye know, that no whoremonger, nor unclean
person, nor covetous man, who is an idolater, hath
any inheritance in the kingdom of Christ and of God.'
Ephesians 5:5

In this fifth verse of Paul's fifth chapter we find ourselves faced
with a solemn warning and an alarming pronouncement concerning unclean living – 'This ye, know, that no whoremonger, nor
unclean person, nor covetous man, who is an idolater, hath any
inheritance' – no place at all! – 'in the kingdom of Christ and of
God.' Here then is a warning that we have got to face. We must
take Scripture as it is. The Apostle felt it necessary to administer
this severe warning to the Ephesian Christians, and we cannot
but conclude that it is necessary as a warning for Christians in all
ages and in all places.

In the first place we are struck by the way in which this warning
is presented. 'This ye know', says Paul – he means that this is
something beyond any doubt, beyond any disputation. This, he
says, is something that is self-evident. How can you be a Christian
at all without knowing it? How can you have learned Christ in
any real sense without being aware of this at once? He says that
no instruction is needed about it. And yet, though he says that,
he does remind them of it. In this modern age I repeat the
Apostle's question. Do we all know what is here stated? Are we
all perfectly clear about this? Is this something that needs no
demonstration or explication to the modern Christian? I can
only answer by saying that, though the Apostle says here that
this is something that ought to be self-evident, we cannot read
the epistles, nor indeed any of the writings of the New Testament,
without being struck by the fact that the writers are constantly

reminding people of such things as this, and doing so in a most solemn manner. In other words, it must be the case that many of us who ought to know certain things do not know them, and that is why we have to go into these things in detail. Now why is there this alarming possibility that we may know these things theoretically without truly *knowing* and understanding and grasping them? People are often surprised at this. They come to me sometimes and say, But fancy having to preach that to Christian people! My only answer is, The Apostles did so; and if it was necessary then, it is necessary now, and it is not difficult to know why it is always necessary. We must look into the matter.

We all stand in danger of being too subjective in our approach to the question of salvation and of redemption. We tend to start with ourselves, and so often we end with ourselves. We want something, and especially happiness, and we regard the gospel as something that will help us in our problem of seeking for it. And it is because we start with ourselves in that way, and with this quest for happiness, never looking at the whole position objectively, that we tend to get into difficulties. We want something, and in an entirely subjective way, we dictate what the something is. And the result is that we forget this other aspect that is infinitely more important, namely, our relationship to God, and our standing in His most holy sight.

Then, too, we are all such experts at rationalising our own sins and failures! Oh! we recognise the thing in somebody else, and we condemn it. But somehow or other, when we do the same thing, there is an easy explanation, and we are perfectly satisfied. We are all experts at that process. We are all on very good terms with ourselves, we do not like to be made miserable, and we do not like condemnation; and therefore we become experts at defending ourselves by adducing reasons and arguments and explanations – the thing really was not quite what it appeared to be! – and so we end on good terms with ourselves.

Once we go along that subjective road it is astounding how brilliant we can become at protecting ourselves and our own interests. In the second chapter of his Epistle to the Romans Paul tells us that we either 'excuse or accuse' in this respect; we *excuse* ourselves, we *accuse* others, about the selfsame things. At the back of it all is the subtlety of the devil, who can come to us as a friend, indeed as an angel of light, and can so easily persuade us, because we want to be persuaded, that what we accuse ourselves of as a sin is not really a sin at all, but just something natural – we were being over-punctilious, we were being hypersensitive in our consciences, we had developed a kind of morbid scrupulosity. And the Evil One comes and he puts it so plausibly, and we, wanting to be right with ourselves, yield to his blandishments. And so we are blinded, and get into such a state that it is necessary for the Apostle to speak to us in terms of the verse that is now before us.

There is a need for us constantly to look at the great statements of Scripture about the ultimate object of Christianity. What is the ultimate object of this Christian message, this Christian faith? It is to make us *holy* – not to make us happy! Happiness is a by-product of Christianity, it is not the central thing. We can never emphasise this too much. It is the differentiating point as between Christianity and the cults. Let me use the technical term – it is the *differentia* of the Christian faith. Here the first thing is *holiness*; in the cults it is happiness. When you examine the cults you find that they are always ministering to your happiness; they are not concerned about your holiness; they want you to get rid of this, that or the other, but do they want you to get rid of *sin*? Many of them do not even recognise the category of sin at all. But in Scripture the first thing, the great thing, the central thing, is that we be made *holy*. This is the great argument of the twelfth chapter of the Epistle to the Hebrews. Because the Lord loves us He chastens us and makes us unhappy for the time being, in order that we may be made holy. He wants us to be perfect. He is preparing us for Himself and for life with Him, therefore, of necessity, holiness must be the first thing and the most important thing. In other words, the thing we need to do increasingly is to look at God and at His view of, and His attitude towards sin and evil. Let us forget ourselves for the time being. We start with *God*; we have come into His presence, we are looking at Him. What HE thinks and says about evil and wrong-doing and about life and living, is what matters. What I feel, and what anybody else says to me, matters little in comparison. And so we turn to our text.

Let us observe the frequency with which the statement that is made in our text appears in the Scriptures. 'Know ye not', says Paul to the Corinthians, 'that the unrighteous shall not inherit the kingdom of God? Be not deceived: neither fornicators, nor idolaters, nor adulterers, nor effeminate, nor abusers of themselves with mankind, nor thieves, nor covetous, nor drunkards, nor revilers, nor extortioners, shall inherit the kingdom of God' (1 Corinthians 6:9-10). And again, later in the same Epistle, we find him saying, 'Be not deceived: evil communications corrupt good manners. Awake to righteousness, and sin not; for some have not the knowledge of God: I speak this to your shame' (15:33-34). And there follows a mighty dissertation on this subject. Then, in the Second Epistle to the Corinthians, we read: 'Be ye not unequally yoked together with unbelievers: for what fellowship hath righteousness with unrighteousness?' – Now answer that! – 'and what communion hath light with darkness?' – who can tell me? – 'and what concord hath Christ with Belial? or what part hath he that believeth with an infidel? and what agreement hath the temple of God with idols?' (6:14-16). The Apostle's questions are put, of course, to show that there is no fellowship, no agreement at all, between opposites; they are eternal incompatibles, and can never be brought together. There is no mean between two opposites, says Aristotle. These things are eternal antitheses. There can never be any grey in the realm where God reigns, it is one thing or the other, black or white, and they can never be mixed. The Apostle John teaches precisely the same thing. In the first chapter of his First Epistle he says: 'If we say that we have fellowship with him, and walk in darkness, we lie, and do not the truth.' And again in his second chapter: 'He that saith, I know Him, and keepeth not His commandments is a *liar*' – there is nothing else to say about him, he is just a barefaced liar! – 'and the truth is not in him'. He is a stranger to truth. And then, in the very last book of the Bible, as if to remind us, just at the very end, of a thing we are so prone to forget, we find it written, 'There shall in no wise enter into it [the holy city] any thing that defileth, neither whatsoever worketh abomination, or maketh a lie: but they which are written in the Lamb's book of life. . . . Blessed are they that do his commandments, that they may have right to the tree of life, and may enter in through the gates into the city. For without are dogs, and sorcerers, and whoremongers, and murderers, and idolaters, and whosoever loveth and maketh a lie' (Revelation 21:27; 22:14-15). Oh! this is an eternal distinction – *without*! – there they are, the people that John is talking about, that have no inheritance in the kingdom of Christ and of God, they are *without*, and outside eternally, and there they remain. They have no entrance into this *holy* city. Our Lord Himself said the same thing in the Sermon on the Mount: 'Not every one that saith unto me, Lord, Lord, shall enter into the kingdom of heaven; but he that doeth the will of my Father which is in heaven' (Matthew 7:21). This is New Testament Christianity. We are not thinking now about our own happiness or subjective feelings, are we? Here is the great, objective, eternal statement. There is a city to enter, and if we want to enter that city, then we must remember that it is a *holy* city and that the entrance to it is controlled by this category of *holiness*. Scripture speaks about holiness without which no man shall see the Lord. 'Blessed are the pure in heart, for *they*' – and nobody else – 'shall see God.'

Now the first question that confronts us is this: What exactly does this statement in the fifth verse mean? The Apostle makes it clear. He is asserting that anyone whose habitual conduct is defiled by such sins as he names has no inheritance in the Kingdom of God. He is not saying that any man who *falls* into any one of these sins is eternally excluded from the Kingdom. It does not mean that, thank God! But it does mean that if such sins are the characteristic of a man's life, if that is his way of living, if that is his atmosphere, if that is the realm in which he is happy and getting what he seeks for, then he has no inheritance at all in the Kingdom of Christ and of God. We have got illustrations in the New Testament itself of Christian people temporarily falling into sin, but that does not become their habitat, as it were; they do not go back to living in sin. These people are not included in these solemn words in verse 5. I say this because the truth compels me to say it. I know that there are people who will clutch on to such a statement, and use it and wrest it, as Peter says, to their own destruction. But I assure such persons that a persistence, a continuance, a settling down in sin, a reversion to it, means that they are not inside the Kingdom. Men and women whose whole demeanour, whose life, is characterised by things contrary to God's law, are not in the Kingdom of God; they have no inheritance there at all. Now why is this, of necessity, true? Why does the Apostle say, 'This ye know'? Well, here he supplies us with a very interesting explanation. He says, 'hath no inheritance in the kingdom of *Christ* and of *God*'.

You will find that the learned commentators spend most of their time, when dealing with this verse, on that particular phrase. They are concerned to say that what the Apostle actually wrote was, 'hath no inheritance in the kingdom of *Christ and God*'; from which many of them deduce, and, I think, rightly, that one of the things the Apostle had in his mind there was to say that Christ *is* God – the kingdom of *Christ and God*! not the kingdom of Christ and *of* God, but the kingdom of *Christ and God*, of the Christ who *is* God. Now, that is a perfectly legitimate thing to say, and yet I cannot but feel that the Apostle was not primarily concerned to say that, though it is true and he says similar things elsewhere. The Lord Jesus Christ is God, He is the Second Person in the Godhead. But I rather feel that the Apostle *was* here saying 'the kingdom of Christ *and of* God', in order that he may emphasise the fact that the kingdom which Christ has opened to us, and which therefore rightly can be called the kingdom of Christ, is also the kingdom of God. And this is the kingdom about which we are speaking, the kingdom in which God is the centre and the soul, in which God is everything, and everything in it must be like God; and 'God is light and in him is no darkness at all'!

Do we not find in reading the Psalms that this truth was known to the Old Testament saints? 'Lord, who shall abide in thy tabernacle? who shall dwell in thy holy hill? He that walketh uprightly, and worketh righteousness, and speaketh the truth in his heart; he that backbiteth not with his tongue', and so on (15:1-3). He is the man who will be with the Lord. And again in another Psalm: 'Who shall ascend into the hill of the Lord, or who shall stand in his holy place?' That was the thing that concerned the psalmist, and he answers, 'He that hath clean hands and a pure heart; who hath not lifted up his soul unto vanity, nor sworn deceitfully. He shall receive the blessing from the Lord' (24:3–5). In a sense, what does it matter whether we are happy or miserable? Does anything matter but this? Do we want to stand in the presence of the Lord? Do we want to ascend that holy hill? Do we want an entrance into that holy, eternal city of God? Do we want to spend our eternity there? That is the question! And the first consideration, therefore, is holiness! 'Be ye holy', says God, 'for *I am holy*'! The thing is so obvious! this you know! 'Our God is a consuming fire'! 'God is light, and in Him is no darkness at all'! Look at our Lord Himself, and you see that He was 'holy, harmless, undefiled, and separate from sinners'. He was such that He could challenge his accusers and say, Who can bring a charge against Me? He could say, 'The evil one cometh, and findeth nothing in me.' He stands out in His holiness, in His sanctity, in His eternal purity.

But a very subtle danger arises at this point, and I have no doubt the Apostle had it in mind when he wrote the very words we are considering. There are people who will argue, 'But wait a minute; are you not preaching the law to us? You are to be a minister of grace, and yet you seem to be preaching pure law. You are reminding us of the Being and the character of God, as expressed in the Ten Commandments and in His moral law; are you not just putting us back under the law? Are you not excluding every one of us from the kingdom of God? Surely you are forgetting the gospel! You have been referring to the original kingdom, and the original law that God held before mankind; but now the Lord Jesus Christ has come, and we are confronted by something quite new; we are no longer confronting the law; all we are asked to do as Christians is to believe on the Lord Jesus Christ. We could not be saved under the law, for the law made it impossible, saying, "There is none righteous, no, not one." But now God has brought in another way which makes it easier for us; we are no longer confronted by the demands of the law and the tremendous holiness of God. It is just a matter of believing on the Lord Jesus Christ, and we shall be saved.' Now that is their argument, but I am bound to say that it is one of the most subtle, dangerous heresies that can ever be offered to men and women. And yet it characterises a great deal of modern evangelism.

[348]

The answer to all this is perfectly clear in the New Testament itself. Christ is God, and He did not come into this world to change God's law; He Himself says specifically in the Sermon on the Mount that not one jot or tittle of the law shall pass away until all be fulfilled. He did not come to destroy the law or the prophets, but to fulfil them. And as the Apostle reminds us here, the Kingdom of Christ is *also* the kingdom of God! It is one kingdom. The saints of the Old Testament are in the same kingdom as we are. They were in it before us. We as Gentiles have been brought in; we were strangers from the covenants of promise and outside all these things, but we have been brought in, we have been made fellowheirs with them, this division as between the old and the new is false; and the argument that the law has got nothing to do with us is a case of the devil appearing as an angel of light. There is but one eternal standard.

In the kingdom of Christ we are brought face to face with GOD! And what is the work of the Lord Jesus Christ? Why did He come? He came to bring us to GOD, says the Apostle Peter. He came, says Paul, and gave Himself for us, 'that he might purify unto himself a peculiar people, zealous of good works'; He came to make us holy! We find a perfect statement of the matter in the Epistle to the Romans: 'For what the law could not do, in that it was weak through the flesh, God sending his own Son in the likeness of sinful flesh, and for sin, condemned sin in the flesh: that [in order that] the righteousness of the law might be fulfilled in us, who walk not after the flesh, but after the Spirit' (8:3-4). It is the kingdom of Christ and of God, and the standard is not lower in the kingdom of Christ than it is in the kingdom of God. The kingdom is one, and holiness is ever the one and only standard. The Lord Jesus Christ did not come into this world to lower the standard or to make it easier than it was before for us to slip into the kingdom, as though we could enter saying, We believe in Christ, and yet be holding on to our sins. Our Lord said, 'Not every one that saith unto me, Lord! Lord! . . . but he that doeth. . .'! And remember the illustration of the house built on the rock and the house built upon the sand. It is introduced by these words: 'Whosoever heareth these sayings of mine, and doeth them, I will liken him unto a wise man, which built his house upon a rock' [Matthew 7:24]; the man that heard Christ's sayings and did not do them is like the man that built his house upon the sand.

But someone may say, 'I cannot reconcile these things in my mind as principles; theologically I do not understand what you are saying. Surely by putting it as you have done, you really are teaching justification by works again. Are you not saying that it is our life that admits us into the kingdom? Are you not saying that if a man is guilty of these things he is outside, whereas if he is not guilty he is inside? Is not that going right back to justification by works? Are you saying in effect that a man is justified by his sanctification? that if he is a sanctified man he is justified, but that if he is not sanctified he is not justified and is outside?' People are often in trouble about this. They are in trouble in exactly the same way about the sixth chapter of the Epistle to the Hebrews. They say, 'Look at those terrible warnings there; we are told that *if* this man who believes goes back, then he is outside for ever; we cannot reconcile this justification by faith only, and this pure grace teaching of yours, with this other emphasis which seems to put it all back upon us and upon our conduct and behaviour. How do you reconcile these things?'

A very important question! We reconcile them by asserting again that God justifies the *ungodly*, not the godly. Justification is by faith *alone*. It was while we were yet enemies that we were reconciled to God by the death of His Son; it was while we were ungodly, while we were sinners. There is no question about that; it is a cardinal doctrine, a first great principle. But justification is only one step, an initial step, in a process. And the process includes not only justification but regeneration and sanctification and ultimate glorification. Justification and forgiveness of sins are not ends in and of themselves; they are only steps on a way that leads to final perfection. And that is the whole answer to the problem. Some Christians persist in isolating these things, but they are not isolated in the Scriptures. 'Whom he called, them he also justified and whom he justified, them he also glorified'! 'But of him are ye in Christ Jesus, who of God is made unto us wisdom, *and* righteousness, *and* sanctification, *and* redemption'! There is the whole process. And the truth is, that if you are in it at all, you are in at every point. We cannot divorce justification and forgiveness from other parts of truth. And the remaining steps are put very clearly before us in the First Epistle to the Corinthians: 'Such', says the Apostle, having given his terrible list of sins – 'Such were some of you: but ye are washed, but ye are sanctified, but ye are justified in the name of the Lord Jesus, and by the Spirit of our God' (6:11). It means that God does not justify a man and leave him there. Not at all! If God justifies a man, God has brought that man into the process. If you can say that you are justified, I say about you that you have been washed, that you have been sanctified, that you have been taken out, you have been removed from the old, and you have been put into a new realm, into a new kingdom; you are in this process of God that is leading to your ultimate, entire perfection. And the verse that we are looking at here is saying that if there is no evidence in our lives of this process into which God puts the people whom He justifies, then we have not been justified, but are merely saying, Lord! Lord! And His response will be: 'I never knew you, depart from me, ye that work iniquity.' For the argument is that when God justifies a man He does bring him into this process, and these things happen to him.

So this would be the way to approach our text, or the early part of the sixth chapter of the Epistle to the Hebrews: these verses are put before us in order that we may test ourselves by them, we who are so ready to say, 'Lord! Lord!' Yes, but listen, says Paul, Know this, 'that no whoremonger, nor unclean person, nor covetous man, who is an idolater, hath any inheritance in the kingdom of Christ and of God'. There have been people in the church who have said 'Lord! Lord!' but were guilty of these things. Read 1 Corinthians 5, and there you will find that there was a member of the church at Corinth who was guilty of such a terrible sin that it was not thought fit to be mentioned, says Paul, even among the Gentiles. Here was a man saying 'Lord! Lord!' and yet guilty of unmentionable sin at one and the same time. This is not a matter of words. Any man can say, 'Lord! Lord!' but if he still goes on with his sin there is no value in it, he is not a justified man. A man who is justified is a man to whom the process has been applied. His whole relationship to sin and evil is a new one. He has been washed, he has been sanctified, he has been justified in the name of the Lord Jesus and by the Spirit of our God.

But our text is more than a test. Do you realise that verses of this kind are a very part of God's way of sanctifying us? Remember our Lord's prayer as found in John, chapter 17. He prayed: 'Sanctify them through thy truth; thy word is truth.' He had already said to certain people, 'If ye continue in my word then are ye my disciples indeed, and ye shall know the truth, and the *truth* shall make you *free*.' Have you realised that it is through such words as these that God sanctifies us? It is a part of His method of sanctification. These warnings, these threatenings, these alarming statements, are the things that God uses to sanctify us; He applies them to us by the Spirit for this purpose. We can all test ourselves as to whether we are Christians or not. How do you react to my text? Does it concern you? Does it alarm you? Does it make you feel ashamed of yourself and your life? Do you say, It is absolutely right and I am ever in danger of relapsing into Antinomianism. If so, I tell you that you are in the kingdom. God has used this verse through the Holy Spirit in order to promote your sanctification. These words come to awaken the true believer, they do not touch the others. The others are just made to feel uncomfortable. They say, 'What you tell me is all wrong, I thought I was justified by faith only.' But they really mean to say, 'I thought that the gospel said that it did not matter if I went on sinning, and that all was right with me if I believed in Christ!' They make the blood of Christ a cloak to cover their sins, they make merchandise of the Cross, they are balancing, putting themselves right. But the man who is really called, the man who is in the kingdom, says, 'This is right, it must be right.'

God is holy, God is light, and in Him is no darkness at all. And these words are employed to further and to deepen and to expedite a true believer's sanctification. I remind you again of the words of the Apostle John in his First Epistle: 'Every man that hath this hope in him purifieth himself, even as he is pure' (3:3). Of course, a man may say glibly, 'I want to go to heaven, I have got this hope in me.' 'You have not!' says John. Here is the test. If you have really got this hope in you – the hope of entering the holy City at the end, and of spending your eternity in it – every man that really has this hope in him, purifieth himself – of course he does, he is bound to – even as He is pure. But the man who has only got the hope on his lips and not in his heart does not purify himself, he goes on living the old life; and the truth about him is that he has no inheritance at all in the kingdom of Christ and of God. He does not belong there. He *says*, 'Lord! Lord!' but speech is cheap and easy.

The question is, Is the hope in our hearts? If it is, we recognise the truth; we say, Yes, we *do* know this, that people who cleave to sin obviously cannot have any inheritance in the kingdom of Christ and of God. There is no contradiction between these statements and the doctrine of free grace and justification by faith only, for the God who justifies goes on with the process. And unless we are giving evidence of being in the process and of being perfected by it, there is but one conclusion to draw – we have never been in the kingdom at all, we must go back to the very beginning, we must repent and believe on the Lord Jesus Christ.

28

The Wrath of God

'Let no man deceive you with vain words: for because of these things cometh the wrath of God upon the children of disobedience.'

Ephesians 5:6

The Apostle in referring to *these things* is referring, of course, to the things which he has just been mentioning – fornication, uncleanness, foolish talking, jesting, covetousness, and so on; all things unbecoming in saints. His primary object here, as we have seen, is to exhort Ephesian believers to live the Christian life truly, down to the smallest detail of their lives. But we see that the Apostle cannot handle even a practical matter like that without relating it to certain general fundamental principles. In other words, he is not interested only in their conduct as such, conduct and morality *qua* conduct and morality; he has a larger and a greater interest, which is characteristic of the whole Christian message. It takes everything that we do in this life and in this world and everything that happens to us, and puts it into an eternal context. In other words, our behaviour in this world is important for three great, eternal reasons. The first is that our conduct affects our relationship to God; not simply our relationship, as it were, to ourselves and to other people, but our relationship to the eternal God Himself.

The second principle is that there are only two possibilities with regard to that relationship to God; we are either in the kingdom of Christ and of God, or else we are outside that kingdom and under the wrath of God, as children of disobedience.

But then there is a third principle, namely, that this relationship of ours to God applies not only to time, but also to eternity. It is important not only for the sake of our life and our happiness while we are in *this* world, it is that which determines our eternal, our endless condition, of either happiness or intense misery and unhappiness.

The unbelieving world has no conception of these three principles which the Apostle here enunciates. It is not concerned about its relationship to God. It does not realise that every human being is either in the kingdom of Christ and of God or else outside it and under His wrath. It does not realise that beyond this life and beyond the grave is another life, that we go on endlessly, eternally in one of two positions, either in bliss unspeakable, or in suffering and agony which even baffles the imagination. And we may well ask how it is that vast numbers of man and women around us are so completely unaware of these three great truths. The answer is to be found in the Apostle's words as recorded in our text.

He says, in the first place, that the people of the world at large are being deceived by vain words. 'Let no man deceive you with vain words'! Man is as he is in sin, and the world is as it is, undergoing all kinds of agonies and turmoils, because it is being deceived. According to the Bible, that is the essence of the human tragedy, the tragedy of the world. All mankind's troubles and problems have resulted from the fact that man at the beginning was fooled, deceived, beguiled, by Satan, who was, says the Bible a deceiver from the beginning. Scripture speaks too of 'the *deceitfulness* of sin'. That is the most horrible thing about it – it inveigles us into evil before we are aware of it. With *vain words* it deceives us.

Modern man glories above everything else in what he calls his knowledge, his learning, his understanding. He believes that he has a true view of life; and in that connection there is nothing perhaps on which the typical modern man so prides himself and congratulates himself as on the way in which he has emancipated himself from religion. Religion, he says, is a kind of superstition which belongs to the infancy of the race; it is characteristic of man in his primitive condition. Its accompaniments and concomitants always have been a spirit of fear and of slavery. Man under religion is a creature of taboos and fears which have all been imposed upon him. But now, modern man feels that he has grown up and has shaken off this incubus; he has got rid of these taboos; he has acquired a scientific, healthy, manly view of life, and is now free to use his intelligence and his learning. Thus, I say, he congratulates himself on the emancipation which he has achieved.

The result of this is that modern man derives and dismisses the old standards, especially the old moral standards. He laughs at them and ridicules them. Modern man not only does, but defends, things which, a hundred years ago, and even more recently, were regarded by most people as unquestionably sinful; indeed he goes beyond defending them, he advocates them. He actually goes so far as to say that a man who does not follow these practices is a man to be pitied; he is still subject to the taboos of religion, still mid-Victorian in his outlook, and has not grown up into full maturity. He maintains that, though in the past these things had been regarded as sinful, and not to be mentioned, by now our researches and our scientific development have taught us that man is a creature, so constituted that he should be giving full expression to these powers and propensities and qualities within him. Modern man's deduction is that what used to be called sin is in fact nothing but a man expressing himself and living a full life, not the kind of mutilated, truncated life of our forefathers, but a man coming into his own and giving evidence of that which is really himself. And so, everything is natural, and we must not speak of anything being unnatural or sinful, for everything a man does is eventually natural, and the final conclusion of modern man is, that *not* to be exercising or giving expression to these natural instincts and powers is – if there is such a thing – sinful, and at the very least, regrettable.

There is also a new tendency in life to explain what used to be called *sin* in terms of variations from the normal, or in terms of disease. The whole idea today is that there is no such thing really as *sin* and that we must not say that people who follow certain practices are sinners. We are told that we must recognise the fact that we are not all identical, and that a man does certain things because that is his make-up. Fundamentally, of course, we are all the same, but when we come to look at ourselves in detail, we find that there are variations in temperaments and in other respects; one man is active, another man is lethargic; one is mercurial and one is phlegmatic; one is more intelligent than another, one is more emotional than another, one is more highly-sexed than another. Essentially all men are made up in the same way, but there are these variations within the normal. This kind of distinction is being pressed hard all along the line – the man was born like that, and therefore he is just to express himself, and if he does not express himself he is guilty of violating his own being and personality!

The balance of his ductless glands is such that he is only doing what is natural to him. And in this way the whole notion of sin is explained away. Sometimes, as I have said, they put it not so much in terms of variations from the normal as in terms of disease. And we cannot but notice that this attitude is creeping even into the arguments in the law courts. A man commits a crime; yes, but the defence claims that he really could not help it at that moment, he is in a diseased condition. This man should not be regarded as a criminal, he should be taken to hospital rather than brought into court! Disease is the cause of his action, and so he is not responsible. It is in such ways as these that the whole notion of sin and evil and wrong, as over against right and truth, is gradually disappearing.

This in turn leads to a relaxation in the whole notion of discipline – discipline in the home, in the school, in the whole of life in general. The old idea was that you taught children to behave themselves, and that you taught them the three R's whether they liked them or not, and whether they were interested or not. But that has now given place to the idea that the problems of education must be approached psychologically, and it is for the child to determine what he is to be taught and how he is to be taught it; everything is to be made nice and interesting. If he does not want to do arithmetic at the moment, you tell him a story; and so on. And thus the whole idea of discipline and of ordering and of governing is disappearing. I am not ridiculing the thing, I am literally stating what is happening. This is what is really believed today. It is being practised in the home, in the school, in connection with work in prisons, and in every aspect of life. The notion of discipline is disliked today and regarded as wrong, for man must be free and allowed to express himself.

[357]

And then, of course, the next step – and it is quite logical – is that the whole idea of punishment is going out. Modern men and women no longer believe in punishment in the home, in the school, or in connection with crime and misdeeds. The newspapers supply ample evidence of this. Crime flourishes; prisons are over-crowded. And how do men propose to deal with the problem? Well, they say, we must not only have more prisons, but we must elaborate our methods and means of treating offenders psychologically. Punishment is outdated; you must put them through this deep analysis, you must discover the hidden springs and motives; they are not criminals; they are either lacking in balance or else they are actively diseased; investigations must be entirely from that standpoint. And then you must try to rehabilitate them by getting them to read good literature, by speaking kindly to them, and so on. The idea of punishment must be abolished.

These ideas have been in practice for some time. And it is very interesting to notice the people who were originally most responsible for them. It is not without significance that the prime mover in this kind of attitude was the man who was one of the prime movers in the appeasement of Hitler. And still they go on doing it. Although it became clear to all that it did not work with Hitler, they still believe it will work with other criminals. It is all the result of this new attitude towards life and towards sin and crime in particular. To sum it all up, the whole situation is being regarded from the standpoint of psychology, and we are told that words like *sin* and *crime* and *punishment* are ugly words which ought to be banished from our vocabulary.

All that I have been talking about you will find set out at great length in the *Wolfenden Report*. Its main argument is that we must no longer talk about certain horrible perversions, as I term them, as being unnatural, for they are natural for the men who practise them! That is the whole basis of the *Wolfenden Report* and of the movement to legitimise the practice of some of these foul, unspeakable perversions in private, if not in public. That is the argument behind it, that they are natural for those people; they are variations within the normal or else the result of disease.

That is the explanation also of a recent action of the Lord Chamberlain who has sanctioned the production on the stage of plays that deal with the subject of homosexuality, as long as they conform to certain rules. But surely, all this is offensive even to the natural man's best and highest instincts. And not only so; the argument I have explained eventually makes of man a beast and insults him. It regards man as a mere collection of ductless glands, nothing more than a collection of impulses and forces and instincts; it overlooks this other thing called the soul, and the spirit, that is in man; it reduces man, I say, to the level of a beast, or indeed even lower than that at times, almost to a machine, and claims that you can manipulate man and his personality by medication – putting in extra doses of this or withdrawing a certain amount of that!

But finally my argument would be this. There is nothing that shows so clearly that all this is but the deceit of Satan and but empty, vain words, as the chaos to which this outlook is leading. Take a look at the modern world, and the state of society, for these ideas have been in practice for some time. I have no doubt at all that when future historians come to write the history of this era in which we live, they will come to the conclusion that the whole cause of our trouble was that the authorities allowed themselves to be influenced by this psychological attitude towards life, at the expense of the scriptural view of life. Education, the home, the hospitals, the prisons – in fact the whole of life – is being governed by this false psychology, which sets aside the idea of man as a being created in the image of God and responsible to God, and who is to obey God's holy laws; all that has been put aside, and man is regarded in this new evolutionary psychological manner.

I have no doubt at all that the world is as it is on the international and on the national level, and in various groups within the nations, because man is still being deceived by these 'vain words' put forward by Satan. As an angel of light he puts the new idea very cleverly into the mouths of educationists, sociologists, and such-like people; yes, it sounds so good and so wonderful, it is so nice and so kind, it seems so much better than the old idea of discipline and order and punishment, and the division into natural and unnatural, and into truth and crime.

It is plausible, it seems very interesting and attractive, but the only term to describe it, I say, is found in my text – '*vain* words'!

But, moreover, the world is as it is not only because it is thus being deceived, but because it does not know the truth about the wrath of God. 'Let no man deceive you with vain words, for because of these things cometh the *wrath of God* upon the children of disobedience.' The sophists to whom I have been referring are particularly sarcastic about this phrase, 'the wrath of God'. Ah! they say, that's so typical of religion! – frightening! alarming! the wrath of God! Our fathers used to be terrified by that sort of thing, and as the preachers thundered from the pulpit about the wrath of God they quaked and they trembled and they decided for Christ, and the churches and chapels were filled; but it does not work with 20th-century man! he has seen through all that! They tell us that he has got the new understanding to which I have been referring. There is nothing, I say, that the sophist is more anxious to ridicule and to banish than this notion of the wrath of God. But there is nowhere, surely, where the blindness of modern man is more evident and where his deception by Satan is more obvious, than just at this point.

Consider for a moment the *fact* of the wrath of God! It is something that is asserted in the Bible from beginning to end. It was taught and preached by the patriarchs, by the kings, by the prophets, by the Lord Jesus Christ Himself, and by the apostles, every single one of them. If you do not believe in the wrath of God, I have only one thing to say to you, You do not believe in the Bible! You cannot believe the Bible without believing in the wrath of God. If you take God's wrath out of it, it is no longer the Bible, it is what *you* think; you have made a bible of your own. But let us be clear as to what the wrath of God is. We must not think of it as we think of man's wrath. Man's wrath is something horrible to witness; it is uncontrolled rage, it is temper, it is violence. But there is nothing uncontrolled about the wrath of God. His wrath is His attitude towards evil and sin, it is His displeasure at sin, it is His settled hatred of sin. The wrath of God is God's declared determination to punish sin. It is the reaction, if I may so speak, of the eternal

God, who is unchangeable and everlasting in His holiness, to sin and evil, to that which originated in the devil and which he has foisted upon the human race and brought into the life of the world. God hates it with all the intensity of His divine and eternal Being. He can have no dealings with it, and He has revealed from the very beginning that He will punish it. That is His settled attitude; it is the meaning of 'the wrath of God'. And, says the Apostle, 'Because of these things' – the evils he names – 'cometh the wrath of God upon the children of disobedience.' And now comes the vital question – How and when is this wrath going to be manifested?

We do well to ask 'When does the wrath of God come? When and how is it manifested?' The first answer to the question is, Now! In the present! Paul does not say that the wrath of God *shall come* upon the children of disobedience; he deliberately uses the present tense, 'cometh'; it is the continuous present; it includes the future, but it is *not only* the future, it includes the present! How does it come in the present? In this way: the moment you sin, at once you feel it. Your conscience condemns you. That is a part of the wrath of God against sin. The feeling of remorse is a manifestation of the wrath of God. Then think of the sufferings that come from sin – physical sufferings. The so-called 'morning after the night before' is a part of the wrath of God against sin, for God has ordained that, if you misuse your body, you will suffer for it. You talk about your pleasure: I remind you of your pain! The physical consequence of sin and wrong-doing is a part of the wrath of God. When man first sinned God cursed the ground; briers and thorns came up, and disease appeared. That was a part of God's punishment for sin, and it is still continuing. Sin and evil produce consequences, and they are a part of the manifestation of God's wrath. Think, too, of the mental suffering, of the agony of mind, of the unhappiness in the world, because of sin! Think of it in terms of family life – the bitterness, the unhappiness and the wretchedness that all come from sin! Think of the confusion in life – the moral muddle and confusion – and all that that involves. Indeed, I can sum it up with a word from the Old Testament: 'The way of the transgressor is hard'! It is God who has so determined that. A man shall not sin and get away with it.

Consider the word uttered by Moses to the two-and-a-half tribes that wanted to settle on the eastern side of Jordan. He said, If you fail to do what you promise to do, 'be sure your sin will find you out'! Sin does find us out. It may take years, but its quest never fails. Then again, there is active chastisement. Read the *Old* Testament; see how God punished individuals; see how He punished nations, even the nation of Israel, His own people. He sent them into captivity! He punished kings, He brought them down! It is written in the histories of the nations and of the world in general. And it is a truth that is taught explicitly in the *New* Testament. For instance, hear the words read at the Communion Service: 'For this cause many are weak and sickly among you, and many sleep.' Because some of you people in Corinth, says Paul, have not examined yourselves before coming to the communion table, some of you are weak, some of you are sick, some of you have died! It was a part of God's punishment of sin. Yes, says the twelfth chapter of the Epistle to the Hebrews, 'Whom the Lord loveth he chasteneth, and scourgeth every son whom he receiveth.' The wrath of God manifested in the present against sin and evil!

But there is something I want to draw attention to on the national and the international level. In the Epistle to the Romans we are told concerning unbelievers: 'When they knew God, they glorified him not as God, neither were thankful; but became vain in their imaginations, and their foolish heart was darkened. Professing themselves to be wise, they became fools, and changed the glory of the uncorruptible God into an image made like to corruptible man, and to birds, and fourfooted beasts, and creeping things. Wherefore God also gave them up to uncleanness through the lusts of their own hearts, to dishonour their own bodies between themselves: who changed the truth of God into a lie, and worshipped and served the creature more than the Creator, who is blessed for ever. Amen. For this cause God gave them up unto vile affections: for even their women did change the natural use into that which is against nature: and likewise also the men, leaving the natural use of the woman, burned in their lust one towards another, men with men working that which is unseemly, and receiving in themselves that recompense of their error which was meet. And even as they did not like to retain God in their knowledge, God gave them over to a reprobate mind, to do those things which are not convenient; being filled with all unrighteousness, fornication, wickedness, covetousness, maliciousness; full of envy, murder, debate, deceit, malignity; whisperers, backbiters, haters of God, despiteful, proud, boasters, inventors of evil things, disobedient to parents, without understanding, covenant-breakers, without natural affection, implacable, unmerciful: who knowing the judgment of God, that they which commit such things are worthy of death, not only do the same, but have pleasure in them that do them' (1:21–32).

And the Apostle says all this to expound what he had said in verse 18: 'For the wrath of God is [has been] revealed from heaven against all ungodliness and unrighteousness of men, who hold the truth in unrighteousness.' He says that that is why the ancient world was as it was. God gave men over to a reprobate mind – mankind rebelled against Him, turned its back on Him, thought it was wise, thought it understood – God gave them over. He took away His restraining grace, and allowed them to wallow in their filth. And do we not feel as we read this terrifying passage that we are reading a perfect description of the modern world? The world is as it is today because it has sinned and because God is punishing its sin!

For a hundred years and more man has been boasting about his cleverness. Since about 1859 with Charles Darwin and his *Origin of Species*, we have been presented with the scientific view! Man no longer a special creation of God, but evolving upwards from the animal! Men turned their backs on God, and on God's view of man and of life and of the world; they took up their own philosophies, and arrogantly rebelled against God. And in consequence, despite education and knowledge and culture, the world has again become what Paul describes in that second half of the first chapter of the Epistle to the Romans. It is what you read in the newspapers, and now the perversions are made legal practice for adults. The downgrade has set in and it will get worse and worse. Men of the world can bring in their psychology and build prisons and do many other things, but they will not find a remedy – God gave them over to a reprobate mind! It is one of God's ways of dealing with this world. When it does not listen to the pleadings of His gospel, God abandons it, withdraws Himself, and the world gets into such a foul and horrible state that at last it 'comes to itself', and begins to plead for mercy, and turns back to God. That is the message of the Bible, and I maintain that this is the one and only adequate explanation of the state of the world at this very moment. I believe we have had two world wars in this century as a punishment for the arrogance and the pride and the vanity and the folly of mankind from about 1864. The whole world had ceased to believe in God, it believed that man was immortal, there was nothing he could not do; by Acts of Parliament he could bring in paradise by legislation. God was not necessary; His truth was dismissed, and relegated to some limbo of forgotten things. And I believe that God has withdrawn His restraining grace and is allowing mankind to reap the consequence of its own arrogant, sinful rebellion. God is showing man what he really is. He is showing him his insignificance, He is showing him his moral nature, He is showing him that he is lost and damned apart from Him and His redeeming grace. As long as the world rejects the message about the wrath of God against sin, things will go from bad to worse. How idle it is to try to be optimistic, and to say that what we want is a spirit of love and of brotherhood and of friendship, while man remains sinful and selfish, and a rebel against God. He has got to be humbled; and God's wrath is being revealed in this very generation in which we live, against all ungodliness and unrighteousness of men.

But God's wrath is not only manifested now, in the present, it will be revealed in the future also at the second coming of Christ, the end of the world, and the judgment of the whole universe! Jesus Christ, the Son of God, the neglected, the derided Saviour, will come back to this world. He will be riding on the clouds of heaven, and He will come to judge the whole world in righteousness. The Apostle announces its certainty to us in his Second Epistle to the Thessalonians: 'When the Lord Jesus shall be revealed from heaven with his mighty angels, in flaming fire taking vengeance on them that know not God, and that obey not the gospel of our Lord Jesus Christ; who shall be punished with everlasting destruction from the presence of the Lord, and from the glory of his power; when he shall come to be glorified in his saints, and to be admired in all them that believe (because our testimony among you was believed) in that day' (1:7-10). The world ridicules this, I know; they call me a fool for preaching it. Let them say what they like. They ridiculed Noah; they ridiculed Lot before Sodom and Gomorrha; they ridiculed John the Baptist; they ridiculed the Son of God; they have ridiculed the prophets always. That does not matter. This is God's Word and God's Truth. Can you not see it being manifested upon the modern world and upon modern man? Well, if you do see it there, believe the rest! The world is under the judgment of God, His wrath is upon it. Christ will return, and He will destroy all evil and sin, and punish all who belong to that kingdom of darkness. There shall be a new heaven and a new earth, wherein dwelleth righteousness. And those who belong to the kingdom of Christ and of God shall be made like Him and shall reign with Him in glory throughout eternity. And this promise applies to all – glory for the saints of God, damnation for unbelievers. The wrath of God comes upon the children of disobedience. If *you* are a child of disobedience it will come upon you, it will come upon the mass of those constituting the doomed, the rejected world. It is universal. It is also individual.

What, then, are we to do? says someone. It is quite obvious, is it not? If you realise that all your suffering and pain and agony are due to the fact that you have disobeyed God, that you are a rebel against Him in your heart and in your life; if you realise it and go to Him and confess it and acknowledge it (which means repentance); and if you then tell Him that you believe His gracious message concerning His only begotten Son, whom He sent from heaven to deliver us from this present evil world that is under His doom and damnation, He will forgive you, He will receive you. As I said earlier, we are all of us either in the world and adopting its mentality and sharing its life, or else we have an inheritance in the kingdom of Christ and of God. And if we are in that kingdom of Christ and of God we have nothing to fear.

Let a third world war come; yes, let the final Judgment come – we are safe, we already belong to Him. There is no smugness about that! But if we do not belong to that world, then we belong to the world that is under His wrath, the world that is revealing His wrath more and more, and that will experience utter, final doom. Oh! there is only one thing to do; it is what the Apostle tells the Ephesians to do – 'Be not ye therefore partakers with them'! Do not share their life! Realise what it is leading to! Turn away! Run from it! 'Flee from the wrath to come'! Humble yourself before God in utter penitence and contrition. Ask Him to have mercy and pity upon you. Repent and believe the gospel of the Lord Jesus Christ. And you will not only be forgiven, you will be given an inheritance in His glorious and everlasting Kingdom. Oh! may God open all our eyes to the truth, and may we dedicate ourselves to unceasing prayer on behalf of a world that is being deceived by vain words. Christian people are called to open men's eyes, to show them the deceit and the folly and the vanity of their position and what they believe. Let us pray to God, then, to give us power to do so. In other words, let us pray for a revival. Let us pray that the Spirit of God may descend again upon the Church today, as He did two hundred years ago, and as He did in 1859, so that she may rise up with such power, and proclaim the truth in such glorious calls and terms that even the dead shall be awakened. You cannot reason with people who are deceived by the devil; it needs the trumpet call of God, it needs the power of the Spirit. Let us therefore dedicate ourselves to incessant, continuing prayer for an outpouring of the Spirit of God, that we may make the truth known to the blinded nations and their leaders, so that they may be saved from the wrath to come, and begin to live a life to the glory of God.

29

Children of Light

'Be not ye therefore partakers with them. For ye were sometimes darkness, but now are ye light in the Lord: walk as children of light.'

Ephesians 5:7–8

Now here the Apostle is beginning a new argument. The theme, of course, is still the same, the importance of right and true and appropriate living on the part of Christian people. We have already been considering one argument, indeed a whole series of arguments, but the Apostle is not content with that, he brings out yet another; and he will have still further arguments to bring forward. Now I am pausing with this just for a moment in order to emphasise this thing which is so frequently forgotten and indeed denied, that this is the New Testament way of teaching and of promoting sanctification and holiness. Sanctification, in other words, is clearly not something which you receive as an experience; you cannot take sanctification by one act. It is something which results from an outworking of the truth. So he presents it in the form of an argument; he states the doctrine, then he says, Now, in the light of that, surely. . . .! 'You were sometimes darkness, but now are ye light in the Lord: therefore walk as children of the light', or as those who belong to the light. Now is it not extraordinary – in spite of this constantly repeated teaching of these New Testament epistles which were specially written in order to deal with the whole question of sanctification and of a holy walk – is it not extraordinary that people still go on teaching sanctification as a gift to be received, something which you have as an experience, something which you take?

Or there is another teaching which is equally popular, which would have us believe that all that is necessary to be sanctified and to be holy is as simple as letting the blinds up and the light in to a dark room. All that is necessary, they say, is for the believer to look to the Lord; he has got nothing to do, there is no problem, there is no struggle, there is no difficulty, he just looks to the Lord, and the Lord does it for him. And that, we are told, is the whole of the teaching of sanctification; people, they say, have always made such a fuss and bother about this, and yet it is quite simple, you just look to the Lord and then He will do it for you, He will be victorious in you, and so on. Well, all I ask is this: if those teachings are true, why were these epistles ever written? and especially in these practical sections, why does the Apostle take the trouble to produce argument after argument – putting the matter first in one form, and then in another?

Surely it is time that we began to consider these things again and to see that this is the New Testament method of sanctification and of holiness; it is to realise the truth and then to apply it. Of course, our Lord Himself had said the whole thing before His death, when He said, 'The truth shall make you free.' 'If ye continue in my word, then are ye my disciples indeed, and ye shall know the truth, and the truth shall make you free.' He prayed at the end (you will find it in John's Gospel, chapter 17), 'Sanctify them through thy truth. Thy word is truth.' Well, that is exactly what the Apostle is doing here. Here is the word of truth, and as the truth comes to us and we see it and understand it, we then must go on to apply it. So he plies us with argument upon argument, building up his case. He has given us positive arguments, he has given us negative arguments, to lead us to obey his injunction to 'Walk in love', and you would have thought that that was enough. But it is not enough; he produces now, in this verse that we are going to look at, yet another argument. Here he bids us walk in the light – walk in *love* before: walk in *light* now. And this is the matter that occupies him from verse 7 right through to verse 14. Notice how he puts it. He says the fruit of the Spirit is in 'all goodness and righteousness and truth: . . . Have no fellowship with the unfruitful works of darkness, but rather reprove them . . . All things that are reproved are made manifest by the *light.* . . . Wherefore he saith, Awake, thou that sleepest, and arise from the dead, and Christ shall give thee *light.*'

[368]

Now as we approach this new section we remind ourselves that the New Testament often speaks of light contrasted with darkness. Obviously, therefore, it is a very powerful argument. The difference between Christian and non-Christian is the difference between being in the light and being in the dark. Let us consider some of the terms which remind us of this. Take our Lord's own terms. He said, 'I am the light of the world.' And He added, 'I am come a light into the world; he that followeth me shall not walk in darkness, but shall have the light of life.' But, addressing His own followers, He also said, 'Ye are the light of the world'; that is to say, because of our relationship to Him, we become the light of the world. And, 'No man', He says, 'putteth a light under a bushel, but on a candlestick.' A Christian is to be like a 'city set upon a hill, which cannot be hid'. 'Ye are the light of the world.' In the prologue to John's Gospel we find the coming of truth into the world expressed in terms of light. Christ, we are told, 'was the true Light, that lighteth every man that cometh into the world'. 'In him was life; and the life was the light of men.' 'The light shineth in darkness; and the darkness comprehended it not.' And so on. Clearly this is one of the major ways in which the New Testament presents to us the whole body of Christian truth, our belief in it, and our belonging to it.

And what is characteristic of the Gospels is equally characteristic of the Epistles. Take that great statement in 2 Corinthians 4: 'If our gospel be hid, it is hid to them that are lost: in whom the god of this world hath blinded the minds of them which believe not, lest the light of the glorious gospel of Christ, who is the image of God, should shine unto them . . . For God who commanded the light to shine out of darkness, hath shined in our hearts, to give the light of the knowledge of the glory of God in the face of Jesus Christ' (2 Corinthians 4:3–6). You find this appearing as a constant theme in all the Epistles of the Apostle Paul. And we find it also in the writings of the Apostle Peter. He says in his First Epistle: 'Ye are a chosen generation, a royal priesthood, an holy nation, a peculiar people; that ye should show forth the praises [the excellences] of him who hath called you out of darkness into his marvellous light.' Again, it is one of the major themes in the First Epistle of John: 'God is light, and in him is no darkness at all', and all that he deduces from that. Thus, I say, we have abundant evidence to show that this is a most important aspect of the truth. And it is not surprising that the Apostle takes it up, therefore, to reinforce and to press home what he has already been saying in our text and context.

The Apostle presents his theme before he comes to draw his deductions, and we can divide his way of presentation into a number of simple propositions, which nevertheless take us to the very heart of the whole matter. The first is this: the difference between the Christian and the non-Christian – and it is an absolute one – is emphasised repeatedly in the New Testament and there should be no difficulty in recognising this difference; all the terminology of the New Testament with regard to what a Christian is can be described in terms of *regeneration* – not merely a slight improvement on the surface, but re-birth; not that you come to a man and take off his rags and put on him a better suit of clothing; not that you make him wash his face and cut his hair. No, no! He has got to be BORN again. There is no more radical term than that! 'If any man be in Christ, he is a new creature', a new *creation*! Here we are taken right back to the origin of everything! A creation is bringing something into being out of nothing. It is not improvement, it is not adaptation, it is creation. A man who becomes a Christian is a man who has been *created anew*. A fundamental term! I emphasise this matter in order to bring out the Apostle's thought in our text. 'Ye *were* . . .; ye *are*. . . .' 'Ye *were* sometimes darkness, but now *are* ye light.' Now these are absolute terms, and we are to test ourselves by whether we know anything about them – *'ye were'* and *'ye are'*. Notice that Paul supplies two further words. He says, 'Ye were *sometimes'*, that is to say, once upon a time. And the contrast to that is, *'now'*. Look back, he says, there, once upon a time, once, that was your position; but *now*! As we have been working through this Epistle we have already had occasion more than once to show how the Apostle glories in the words, *but now*. We considered them in the second chapter, where Paul – using them with such force and power – reminds the Ephesian saints that in past time they were 'without Christ, being aliens from the commonwealth of Israel, and strangers from the covenants of promise, having no hope, and without God in the world: BUT NOW....'! Thank God, he says, you are no longer in your former state. NOW! And then later on in that same chapter he says, '*Now* therefore ye are no more strangers and foreigners, but fellowcitizens with the saints, and of the household of God.' Ye were: ye are! Sometime: now! And that is the difference, I say, between not being a Christian and being a Christian.

Next we notice that Paul proceeds to contrast *darkness* with *light*. You cannot mix light with darkness. They are eternal opposites. He tells the Corinthians that 'There is no communion between light and darkness'. And he wants the Ephesians to realise that they are no longer darkness but light in the Lord. Now let me make this perfectly clear. He is not concentrating on the way in which we passed from darkness to light, or the exact time at which we did so. Many people are troubled because they cannot put a finger on a particular moment or on a particular text or a particular occasion. But that is not the point. The question that the Apostle asks is not when or how exactly did you pass from what you were to what you are; but rather: Can you say about yourself, I am *this*, I am no longer *that*? The thing he is concerned about is that we are light and not darkness. It may happen suddenly, it may happen gradually. In some people's case it is like switching on an electric current; suddenly in the midst of darkness there is a blaze of light. With others it is very much like what happens in nature: across the darkness of the night there comes the first streak of dawn – the first promise of the light of day. Do not be concerned about the time. The time element does not matter at all, nor the exact method of the process. The analogy of birth confirms what I am saying. It does not matter whether your new birth has taken a very long time to bring about. The question is, Are you alive or are you not? If you are the merest babe in Christ you are *alive*.

The Apostle tells us that we are either light or darkness, one thing or the other. We are either Christians or we are not Christians; there is no mean between them. You cannot be half a Christian. The road to hell is paved with good intentions. I have used the illustration before, let me use it again: you may be standing in a bus queue. The bus comes along, and the people go in; and then to your utter dismay, suddenly the conductor holds up his hand; the man in front of you was allowed in, but you were not. It is no comfort and consolation to know, is it, that you would have been the next if there had been yet place for one? The point is, you are not on the bus; you very nearly got on the bus, I know, but you did not, and it is no consolation to know that you very nearly did. We are either in the bus or else we are left standing in the queue. We are either Christians or non-Christians, we are either light or darkness.

The Apostle is telling us, of course, that this is something that is so clear that we should know it. And not only should we know it, but everybody else should know it. He cannot apply his argument if we do not know it. If we are not quite certain whether we are light or darkness, how can we listen to the argument which applies to those who are light? Throughout the New Testament there is a clearly-marked distinction between the Christian and the non-Christian, between the church and the world. And the whole tragedy of the church today is that this distinction has become lost. The Protestant Reformers said that the Christian Church carries three marks. She is a place in which the true doctrine is preached, the sacraments are administered, and discipline is applied. But there has been confusion. Teachings have come in which have blurred these lines. Morality has come in and has become mixed up with religion. The standards have been lost. It is assumed that if a man lives a good life he is a Christian. But is that enough? is the man himself certain? is everybody else quite certain? The Apostle, I say, is striking this tremendous point right home, by saying you have got to realise that the difference is between light and darkness. You were . . . you are; sometimes . . . now. Darkness . . . Light! So that the question we ask ourselves is this, Are we light in the Lord? Are we newborn babes, if no more? I leave it at that. But the Apostle goes on pressing it.

We next proceed to look at the *nature* of the difference between the Christian and the non-Christian. And here the Apostle's terms are unusually interesting. He says, 'Ye were sometimes *darkness*, but now are ye *light* in the Lord'. He does not say, At one time you were *in the dark*; but simply, You were *darkness*. He means that not only were they in the dark, but that the darkness was in them! And then, on the other side, he does not just say, You are now *enlightened*, or you are *in the light*; no, he says, You are *light*! Once they were darkness itself! Now they are light itself! What does he mean by this? Let me put it in this way. This is one of the most urgent matters from the standpoint of evangelism – when I say evangelism, I not only mean preaching, I mean our conversation with people about these matters. A statement such as this is very important as we must understand the exact condition and position of the man who is not a Christian. The Apostle assures us that he is not only in the dark, but the darkness is in him! He himself is darkness, he is part of the darkness; that is to say, sin.

The Apostle is much given to working out this idea. In the first chapter of Romans, for example, he speaks of those whose 'foolish heart was *darkened*'. It was not simply that they were in the dark, but that their very hearts became dark in and of themselves. Again, in the fourth chapter of Ephesians, unbelievers are described as 'having the understanding *darkened*'; a kind of darkness has entered the mind, the heart, the outlook, the whole seat and centre of personality. One of our hymns has a verse which puts exactly the same point: 'O, how shall I, whose native sphere is dark, whose mind is dim. . . .' How can such a man 'before the Ineffable appear' and on his 'naked spirit bear the uncreated beam?'

The trouble then with man is not simply that he is in a dark world, but that the light that was in him has gone out! God put a light into man. When God made man He breathed into him His Spirit; man became a living soul, and he was in communion with God; there was a light in his soul. Sin has put out the light. It is not simply that we are in a dark world, but that there is darkness within us, in our very being and constitution. Listen to our Lord's words in the Sermon on the Mount: 'The light of the body is the eye: if therefore thine eye be single, thy whole body also shall be full of light. But if thine eye be evil, thy whole body shall be *full of darkness*'! Because the eye of the soul and the spirit has become opaque and darkened, no light goes into the body, and the result is that the whole of the body, the mind and the heart, the whole personality, is *full of darkness*. It is just another way of saying what the Apostle said of the non-Christians at the beginning of chapter 2 in this Epistle to the Ephesians: 'You hath he quickened, who were dead in trespasses and sins' – not merely in the dark, but *dead*, without a spark of life in you. That, says the Apostle, is exactly, what you were. And again, our Lord has put this very clearly in John's Gospel: 'And this is the condemnation, that light is come into the world, and men loved darkness rather than light, because their deeds were evil.' Light has come! Why do men not believe it, why do they not turn to it? They 'love darkness rather than light'! Darkness is in their hearts, and darkness is in their minds. They *love* darkness, they enjoy it; it is the thing that appeals to them; darkness is within them. 'Ye were sometimes darkness', says Paul.

And then, on the other hand, Paul does not say about the Christian simply that he is being enlightened, or that he has come into the light. That is perfectly true, but he says something much more wonderful: 'Now are ye *light* in the Lord.' The light has entered into him! has irradiated the whole of his being! has possessed him! has lighted him up! 'God, who commanded the light to shine out of darkness, hath shined in our hearts, to give the light of the knowledge of the glory of God in the face of Jesus Christ.' Our hearts have been made *light*, the light has been put *into* them. 'Light is sown for the righteous', says the Old Testament psalmist. The Christian, therefore, is not merely a man who has the eyes of his understanding enlightened; he has that, but he has more; his eye has been made single, with the logical consequence that his whole body also is *full of light*. The Christian is a man who has been filled with light. Now why is this so important? For one thing, it emphasises the radical difference between the non-Christian and the Christian. It shows us that the change that the man undergoes when he becomes a Christian is the profoundest change in the world. It affects the vitals of his being, the seat of his personality, the heart, the understanding, the affections, everything.

This truth is also of tremendous importance in the matter of evangelism, and in this way. There is a false school of evangelism, which assures us that all the preacher has to do is to hold the truth before people. Its adherents say that man has got it in him to understand and to believe and to accept the truth. So all we need do is to hold the truth before him, present it logically and clearly, bring out our arguments, put it as strongly as we can, supply eloquence, and so on. But the chief thing, they say, is to present the truth to him, for he has got the capacity and the power to believe it and to take it; and that is all that evangelism really means and does. I agree that it is vital in evangelism that one should present the truth; but that alone is not enough. Our Lord has dealt with the matter in a verse I have already quoted: 'This is the condemnation, that light *is come* into the world, and men loved darkness rather than light, because their deeds were evil.' Men's natures are wrong. It is not enough to hold the truth before men, they hate the truth, they prefer and love the darkness! So it is not enough merely to teach people. I remember one quite well-known man who used to say that all that was needed was to put up posters, to plaster London with texts of Scripture, and tremendous things would happen. I suggest to you that nothing would happen necessarily. God sometimes uses that method, but merely to confront people with texts of Scripture in and of itself cannot save a single soul, neither can any preaching of any type or kind, the reason being that the unbeliever is *darkness*.

The difficulty with the non-Christian is not merely that he needs to be shown light, but that, in addition to showing him the light, you have got to enlighten *him*. He needs to be born again, the Holy Spirit must do an operation *in* him, for 'the natural man receiveth not the things of the Spirit of God; they are foolishness unto him'. You can put the truth before him, quote your verses, bring your arguments, but they remain foolishness to him, 'neither can he know them, for they are spiritually discerned'. Not only must we present the light and the truth, but we must pray that the Holy Spirit may enlighten the mind and the heart. It is a dual operation; which fact causes me to say once more, that nothing short of a mighty revival and the visitation of the Spirit of God can deal with the present situation. Bibles are still being sold on a large scale; books on these matters are constantly being produced and are being read; education is being promoted here, there and everywhere; yet the position goes from bad to worse, for even gospel truth, if it does not come to men and women in 'demon-stration of the Spirit and of power', will achieve nothing. The father of the evangelism which imagines and thinks that it is sufficient simply to hold the truth before people, was truly a great man, named Finney. That was exactly what he taught. He did not believe in original sin, but believed that all that needed to be done was to hold the truth before people. This done, he said, they possess the ability to believe it and take it in. But they cannot! They are *darkness*! And because they are darkness and not merely in the dark, to hold the light of the truth before them is not enough; they need to be changed at the centre of their being, they need to be made *light*. The operation of the Holy Spirit is essential. The princes of this world did not recognise Him when He came, for if they had done so, they would not have crucified the Lord of glory.

How does anybody believe these things? In this way, says Paul: 'God hath revealed them unto us.' How? by the preaching or by the written Word? No, 'by his Spirit: for the Spirit searcheth all things, yea, the deep things of God'. We must never separate the Word and the Spirit! Man needs not only light from outside, he needs light *within*. It is the work of the Spirit to open the Word and to open the heart to receive it. Remember the story of Lydia, the first convert in Europe of the Apostle Paul? How did she become a convert? The Books of Acts tells us: 'whose heart the Lord opened, that she attended unto the things which were spoken of Paul'. A true evangelism is one that is utterly dependent upon the power of the Spirit to put light into man. He needs to be made *light*, he not only needs to be enlightened.

But still another factor operates to bring about this change, this transition. What is it that accounts for this difference between the Christian and the non-Christian? Well, fortunately the Apostle tells us: 'Ye were sometimes darkness, but now are ye light in the Lord.' '*In the Lord*'! It is all *in* the Lord. There is nothing without Him. The Lord Jesus Christ is the Alpha and the Omega, the Beginning and the Ending. He is All, and in all. There is nothing without Him. All is in Him. Let us go back again to the Second Epistle to the Corinthians where Paul puts it so gloriously and beautifully. We were 'sometimes darkness'; how have we become Christian? In this way, says Paul: 'God, who commanded the light to shine out of darkness,' – that is how I became a Christian, he says, it was nothing less than the action and the operation of God who at the beginning, when the Holy Spirit brooded over the chaos, when the world was without form, and void, said 'Let there be light'. 'God, who commanded the light to shine out of darkness, hath shined in our hearts.' He has not merely put us into an atmosphere of light, but has shined into our hearts! A kind of X-ray, the most powerful imaginable! 'Hath shined in our hearts.' What for? 'To give [*or* to reveal] the light of the knowledge of the glory of God in the face of Jesus Christ'!

It is not surprising that Paul put it like that, is it? Remember what had happened to him. Go with him along that road to Damascus as he sets out from Jerusalem breathing our threatenings and slaughter, a non-Christian and a persecutor of Christians. It was the darkness inside him that made him breathe out threatenings and slaughter, that made him feel ravished at the mere anticipation of massacring innocent Christian people; it was darkness manifesting itself, the darkness in his soul! And then he saw the light, above the brightest shining of the sun; and not only the light, but a Face! 'Who art thou, Lord?' Whence comes this radiance, this light, this glory? Whose is that Visage? Who art thou, Lord? You have lightened me, I have never seen anything like it, Who art thou? And the answer was, 'I am Jesus, whom thou persecutest'. He had already seen that He was a Lord, a divine Person, and now he comes to see that He is indeed the eternal Son of God, co-equal, co-eternal with the Father. And through Him and by looking into His face, he has seen God – 'the light of the knowledge of the glory of God in the face of Jesus Christ'! The Apostle had to see the Face in order to be an Apostle and to be a witness of the resurrection. We shall not have that direct vision which he had, and which was so glorious that it blinded him; but I can tell you this, that no man can be a Christian without something of that light which is in the Face of Jesus Christ coming into his heart and into his soul. 'But now are ye light in the Lord'!

'No man hath seen God at any time; the only-begotten Son, which is in the bosom of the Father, he hath declared him.' Yes, but more, He shines into our hearts. He enters into them, and we are in Him. Now are ye light *in* the Lord! We do not merely believe in Christ, we are joined to Christ, we are *in* Christ, and Christ is in us, the hope of glory. There is an indissoluble link. He is the Vine, we are the branches. We are in Him, participators, partakers of His very life and light and glory. He makes us *light*. It is entirely and altogether and exclusively in Jesus Christ. A Christian is not merely a man who believes the teaching, accepts the Christian ethic or the Christian morality, and who then proceeds to apply it to his life. Many good and moral people are doing that, but they are not Christians, for they are not made light. They are simply borrowing a little of His light, as Gandhi and others did. But that does not make a man a Christian. What makes a man a Christian is not that he has seen a certain amount of light and taken hold of it and applied it, but that he has been *made light*; that he is *in* the Lord, *in* Christ, and Christ in him; that he has thus derived his life and his energy and his power and his everything from the living Head. We are the body of Christ, and members in particular. He fills us with life and light and power, and so we are enabled to practise it. *We* do that. We do not just do nothing and passively look to Him. He enables *us* to act; therefore 'walk as children of light'.

Thank God the Apostle put it like this, in order that we may realise that the difference between a Christian and a non-Christian is an absolute one; in order that we may realise that we are not merely looking at the light; thank God, we are, but the light is within us. We are no longer darkness; I cannot honestly sing any longer, 'O, how shall I whose native sphere is dark, whose mind is dim'. Thank God, it is not dim. The light of the knowledge of the glory of God in the face of Jesus Christ has entered; I see, for my mind and my heart have been filled with light. I have infinitely more to learn, but I am no longer darkness, I am light in the Lord. As He is light, we are light. As He is the Light of the world, we are the light of the world. We are lamps, we are luminaries, the light is in us, we are not merely reflecting it, it is within us. 'Now are ye light in the Lord.'

30

The Unfruitful Works of Darkness

'For ye were sometimes darkness, but now are ye
light in the Lord: walk as children of light: (for the
fruit of the Spirit is in all goodness and righteousness
and truth;) proving what is acceptable unto the Lord.
And have no fellowship with the unfruitful works of
darkness, but rather reprove them. For it is a shame
even to speak of those things which are done of them
in secret. But all things that are reproved are made
manifest by the light: for whatsoever doth make
manifest is light.'

Ephesians 5:8–13

We continue our study of 'darkness' and 'light' by asking how we
may know whether one is darkness or whether one is light; and
the answer is that this shows itself along three main lines. First
of all, darkness shows itself in the mind, in the intellect and
understanding. We have a habit, have we not, of associating
ignorance always with darkness? We speak of The Dark Ages,
before the Renaissance in Europe and the rediscovery of Greek
philosophy and learning, and so on. In other words, we are all
familiar with this equating of darkness with ignorance; the things
are synonymous in our ordinary parlance. On the other hand we
tend to speak of people who have knowledge as people who are
enlightened. Certain historians refer to the whole of the 18th
century as The Age of Enlightenment because it experienced a
recrudescence of knowledge and of learning, the new birth of an
interest in philosophy and kindred subjects.

Darkness, as opposed to light, adversely affects the mind, the
intellect, the understanding, and all the faculties that are concerned with knowledge; and the Bible of course, above every-

thing else, uses the term in this sense. And so when the Apostle says to Ephesian believers, 'Ye were sometimes darkness', he means there was a time when their minds were dark, and they were grossly ignorant. And this remains true of every person who is not a Christian. He or she is just ignorant – there is no other word for it – lacking in certain vital knowledge, and blinded by sin. But of what are they ignorant? In the first place, they are ignorant of God! 'The fool hath said in his heart, There is no God.' He says there is no God because he lacks the knowledge of God. That is typical of ignorant people always, is it not? You give them a piece of information, and they say, I don't believe it! I can't believe it! It isn't true! They are not proving the information wrong, they are just telling us a great deal about themselves. I once heard a man put it very well. He said, 'When a man tells me that he sees nothing in Beethoven, he is telling me nothing about Beethoven, but he is telling me a great deal about himself!' And that is the exact point which we make here. The non-Christian, the unbeliever, is ignorant of God. If only men and women knew God, and knew the truth about God, they would not continue to live as they do. They know nothing about His holy character, they talk of God glibly, they express their opinions, they do not hesitate to criticise Him. If they had but some dim, vague, glimmering notion of God as He really is, they would put their hands upon their mouths as Job of old did, and they would remain silent.

It is the appalling ignorance about God that makes people talk as they do. We can at least say this for the Jews that, even at their worst, they knew certain things about God; they knew that God was so great and so mighty and so holy, that they never even dared to use the word JEHOVAH, they spoke about 'The Name'. That was their way of indicating their knowledge of the glory and the majesty and the holiness and the might of God. And non-Christians are not only in darkness, they *are* darkness; they do not know God, and the more they talk, the more they express their ignorance. They are ignorant of God and His laws. In the same way they are ignorant of the real truth about themselves, ignorant about the value of their souls. Cast a glance at people living in pleasure and in sin, plunging into it, glorying in it, revelling in it. The real trouble with them is that they do not know the answer to this kind of question, 'What shall it profit a man, if he shall gain the whole world, and lose his own *soul*? or what shall a man give in exchange for his *soul*?' They do not realise that there is within them this thing that has been placed there by God, which is greater than the whole world, the most precious, the most wonderful thing of all; they are completely ignorant about it, they live as if they had not an immortal soul; they live on the animal level. We know such people; we read about them; they are found in all classes of society. In spite of their knowledge of many another subject, they are ignorant of this.

In the same way, they are ignorant of the true meaning of life, its object and its purpose. What is life? What are we meant for? What is the whole object of our being in this world, what is the end to which all this is leading? On such themes they are completely in the dark. Their whole notion of life, as stated in the Scriptures, is 'Let us eat and drink, for tomorrow we die'. What an insult to life and living and to human nature! Are we but animals? Eating, drinking, gambling, indulging the natural instincts – do these constitute real life? Non-Christians often think so! They are content to remain completely ignorant about the purpose of life, and what happens beyond it. The Bible says, 'It is appointed unto men once to die, but after this the judgment.' According to Scripture, life is a tremendous thing, full of responsibility of the most momentous character. All we do and all we say is being recorded. All our actions are known unto God. The Book of Revelation puts it pictorially and says that the *books* will be produced and will be opened. We know of responsibilities, do we not? We know that Ministers of the Crown have a great and a dread responsibility, and the higher they rise the greater their responsibility, the Prime Minister being responsible to the Queen herself. And every one of us, as Scripture tells us, is directly and immediately and personally responsible to God. We shall have an audience with Him, and shall have to give an account of the deeds done in the body whether they be good or bad. A judgment! But unbelievers are entirely ignorant of the things of God. That is why they live as they do. And ignorant not only of God, but equally so about the Lord Jesus Christ, the eternal Son of God, and about the reason for His coming into this world.

They are ignorant of the need of salvation, so they are not interested in salvation.

Christians have tested this often. If you have not, it is about time you did test it. Try to discover what people really do know about Christianity and about the Lord Jesus Christ. It is almost incredible, that although the Bible and other Christian books are openly available, and although they have been brought up in a so-called Christian culture, and have in many cases a vague sense of its value, yet they remain completely ignorant of the real Lord Jesus Christ and His way of salvation. They are ignorant of His Person and of His work, ignorant of the one and only way whereby we can be reconciled to God and saved and made safe to all eternity. Put certain simple questions to the man in the street – Have you realised you have got a soul? Have you realised the truth about God, and that you have got to meet Him and face Him? Have you realised day by day the responsibility of living, the preciousness of this gift that God has given to you? Do you think of yourself as one who has been made and created in the image of Almighty God? What is your view of yourself? Have you thought about your death, and about facing God and giving Him an account of what you have done? The answers, if any, that you will get to such questions will, I am certain, only confirm the truth of what the Apostle tells us about the appalling ignorance of mankind. A darkness that may be felt!

But darkness not only affects the mind, it also affects the heart and the emotions. Non-Christians are not only ignorant of the truth, they do not want to hear it, they are unresponsive to it, they are hard. Even if they do hear it they think it is boring. Many of them sit in judgment on the preacher; but what is really happening is that they themselves are being judged. The man who is bored by the preaching of the Gospel is simply making a tremendous proclamation about himself! There is no more terrible state conceivable than that of the man who considers that the truth of God, the glories of the Gospel, are just boring, dull, uninteresting, fatuous, something to be dismissed out of hand. But that is the position of the unbeliever. Our Lord Himself tells us so. 'This', He said, 'is the condemnation, that

light is come into the world, and men *loved* darkness rather than
light, because their deeds were evil.' It is not only the mind that
is dark, the heart also is dark! Can anything be worse than that a
human being should have a heart that *hates* the light, detests it,
abominates it? But that is what sin does to us; that is the influence
of the devil upon us all.

But we must move on to consider the will of man in this regard,
for this is the thing which the Apostle is emphasising in this
paragraph above everything else. We have got an adage which
reminds us that 'As a man thinks, so he is'. It is absolutely true,
although we often tend to forget it. Everybody today who is
alive and doing this or that is proclaiming exactly what he or she
thinks! Everybody is a philosopher, everybody has got a philosophy of life, and we show what our philosophy of life is by the
way in which we live. Our actions always correspond to what
we think and what we believe. Therefore, if people are living a
superficial, bubble kind of existence, they do so because that is
the sort of mind they have. It is their failure to think that causes
them to live a superficial kind of life. And this leads me to say
that the problem of immorality or vice or crime can never be
tackled directly. Conduct is the result of the point of view, so
you can never deal with conduct directly. To try to do so is the
fatal blunder of every non-Christian system. And we are seeing
the failure on all hands. Men refuse to recognise the fundamental
principle that as a man *thinks*, so he *is*. Therefore, it is of no use
trying to control his behaviour if his thinking is wrong.

For a long time we were told by non-Christian thinkers that
the one great cause of crime was poverty. But at the present time
what they are telling us is that the one great cause of crime is
prosperity! Young people, they say, are earning too much
money and they do not know what to do with it. They say it is
this prosperity that has brought about the crime wave! Do not
misunderstand me. We should all be concerned about the problem
of poverty and the distress it often causes. But I am simply
concerned at the moment to point out the pathetic fallacy of
non-Christian thinking, which will not face this central truth,
that it is a man's total attitude towards life, himself, God, and
their relationship, that ultimately and inevitably determines and
controls conduct and behaviour. The Apostle puts it very clearly

in the first chapter of his Epistle to the Romans, where he says: 'The wrath of God is revealed from heaven against all ungodliness and unrighteousness of men.' Notice the order! Ungodliness first! It is ungodliness that leads to unrighteousness. And to try to deal with unrighteousness without dealing with the ungodliness is a sheer waste of time and energy and money. So let men bring their new Acts of Parliament, let them enlarge their prisons, let them invoke the schoolmasters and all the social agencies, it will avail them nothing; it never has done, it never can. There is only one thing that can deal with this whole question of morality and behaviour, and that is that men and women be brought out of darkness into God's marvellous light, that they cease to be darkness and become light in the Lord. History proves my contention, the contemporary situation is demonstrating it anew and afresh.

But how does darkness manifest itself in the realm of the will? Again, this is something that you find almost endlessly in the Bible. Notice the terms. People who live an evil life are described as 'children of the night'; 'they that be drunken are drunken in the night'; they are children of darkness, children of night. What is a Christian? He is a child of the light; 'children of the day', says Paul. We are not in darkness, we are children of the day, children of light! Notice the difference in the terms used. And indeed, quite apart from Christianity, the general observation of mankind seems to have discovered the difference. We hear and read about the *night life* of London. It is something that happens in the night, in the dark, the *night life of London*! It is a perfect description. The Apostle puts it here still more clearly; he refers to 'the hidden works of darkness', and says that 'It is a shame even to speak of those things which are done of them in secret'. He talks about 'the unfruitful works of darkness'.

The Apostle Paul was very fond of emphasising the contrast between the fruit of the light and the unfruitful works of darkness. He uses very similar terms in the fifth chapter of Galatians (verse 19) saying: 'Now the *works* of the flesh are manifest, which are these' – then comes that terrible list. Then he says, in verse 22, 'But' – not the *works* of the Spirit – 'the *fruit* of the Spirit. . . .'

[384]

There is a contrast here between works and fruit. This is clearly a difference which is not accidental. The Apostle obviously has a very profound meaning to convey to us, but he is putting it in this particular form, and invariably he talks about the *works* of darkness. Why? It seems to me that the only deduction we can make is that there is something about the evil life of darkness which (to use the term in its right meaning) is artificial. It is a sort of artifact produced by man. In other words, it is not man's natural life, not the kind of life that man was meant to live. It is true of what we call, and boast of, as 'civilisation'. We can say with assurance that God never meant people to live as, for instance, we live in this city of London. God never planned a place like London, or Chicago, or New York, or Paris, or any one of these great cities, or indeed even any one of our villages as we know them today. God never meant life to be like that! This is man's artifact, that which man has produced. The first person who built a city was Cain, the man who murdered his brother. He had become darkness and he began to express it, and he soon built a city, and began city life. That is not God's intention for man at all. The monstrosities that man has produced are not God's production at all. So the Apostle talks of this as the *works* of darkness. It is something mechanical, something which is organised.

Perhaps we see this today more clearly than mankind has ever seen it before. The newspapers of today are becoming more and more the finest commentary that I know of on the Bible. In them we see the utter artificiality of the life lived in darkness. There is nothing real there at all, but something has been erected and put up; it is all man's work, man makes it. And so life goes on, and it is called civilisation. But the Bible calls it 'the works of darkness'! And is there not something tragically mechanical about it all? The most awful thing, it seems to me at times, about the life of sin is its mechanical character, the way it goes on repeating itself, like a machine. Nothing new, nothing artistic about it! It churns out the same old thing day after day, the same sin, the same temptation, the same vice, the same ugly thing that gets you down. Mechanical, repetitive, it is just like a machine, it is machine-produced, it is '*works*'. It is the same as the difference between a machine and a flower or anything which has real life

in it. 'The works of darkness'! And we all get involved in it, in
the machinery. Our lives are organised for us, people do not
think any longer, they just do what is 'the done thing', that which
everybody else is doing. Originality is excluded from it; people,
irrespective of their real interests, just drop into it. And we all
look alike, dress alike, and are mass-produced in every respect.
We are made to enjoy the same things, believe in the same things,
do the same things. 'The works of darkness' is a perfectly accurate description of non-Christian life! How contemporary
God's book is!

And then let me take a look at Paul's second word. He talks about
the *unfruitful* works of darkness. He is not only contrasting the
machine with real life and growth, but he is looking at another
side of it. He says that there is no value to be found in a life
lived in darkness. He says the same thing in his sixth chapter
written to the Romans: 'For when ye were the servants of sin,
ye were free from righteousness. What fruit had ye then in those
things whereof ye are now ashamed? for the end of those things
is death.' What fruit had you *then*? None at all! That is the
appalling thing about this life of sin, this life of darkness. It is of
no value to the man himself. It does not add to his mind, his
understanding, his knowledge, his purity, his cleanliness. It takes
his money, it takes his energy, and leaves him an exhausted hulk
at the end of his life. The life that started with such glamour
may end in a gutter. The beauty with which it started becomes –
oh! just a raddled face. It is a valueless life, there is no fruit, no
profit in it; it takes everything from you.

We see it illustrated in the case of the prodigal son, do we not?
He started off with his pockets full of money; he ended with
nothing, empty pockets, no friends, nothing at all. That is the
life of sin, it takes from us, it is unfruitful, it is of no value to the
man himself! And what is even worse is that it is of no value to
anybody else. It makes no contribution. And that is, I suppose,
the final charge that will be brought against the present generation. What are we really contributing even to the story of humanity and of the human race? There is nothing ennobling,
uplifting or stimulating about it. It does not make people rouse

themselves to high achievement. We are not interested in achievement, we are interested in ease; our interest is leisure; we have even lost interest in work! It is the time in which we are not working that interests us. And then how do we spend that time? Is it some active interest? is it something that improves the mind or enlarges the heart? Not at all! Passive, mechanical entertainment always! It is unfruitful altogether, it has no contribution to make to others, even as it fails to produce any fruit in the persons themselves. Indeed it never leads to any kind of growth except the growth of some noxious weed. It produces a garden of the soul which is a mass of weeds and thorns; and there is no fruit there, nothing to eat, nothing to live on. It does not help you in the present, if you are taken ill, or find yourself lying on a sick bed, or facing death and eternity, for though you hope and expect to fall back on your reserves, you find you have nothing at all! Remember the words that came to the rich fool, who was congratulating himself and saying, 'Soul, thou hast much goods laid up for many years; take thine ease, eat, drink, and be merry'; but God said unto him, 'Thou fool! this night thy soul shall be required of thee, then whose shall those things be which thou hast provided?' – they are not yours, you cannot take them with you, you are bound to leave them behind you.

It is because people do not think about these things that they go on living as they do. Isn't life wonderful! says the young person. Is it? Examine it, my friend; see what it is going to lead you to, go on to the end! Is there any fruit for you or for anybody else? No! These transient things are completely and entirely unfruitful. And this is not only true on the personal level; it is true on a wider level in the case of countries and nations and empires. It is a fact of history that what finally produced the decline and the fall of the great Roman Empire was this sort of thing. Rome went down and collapsed because of internal rot. Gibbon will teach you that! The secular historians bring that out! Collapse came when the people became indolent and lovers of pleasures; they built their marvellous baths of gold and of silver, and they spent their day lolling in them, and had their sweet music played to them as they did so. The whole race became indolent, and slack, and lost its ambitions and the sense of its own mission and greatness. Such a life, as the Apostle says, is always *unfruitful* in every respect. And what alarms one is the question: Are we witnessing something like this in this very country of ours at the present time? Is not this rot the whole essence of the trouble? Neither morality nor even political idealism can be maintained apart from some grand motive or some noble view and conception of man. And we are as we are today, and we are witnessing what we are witnessing, because about the middle of the last century people began to listen to men like Charles Darwin and others, who maintained that man was no special creation of God! – if there is a God at all – man stands at the end of a process! So the view of man becomes degraded; and men forget God.

Of course for a while men can live on the capital of the Evangelical Awakening, and can carry on with their morality and their work and their political idealism, but it does not last very long. Once the real motive has been lost you get what we are witnessing today. The unfruitful works of darkness! They have a kind of inevitable consequence of their own; it is not fruit; it is just the smashing up of the machine. Our Lord Himself gave us the warning in the Sermon on the Mount, when He said, 'Enter ye in at the strait gate; for wide is the gate, and broad is the way, that leadeth to *destruction*'! The machine has become master, and the whole thing has blown up and been smashed to pieces. The unfruitful works of darkness inevitably lead to destruction.

Lastly, we look at the word that Paul uses in verse 12: 'For it is a *shame* even to speak of those things which are done of them in secret.' The manifestations of the godless life are darkness in the realm of the will also; they are works, they are unfruitful; yes, and they are shameful. Those who do them are ashamed of their practices, so they prefer to follow them under cover of darkness. Man, after all, whether he believes it or not, was made in the image of God, and he shows it when he least suspects it. Though he does not believe in God, and does not believe in his own soul, though he is fallen and degraded, this sense of shame is in him still. Thank God for that! Man is not an animal, man is not a machine; there is this in him that remains and abides. Though marred and ruined, there is something of the image left, and man, even at his lowest and his vilest, still knows something about a sense of *shame*. And it is the business of the Christian in terrible, godless days like these to start with people on their own level and to say to them, Tell me why you do not practise things like this in broad daylight? And then start from this sense of shame and try to bring them to see how their whole view of themselves, and of God, and of life, is based on utter ignorance, which, if it be not enlightened, will lead them to disaster and final doom.

Oh! the love of God, that, looking upon such a world of darkness and of ignorance and of shame, He should have sent His only begotten Son into it, to be the Light of the world, and by dying upon the cross to deliver us from it and to translate us from the kingdom of darkness into the kingdom of His dear Son! But, Christian people, may I put it to you like this: Are you concerned about the masses that are in this darkness? I know you feel a sense of disgust with respect to them; we all do; but if you merely feel a sense of disgust, and gather up your skirts, and walk on the other side of the street, you are almost as bad as they are. The Levite and the priest did just that, and no more, when they saw the wounded man by the roadside. That is of no value. If we realise that the people we encounter are living worthless lives because of this world's tragic ignorance and darkness, then, I say, as Christian people it should move us to say, What can I do for these people? how can gospel light and knowledge be brought to them? And I say once more that there is *nothing* that can deal with the situation but such an outpouring of the Spirit of God, such a visitation of God's Spirit in revival, as was experienced during the Protestant Reformation, and in the Puritan Period; in the 18th century under the preaching of Whitefield and the Wesleys; and also under Romaine and others here in the city of London; and again in 1859. And therefore it seems to me that the way to test whether we really do take these things seriously is to ask ourselves whether we are praying God to send us such a revival. Let us ask God to pour out His Spirit upon us, that the Church may be so filled with power that the men and women of this apathetic, godless, dark, ignorant, shameful generation will be compelled to listen, and compelled to think, and compelled to face God and their own eternal destiny.

[389]

31

The Fruit of Light

'(For the fruit of the Spirit is in all goodness and
righteousness and truth;) proving what is acceptable
unto the Lord.'

Ephesians 5:9–10

Having reminded the Ephesians of what they once were – 'Ye
were sometimes darkness' – Paul next proceeds to remind them
of what they now are and what is now expected of them – 'Now
are ye light in the Lord; walk as children of light'. We must
therefore work out the teaching in detail so that we may realise
not only the difference between the Christian and the man who is
blatantly and obviously not a Christian, but the difference also
between the man who is a true Christian and 'light in the Lord',
and the so-called good, moral man, who is not a Christian. This
becomes important because of this ninth verse, where we are
told that 'the fruit of the Spirit is in all goodness and righteousness and truth'. There is a type of man found in the world who
is not a Christian, who tells us that he is not a Christian, and who
almost boasts of the fact that he is not a Christian. But on the
surface he seems to be a good and righteous man who is interested
in truth and in integrity, in other words 'a good pagan'.

I have often referred to a book, called *The Failure of the Good
Pagan*, by Rosalind Murray, and I commend it to you again. It is
an exposure of this good, moral man who is not a Christian, and
who is ultimately, I suppose, the chiefest enemy of the Christian
faith. He may be a religious man, because you can be religious
without being a Christian, and it is very important to differentiate
again between these two. It is only as we see the characteristics of
the light that we shall be able to draw these all-important distinc-
tions, because – and I say it again – the Christian is not merely a

[390]

man who has received a certain amount of enlightenment, he *is*
light; 'but now *are* ye light *in* the Lord'.

We must ask therefore, How does this light manifest itself? It
does so, first and foremost, in the mind. Biblical truth comes
primarily to the mind, to the intellect, to the understanding; it is
not some sort of vague feeling people get. Vague feelings may
have nothing to do with Christianity at all. This is always a
matter of truth, so we start with the mind. And the first thing
we have to say about the Christian is that he shows that, since
he has become light in the Lord, he has a knowledge which he
lacked before. Darkness is characterised by ignorance: light is
characterised by knowledge and understanding and, above all,
by a knowledge of GOD; not merely a knowledge of certain
things concerning God, or a knowledge *about* God. That is
accessible to all. But this man has got a further knowledge. He is
in the position described by our Lord in John's Gospel: 'This is
life eternal, that they might know thee, the only true God, and
Jesus Christ whom thou hast sent' (17:3). It includes a knowledge
about God, of course; but it goes beyond that; it includes an
apprehension and a knowledge of God open only to the Christian,
and which all others lack.

Paul told the Corinthian Christians that 'the natural man
receiveth not the things of the Spirit of God, for they are foolishness unto him: neither can he know them, because they are
spiritually discerned'. That is to say, a man may have great
intellectual powers and reasoning ability, but, if he is not a
Christian, he is entirely ignorant of spiritual truths; he sees
nothing in them, he does not understand them. The spiritual
faculty is *the* thing that differentiates the Christian from everybody
else: it gives him an insight into, and an understanding and
apprehension of, spiritual truth. Now all non-Christians lack this.
They have minds, they have intellects; if you present them with a
political situation they can understand it and can reason about it,
they can take it in; they can do the same with poetry, with music,
with sociology, science, and a thousand and one other subjects.
But when you bring them to the realm of spiritual truth they
have no faculty which enables them to understand. They see

nothing in it, it is foolishness to them, it is all a lot of nonsense, they dismiss it with a wave of the hand. There are many such people, and they are given great prominence on radio programmes and on television. But have you noticed their ignorance of spiritual truth? Have you noticed their complete failure to think spiritually? They cannot help it, of course; they are blind, they are lacking in the faculty, they are not light in the Lord, they are darkness! They are afflicted by this ignorance, their foolish hearts are darkened, their minds are blinded by the god of this world.

You see, belief in Christ and the gospel is not a question of intellectual capacity at all. People think that certain persons are not Christians because of their great brains, their great intellectual capacity. And alas! many a Christian tends to think like that and is rather troubled by the fact that these great men are not Christians. But, you see, that is a denial of the whole of Christianity. It does not matter how perfect the instrument is, if it lacks this spiritual quality, this spiritual faculty, it amounts to nothing at all. 'The natural man receiveth not the things of the Spirit of God, for they are foolishness unto him.' He is 'darkness' he is not 'light in the Lord'. But the moment a man becomes a Christian, the first thing that he becomes aware of is that he has got a spiritual faculty; he now possesses an understanding in the realm where formerly he was such a stranger and felt himself to be an outsider. He begins to have an apprehension of God, the being of God, the truth about God, and in addition he begins to realise that he has a soul.

It is only the man into whom the light has entered who really becomes concerned about his soul. Other people are not concerned about the soul at all. They think of man as an animal, and they think that death is the end. They think they are paying themselves a compliment by talking in that way, but they are denying the highest thing that is in man, the soul! But you need a spiritual apprehension to be aware of the fact that you are a soul, and that 'Dust thou art, to dust returneth, was not spoken of the *soul*'! This imperishable thing! Ah! but, they say, when you dissect a body you cannot find an organ called the soul, and they think themselves clever in dismissing the idea. Sheer ignorance! These things are spiritually discerned; it is only the Spirit who

can reveal unto man the deep things of God, but the Spirit does –
to Christians!

Furthermore, because Christians are 'light in the Lord' they
have an understanding and an apprehension of the fact of sin!
Non-Christians do not know what it means to be a sinner; the
whole notion seems to them to be monstrous and to be ridiculous.
They explain the whole of conduct in terms of environment or
heredity or upbringing or things like that; they are not aware of
the fact that there is a principle of evil in man, which vitiates all
his judgments, a bias, a tendency towards evil. Paul calls it a
'law in our members', ever dragging us down. It means nothing
to them, they know nothing about a spiritual conflict within. But
the moment a man becomes a Christian he becomes aware that
he is the seat of this tremendous battle and fight; he is aware that
he is a sort of enigma; he is aware of these forces struggling
within him, some for the soul, some against.

And then, the Christian man is taught by the Spirit to look at
the Lord Jesus Christ. Other men, in darkness, look at Jesus
Christ, whom they only call *Jesus*, of course. That is characteristic
of them, to call Him *Jesus*. Christians should not call Him *Jesus*;
He is the *Lord Jesus Christ* to the people of light! But the non-
Christians look at Jesus, and they see but a man, a carpenter, a
mere teacher, and so on, a pacifist or something like that, and
that is all they see in Him. You need to have eyes enlightened by
the eyesalve of the Holy Spirit before you can really see Him and
begin to see the marvel and the mystery of His Person. You see
the divine, you see the human; you see the divine nature, you
see the human nature; you see the two there together, they are
unmixed, they are both there but they are not mingled. You look
at the marvel and the mystery, and you take your stand with the
Apostle Paul and you say, 'Great is the mystery of godliness!
GOD was manifest in the flesh'! Now to the Christian this is the
greatest thing in life. It is no longer something ridiculous which
he dismisses and says he cannot understand scientifically; it is to
him the most marvellous and the most glorious truth of all, that
the Incarnation has taken place. '*GOD* was manifest in the flesh',
'the *Word* was made flesh and dwelt among us', and so he con-

templates the Person of the Lord and the truth concerning Him, and it moves him to wonder and to worship.

And likewise with the way of salvation. The man who is light in the Lord is a man who knows the way of salvation, and he can explain it to others. This is not merely the teaching of the Apostle Paul. The Apostle Peter, in his First Epistle says the same thing: 'Be ready always to give an answer to every man that asketh you a reason of the hope that is in you, with meekness and fear' (3:15). Now the Christian can do that, for he has an understanding of the one and only way of salvation. Let us work it out, the whole of this great and glorious truth. The Christian is a man who comes to it with a new mind, he is light in the Lord, this Book means everything to him, he sees this extraordinary truth in it, and he has an increasing understanding of it.

In addition, the Christian not only has this new understanding and apprehension, but he has a *heart* that can respond to it. Some seem to be so constituted that they can take a kind of intellectual interest in the Bible, but their hearts do not respond to it. Certain people are interested in the Bible as literature, or as philosophy, and so on. But they are not gripped and moved by the truth. But a man who is light in the Lord, his heart is light! And he is a man who *feels* the power of the truth, the power of the word that is found here; he is moved by it. Now this is of necessity true of the Christian. He is light in the Lord, and the whole man is light in the Lord. As the Apostle puts it in writing to the Romans, 'he has obeyed from the heart the form of sound words' delivered to him. The complete man is engaged. And so I emphasise that the Christian is a man who shows that he has got light in his heart. His emotions are engaged, he desires holiness. He *must* desire holiness. I am not saying that he is sinless and perfect. Not at all! But though he sins he desires holiness, he hungers and thirsts after righteousness. The desire of his heart is to be delivered from sin. It is to know God and the Lord Jesus Christ, to know the Bible, to know the truth. This is the relationship of his heart to these matters. His heart has become light in the Lord.

But now we must consider the third aspect, which is the will. This is the realm about which the Apostle is particularly concerned in this section with which we are dealing. Every aspect is there, but this is the thing which he emphasises supremely. Here

[394]

we come to character as it shows itself in expression, in action. In verse 9 we read, 'For the fruit of the Spirit is in all goodness and righteousness and truth.' In one respect this translation in the Authorised Version is unfortunate. The translation most in accordance with the best manuscripts is: 'the fruit of *light* is in all goodness and righteousness and truth'. Of course, it amounts to the same thing; it is the Spirit who gives the light, there is no light apart from Him, and it is not surprising therefore that the Name of the Spirit came in at this point; so take it 'fruit of the *Spirit*', or 'fruit of the *light*'; it is equally true in both cases.

We have already seen that the characteristic and significant word in relation to darkness is 'works': 'Have no fellowship with the unfruitful *works* of darkness.' But when he speaks of the light and the manifestations of light, he no longer speaks of *works*, but of *fruit*. We must therefore look into the significance of this change in the use of terms, contrasting 'the fruit of the light' with the 'works of darkness'.

The great characteristic of the life of the true Christian is fruit, and this tells us that it is only when a man becomes a Christian that he really becomes natural. It is only the Christian who begins to approximate to what a man is meant to be, that is to say, what man was in his first creation. He was made and created in the image of God, he was made upright, he was given original righteousness; but as the result of the Fall and sin all that has become lost. And the trouble about man in sin is that he is a monstrosity, he is un-natural. If you want to read what is perhaps one of the greatest expositions of this which you will find in the whole Bible, I urge you to read Psalm 104, and there you will see the psalmist speaking of Creation and telling us how everything displays the glory of God – the mountains, the rivers, the birds, the trees, the cedars of Lebanon that are full of sap. On and on he goes. And then, having described the various works of creation, he looks at man, and he feels there is only one thing to say about him – 'Let the *sinners* be consumed out of the earth, let them disappear out of sight.' Why? Because the sinner is a monstrosity in God's universe. He has become un-natural. But when a man becomes a Christian, the first thing that is true about him is that he becomes natural. And he begins to function as he was meant to do. The business of a fruit tree is to produce fruit; that is the natural order. But how often do we think of the Christian in these terms? On the other hand, non-Christians are unnatural, they are monstrosities, they are a denial of the true being of man. It is Christianity alone that makes us *men* worthy of the name.

Again, there is never anything artificial or mechanical or machine-like about the life of the Christian. The life of the Christian is rather reminiscent of the way fruit grows on a tree. The Christian should never give the appearance of being machine-like, or machine-produced. Christians cannot be produced to order, neither can their life or their activities and actions. Now this, to me, is of tremendous importance. It is here we see the real difference between Christian behaviour and living on the one hand, and the kind of conduct and behaviour that characterises the devotees of the cults and false religions on the other. The latter are always machine-made, they are always produced to order. The life of the Christian should never give the impression that he has imposed a certain number of things upon himself. His life is comparable to a tree, whereas the life of the cults and the false religionists resembles a Christmas tree. In the case of the Christmas tree, you have to hang the fruit on to it, the gifts and the presents. It is an artificial tree. But the characteristic of the real tree is that the fruit grows out of it, you do not hang it on to the branches. So the Christian and his manner of life should never give the impression that he has imposed upon himself a certain line of conduct and of behaviour. The cults may simulate reality. It is very difficult at times, is it not, to tell the difference between a living flower and an artificial one? People are very clever, they can make an artificial rose in such a manner that, at first glance, it can almost deceive the expert. The devil becomes an angel of light, and he counterfeits the true, but it is still artificial, it is still without life, it is something manufactured and made. We are never to give that impression. Our fruit is to be 'the *fruit* of the light'!

But, to carry the analogy further, there should always be a suggestion of the element of steady growth and of development in the life of the Christian. Without pressing the analogy, let us continue to look at it in terms of this fruit tree. You go to bed one night, having looked at the tree just before you went in, and there it was, just the branches and the leaves, nothing more. Next morning you get up and open your door and go out into your garden, and there you see the tree covered, teeming, with fruit fully developed. That never happens, does it? No, no, you get buds; later you see flowers, then you get just a suggestion that fruit is on the way; then that fruit begins to develop until finally it reaches maturity. That is the Christian – the fruit! It does not happen suddenly, it is not imposed, it is not ready-made. But, I find far too many ready-made Christians, with regard to conduct. First of all, a person is taken to an evangelistic meeting and there he gets saved; next, he is taken in hand for instruction, and he is told what to do. Almost at once he is perfected, an example of a Christian ready-made and mass-produced. But *that* is *not* Christianity. I say it deliberately, that is *not* Christianity. It is what the cults do, it is what false religions do, it is what legalism does. Religion can do it. But true Christianity produces genuine *FRUIT*, and in its production there is always the element of growth and of development, leading to maturity.

It is also characteristic of fruit that, while essentially, of course, all the fruit is the same, it is equally true to say that there are always individual differences. Look at an apple tree teeming with apples. Well, you say, they are all apples! I agree, but they are not all identical in shape, or in the colour; there is a little more red in one, a little less in another, and so on. There are all sorts of minor differences and variations in the fruit. And this is always the characteristic of true Christians. But it is not the characteristic of the followers and the devotees of the cults and the false religions. They are always the same, they are mass-produced. When you see one, you see them all; they are like postage stamps; they are all identical, machine-like, rubber stamped.

Sometimes one can tell the very organisation in which a man became a Christian. He has a certain stamp on him, a sameness in expression, in behaviour and everything. But we must protest against all this in the name of the Spirit, and because of the liberty of the Spirit. Christians are fruit, the *fruit* of the light! And

[397]

we must never allow anybody to impose a mould upon us. We are called into the glorious liberty of the children of God. It is a tragic thing to see young Christians conforming to a mould and to a pattern. I have seen it evidenced even in matters of dress, in the way they pronounce certain words, and so on. Let us remember, I say, that we have got life, that we are fruit, and that one of our characteristics is the liberty which leads to variety and variation.

Let me also remind you, again, that fruit always comes from within outwards. In a sense fruit is an expression of the life of the tree that produces it. It is something that comes out of the character, out of the nature, out of the life! And so it is with the Christian. In consequence we must never impose forms upon the Christian. And not only forms of conduct and behaviour! There are people who would even impose upon you what you are to do with your life; they may try to make you become a foreign missionary, or a home missionary, or a cog in a piece of church machinery. Do not let them! Never do anything because anybody else tells you to do it. Fruit must come out of yourself; it must come out of your own light, your own experience, your own life, your own vitality. Everything must be the result of what we *are*, and we do not make ourselves what we are by what we do; we do what we do because we are what we are. Fruit always comes from within and is the expression of the true nature. 'Ye were sometimes darkness, but now are ye light in the Lord; walk as children of light; for the fruit of the light *is*. . . .' That is the order of things!

I would even go further and contend that not only must we not allow other people to dictate to us and to impose things upon us, we must never even force ourselves. This is very important in regard to guidance. I have often said it before, I will say it again: You must never decide to do anything solely in terms of your mind and your understanding. People who teach that the need is the call are really denying this principle. The need is not the call. If the need were the call, then every Christian man or woman should give up all secular employment and go straight into wholetime Christian work. The need is not and never has been the call. The need is a part of it, it comes into it, but it is not a call until I know something of this inward constraint, this pressure of the sap rising up within me which makes me say with Luther, 'I can do no other'. These things come from within, as an expression of the nature. Hence the New Testament always puts its main emphasis, not upon what we do, but upon what we *are*. But the whole prevailing theory today in the Church, and alas! even in evangelical circles, is the exact opposite. Let's be getting busy! let's get going, people say. But the decision to act, to decide to get going, does not belong to us. God has put certain principles within us. The light in the mind and heart and will, that is the dynamo, that is the thing that gets us going, the pressure from within. And what we are called upon to do is to cultivate the soul. If we cultivate the soul truly, the fruit will appear; the conduct, the behaviour, the vocation, and all these other things, will come out of it!

There are too many hot-houses in the Christian church, and too much apparatus for forcing growth. That is a marked characteristic of life today, is it not? And it will perhaps be one of the major problems for civilisation in a few years. Have we not seen it, for example, in the matter of egg production? how they use artificial light in the pens in which the hens are kept, artificial light throughout the night so that the poor birds are forced to produce! It is a violation of nature, it is wrong. And it is wrong in the spiritual life also. We are not to have our eye primarily upon production or upon the quantity produced! We must ever be concerned about our capacity to produce, and about the quality of what we produce. As Paul puts it in writing to Timothy, our business is to see that we are vessels that are fit for the Master's use. Let's get going! men say; let's get busy! Familiar terms! But that is machine-like, as if they were starting off some mechanism. It is not the Christian way. Our business is to be vessels that are fit and meet for the Master's use. Let us think of ourselves as living trees, with the nutriment, the sap, the life. Our Lord is the Vine, and we are the branches. As long as we look at the truth in this way, we shall be able to avoid most of the pitfalls, so dangerous to the individual soul and experience, and equally dangerous to the whole Church and her life and activity.

I conclude by reminding you that it is no longer a matter of works, it is now a matter of fruit. We are *His* workmanship, created anew *in* Christ Jesus *unto* good works. That is the way. A man must become light in the Lord; and when this happens he will begin to produce the fruit. Is it not the tragedy of the modern Church that she is full of works and activity and activism, but that there is such little fruit, this glorious fruit of the light and the Spirit, to be seen among us? Let us be clear then that our fundamental concepts are true and clear and biblical, and let us realise that we are branches of the true Vine, and are meant to produce fruit to the glory of God.

32

Acceptable unto the Lord

'For ye were sometimes darkness, but now are ye
light in the Lord: walk as children of light: (for the
fruit of the Spirit [*or*, the fruit of light] is in all
goodness and righteousness and truth;) proving
what is acceptable unto the Lord. And have no
fellowship with the unfruitful works of darkness,
but rather reprove them. For it is a shame even to
speak of those things which are done of them in
secret. But all things that are reproved are made
manifest by the light: for whatsoever doth make
manifest is light. Wherefore he saith, Awake thou
that sleepest, and arise from the dead, and Christ
shall give thee light.'

Ephesians 5:8–14

We continue with our study of the Christian as a person who is
'light in the Lord', and in verse 9 we find the Apostle telling us
that the light in question shows itself in certain ways. He seems
here to be holding a sort of prism under the light. And what the
prism does of course, is to break up the light into its component
parts. It thus produces a sort of spectrum which Paul demonstrates
in the words, 'the fruit of light is in all goodness and righteousness
and truth'. His actual exhortation is, 'But now are ye light in the
Lord: walk as children of light, proving what is acceptable unto
the Lord'; but lest they should be forgetful of the characteristics
of the light, he divides it up for us here (in a parenthesis) as a
prism divides the natural light, into goodness, righteousness, and
truth, – *all* goodness, *all* righteousness and *all* truth – and we
must look carefully at these three most important words.

The first is *goodness*, and then comes *righteousness*. Paul was very much interested in these two words, and he often puts them together, as for example in the fifth chapter of Romans, although there in a different order. He is showing how 'God commends his love toward us in that while we were yet sinners Christ died for us'. That, he says, is truly amazing, astonishing, almost incredible, because you do not find that sort of thing among men. And then he puts it like this: 'for scarcely for a righteous man will one die: yet peradventure for a good man some would even dare to die'. Here he takes the righteous man first and then mentions the good man; but in Ephesians he starts with the good man and continues with the righteous man. And it is easy to see, I think, why the order of the two words is not the same in both cases. The Apostle is working up towards something in Romans 5, but in our Ephesian text he is working from above downwards; so he starts with the word *goodness*. 'The fruit of light is in all *goodness*.' What is goodness? Here is a word that we tend to use glibly, thoughtlessly and lightly, but it is a very great word. Goodness is one of the characteristics of God Himself. 'God is good to all.' 'The earth is full of the goodness of the Lord.' Or take it again as the Apostle defines it somewhat in the second chapter of his Epistle to the Romans: 'Despisest thou the riches of his goodness and forbearance and longsuffering; not knowing that the goodness of God leadeth thee to repentance?' – the goodness of God! God is good!

Goodness means benevolence. It is always indicative of a perfect balance in the various parts of the personality. A good man is a balanced man, a man in whom everything that is noble and excellent works harmoniously together. He is not angular; the various attributes of his person and his personality are to be seen in this perfect blending. And the result of this is, of course, that he is a man who is concerned to promote the happiness of all around him. He is not selfish, not self-centred, but because he has this balance himself he is concerned about others. And this is the great characteristic of God also; it is the goodness of God that leads us to repentance; it is God looking upon our misery, our unhappiness, and all that is true of us as the result of sin; it is that in God which leads us to repentance. God is good to all, He makes His sun to rise upon the evil and the good and sends His rain upon the just and the unjust. Although men are evil and unjust He does this for them. The goodness of God leadeth to repentance.

In man we see a very pale reflection of the same thing. The good man is a man who thinks about love and beauty and truth. And therefore, as he looks out upon his fellow men and women, he is concerned in turn to alleviate suffering, to mitigate wrongs. He is always looking for opportunities to do this, his heart is full of benevolence, he is concerned about benefitting others. It is a complete contrast, therefore, to the unfruitful works of darkness, which are of no benefit or value to anybody. The sinner is no benefactor, he is purely selfish, he is out to satisfy and gratify his own lusts and desires. His attitude is – I want this, and because I want it I must have it. He may cause intense suffering to others, but it does not count with him at all. That is the exact opposite of goodness and of benevolence. You see, the terrible thing about sin is that it turns a man right in upon himself, making him self-centred, self-interested, selfish. So, says the Apostle, the first thing that you see as you hold up this prism to the light is that the man who is 'light' is full of goodness, this thing that goes out to others and is concerned about helping them and improving their lot. God is good to all. And the Christian in turn should be good to all. Christ says, 'I am the light of the world', and goes on to say, 'Ye are the light of the world'. As He was good to all, we must be good to all in the same way.

The second term is *righteousness*. This differs from goodness in that it brings in legal notions and conceptions. Righteousness means conformity to law, and is a narrower term than *goodness*. Righteousness is something that you think of in terms of the prescriptions and the demands of a law, and conformity to that law. It means uprightness, and a manifesting of justice. It means in fact being right. You test the rightness, the uprightness, of a wall or a door by using a plummet or plumb-line. That supplies the whole idea of *righteousness*. And the Apostle is saying that righteousness is the characteristic of the Christian man. He is right and just in and of himself: in his own handling of himself what he does is upright and just, and he is fair also in his treatment of others; he never violates the rules or the laws with regard to them; he never does them any wrong; and he respects their rights and possessions. In other words, we can think of righteousness in terms of the Ten Commandments and what we are told about not *coveting* the things that belong to a neighbour. The man who has light in him is never guilty of coveting his neighbour's possessions and rights. Now, we are not thinking so much of benevolence at this moment, but of that which is right and true and just, that which is indicated by God's moral law. In other words, he is not a selfish man, neither is he a man who is governed by prejudices. He is not governed by his impulses and his thoughts, he wants to know what is right, what is just, what is equitable, what is really fair to his fellow-man. He loves his neighbour as himself. Righteousness lies in a perfect conformity to the law, not to the letter only but also to the spirit.

A common characteristic of the non-Christian life is lawlessness, every man for himself, with no thought of caring about other people's rights. We see much of this in the life of society today. In fact, most of the troubles and problems which are confronting the politicians and others are due to an absence of this righteousness; not only is there no goodness, there is no righteousness; and these things, of course, always go together. I have already reminded you how the Apostle puts it in the first chapter of his Epistle to the Romans: 'For the wrath of God is revealed from heaven against all ungodliness [first] and [then] unrighteousness of men.' The absence of godliness is always followed by the absence of righteousness. There is no greater fallacy than that which has characterised the moral teaching of the last hundred years or so, namely, that you could shed the godliness and hold on to the righteousness; that you could dismiss the Bible but still get the conduct that the Bible inculcates. It just cannot happen. Once you lose godliness you will always lose righteousness. So the Apostle is reminding the Ephesian believers that, conversely, to come back to God, to have this light of the knowledge of the glory of God in the face of Jesus Christ shining in our hearts, leads not only to the goodness that characterises God Himself, but in turn leads to righteousness in character and in conduct in every sphere of life. In other words the Christian is a man whose life is governed by principles. He knows what he is doing, and he knows why he is doing it. He is not just conforming to a pattern, he has reasons, he is working out his doctrine, he is a righteous man because he knows that the law of the Lord is perfect [right], converting the soul, as the Psalmist tells us.

The Apostle's third word is *truth*. 'The fruit of the light is in all goodness and righteousness and *truth*.' And this again is a most important and vital element. By 'truth', in this context, Paul means a series of contrasts with what he has been saying about the non-Christian life. He has said in verse 6, 'Let no man *deceive* you with vain words.' In verse 12 we are told that 'it is a shame even to speak of those things which are done of them in *secret*'; elsewhere he talks about the '*hidden* things of darkness'. Well now, truth is the exact opposite of all such things as these. The characteristic of the life of the Christian man is that there is no deceit in it, nothing hidden or underhanded or dishonest, nothing that savours of hypocrisy or pretence. No! its characteristics are that it is open and above-board, pellucid, and transparent. Indeed, as the Apostle points out, 'All things that are reproved are made manifest by the light: for whatsoever doth make manifest is light.' That is not the best translation, as I shall show you, but there is that meaning to it. You cannot conceal anything when light comes. Imagine that you are walking along a dark country road. Suddenly a car comes with its headlights ablaze, and at once everything becomes visible, and you see all sorts of creeping things disappearing into the shadows. Light exposes everything, and that is the effect of truth within the personality. The Christian is an open man, who has nothing to conceal or to hide. He does not pretend to be something that he is not. He is what he is by the grace of God, very different from that other type of man, whose whole life is lived in deceit. The non-Christian trusts nobody, and nobody trusts him; you cannot believe him, you never know when he is speaking the truth. Adam and Eve, after they had sinned, covered themselves with fig leaves and went behind the trees of the garden to hide themselves from God, and the ungodly man still does the same thing in his own way. That is always the characteristic of the life of sin – hidden! untrustworthy! deceitful! But the Christian is the exact opposite of all this, there is a transparency about him; you know your man, as it were; he is all above-board, he is not hiding anything, there is no pretence, he is sincere. In his First Epistle, Peter describes him as without malice, without hypocrisy, without guile, which is saying the very same thing that the Apostle Paul is dealing with at this point in the Epistle to the Ephesians. The Christian is what he is because of the truth of God, for this truth has entered into him and possessed him; so his life is characterised by truth in all its varied and glorious manifestations.

We can sum up what the Apostle is telling us about light by saying that it is the most beneficent thing in the world. It is a wonderful thing in itself. And, oh! the good that it does! Nobody likes a day of fog, but we glory in the light and the sunshine. Light! It heals our bodies. It brightens everything, and even works into the deepest parts of our physical constitutions. Our Lord has told us, as I have reminded you, that we in turn are the light of the world, and we are to irradiate this beneficence among our fellow men and women. We have also seen that light always exposes that which is wrong, brings it into sight and condemns it, as it were, and shows us what is right and true and good. And light is that which makes everything open and plain and clear. A man is studying a portion of Scripture and he does not understand it. I would like some light on this! he says. Light opens things out, makes everything plain and clear and pellucid. And Christians, according to the Apostle and to the New Testament everywhere, are to be characterised by these qualities. When we visit people they should feel when we leave, It was good for us that they came, we are feeling better for their visit. In the same way, by being what we are, we should be a rebuke to evil, and manifestations of the just and the true, the holy and the upright life. Above all we should bring this element of openness and of truth into all our dealings and all our associations.

Here Paul closes the brackets, the parenthesis, and ends his sentence proper '. . . but now are ye light in the Lord, walk as children of light . . .' with the words: 'proving what is acceptable unto the Lord'. In certain ways this is the key to it all, the key to the three things mentioned in the brackets, for it provides the

[406]

overriding principle which, if we observe it, will guarantee the three manifestations of the light within us. A parallel statement of the Apostle's is found in the twelfth chapter of his Epistle to the Romans: 'Be not conformed to this world: but be ye transformed by the renewing of your mind, that ye may *prove* what is that good, and acceptable, and perfect, will of God.' In both passages the word *prove* occurs. It is a term that was employed in the testing of precious metals; when you wanted to differentiate between one metal and another you were given a lump of the material, and asked to identify it. You then tested it by applying various acids, and observing the response. You were *proving* the metal, that is, you were testing it and discovering what exactly it was, by applying the tests. The Apostle uses the same word in our text: '*proving* what is acceptable unto the Lord'.

The great characteristic of the life and conduct of the Christian is that he sets himself to discover what it is that really pleases the Lord. That is what he wants to do, that is his grand, ultimate motive. This is all-important and we must emphasise it in a very special manner, for in looking at conduct and behaviour we need not only to differentiate between the Christian and the flagrant, obvious sinner, but also between him and the so-called good, moral man, 'the good pagan', if you like. Verse 10 supplies the ultimate acid test. When you look at the lives of the two men you cannot easily see much difference between them; they both seem to be good men, righteous men, men who are characterised by truth. And yet one of them is a Christian and the other is not. How are we to discern the truth concerning them? I know of no better test than the one supplied in this tenth verse. Here is something that is true only of the Christian, never of anybody else. It is *the* characteristic of the Christian, that he is always proving what is acceptable unto the Lord. Let me explain. Here is a man who is not concerned about and interested in goodness, righteousness and truth in and of themselves. He is not interested in them as abstract virtues, nor as abstract absolutes that govern his conduct. On the other hand, non-Christians may be interested in these things in and of themselves. I believe in goodness, I believe in righteousness and justice, I believe in truth and in truthfulness, says the good pagan. He sets them up as his code and he lives according to it. Let us grant him everything that he claims; he may succeed very well. But all I am saying is this, that if that is all he is able to tell me, I tell him that he is not a Christian. That is just excellent paganism. It is the teaching of the great Greek philosophers before Christ; they inculcated these virtues as principles, abstract principles. But the Christian is not interested in them as abstract principles. He is interested in them because he knows they constitute the will of the Lord. It is the Lord who interests him, and because the Lord is characterised by these things and is anxious that His people should be also, the Christian is interested in them. The Apostle goes further therefore and adds this differentiating truth – 'proving what is acceptable unto the Lord'.

Again, the Christian, unlike the good moral man, or the good *religious* man who is not a Christian, is not living this kind of life in order to please himself or to live up to his own standard or his own code. There are many men who do that. It is no part of my business to criticise them, but it is very much my business to show that they are not Christians. This is one of the most subtle points we can ever encounter. There are men who say, Well now, I believe in having a standard, I believe in having a code, and I am going to do my utmost to live up to that code; I am going to be unhappy unless I succeed. But the man is doing it to please himself, he is doing it in order to live up to his own standard. He says, A man has got to live with himself! I would lose my self-respect if I did not do this, I would be ashamed of myself if I did not, I am not content to live anyhow. I believe in living up to that mark and to that standard. Yet the whole time his motive is to please himself and to conform to his own standard and to his own code, and this is very different from the Christian's ambition to prove, and to prove always, what is acceptable unto the Lord!

But I must go further. There are many people who are living what is commonly called a good life simply because they are afraid of what people will say if they live otherwise. They are afraid of being found out and condemned, they are afraid of losing the good opinion of their neighbours, they fear adverse publicity if they falter; and this fear and this concern for the good

opinion of other people governs the whole of their lives. They
are governed in all their conduct by what other people think or
say or do about them. The Christian is different. In his First
Epistle to the Corinthians the Apostle says, 'With me it is a very
small thing that I should be judged of you, or of man's judgment;
yea, I judge not mine own self . . . He that judgeth me is the
Lord.' That is Christianity! Paul is not governed by what other
people are going to say, he is not even governed by what he is
going to say about himself. 'I judge not mine own self.' Say what
you like, says Paul, it makes no difference to me; I have committed my judgment to the Lord. Such is the Christian; he proves
what is acceptable unto the Lord!

But we must go one step further. The Christian man whose life
is characterised by goodness and righteousness and truth is not
even a man who is trying to live a life in conformity with and
according to the teaching of the Lord Jesus Christ Himself
because he thinks that that is the highest and the best. Now again,
there are many people who do that. They read the ethics of the
Greek and other philosophers, and then they come to the Sermon
on the Mount, and they say, Here is the acme! here it is at its
highest and its finest! there has never been such ethical teaching
as this! Very well, says the man, I am going to live my life
according to the dictates and the teaching of the Sermon on the
Mount, the highest, the noblest concept I have ever encountered.
Is he a Christian? Well, all I say is this, that if he stops at that point
he is not a Christian, for the Christian is a man who is governed
by the need to 'prove what is that good, and acceptable, and
perfect, will of God'. We must be absolutely clear about this. The
thing that proves that we are Christians is that, over and above
everything else, our ultimate, our final consideration is our desire
to seek and to know, to discover, the will of the Lord, in order
that we may please Him. It is this personal relationship to this
blessed Person.

That is, as I have been saying, the *differentia* of Christian ethics,
that puts it into a category entirely alone. Its motive, its main-
spring, the most important thing about it, is that none but the
Christian can claim or even speak about the desire to live to the
Lord's glory and to His praise, and to please Him in all things;
as this Apostle puts it, 'even as I please not myself'. His obedience

was always to please the Lord and to live for the Lord's sake.

Why? Well, surely this must be true. A Christian is a man who realises that he owes everything that he is, and has, and hopes to be, to this Lord, to the One who so loved him while he was yet in darkness, while he was yet a sinner, while he was yet ungodly, while he was yet an enemy, so loved him that He gave Himself for him. His body was broken, His blood was shed, that he, a sinner, might become light in the Lord. He is a man who says to himself, 'I am not mine own, I have been bought with a price'. He is not a free agent, he is, with the Apostle Paul, the bondslave of the Lord Jesus Christ, who died that he might be forgiven, who died that he might be made good, who died that he might have a hope of entering into heaven. It is the Lord! this One who has given him everything, HE is the motive, it is to please Him. The Christian's motive is not to live up to a certain code of morality, it is not to avoid the criticism of others, it is not to be on good terms with himself, it is not to be a paragon of all the virtues, it is not to cut a great figure or have a great name among men. No, no! He says, 'Let nothing please or pain me, apart, O Lord, from Thee.' 'Proving what is the acceptable will of the Lord'! The Apostle expresses the same thought in writing to the Corinthians: 'Whether, therefore, ye eat or drink, or whatsoever ye do, do all to the glory of God'! That is in 1 Corinthians 10. Read it again. '. . . conscience', he says, 'not thine own, but of the other'. 'All things are lawful for me, but all things are not expedient.' What does he mean? Well, there is that weaker brother! Why should I consider him? Because Christ has considered him! 'Whatsoever ye do' – he works it up to a great climax at the end – 'whether ye eat or drink, or whatsoever ye do, do all to the glory of God'. It is only the Christian who does that.

The Christian is a man who is not interested in abstract virtues as such, even though they be goodness, righteousness, and truth; he is interested in them only because he is interested in the Lord. Christ died that we might be the light of the world, that we might be reflections of Him, that we might be like a city set upon a hill which cannot be hid, and like the light which is not put under a bushel but in a prominent place so that it irradiates its light throughout the entire room! Let your light, He says, so shine before men that they may see your good works, and glorify your Father which is in heaven. Yes, says the answer to the first question in the Shorter Catechism, 'The chief end of man is to glorify God and to enjoy Him [as you are doing it] for ever.'

'Proving what is acceptable unto the Lord.'

33
Exposed by the Light

'Be not ye therefore partakers with them. For ye
were sometimes darkness, but now are ye light in the
Lord: walk as children of light: (for the fruit of the
Spirit is in all goodness and righteousness and truth;)
proving what is acceptable unto the Lord. And have
no fellowship with the unfruitful works of darkness,
but rather reprove them. For it is a shame even to
speak of those things which are done of them in
secret. But all things that are reproved are made
manifest by the light: for whatsoever doth make
manifest is light. Wherefore he saith, Awake thou
that sleepest, and arise from the dead, and Christ
shall give thee light.'

Ephesians 5:7-14

We continue our study of the practical applications of the
Apostle's doctrine, having already considered how Christians
who are 'light in the Lord' should comport and conduct themselves. There remains, however, the problem as to what our
attitude should be towards the darkness itself that is still round
and about us. After all, Christians are not people who live in some
kind of glasshouse. We do not live an isolated, segregated life,
we have to live this Christian life in the world; that is the New
Testament teaching about this matter. There is an erroneous
teaching, of course, called monasticism, which says that Christians
should go out of the world and segregate themselves and live in a
type of enclosure with some sort of a curtain round them. But
this is a false view of Christianity, a false asceticism, which is in
many ways the enemy of Christian truth, because it robs the
gospel of one of its greatest victories, namely, that it enables us,

in the same world in which we lived before, to live a new kind of life. Most of us, if not all of us, know very well the feeling that gave rise to monasticism; we must often have longed to be able to get away from difficulties and problems and people, everything that tends to irritate us and upset us and to get us down. We understand the feeling of the psalmist when he cried out and said, 'O, for the wings of a dove' that I might fly from it all. That is the spirit that leads to monasticism, but it is not Christianity; and thank God it is not! He gives us the help that enables us to live the Christian life, a Christlike life, in the midst of our problems and trials.

The problem is illustrated by the way in which our Lord dealt with the man who lived in the country of the Gadarenes, the man who had a legion of devils in him. Our Lord by His power exorcised these devils, drove them out of the man, and we see him seated, clothed, and in his right mind. Suddenly he saw our Lord departing, at the request of the people, and about to enter into a ship. The man ran after Him, expressing a desire, beseeching Him that he might be allowed to go with Him. But our Lord refused his request; He said, No, go back to your home town, go back to the very place where you have suffered so much and where you have lived in this terrible condition. It sounds preposterous that our Lord should send this man alone and apparently utterly defenceless, back to the city and the place of his former devil possession and misery; He does not allow him to go with Him. Now the man's desire was very natural, was it not? He must have thought to himself, Oh! if He is going to leave me, the devils will come back again, my only place of safety is to be with Him. Let me go with you, he says. No, says Christ, go back! He sends him back to the very place of his hopeless misery. Why does He do that? The answer is supplied by the Lord Himself: Go and tell your friends, He says, what God has done for you; go and witness and testify there. So He sends him back to witness and testify at home. But He sends him back with a power within him that the man had not yet realised.

Now that is Christianity! We do not go out of the world, we are still to live in it, and in the midst of our former surroundings we are to live the Christian life. And here, in his Letter to the Ephesians, the Apostle tells us how we are to do it. Surely there is nothing that is more urgently important for Christians, on the practical level at the present time, than just this matter. The world is becoming more and more godless, irreligious, and indeed actively, positively, pagan. We are more and more back in the conditions that obtained in the city of Ephesus two thousand years ago; and it becomes a very difficult and perplexing problem for Christian people to know how they are to conduct themselves as they meet in business and in their professions, in politics and in almost every situation today, with men and women who are godless and irreligious, pagan in their outlook and in their practice. What is to be our attitude towards them? what is to be our relationship to them? The Apostle answers the question in three very striking statements in this fifth chapter.

The first is in verse 7 where he says, 'Be not ye therefore partakers with them.' You once were darkness, he goes on to say, and then you did partake with them; but now you are light in the Lord, do not partake with them in those sinful things any longer. In our conduct and practice there are certain things that we are to avoid completely and entirely and absolutely, and there is no qualification to that. We are not to touch these evil practices, not to participate in them at all; we are to finish with them completely, and make a clean cut. Now those are the things that the Apostle has been describing in the previous verses. But let me emphasise again that the Apostle felt it necessary to give this warning, even to converted Christian people at Ephesus. We must get rid of any magical notion of the Christian life. Some of these evil things were still tempting believers in Christ, and some of them were falling to the temptation. Paul had to write the same things to the Corinthians. The Apostle has to tell them positively not to do certain things they formerly had done. Why? Well, the explanation is that when we are converted we do not understand everything about the Christian faith, and we have to learn things, we have to go from step to step and stage to stage. The philosophy of the world in which we live becomes so deeply ingrained in us that occasionally it takes some time for the applied Christian truth to enlighten us in all things. These new Christians had been so accustomed to regarding certain things as quite normal, quite natural, not wrong in any way, that they had to be taught that these things were sinful and vile, and that they must not touch them. And so you will find much of this kind of instruction in the pages of the New Testament. The Christian is not a man who is suddenly and immediately, in one act, delivered out of all sin. No, no! He is sanctified by the truth, by the teaching which we have in passages such as this.

But we move on to the second injunction (in verse 11) which is not so plain: 'and have no fellowship with the unfruitful works of darkness, but rather reprove them'. What does that first part of the sentence mean? There is an important difference between 'not being partakers' and 'having no fellowship'. The Apostle did not use the same word in verse 11 as in verse 7. All that we are told in verse 7 is that we must not join with sinners in the practice of evil things, but the doctrine does not stop at that, it goes much further. Verse 11 tells us that we must not even display an interest in them. To be still more practical, we must not even talk about them in the wrong way. We all know the distinction in practice. It is one thing not to do these things; it is a very different thing not to be interested in them. And there are many Christian people who are very much interested in forbidden things, in things of which the Apostle says that it is a shame even to speak of them, – of 'those things which are done of them in secret'. They would never do them, but are we clear that it is equally a shame even to read about them in the newspapers and in the modern novels, and in the books and the journals? Have you not noticed the interest some Christian people show, who would not dream of being partakers in these things, but sometimes you watch them and your notice the interest in their faces, the gleam in their eye, as they listen to a conversation about these practices. They may even pretend, of course, that they are taking a psychological interest in them, that they must be familiar with the facts, otherwise of course they cannot help people. That may be the cloak for having a kind of enjoyment of these things in the mind and in the imagination and in the heart; they are having fellowship with them, they are really enjoying the talk and the conversation, and so they allow people to say things in their presence that should not be said. The Apostle makes it absolutely

[415]

clear that the Christian is not only not to engage in evil practices, he is not to enjoy the so-called jokes about these things, he is no longer to consider them clever or funny or amusing or entertaining. He is to have no fellowship whatsoever with them. He is never to connive at them, but to show to others that they belong to a realm to which he no longer belongs.

The first Psalm abundantly confirms what I am saying: 'Blessed is the man that walketh not in the counsel of the ungodly.' That is the first thing he is not to do! In other words his life, his living, his conversation, his general manner of conduct, is not to be after the counsel of the ungodly. But it does not stop there. The second thing, 'nor standeth in the way of sinners', is something a little more subtle. He must not half walk with them either; he must not stand with them on the street corners and give a welcome to the ideas which they represent, in any shape or form; he is not to have a secret longing or hankering after those things which he no longer takes part in. And the third thing: he is not to 'sit in the seat of the scornful'. By sitting there he is giving the impression that after all he has still got some sort of an interest in these matters and that there is something in him which still responds to them, something there which still makes an appeal to him. No, says the psalmist, he is to have no fellowship at all with the unfruitful works of darkness. That, then, is the general statement of the principle. But this is a very delicate matter to handle, it is a very difficult principle to put into practice in daily life and living; it can be seriously misunderstood.

I must show therefore exactly how this teaching is to be put into practice, because if I leave it at this point there are those who may say to me, Are you not teaching a kind of monasticism? are you not telling us to have nothing at all to do with sinners, with people who are not Christians? We are not to walk in their counsel, we are not to stand on the street corners with them; we are not to sit in the seat of the scornful. Are you telling us therefore that we are to spend the whole of our time with Christian people only, and never to have any conversation whatsoever with those who are guilty of living a life of sin? The answer to this perfectly fair question is to be found in the fifth chapter of Paul's First

Epistle to the Corinthians and it is a very important statement: There Paul says, 'I wrote unto you in an epistle not to company with fornicators: yet not altogether with the fornicators of this world, or with the covetous, or extortioners, or with idolaters; for then must ye needs go out of the world. But now I have written unto you not to keep company, if any man that is called a brother be a fornicator, or covetous, or an idolater, or a railer, or a drunkard, or an extortioner; with such an one no not to eat. For what have I to do to judge them also that are without? do not ye judge them that are within? But them that are without God judgeth. Therefore put away from among yourselves that wicked person.'

The context is important. The Apostle is dealing here with the case of an incestuous person who was in the membership of the church at Corinth, and he tells them to put this incestuous person outside the fellowship; they must excommunicate him and have no fellowship with him. But then he realises that they might misunderstand what he says, so he takes it up and expounds it. He says, 'I wrote to you in an epistle not to company with fornicators', which is equivalent to saying, 'Have no fellowship at all with the unfruitful works of darkness.' But be careful, he continues, how you carry that out – 'yet not altogether with the fornicators of *this world*, or with the covetous, or extortioners, or with the idolaters of this world, for' if you did that, then you would have to go out of the world altogether and segregate yourselves and become monks and hermits and anchorites. But, he says, I am not telling you to do that! In other words, he is not telling them to break off all communications with sinners outside the church. And he supplies a very good reason for his qualification. As Christians we are to be the light of the world, and the salt of the earth; we are to remain in society, and it is through us and our life and conduct and behaviour, our words and our teaching, that sinners have a hope of becoming Christians and of being delivered from the wrath of God. Therefore, we are not to cut ourselves off entirely from them. They are living a life of sin; yes, but, says the Apostle, if you are to have nothing at all to do with them, you would have to go right out of the world. Christians would have to live in communities of their own and would never have any dealings at all with non-Christian people. So the

[417]

Apostle explains the distinction that he draws; if a person who belongs to the Church becomes guilty of evil practices, they are not to have any fellowship with him at all. Why? Because more is expected of him! He is a Christian, he must be reprimanded, he must be dealt with and punished. Paul talks about handing such a person over to Satan, for the destruction of the flesh, that the spirit and soul may be saved. But he does not tell us (and this is the thing I am anxious to emphasise) that we are to have nothing to do with outsiders whom we know to be guilty of sin.

How do you reconcile these statements? asks someone. I do it like this. We are to maintain contact with sinners in exactly the same way as our blessed Lord and Saviour did. He was called 'the friend of publicans and sinners'. He sat with them, He ate and drank with them; they drew near to Him and He did not refuse them, He did not reject them; He mixed with them, He spoke to them; yes, but He did it in such a way that He had no fellowship whatsoever with the unfruitful works of darkness. In other words, as our Lord sat there and mixed with the publicans and sinners, they did not indulge in evil and foul and suggestive talk; they did not do that in *His* presence, there was something about Him that prohibited that. And the Apostle is telling us that, while we maintain our contacts with non-Christians for the good of their souls and for their salvation, we do not have any fellowship in their outlook, or in their talk. Most of them recognise our position and our profession of the name of the Lord. We can discuss other matters with them, but if they tend to bring in ugly and unclean things we are to show our disapproval, we are to show that we have no fellowship with them, we do not enjoy such things any more. The line is sometimes a very difficult one to draw, but I think we will always know when the time comes to do that. We can have fellowship with them without enjoying the things they are doing. Let us maintain our contact with them, and our hold upon them, for their good and for their benefit, but let us have no fellowship with the unfruitful works of darkness in any shape or form. We must make it plain and clear to them that though we are interested in them as persons and as human beings, and though we may share certain common interests with them, we have no interest whatsoever in that which is sinful and harmful in their lives.

But we observe that the Apostle's teaching does not stop even at that point. Our attitude should not be negative only, it is to be positive. He says, 'Have no fellowship with the unfruitful works of darkness, but *rather reprove them.*' Here again is a word that can be very easily misunderstood. *To reprove* does not simply mean to reprimand, or to condemn, or to denounce. It is very easy to do that. We think that to reprove means to show our disgust, to denounce the thing, to reprimand it, to condemn it out of hand, to be severe about it. But that is not what the Apostle meant at all. That was the attitude of the Pharisees who, when they saw these things, gathered up their robes and took themselves away. That is the typical pharisaical attitude, and in many ways it is the exact opposite of the Christian attitude. It is purely negative. I agree that it is very difficult not to act in this way at a time like this when you see and read about disgusting and foul things. How difficult it is not to show horror, detestation, and abhorrence, and not just to denounce it root and branch while keeping to the other side of the road. But that is not the Apostle's meaning.

Neither does reproving simply mean that you apply moral teaching to the problem. Morality has got its teaching, but it is a teaching which is almost entirely negative. It denounces evil things just because they are bad for the person and bad for society; and there it stops. Morality goes to a man who perhaps is guilty of drunkenness, and it gives him a lecture on the evil effects of alcohol on the body. It goes on to give statistics about the evil effects of alcohol on production in industry, and upon human relationships, and upon the wealth of the country, and a thousand and one other things; perfectly true statements, every single one of them; but at that point it stops. In a sense it is reproof. But it is not truly so; it is merely the negative application of moral teaching.

What then does the Apostle mean when he says 'But rather reprove them'? Well, the real meaning of the word – and this is not my theory; you may check me – is *to convince by means of evidence*, to convict by means of giving enlightenment and understanding. It means that we are to throw light upon these things in such a manner that we really shall convince the person to whom we are speaking of the nature of what he is doing and what it means to his immortal and eternal soul. We are not just to

[419]

denounce evil things in and of themselves; instead, we are to throw upon them the whole light of the gospel. We are not to address non-Christians about particular evils alone; but, in a loving and sympathetic and understanding manner, to talk to them about themselves and their souls and their whole relationship to God. The tragedy about a man who is the slave of drunkenness is not simply that he is drunk, and that the consequences are bad in a social sense, but that the man's relationship to God is altogether wrong. The Apostle tells us that 'no whoremonger, nor unclean person, nor covetous man, who is an idolater, hath any inheritance in the kingdom of Christ and of God'! That is the point! And rightly to reprove means to throw the light of the gospel upon a man and his whole situation. We must get him to realise that he is *darkness*, that he has darkness within him, that he is dwelling in darkness, that his whole relationship to God is wrong, and that, if he goes on living like that until his death, then he will go to perdition. Do what the Lord Jesus Christ did with the publicans and sinners; He did not simply denounce their sins; He preached the gospel to them; He showed the love of God to them, having made them realise the character of the things that they were doing. Such is the meaning of this word *reprove*.

And that is what you and I are called upon to do. We are not to cut ourselves off from these people; we are not, as self-righteous Pharisees, just to show our disgust and our abhorrence or our superiority and our cleanliness. God forbid that we should ever do such a thing, or that the Church of God should ever do such a thing! She has done it far too often in the past. She did it in the Victorian period, and I believe she is still doing it. The masses of the people, the so-called working classes, are outside the Christian Church today, and it is partly because we are far too ready to give the impression that we are just respectable people, not Christian people. We are to reprove in this right way, we are to talk the Gospel to these people; not to preach at them but to talk the Gospel. They will know that we are different, that perhaps we once took part in certain things but that we no longer do so. Our business is to let them know about the change that has come to us. We are to give them glimpses of a better life, a purer and a cleaner life, yes, and a life which is much more enjoyable.

The tragedy is that they think that our life is miserable and unhappy and at best boring. And we must not blame them for thinking in that way. If we look miserable as a company of people, they think that it just means that we give up everything, and that Christianity, to use the words of Milton, means 'to scorn delights, and live laborious days'. It is because we do not show the joy of the Lord and the joy of salvation that they get this wrong notion of Christianity. We are to reprove them by showing that Christianity means a life of enjoyment, a life of happiness, a life of peace. We get greater enjoyment here than they have ever known, or than we ourselves ever knew when we lived as they do. Flash the light of the gospel upon them.

The Apostle goes further, in verse 13, when he adds, 'But all things that are reproved are made manifest by the light.' He means that when anything is exposed and reproved by the light, it is made visible and clear. Flash the light of the gospel upon it, 'for whatsoever doth make manifest is light', which can be translated, 'whatsoever makes things plain is light'. While we continue to hold conversation with unbelievers, while we maintain a social contact with them, we must desire to make them begin to feel that they are missing something tremendous. Why did publicans and sinners draw near to the Lord Jesus Christ? He was absolute purity and holiness, yet He acted like a magnet on them and they drew near unto Him. The Pharisees hated them, denounced them, and kept apart from them, but when publicans and harlots saw the incarnate God walking before them, they drew near unto Him. Oh! there is something attractive about holiness; it makes us feel very unworthy and unclean when we look at it; it makes us see the things we are doing, as negative denunciation never does nor ever can do; it shows us our need, and at the same time it gives us a glimpse of something that is so different from our past, so much better, so much more wonderful than anything we know. Holiness ought to be attractive, it ought to be loving, it ought to be enticing, it ought to be charming, it ought to draw people. That is what is meant by *reproving*. We are to reprove the unfruitful works of darkness by

[421]

being light, by being what we are, in our conversation, in our speech, in our exposition of the gospel.

You will find that non-Christians sometimes quite deliberately try to annoy you; they will do things to shock you; they will do everything they can to make you denounce them. Resist the temptation! Do not let them succeed! Never be merely negative and denunciatory. But rebuke by showing something of the light of the knowledge of the glory of God in the face of Jesus Christ. Radiate upon them the light of the gospel. Remember that Christians are the light of the world; in your light they will see themselves and what they are doing as they have never done before, and they will long to be cleansed, to be washed, to be purified, to become holy, as you are holy, but above all as Christ is holy. Do not be partakers with them, have no fellowship with what they are doing, reprove them as 'light in the Lord'.

34
The Fool and the Wise Man

'See then that ye walk circumspectly, not as fools, but
as wise, redeeming the time, because the days are
evil. Wherefore be ye not unwise, but understanding
what the will of the Lord is.'

Ephesians 5:15, 16

Instead of considering the whole of this section, we shall look first
of all at verse 15: 'See then that ye walk circumspectly, not as
fools, but as wise.' The apostle has reminded us in the 14th verse
of what we are to be and how we are to conduct ourselves in
general as Christians, and now he proceeds to show us how we are
to do all this and, indeed, the importance of doing all this, in
actual practice. That, then, is the connection which this verse has:
this word 'then' reminds us immediately that it connects with
what has been going before and I believe it connects directly with
verse 14. But not only that, it connects, as I am saying, with the
entire paragraph in which he has been dealing with this subject
of light.

What then does he tell us? Well, here is an exhortation: 'see
then', take heed, beware, be careful. This, he says, is tremendously
important. See to it then, make certain that you do it, take heed to
this matter. Give it your undivided attention. It is an arresting
statement; it is a command, it pulls us up as it were. He is addressing us and asking us to listen for all we are worth. 'See then.'
What then does he tell us? To what must we pay attention? In
what respect have we to take heed? Well, he says, With regard to
this walk of yours, see then that ye walk circumspectly. This
word, 'walk', is, of course, a characteristic New Testament word.
It refers to the whole of our conduct and behaviour and demeanour. It is an inclusive term and there are many such terms in the

New Testament. You will see one, for instance, in the next Epistle, the Epistle to the Philippians, in chapter 1, verse 27, where we read in the Authorised Version, 'Only let your conversation be as becometh the gospel of Christ'. 'Our conversation' has by now come to have a different connotation for us. We think of conversation as being only a matter of speaking, but conversation, like walk, is an inclusive term which takes in the whole of one's behaviour and activity, the whole of one's life amongst other people. That is our walk.

What the Apostle is concerned about, therefore, is that we should live in such a way that we shall ever be acting as the light, both in our own personal conduct and behaviour and in our effect upon others. But here the question arises, How are we to do it? How are we to walk in this world, even as the Lord Jesus Christ did? 'As he is so are we in this world' – we are to follow His steps. That is what we are called to do. We are called in our way to function as He did when He was here in this world of time. How can we do this? That is the thing the apostle is concerned about and it is with this that he deals particularly in this statement. The first thing he tells us is this: we do it by not being fools, by not being unwise, but by being wise and by manifesting and exercising wisdom.

It seems to me that the apostle divides up what he has to say into three main sections.

First, what is wisdom? We cannot behave as wise people if we we do not know what wisdom is. Secondly, he tells us that the Christian can be addressed as somebody who is wise. 'Walk', he says, 'not as fools but as wise; because you are wise act as wise people.' And, thirdly, he tells us how this wisdom which is in the Christian manifests itself; or, if you prefer it, we see the results to which this wisdom leads.

Let us start then with this first matter which is obviously the key to everything else. What is this wisdom about which he is speaking? Now all who are familiar with their Bibles will know that this is a very great word throughout the Bible, the Old Testament as well as the New. The Old Testament has a great deal to say about this wisdom. Indeed, we actually call some of the books of the Old Testament the Wisdom Literature, or the Wisdom Books. Those great moral statements, those affirmations, those books of instruction are the Wisdom Literature. And, of course, it is an essential part of the biblical teaching. What the Bible says about the man who is not a child of God, and who is not a Christian, is that ultimately he is a fool. 'The fool hath said in his heart, There is no God.' 'Be not like the mule,' says another Psalm. Do not be like a mule, you are a child of God. And you will find that running right through the whole of the Old Testament, this constant reference to wisdom. The Christian life is the only sane life according to the Bible. The whole trouble with the unbeliever and non-Christian is that he is a fool. He is lacking in wisdom and in understanding.

We find exactly the same everywhere in the New Testament – for example that great paragraph from the end of 1 Corinthians, chapter 1, where Paul glories in this wisdom. As we have seen the apostle saying at such great length in this practical section of Ephesians, the whole trouble with unbelievers is that they have their understanding darkened. They are alienated from the life of God through the ignorance that is in them. It is always the same. We are looking, therefore, at something which is a key word in the whole of the Bible, and there is a sense in which we cannot understand the great message and exhortation of the Bible unless we are clear about this whole question of wisdom.

What, then, is it? Now in a most interesting way, the Apostle, in this very context, introduces us to the whole subject. The very way in which he puts it gives us an indication as to how wisdom is to be defined. In verse 14 he has already told us that we have knowledge, we have light – 'awake thou that sleepest and arise from the dead and Christ shall shine upon thee'. No man can be a Christian without Christ shining upon him, and we saw that this meant that Christ gives him this knowledge, this understanding. So then, a man who is a Christian is a man who has knowledge, he has light. But here the Apostle goes on to say that we must exercise and display wisdom. I think we can rightly and legitimately deduce from this that wisdom is not synonymous with knowledge and with light. This is where we come to what is, of course, the most vital distinction. Wisdom is not merely knowledge or ability or intelligence or even genius. You can have all those and still not have wisdom. It is not even goodness. Here is something the Bible keeps on repeating. We must not think of wisdom as being merely the possession of knowledge. We must not think of it as merely meaning that a man has got great ability, natural powers and faculties and propensities. A man may even be highly intelligent to the point of being a genius, and yet he may lack wisdom.

What then is this wisdom, if it is not synonymous with intelligence and ability or even with genius or goodness?

Well, we can put it roughly like this: it is the power and the ability to apply all those things. It is the faculty for making use of your intelligence and knowledge and for bringing it into relationship with the ordinary practical daily things of life. There, as I see it, is the essence of this word. Wisdom, of course, is very similar to judgment, and again we are familiar with the difference between the mere possession of knowledge, and judgment. They are not the same thing at all. There are people who know a great deal. They have wonderful memories and they can remember all sorts and kinds of facts but they have no judgment. Consequently they cannot harness their knowledge, they cannot apply it, they cannot bring it to bear upon particular problems. They are like gramophone records, they can repeat information but they cannot apply that information, and therefore you say, 'Ah well, yes, he is a very learned man but he has no judgment, he is really lacking in wisdom.'

Think of this in various realms in order to see the difference. Let us go for a moment to the realm of legal matters. You will find, if you read the biographies of men who have become prominent in the legal world, that there is often a kind or a type of man who is a brilliant Advocate, but who, if elevated to the Bench, makes a very poor judge. I was reading recently about a famous Lord Chief Justice of whom this was true. Why was this so? Because he was still acting as an Advocate when he was on the Bench and it is a poor Judge who takes up one side or the other and becomes an Advocate. He could not cease to be an Advocate and he was therefore a bad Judge. Now that is a lack of wisdom, and of judgment. You see they are entirely different things. Or take it in the realm of business. There is the type of man who makes a very good executive in a business but he does not always make a good manager or chairman. There are men who seem to be born to be secretaries but not to be presidents;

men who, when they are put into a position where they have to take responsibility and arrive at decisions, cannot do it. That is the difference between knowledge and intelligence on the one hand and wisdom on the other. There is something extra here, a further quality. It is this capacity to take all the knowledge and ability one has, and then to apply it.

Or, again, in the realm of music, there are men who are quite good technicians – good performers. Good performers in the sense that they are accurate, they never make any mistakes and so on. But they may not be good musicians. They may not be good critics. They may lack this facility of really getting at the soul of what they are playing. They are mechanics, as it were, mechanically correct, which is both good and essential, and they may have the dexterity and the agility that is necessary. Ah, yes, but they lack the final thing, the thing that ultimately counts. It is the difference between them and the man who seems to have this wholeness of view, this depth of understanding, this ability to take all that he is and all that he knows and has and to bring it to play upon a given situation.

Now, you may recognise at once that this is all tremendously important in every realm and department of life, but it is supremely important with respect to the Christian. Hence the Apostle's exhortation, 'See that ye walk circumspectly, not as fools but as wise'.

Let us go into this a little bit further. We are called to this. We cannot behave as lights, we cannot be true representatives of the Lord Jesus Christ, unless we possess this wisdom and are manifesting it. So we must go beyond my general statement to a more particular analysis and definition.

Let us take the Apostle's own contrast. You see this in his method. He throws out a negative. I want you to live as wise people, he says. Yes, but you notice he slipped in his negative first, 'not as fools'. He expects us to take this up and to analyse it. How am I to know what a wise man is like? How am I to behave in a wise manner? Don't be a fool, he says, don't behave as the foolish man behaves. So I can arrive at a positive definition of wisdom by contrasting it with folly. What are the characteristics of the man who is described in the Bible as 'the fool', a foolish person, an unwise person? Here are some of his characteristics.

[427]

These are the things which we have to fight constantly in order that we may behave as wise people.

The first characteristic of the foolish person is that he or she is generally governed by feelings. Everything is estimated in terms of feelings instead of reason. Fools cannot give you reasons. Let me take a rather obvious illustration. It is the sort of person who votes for a Member of Parliament just because they feel he is nice looking or something like that. No real reason at all, but he looks a nice man, vote for him. Governed by feeling!

But you see that applies right through life. There are so many people who are governed entirely by their feelings and they do not want to use their minds and their brains. Even in a religious service they just want happiness and enjoyment. They want to have a good time, as they call it, to get excited, to work themselves up by singing hymns and songs and choruses, and to keep on repeating and repeating until they are in a state of mental intoxication. They do not want to be made to think. Life is hard enough as it is, they say, without having to struggle with this thought and that, so let us have more singing and less preaching and so on. Feelings! Just a riot of enjoyment – that is a foolish person. Do you see the relevance of all this to the state of the church today? It does not matter how crowded your churches are in whatever country you belong to. What I want to know is, what happens when the crowd gets there? How is the time spent? And, alas, one sees and hears more and more music and entertainment and less and less of teaching and doctrine and true understanding. That is one of the characteristics of folly.

Another mark of the foolish man is that he is always governed by desire. I must have what I like, and what I like is right. If that thing appeals to me, that is what I am really happy with and I must have it. Reason does not come in, nor does understanding; nothing but desire. You can think this out for yourself. It is one of the great problems in the world today that society is being governed by desire, hence the breakdown of marriage and everything else. People are being directed and determined solely by these innate desires that are in us all as a result of the fall and of sin. Now the foolish man is the man who is governed by these at the expense of everything else.

Take it again in a slightly different form. The foolish person is

[428]

always the person who acts and is governed by impulses and instincts and, of course, he generally prides himself on this. 'I'm not one of those people who read a lot and think and meditate, you know. I get an idea and I do it.' Impulse! Instinct! And it is thought to be rather wonderful. I remember once reading a book by a man who was advocating this. For him this was the solution to all the problems of life. Our problem, he said, has been that we have lived too much in the realm of the cerebrum, the higher part of our brain and intelligence and understanding, instead of living on a more instinctive level. And he went on to say how he had written a book in that way – deliberately shut out his higher control and inhibitions, as he called them, and had just written down what appealed to him. Impulse! Instinctive! Yet there are people whose whole life is governed by that. You never know what they are going to do next. An idea will come and they act on the impulse.

Or again there are those who obey some instinct that is within them. They cannot explain it and, of course, sometimes this is elevated almost into the supreme virtue. There are people who really believe that instinctive judgments are better than judgments which are based upon reasons and understanding. I know what they mean up to a point. I have heard such men say that when they want to make a really important appointment in their business or in their office they always trust to the instinctive judgment of their wives. Well, there may be something in it! But all I am saying is that if you elevate that into a principle, you are surely doing something that is dangerous from every standpoint and it is certainly contrary to the teaching of Scripture.

We must now go up the scale a little in our definition of folly. The foolish person is very often governed by zeal. It becomes a little more subtle at this point, doesn't it? We are rather fond of zealous persons and I think that is right. We should all be zealous. But there is a grave danger if we are governed by zeal. Zeal and sincerity are wonderful but they are never meant to be in control and if you put them in control, there will be disaster for certain. But there are many people who are governed by their zeal. They see something and they want to do it, so they rush on without considering anything else. They assume that because they are zealous they must be right. Oh, no, you can be sincerely wrong.

You can be zealous in a false cause. We say 'fire is a good servant but a bad master' and the same is true of zeal. Zeal can lead to fanaticism, to cruelty, to persecution. Zeal has been one of the most devastating influences in the long history of the Christian church. Zeal, I say, which is not under control, and which is not governed and guided by wisdom and by understanding. But the foolish person trusts to his zeal. He is right, he is sincere. If he is sincere he must be right. How often we have heard that in this century. It does not matter very much what a man believes as long as he is sincere. And so the foolish person rushes madly into trouble because he has exalted and elevated zeal to the supreme position.

What all this amounts to is this, that the foolish person is one who does not think adequately. He does not think right round a subject; in particular he does not think ahead. He is concerned only about the particular moment. That is the essence of a fool, isn't it? Here is something confronting him. He rather likes it, it appeals to him. I want that, he says, and I am going to have it. He does not think ahead at all. It is just this immediate moment, this second in which he is alive. At this point we are touching a subject which could be handled at very great length because it is one of the most popular philosophies at the moment. It is existentialism; this moment is all that matters, this immediate moment.

There is a sense, of course, in which that is right and true. There are certain moments of ultimate final decision, a moment of conversion, and so on. But if you elevate the present moment into a controlling universal principle, it becomes devastatingly dangerous because I am not alive only at this moment. I will be alive at the next moment, and the next, and the next; and my decision now has a bearing upon and a reference to them. If it does harm to them it is wrong now, though it may appear to me to be right at this given moment. But the fool never thinks ahead. He is concerned exclusively with the immediate. Nothing else matters.

We can put this in a slightly different form. The fool does not consider consequences. This is wisdom, that you look all round your subject, you consider not only the immediate results but the remote results, the possible consequences. The fool is impatient of all this. I want it now, he says. This is the moment, this is life. Oh, he says, if you keep on looking at possible consequences you will never do anything at all, and so he lives for the moment. What tragedies there are in the world today, what heartbreak there is because people have lived for this existential moment and have refused to consider what their real conscience and the relics of wisdom within them are urging them to do with respect to the consequences.

I have already anticipated the next negative which is this – and you see they all belong to one another. The extraordinary thing is that there is a sort of consistency in the fool. Everything he does is of a piece. Because he will not look ahead and, because he will not consider the consequences, he is always impatient. That is a great characteristic of anybody lacking in wisdom. It is the whole difficulty with a little child. The child wants to act at once. He is impatient. You sometimes try to teach him in that way by holding something back from him, but he cannot control himself, he wants it immediately. Lack of wisdom is characteristic of a child. So when you see an adult who is like that you say, What a foolish person! Impatient! You see you can be impatient in a good cause as well as in a bad one. A man may see a certain goal which is desirable, but then, because he lacks wisdom he rushes (as we say) like a bull at a gate. He does not wait, he does not see that the right way to get it is to go carefully and to make sure of what you are doing. He rushes madly in and does more damage and harm to his own cause than the man who is an active and a militant opponent of his cause. Why? Just because he is impatient, and cannot wait for the right and appropriate time and moment for things to happen.

In many ways the real trouble with the foolish person is that he only sees one thing at a time. And this monopolises his attention. He is blind to everything else. There are men who see only one doctrine and everything else is forgotten. The others are there, nevertheless. But because of concentration on one element the whole thing becomes lop-sided. This is the final point. The fool always lacks balance. He is lop-sided and therefore there is an ugliness always about folly. Now then, says the apostle, 'See that ye walk circumspectly, not as fools . . .'.

What, then, is it positively? Well, even here I cannot leave the negative. Because if I were to say that the wise man is just the man who is not guilty of all those things, I would not be saying the truth about wisdom. So I need some further negatives. Let us look at it like this. What is wisdom? What is the wise man? Well, let me say that wisdom is not mere fact. You see the importance of this negative. It is not merely what we call worldly-wisdom. The contest is always between this wisdom and the wisdom of the world. It is not mere discretion. This is to me tremendously important. Wisdom does not merely mean a cautious spirit. There are many men who are most cautious and canny and careful but they are not wise men. They often give the appearance of being so, and they are often credited with being very wise men. You know the sort of man who sits quietly and says very little. Animated conversation is going on. Questions are debated and discussed, opinions are asked for and are considered. This man sits and says nothing, he looks on. He is thought to be a man who thinks profoundly and who, therefore, does not speak very readily. Now that sort of thing is often equated with wisdom but it is altogether wrong. Francis Bacon has put this right surely once and forever, 'Silence is the virtue of fools'! And how right he is! That is why I am going on with my negatives. So you cannot say that a man is a wise man simply because he does not talk much. But I will tell you how to know whether he is wise or not. Listen to what he says when he does talk, and you will see the difference. The wise man is one who has a contribution to make and he makes it. But that dull fellow has no contribution to make! He has nothing to say, but in his pomposity he is often regarded as a wise man. No! No! Let us be clear about this. It does not consist in mere silence or even in mere absence of those things which we have been talking about and have been describing. It is not your canny careful fellow who spends so much of his time in calculating that he does nothing at all. No, that is not wisdom.

What then is wisdom? Let us look at it like this, positively. The wise man is a man who always thinks. He does not act merely on the basis of instinct or impulse or desire. No, he is a man who insists upon thought and reason and meditation. But I must add to that. He is a man who thoroughly examines every proposition by which he is confronted, or every situation into which you lead him. He is a man who first and foremost listens to all the evidence. He is unlike that Judge on the Bench who becomes an Advocate and takes sides at the beginning of a case. The wise man refuses to do that. He holds himself back and listens to the evidence on both sides. He gives the argument a fair hearing from every conceivable angle and he does so with great patience.

I sometimes think that the hallmark of the wise man is that he is always a good listener. Remember that he is not, as I have been saying, a man who does nothing else, and of whom you can say, 'Silence is the virtue of fools'. Yet the wise man is an extremely good listener. Why? Well, he is gathering his facts, he is getting the data together. He says, I cannot arrive at a judgment without having all the data before me, so he is very patient. He does not rush. He does not charge in immediately. He looks right round his subject and having gathered all his evidence, he then proceeds to sift it, to weigh it and to evaluate it. And that takes a little time. But this man does it, he insists upon it. It is, again, one of these essential hallmarks of wisdom. It may take a long time or a short time – that depends upon the man and his experience and his circumstances – but he is a man who never acts without having made his review of the total situation.

We could illustrate all this from the history of the church. How often has error been brought into the church quite apart from what happens in the world. Some men suddenly become full of one idea and, at the expense of everything else, are carried away by it. No, no, there is a completeness, there is a wholeness, there is a balance, there is what the Apostle Paul calls 'the proportion of faith'. All these things must be held as a whole and the man who has wisdom is the man who does that. He has doctrine and practice. Not only doctrine, not only practice, but both, and always going together. It is the same in everything. So the wise man is one who sits and weighs his evidence.

Then, having weighed the evidence, the wise man relates it all to fundamental principles. Here is the secret of wisdom. You see, even having taken his time and having been patient and having gathered all his facts and marshalled all the evidence; having looked at it all round, sifted, analysed and collated it and put it into its appropriate departments, even then he does not arrive at his decision by himself and immediately. No, he takes all this and

[433]

he examines it in the light of certain fundamental eternal principles. You see he is subjective no more, he is always objective. That is the whole essence of wisdom. The secret of wisdom is that one keeps one's self out – what one is by nature and by instinct – and all along one is relating what one finds and discovers to the great fundamental certainties. These are things wh:ch are axiomatic and about which there is no discussion. All is related to them, and in the light of these principles the verdict is arrived at and is promulgated.

That is the essence of wisdom. The apostle says it all here, of course: 'See that you walk circumspectly, not as fools but as wise, redeeming the time because the days are evil. Wherefore be ye not unwise but understanding what the will of the Lord is.' That is the ultimate. There are the eternal principles, and all that I am aware of and have discovered must now be put into the light of these eternal principles. In other words, though I have collected the facts so carefully and sifted them and so on, I do not let my mood decide what my verdict is. Taking a firm grip upon my feelings, my desires and everything else, I take this situation, this thing, this condition, this proposal that is put before me and I hold it there in the light of these eternal principles. And I listen to what they have to say. My decision, my action, the whole of my life is determined by that and by that alone.

Now, of course, having arrived at my decision in that way and being sure of myself, because of my principles, I proceed to put them into practice with enthusiasm, with zeal, with energy and with all the vigour that God has given me. But you see the difference between having sincerity and zeal as hired servants and not as masters; as instruments to carry out that which is right instead of determining what is right. A man is thus not governed by excitement or zeal or enthusiasm or impatience, but always by his knowledge of and his desire to serve and to be governed and controlled by the truth of God as it is in Christ Jesus our Lord.

We must examine ourselves in the light of this. Is our theological life governed by wisdom? Is our practical daily life and living governed by this wisdom? Is this how you act in your contact with non-Christians? I am thinking of relatives you may have who are not Christians and you are so anxious that they should be. Do you rush in and perhaps do irretrievable harm? Or do you approach the problem with wisdom? Do you stop to think? Misguided zeal and enthusiasm are responsible for grievous harm. The Christian is to be wise. He that is wise winneth souls. Yes, it is the wise man who does. The other can have immediate, flashing, startling results, but they do not last. Seek wisdom, seek understanding and, as I have said, in the still more ordinary affairs of life, in a city like London, in the world as it is today, when things are meeting us from all sides and directions, are you living in a wise manner, or are you governed by impulse, instinct, desire? Is your every action and thought, and all that you are and do, always brought into relationship with the eternal principles, with the truth of God, the message once and forever delivered and committed to the saints? See then, children of light, see then that you walk circumspectly, not as fools, but as wise; as made wise with the wisdom of God, as men who can say, 'We have the mind of Christ.'

35
Walking Circumspectly

'See then that ye walk circumspectly, not as fools, but
as wise, redeeming the time, because the days are
evil. Wherefore be ye not unwise, but understanding
what the will of the Lord is.'

Ephesians 5:15, 16

We have been considering what this wisdom is, about which the
Bible says so much. I have suggested, however, that beyond that
the Apostle says two other things. The first thing is the wisdom
itself, the second is his proposition that every Christian has that
wisdom and the third, how this wisdom is manifested.

We come now to the second point – the Apostle's assertion that
all who are Christians are possessors of this wisdom. You notice
how he puts it; 'See then that ye walk circumspectly, not as fools
but as wise', by which he means, You must not behave as fools
because you are wise. The fact that you are a Christian means that
you are wise. It is precisely because of this that he is able to say to
them negatively that they must not behave or walk as fools or
unwise people.

The Bible, you see, divides the whole of mankind into two
groups. It has many different ways of describing them but they all
come to the same thing – Christian and non-Christian, belonging
to Christ, belonging to the world. Yes, but this further distinction
is equally true. Wise, unwise. You have it all in our Lord's famous
parable at the end of the Sermon on the Mount – the wise man
who built his house on the rock, the other man who built it on the
sand, the foolish man. The wise virgins, the foolish virgins. That
is a fundamental division. You find it in precisely the same way in
the Old Testament. All the patriarchs and prophets were wise
men; sometimes they were even called 'seers' for that reason.

This, therefore, is something quite basic to our own understanding of the Christian life. The apostle's appeal to the Christian is always in terms of his being wise, his being made wise in contradistinction to this other man.

Now, this is a very astounding claim and the Apostle never ceases to rejoice in it. You will recall how in the first chapter of his First Epistle to the Corinthians he plays on this notion and he exults in it. 'The Greeks seek after wisdom', the great characteristics of the philosophers is that they are always looking for wisdom, for ultimate knowledge and understanding. The whole business of philosophy is to try to discover this wisdom and the Greeks spent all their time in trying to find it, but they did not succeed. It always eluded them, in spite of their great genius and ability. It has been the same, of course, ever since, the world has always been chasing after wisdom.

All the so-called culture of the world is concerned about this, all the clever talk and writing of books by clever and learned men who are not Christians. That is what they are all doing, they are seeking for this wisdom. It is, of course, right that it should be sought, because any man who thinks can see at once that there is something radically wrong in this world. He wants to find out what is wrong, and how it can be put right. That is the search for wisdom and the extraordinary thing is that the world with all its ability and cleverness cannot find it. It is seeking for it today as busily as it has ever done. People are still reading the old Greek philosophers, they are trying to go beyond them and to build upon them and they bring out their systems. There are fashions even in philosophy. In recent years philosophers have continued to try to find the meaning of language in order that it may be used correctly. This great quest for wisdom is still going on and yet the apostle reminds us here that what the world with all its genius and brilliance cannot achieve, and cannot succeed in doing, is already in the possession of the Christian. The Christian is a wise man. He has found the wisdom that the world is looking for. He is not seeking any longer, he has found it – it has come to him.

You read those first two chapters of the First Epistle to the Corinthians and you will find it. The Jews require a sign, the Greeks seek after wisdom, we preach Christ crucified. Why? Because Paul says, He is the wisdom of God and the power of

God. 'But of him', he says again, 'are ye in Christ Jesus, who of God is made unto us wisdom.' Wisdom! We have the wisdom, we have it in Christ. God has put this final wisdom in His Son. This then is the tremendous claim. I wonder whether as Christians we are as aware of it as we should be. If we are Christians, in the true sense, we have this final wisdom. We have the knowledge and the understanding about life and all its attendant circumstances which the world is vainly seeking to discover. What the world in all its wisdom has failed to do has already happened to the Christian.

Let us now just for a moment look at this. How has it happened to him? Well, it has happened because his eyes have been opened to that final wisdom which is in the Lord Jesus Christ. As Paul puts it in the second chapter of the Epistle to the Colossians 'In whom are hid all the treasures of wisdom and knowledge'. It is all in Christ. The answer to the problems of the world are in the Lord Jesus Christ. That is another staggering claim, isn't it? But it is the claim we make as Christians. There is not a problem confronting the individual or the whole of society today but that the answer is in Jesus Christ. Everything! I do not hesitate to assert that. The apostle says that *all*, all the treasures of wisdom and of knowledge are hidden in him. It is all there. And if men and women only knew him they would be possessors of this wisdom.

To be a Christian, then, means that you are in that position. A Christian is a man whose eyes have been opened to the truth, to the wisdom as it is in the Lord Jesus Christ. He has come to see these great principles which govern the whole of thinking and the whole of life. Whether you like it or not, Christianity is the only complete philosophy. It is not a human philosophy, Paul denies that in Colossians 2 as well as in 1 Corinthians 2. It is not the wisdom of this world, but it is wisdom none the less. It is our business as Christian people to realise this. It is a perfect and a complete system of thought and of understanding. We do a great disservice to the Christian cause if we do not grasp this and if we live only in the realm of some comfortable little feeling. We are supposed to give a reason for the hope that is in us. It behoves us, if we are to function as light, to show that in Christ is all the wisdom and knowledge we need. The Christian is a man whose eyes have been opened to this and he sees these great eternal and fundamental principles with regard to the whole of life and the whole cosmos, the whole of history – with regard to everything.

There is another way in which this wisdom comes to him. He has in himself a new principle of life. Now that is tremendously important. It is not merely that his eyes have been opened to that objective wisdom which is there outside him in Christ. No, there is at the same time a new principle of life in him. And you see how important this is. We have made an analysis of the foolish, unwise person and we have seen that he is foolish because he is the creature of certain impulses and instincts that are within him. We all have them in us, these urges and drives, and they are stronger than our own will or our own natural understanding. That is why, as I was indicating, men who may be very learned and knowledgeable, may be utter fools in their life and practice because of these other forces. So in order to become truly wise, I require not only the knowledge, the objective wisdom which is there, but I need something to operate within myself, and here it is in Christ, new life, a new power and a new principle. We are partakers of the divine nature. There is now in us a positive principle which is working in the direction of truth and wisdom and pleasing God, and it keeps at bay the other forces and powers that are in us by nature and as a result of the fall. That is why the apostle addresses us as wise. We must not think of the Christian merely as a man who has changed his point of view. He has done that, of course, but that is not the only thing. Thank God, there is this other thing, regeneration. The Christian has a new mind, a new ability, a new power, a new principle of life and they work together with the knowledge he now has.

Thirdly, the Holy Spirit of God is resident within the Christian. That is plainly taught everywhere in the New Testament. The Christian is a man in whom the Holy Spirit dwells. 'Know ye not', says Paul again to these Corinthians, 'that your body is the temple of the Holy Ghost which is in you?' Because he is in us, we are aided in this matter of wisdom. How can I control these forces that are within me, this impulsiveness, this tendency to act on intuition and feeling and so on? What can I do about these urges? The Holy Spirit is the answer. Writing to Timothy, who tended to listen too much to his feelings and his moods instead of applying this wisdom, the apostle says, 'God hath not given us the spirit of fear; but of power, and of love, and of a sound mind.' Discipline – wisdom, if you like – that is the character of the spirit that has been given to us, he says. Not the spirit of fear. No, the characteristic of the Spirit is that he gives power, he gives the ability to keep these other things in check. He stimulates the love which is so essential in these matters. Above all, there is this soundness of mind, this wisdom, this discipline and this orderliness.

Here, then, are three reasons, without going any further, why the Christian can be regarded as a wise man. You see he is altogether different from the man who is not a Christian. The man who is not a Christian is blind to the truth. He has not got a principle of new life in him. He is not regenerated and the Spirit of God does not dwell within him. What chance has he of being wise? He has none at all. He is the victim of himself and the world in which he lives. He is a fool and he cannot help himself. But not so the Christian. Everything about him separates him, puts him on another side and in a different category and here he is, he is a wise man. This is the apostle's astounding claim.

There is something rather sad, isn't there, about the fact that as evangelical Christians we far too often give the impression that to be Christians just means that we spend a lot of our time in singing choruses and in being bright and breezy and happy; telling little tales and stories, joking and making people laugh. My dear friends, in Him who is in us and in whom we are, are hid all the treasures of wisdom and of knowledge. And you and I must show that. We are misrepresenting Him if we do not. The charge constantly brought against us as evangelicals is that there is nothing for the intellect, that we are anti-intellectual, and obscuranist, that we are burying our heads in the sand, that we are not facing problems, not displaying this wisdom and this knowledge. Shame on us if it is true! The Christian is a wise man. He is a possessor of this ultimate wisdom and he is to show it and to make it manifest. As he does so, he will be calling to the unbeliever, 'Awake thou that sleepest and arise from the dead and Christ will shine upon thee.'

Let us go on to the next matter. How does this wisdom that the Christian now possesses show itself? Here, the apostle descends to our weakness and he divides it up for us. The first thing he tells us is this – the primary characteristic of a man who is wise in this

Christian sense is that he walks circumspectly. 'See then that ye walk circumspectly, not as fools but as wise'. What does this expression mean? It is a term which really means 'accurately', carefully, because you cannot be accurate unless you are careful. Circumspectly – accurately, carefully – what do these words suggest? They suggest that a man looks before he leaps. He looks round, examines carefully, does not go rushing madly in a head-long or impulsive manner. He has an idea, he has read something in a book and at once he has done it – not at all! He looks, he examines, he inspects, he is careful. Indeed he is a complete contrast to that foolish man whom we have analysed at great length in order that we might be clear about this matter. Do not despise the negatives; they are all important. It is because we forget the negatives that we are so much as we are. This wise man who walks circumspectly is the exact opposite of the fellow who is governed only by instincts and impulses and desires and a mad zeal – that is the man who is lacking in wisdom. To walk circum-spectly means that you walk strictly according to a rule. Oh yes, the wise man always has a rule. I have hinted already that he always relates everything to certain fundamental principles. He knows what he is doing, he knows why he is doing it, he can give reasons for it – that is the essence of wisdom.

The wise man is the man who realises that many things have to be considered before he acts. Now this is not, as I said, the canni-ness or the ultra-carefulness of the man who never does anything at all – 'he who regardeth the wind will never sow'. It is not that. It just means that he realises at once that he is not a separate unit in life but that he has his relationships with others, that no man liveth unto himself, no man dieth unto himself. You know, most people do not think like that. They only think of themselves and they do what they want to do. But the wise man stops and realises that there are other people who are going to be involved in how he lives and what he does. I do not live to myself and I cannot. I must therefore look around and consider these many other factors. The Christian, in order to walk circumspectly, is constantly reminding himself that he is a Christian. He should remind himself of that every morning as he wakes up, every morning as he goes to his front door out into the world. In the same way, he must realise the condition of others. If we do not think of others and their position, we shall not act as light with respect to them, we shall not awaken them out of the darkness and the death in which they are, and bring them to the light of Christ.

No, walking circumspectly means that you look round, you see that there are certain pitfalls, and if you put your foot in, you sink. You inspect before you move, you take a general view and only then you begin to walk. The Apostle, of course, is very fond of this whole notion and he says it in different epistles. Listen to it again in Colossians chapter 4 verse 6, where he says, 'Let your speech be alway with grace, seasoned with salt, that ye may know how ye ought to answer every man.' That is what it means to walk circumspectly. In other words we have to make assessments, we have to consider these other people. What, we must think, would be the effect of this action of mine upon them? You see there are many things that are perfectly legitimate for the Christian, but he will not do them because of the effect they have upon others. The apostle puts that in 1 Corinthians like this – 'Conscience, I say, not thine own, but of the other'; he also says, 'All things are lawful for me but all things are not expedient.' Now the wise man is aware of that. The other man says, 'Well, if this is right, I have a right to do it, what does it matter?' and he does it. Ah, but he has offended his weaker brother for whom Christ died, and he has done great harm in the church and to those who are outside. Walking circumspectly means considering how it is going to affect others. That is a part of exercising wisdom.

The Christian, therefore, is a man who has to exercise great tact and great patience. He sees the truth very plainly and his instinct, of course, is to *make* everybody else see it. Have we not all known this? We are concerned about somebody and try to explain the Christian truth to them. It is so simple and elementary to us, but this other person cannot see it and you feel you would almost like to box his ears to make him see it, but, of course, if you do that he will never see it. That is where the patience and the wisdom of the Christian comes in. The Christian must say to himself, 'Now this man is a highly intelligent man, why then doesn't he see this point? 'Ah,' says the Christian 'I know why he doesn't see it, he is blinded by the god of this world. He can't see it. "The natural man receiveth not the things of the Spirit of God: for they are foolishness unto him".' The Christian realises this. So he is careful how he speaks. He does not bombard people nor bludgeon them, he does not ram the truth down their throats. No, he is a wise man.

The Christian also has to consider different types of people. He realises that they are not all identical. So he varies his approach; not his message, but his approach. The Apostle Paul tells us that he did that. He says, 'I speak to them that are under the law as under the law myself. I speak to those who are not under the law as not under the law. To the circumcised in one way, to the uncircumcised in another. I am made all things to all men that I might by all means save some.' You and I must do that too. There are different types of people with different gifts and abilities. They are in different positions. It is our business to present the truth in such a way that it will have something to say to all. Not only to one type but to all types. If we fail to do that we are not walking circumspectly. If we say, Well this is my method and I am always going to use it, that is how a foolish man behaves. He does not look around and consider. He does not see the situation. He has not got a real, profound love of souls. He is only concerned about himself and what he does and what happens to him – how tragic it is!

Now it is necessary for us to know these things in the church, and it is the business of every church member to understand them. If something does not appeal to you, remember it may appeal to somebody else, and that is why there are these constant appeals to us to bear with one another. We must grow together. We are at different stages. If you do not quite understand something, then believe that somebody else does, and try to get there yourself. That is how we grow in grace and in the knowledge of our Lord. That is wisdom, that is walking circumspectly. It involves all this, this great tact and patience, this ability to diagnose and to understand, this ability to present the truth.

Read the Acts of the Apostles and you will see it magnificently in some of those great dramatic chapters. Read for instance, the 26th chapter and notice now the great apostle walks circumspectly. Here is the Apostle Paul appealing before King Agrippa and his wife and Festus and his wife. 'Paul stretched forth the hand, and answered for himself: I think myself happy, king Agrippa, because I shall answer for myself this day before thee touching all the things whereof I am accused of the Jews: Especially because I know thee to be expert in all customs and questions which are among the Jews: wherefore I beseech thee to hear me patiently.' What magnificent wisdom! What circumspect walking that is! You see, if he can say anything favourable he says it. He is anxious to win that man, he does not attack him. No, he meets him exactly where he is and starts from that point. He is trying to win people to the truth. He does not say, Here I stand! You end by saying that very often, as Luther did, but you do not start like that – this is wisdom. We all need to work that principle out in detail for ourselves.

The essential feature of wisdom is that it realises that knowledge is to be applied, and that if it is not applied in an appropriate manner it will probably do more harm than good. Theoretical knowledge, academic knowledge, in and of itself, can be quite useless. There is a type of man who denies his message by his method. The wise man has a consistency between message and method. He is always applying his message, it comes out in everything that he does. That is the essence of wisdom. This is the first thing that the apostle tells us; we must walk circumspectly.

The second point tells us why we must be so circumspect. The Christian, because he is wise, is a man who has a correct view of life in this world and of the state of the world. He redeems the time because the days are evil. Nobody knows that but the Christian. To a non-Christian the days are wonderful; they have never been better. What is the phrase? 'Never had it so good'. The days are not evil, there is plenty of work, plenty of money, plenty of everything. Ah, but the man who has wisdom is the man who says the days are evil. It is the wisdom of God alone that enables a man to say that. The world is wonderful, says the other man. The days are evil, says the Christian. This, of course, is perfectly expounded by the Apostle himself in the next chapter in verse 12. He says, 'We wrestle not against flesh and blood but against principalities, against powers, against the rulers of the darkness of this world, against spiritual wickedness in high places.' You see, what he means is that the world is evil. The days are evil, not in an abstract sense; he means that this world is pernicious. This world is in the control of powers and forces and factors that are hostile to God and in active opposition to God. That is what he means.

[444]

He had already said this, of course, at the very beginning of chapter 2! 'You hath he quickened, who were dead in trespasses and sins; wherein in time past ye walked according to the course of this world, according to (governed by) the prince of the power of the air, the spirit that now worketh in the children of disobedience'. The days are evil. Now, it is only the Christian who understands this; but the Christian understands it at once. He realises that behind men, and the things that men do, is this other awful, evil, infernal power which is intent upon bringing to ruin God's glorious creation and everything that is in it. It is pernicious; it is actively evil. If a man does not realise that, he cannot possibly walk circumspectly in this world. He cannot possibly live as he should be living. If a man objects to this and says, 'Well I don't see it, that's rather a pessimistic view. Of course, that's typical of the Bible, that's the old Puritanism. Everything will be black and dark. But the world isn't like that. The world is wonderful, it's bright; let us have a good time, especially when we are young'. A man who thinks like that will never be a light to anybody. He will never awaken any poor, damned soul from under the wrath of God and from the hell to which he is speeding.

We must understand that this world is the seat of conflict of two mighty spiritual powers and forces. God and His Christ, the Host of Heaven, the Holy Spirit, and on the other side, the Devil and all his powers and emissaries. And you and I are involved in this conflict. The days are evil. We must realise that with regard to ourselves. That is why the Apostle will tell us in the next chapter that we must put on the whole armour of God. Nothing else will suffice us. 'Above all', he says, 'taking the shield of faith wherewith you shall be able to quench all the fiery darts of the wicked.'

Do you not feel sometimes that this is true? Are you aware of the fact that the days are evil? Do you, with John Bunyan, regard the world as it is, and without Christ, as a City of Destruction? Do you see the hellish power that is behind the appearances? Can you not see it as you look at your popular newspapers every morning? Do you not see the evil that is at the back of it? Everything is done to make money – and they will pander to anything, to films, sex and everything else. It is simply a matter of making money. And it is this evil power that does it. Nothing counts, principles do not count. Oh, the vileness and the pernicious character of life in this world! And, you see, the man who walks circumspectly is the man who realises that and says, 'I have got to be careful. I must be careful about what I read. There is so much literature about me in various forms that can harm my soul and blunt my taste, take down my barriers, undermine my resistance and affect my judgment.' There is so much of it, there is nothing more difficult than for a man to keep straight and true and pure in this modern evil world. The days are evil!

The Christian sees that, so he says, I must walk circumspectly. Then, when he realises the condition of those who are the ignorant victims of this evil power, he knows that he must redouble his efforts and be careful. Men of .he world do not know this, they are not aware of it. They regard these things as having a good time, they boast of it. They boast about drunkenness, the thing that causes so much unhappiness and breaks down families. They make jokes about it. It is said to be wonderful and you are out of step, behind the times, if you do not do such things. They do not see that it is just this evil power that has got them. But you and I are to think for them, we are to cater for them, we are to do all we can to deliver them and to get them out of this malign and evil power that is controlling them. The days are evil. They never were more evil. And it is the wise man alone who looks on and sees it all for what it is. Are we clear about the state of the world? Have we got this great distinction in the forefront of our minds between the world and the church, between the kingdom of darkness and the kingdom of light? It is basic to Christianity and you and I must grasp it.

Let me say just a word on the last thing – Redeeming the time – which is the other characteristic of this wisdom. The Christian is a man who, because of all these things, redeems the time. What does this mean? Well, we must be careful about this. It does not merely mean that he uses his time in the right way. It includes that, of course. But there is something much more than that. Time here does not so much mean time in terms of calendars – a space of time from January to December. No, it means *opportunity*. Redeeming the time should be translated, 'buying up the opportunity'.

This is a very profound thought. Here is this wise man, this

[446]

Christian. How does he show his wisdom? This is one way. He views his life in this world as being a great opportunity. Thereby, of course, he is absolutely different from the non-Christian. The non-Christian views life in this world as a place in which a man settles down, does as well as he can for himself and enjoys it to the full. But that is not the Christian's view. The Christian realises that this is a passing world and that he is nothing but a journeyman in it. Here are the New Testament terms – 'I beseech you', says Peter, 'as strangers and pilgrims . . .'. That is what you are, you are strangers and pilgrims. You are but sojourners here. This is not your home. 'Our citizenship', says Paul to the Philippians in chapter 3, verse 20, 'is in heaven'. That is where we belong. In this world, I am a man away from home. I am a stranger here, I am just on a visit. Strangers and pilgrims, travellers and sojourners, men who are on the move. 'I nightly pitch my moving tent a day's march nearer home'. Home! Home, I belong there, not here!

That is the position of the Christian. This is not real life to the Christian. The real life is coming. As Paul says in Romans 13, 'The night is far spent, the day is at hand.' That is what the Christian is looking for. That is the realm to which he belongs, but here he is in an evil world and he says, Ah, while I am here, I must make use of the opportunity. It is a temporary place of opportunity. I am out of it in my spirit but I am still left in it in a physical sense, so what am I to do here? Well, I am going to make use of my time here to show the glory of God. We shall leave it at that now because I want to work out in detail how the Christian really does all that.

We are called to do this and, at a time like this especially, when it is no longer the custom for people to go to places of worship, the responsibility of the individual Christian is greatly increased. People will not listen to the gospel today. Very well then, let them see it in your life. Let them see the light as they look at you. That is what the Apostle is urging.

We have been looking at the principles that will enable a man to walk in such a way that he will act as light to others. He is a man who is looking around; he is walking circumspectly. He has principles by which he can assess everything and he has come to the conclusion that the days are evil. He sees the hell behind the facade, he sees the misery and the wretchedness and the devil who is there. All these things guide him in his own personal deportment, and in his behaviour towards others. And then he says to himself, I am here to represent my family, I am here as a representative of my Father, I am here as a representative of His Son, the Holy Spirit and all the angelic host. I belong to His family and I must regard my time in this world primarily and essentially as an opportunity to tell men and women that there is another life, a life of glory, a life of holiness, a life shared with God. I see these poor people round and about me in the bondage and the clutches of sin in its different forms. I do not care what form it takes, I am to try to bring those people to the light, I must try to awaken them, I must be all things to all men that by all means I may save some. I must therefore show this wisdom in all its variegated forms and shapes and colours. Let the whole spectrum become manifest in and through me, so that by any means, somehow, some poor soul who is a victim of evil and of sin may be awakened from his sleep, may arise from the grave and the death of sin and begin to look into the face of Jesus Christ and see the light of the knowledge of the glory of God.

36
Redeeming the Time

'See then that ye walk circumspectly, not as fools, but
as wise, redeeming the time because the days are
evil. Wherefore be ye not unwise, but understanding
what the will of the Lord is.'

Ephesians 5:15, 16

We come back to this important statement once more because
in it the Apostle is saying something very important. His great
concern is that all Christians should realise the difference between
themselves and those who are not Christians. The Christian has
the wisdom of God in Jesus Christ. He knows things, he has an
insight into life which nobody else has, and what he has to do,
therefore, is to walk circumspectly. We have seen that. He has to
understand the condition of the world in which he lives – the days
are evil. It is only a Christian who can say that. The non-Christian
even resents that statement. He believes that the world is wonderful, that life is amazing. No, says the Christian, the days are evil.
And so we saw that the Christian regards his life in this world
primarily as a great opportunity – an opportunity of behaving as
light, an opportunity of witnessing to the grace of God in the
Lord Jesus Christ. In this way he redeems the time, buying up the
opportunities.

That, then, is the thought we must have in our minds as we
proceed to consider how the Christian uses his life in this world as
an opportunity to disseminate the knowledge and the light which
comes from God in the face of Jesus Christ.

The first thing, therefore, which we must emphasise is that he
must indeed redeem the time. The meaning of the word, redeem
is that of buying up something, and especially the idea of buying
it for ourselves. If you like, it is the picture of a man who is

looking for a bargain. He wants to buy something for himself and he is watching the goods on the stall, or in the shop window. He is anxious to get that bargain, so he looks around and shows great keenness.

Now that is the exhortation which the Apostle gives us here as Christians. Realising what you are, he says, and that the days are evil, and understanding the condition of the world in which you find yourselves, be like men who are watching for opportunities. Be ready to grasp them and to take hold upon them. That is quite a familiar picture of the Christian in the New Testament. The Apostle Peter puts the same thing in his own language in these words in the First Epistle, chapter 4, verse 3. He says, 'For the time past of our life may suffice us to have wrought the will of the Gentiles, when we walked in lasciviousness, lusts, excess of wine, revellings, banquetings, and abominable idolatries.' Surely, the Apostle Peter is arguing, it is almost unnecessary that I should plead with you about this. You have already spent sufficient of your time in this world doing those other things, wasting it and throwing it away. Well, he says, don't do that any longer. You have wasted so much of your life in this world with rubbish and nonsense. Not any more! Be alive, alert, seek every opportunity. Hold on to every minute and every second, redeem the time. In the light of the fact that you wasted so much and allowed so many glorious opportunities to slip by. Don't do it any more.

Paul is not merely exhorting us not to waste our time. He is very positive. He says you must go out of your way to seek opportunities. You see, it is so much stronger than the negative, though the negative is, of course, included. You cannot do this if you are wasting your time. But it is not only that. Be alert, be alive, seek opportunities. Look for them and take them eagerly every time you are presented with one. This, of course, is all-important, because the days are evil and because of the conditions in which we find ourselves.

Now it seems to me that here the Apostle is exhorting us to buy up the opportunities for two main reasons. The first is for our own sake. Then, secondly, for the sake of other people.

Let us consider the first of these. You are to redeem the time, says the Apostle, for your own sake. How am I now then to see to it, during the remainder of my brief life in this evil world, that I buy up the opportunities?

Let us see first what he tells us negatively. Then we shall see how he refers us positively to what the will of the Lord is. We find very practical advice and instruction with regard to this in the first Psalm. If I am to redeem the time there are certain things I must not do. I must not walk in the counsel of the ungodly. I must not waste my time in standing in the way of sinners. I must not loiter about in the sort of place where I know that they are likely to be passing along. Neither am I to sit in the seat of the scornful. If I do those three things, far from buying up the opportunity, I am wasting opportunities. Here is God's instruction. 'Blessed is the man that walketh not in the counsel of the ungodly.' You know their outlook, you know their view of life. Have nothing to do with them. Do not have any interest in their philosophy, their counsel. Do not invite sin, or, as Paul puts it in writing to the Romans, 'make no provision for the flesh'. If you put yourself in the way of sinners, the end will be that you will be sinning with them. Therefore, if you know of literature of a type that is likely to harm you, do not look at it. Throw it into the fire. Have nothing to do with it. Do not spend too much of your time reading unsavoury details about law cases in newspapers. They do not do you any good. That is standing in the way of sinners and if you stand there you will be carried along with them before you realise it.

The same is true of sitting in the seat of the scornful. The Apostle Peter puts this quite plainly to us in his First Epistle in the second chapter, verses 11 and 12: 'Dearly beloved, I beseech you as strangers and pilgrims'; that is what you are, you are strangers and pilgrims in this world since you have become Christians, 'I beseech you as strangers and pilgrims, abstain from fleshly lusts, which war against the soul; having your conversation honest among the Gentiles.' That is the same thing, exactly. There, then, are the negatives.

What about the positive? Well, go back again and you will find it all in the first Psalm. Here is the blessed man – 'but his delight is in the law of the Lord; and in his law doth he meditate day and night'. You see, this man is not wasting his time with unworthy and harmful literature. Rather he spends his time in the law of the Lord, and he meditates in it day and night. He is not like the man who says he is so busy that he really has no time for Bible study and for reading good books. But how is he so busy? Does he spend more time with his newspaper than with his Bible? Then, he has no excuse any longer. Let him give the time he was giving to his newspaper to the law of the Lord instead. The Christian meditates on the law of the Lord day and night. This is his delight. He says, I want something that will build me up and help me and enable me to function as light; so he is a man who is very careful about the portioning of his time. He does not fritter away his time and find at the end of the day that he has not read his Bible, scarcely prayed to God or done anything else, because his time has gone with the frivolities of the things of this present world. No, no, this is the man who buys up the opportunity. He has to discipline himself. He says, I must do this, I insist on this. I am doing so at all costs. Never was this more necessary than it is today.

Or take another exhortation which is given by our Lord Himself. 'Lay not up for yourselves treasures upon earth, where moth and rust doth corrupt and where thieves break through and steal.' Do not spend your time in this world doing that. What then? Well, 'Lay up for yourself treasures in heaven where neither moth nor rust doth corrupt and where thieves do not break through nor steal.' You are a pilgrim of eternity, that is where you are going. Well then, do not spend all your time in laying up treasures in this world, because you are going out of it; you are going to decay and you will leave them behind you. Look ahead, prepare ahead, lay up treasures there, redeem the time. Buy up the opportunity.

Take the similar exhortation in Luke's Gospel chapter 16, verse 9: 'Make to yourselves friends of the mammon of unrighteousness; that, when ye fail, they may receive you into everlasting habitations.' What does he mean? It is a comment on the parable of the Unjust Steward. What was the characteristic of that steward? It was his wisdom. As our Lord says, 'The children of this world are wiser in their generation than the children of light.' Here was a man in trouble and he jumped at an opportunity. He said, Now, before the sentence drops on me I am going to prepare for the future; so he went to customers and said, How much do you owe? One man said, I owe this much – so the steward said. Write down much less, half that. And so he went on. What was he doing? He was preparing himself for the calamity that was about to descend upon him. He was a wise man. He saw what was coming and he acted immediately, redeeming the time. You and I are to be like that. So our Lord says, use your money in such a way in this world that when the end comes, you have your preparation already made there, so that when you cross right over into the other world there will be many who are ready to receive you and to rejoice at the sight of you. You see you are living in this world in such a way that you are really making preparation for that next world. You are buying up the opportunity.

I could quote Scripture almost endlessly to you in this connection, but let me mention just one passage – a very striking one at the end of the thirteenth chapter of Paul's Epistle to the Romans: 'And that, knowing the time, that now it is high time to awake out of sleep: for now is our salvation nearer than when we believed. The night is far spent, the day is at hand: let us therefore cast off the works of darkness, and let us put on the armour of light. Let us walk honestly, as in the day; not in rioting and drunkenness, not in chambering and wantonness, not in strife and envying. But put ye on the Lord Jesus Christ and make not provision for the flesh, to fulfil the lusts thereof.' These are all different ways, you see, of telling us to rouse ourselves, to realise who we are and what we are and to clutch at every opportunity. Be alive and alert. Regard this world as but an opportunity of pleasing Him. Make to yourselves friends, even with the mammon of unrighteousness; lay hold on eternal life.

If anything further is needed to press upon us the urgency of doing this, think of this: 'We must all appear before the judgement seat of Christ.' Christians, we must 'give an account of the deeds done in the body, whether good or bad'. Very well, says the Apostle, knowing the terror of the Lord I persuade men. What he means is this. He knows that he will stand before his Lord. It is not that he is in danger of losing his salvation. It is not judgment in the sense that our eternal destiny is going to be determined. He is talking to people who are already Christians and whose eternal destiny is safe. This is a kind of judgment of reward. The one who came from heaven to earth for us and died on that cruel cross of shame on Calvary's hill; who spared not himself, who endured the contradiction of sinners. He who even bore that agony in the garden and on the cross, He will look at us – and what He will look for is this: how we spent our time in this world after we realised what he had done for us. It is the terror of love you see, not the fear of torment. You will look into that beloved face and into those eyes and you will realise, as you have never done before, what He did for you. Then you will realise with shame what you did not do for Him. Oh, says Paul, buy up the opportunity, do not waste a second. Keep that in the forefront of your mind.

The Apostle John says exactly the same thing in his First Epistle, chapter 3: 'Beloved now are we the sons of God, and it doth not yet appear what we shall be; but we know that, when he shall appear, we shall be like him; for we shall see him as he is.' Then he immediately adds, 'And every man that hath this hope in him purifieth himself, even as he is pure.' That is precisely what the Apostle Paul is saying here. You are children of the light, he says, and of the day; you must not walk as if you are still in darkness. No, realising what is coming, you know you have not a second to waste. Buy up every opportunity. Make full use of the time you have got left in this world. And then, finally, to cap it all, there is a great statement in the book of Revelation in chapter 14 and verse 13: 'Write' – you must have heard this at funeral services, have you ever realised its significance? – 'Write, blessed are the dead which die in the Lord from henceforth; Yea, saith the Spirit, that they may rest from their labours; and their works do follow them.' Here it is again. Thank God, the works that follow us are our good works! They are the works that we have done as we have been buying up the opportunity or redeeming the time. It is all being recorded, nothing will be forgotten; you will hear the blessed words: Come, blessed of the Lord, come, good and faithful servant, enter into the joy of the Lord. Enter into the kingdom that has been prepared for you before the foundation of the world. It is an amazing thing this – 'their works do follow them'.

Very well, then, here is the exhortation in the light of all that. In order that you may have that reception, that you may hear that encomium, redeem the opportunity. What a wonderful thing it will be to hear those words, 'Come ye blessed of the Lord.' Work it out in terms of Matthew 25, of the people who visited Him in prison by visiting His people in prison and giving them food and drink and clothing. You see, they bought up every opportunity, they were living in the light of this and they redeemed the time. That is the exhortation. There it is with regard to ourselves, but we do not live for ourselves only, though we must start with that. We shall be of little value to others unless we realise all this about ourselves, and so the Apostle has put that first.

But then we come to the second application – our relationship to others in this world. We are to buy up the opportunity with regard to them. How do we do so? The first thing we must do is to realise their state and their condition. They still belong to this evil world. They are still in darkness and in a state of sin. But we know something more. We know that the whole time they are looking at us and observing us. We all know that from personal experience. Moreover, the newspapers shout it at us. Have you not noticed how, if there is a man in a court on some criminal charge, if they can find that he was a Sunday-school teacher thirty years before, they will always mention it. They may even put it as a heading 'Sunday-school teacher on trial' though he has not been there for thirty years perhaps. They are watching. They say. Those people claim to be different. Very well, let's see how they behave, let's see how they live. That is the common argument isn't it? Why should I be a Christian? Why should I join you at church? Look at the people who go!

Still more important, people are judging Christianity by what they see in us. Not only that, they are judging Christ by us, they are judging God by us. We stand for God and for Christ, for the Gospel of salvation, for the whole of the Christian message. We are its representatives. They judge it entirely by that they see in us. They do not read the Bible, or books about the Bible. We stand for it. So they are observing us! You see why the Apostle says we must redeem the time and buy up every opportunity. God has often brought people to repentance and to salvation simply by leading them to observe other Christians and they have felt a sense of condemnation, and at the same time a sense of something attracting them. This is the reason we are to be careful says the apostle.

What, then, are we to do? How are we to redeem the time? We are to live in such a way that we will silence all criticism. Peter puts that perfectly in 1 Peter 2:11–12; 'Dearly beloved, I beseech you as strangers and pilgrims, abstain from fleshly lusts which war against the soul.' They are harmful to you, so do not do it for your own sake. But then he goes on, 'Having your conversation honest among the Gentiles: that whereas they speak against you as evildoers, they may by your good works, which they shall behold, glorify God in the day of visitation.' Live in such a way, he says, that you will disarm their criticism. There will be nothing to say. Though they have been speaking against you as evildoers, your very good works will answer them and they will have to admit that they were wrong.

That is obviously the first thing; but we must go beyond that. We must not only live in such a way that we silence criticism. We must positively live in such a way as to attract these people and to make them feel that they are missing something great and wonderful by not being Christians. There is to be that about us which was in the Lord Himself, which attracted people like a magnet. Do you see those poor men possessed with devils? When they saw Him, they ran to Him. They had lived up in the mountains and amongst the tombs. They were running away from people, but when they saw Him they ran to Him. 'Then drew nigh unto him publicans and sinners', we read at the beginning of Luke, chapter 15. It was always the effect he had, the Pharisees did not attract people but Christ did. There was something about Him that made them feel they would receive understanding and sympathy. The woman that was a sinner in the city went and fell at his feet, washed them with her tears and wiped them with the hairs of her head. That was His effect always, and you and I are to live in that kind of way.

But how do we do so? What kind of a life must we live? The first essential, I would say, is this. It must be an ordered life. It must be a disciplined life. One of the things that does most harm to the Christian cause is an erratic Christian. You know the sort of man who comes rushing in and makes us feel for a while we have never been Christians before. But it does not last more than a few weeks, then he suddenly disappears completely. Then back again he comes! There is nothing which does such serious disservice as that. The world is watching and it smiles when it sees such a person coming back again. Well, thank God, it is not the world who decides such a man's destiny, and if you have been an erratic Christian, let me assure you that if you have come back and come back truly, God will receive you and you will have another opportunity. But do not go on behaving like that; 'Go and sin no more'. But we must not be erratic or changeable or unpredictable, if we claim that we are wise. We do not live by *ad hoc* legislation. We have a great plan and we live steadily according to it. If I may borrow words from Matthew Arnold (and multiply them by infinity!) – the Christian is a man who sees life steadily and he sees it whole, and therefore he is not erratic.

Or, look at it like this. We must live a life that is not characterised by stumbling or falling in any way. A stumbling or a falling Christian is a very poor recommendation for the Gospel because the world can stumble and fall into sin in any shape or form, sin in temper, anger, lack of control, lack of sympathy and of understanding: A man who does that is not redeeming the time. He is not recommending Christianity, nor God, nor the Lord Jesus Christ. No, the great characteristic of the life of a Christian is to be consistency. There must be no violent reactions one way or another. Listen to a psalmist describing this kind of good man in the 112th Psalm: 'He shall not be afraid of evil tidings: his heart is fixed, trusting in the Lord.' You see, times of crisis always help to show what a man really is. It is one thing to be a theoretical Christian, but the real test is what you are like when things go wrong. Suddenly you are taken ill and if you are alarmed and do not know what to do, the world says, I thought he was a Christian but it doesn't seem to help him very much. What are you like when sorrow or bereavement comes to your home? What are you like when a war breaks out? You see, it is by our reactions that we betray what we are. Our Lord said, 'By thy words thou shalt be justified and by thy words thou shalt be condemned'. Something happens, and you speak instinctively and you have shown exactly what you are in the depths. The Christian is steady; he shall not be afraid of evil tidings. His heart is fixed, trusting in the Lord.

Of course, you see, when things have been going well this man has been talking to himself and saying, 'Well, yes, thank God, things are going well. God is gracious and kind to me. I don't deserve even this. I can't understand why he blesses me as he does, but he does and I thank him for it. But I know that in an evil world like this you never know when things go wrong. Sin has brought in all sorts of consequences and complications and I am part of the world and I am subject to these things. At any moment they may come to me.' So, when they come, he is not taken unawares. He has thought ahead, he has seen it all. It is all right, he says, this is a part of my lot in this world; in this tabernacle we do groan being burdened, earnestly desiring to be clothed upon with our house which is from heaven. His heart is fixed. He is a steady man. He has a balance in his life. He has reserves that nobody else knows anything about. He is on a rock, on a foundation, and though the whole world may be convulsed in final calamity, this man is steady, trusting in the Lord. That is the sort of life we are to live.

Think also of redeeming the time as it is applied practically in the matter of speech. This is so important. You not only live like this because you know other people are looking at you, but when you are in conversation with them you are full of wisdom, discretion and understanding and you watch for your opportunities. You may be sitting in the train next to somebody, or talking to somebody over the garden wall. They begin to express their opinions and you are able to buy up the opportunity. They may start by saying, 'Isn't it awful?' You do not just say, 'Yes isn't it?' You say, 'But why is it awful do you think? What is the cause of all this?' You have taken your opportunity. Let them speak. You do not suddenly go to them and say, 'Are you saved?' Oh, no, you have to be wise – he that is wise winneth souls. Listen to their conversation. If they express a criticism or an opinion, be ready to use the Christian message. Lead them on to it, starting from where they start, gradually leading them on and linking what is said to eternal principles.

Or they may ask you questions. What a heaven-sent opportunity! If we only look at it in this way, it is amazing how constantly people are presenting us with these very opportunities. Yes, but are we buying them up, are we looking for them? Are we always ready to take hold of and to improve the occasion? That is what the Apostle is telling us to do. Or again, we must keep our eyes open and watch what is happening to people. Here is a man who has taken ill, a man whom we have known and who has no interest in Christian matters. It is a wonderful thing to go and offer him a little sympathy, to try to help him in some practical way and then you will soon be given your opportunity to improve it. Illness, sickness, accident, death, misfortune, all these things are constantly happening to people and there we find our opportunity. When their hearts are tender, let us be there and let us be ready. Redeem the time, buy up the opportunity!

Then, finally, we must be governed by our understanding of what the will of the Lord is. 'Wherefore be ye not unwise, but understanding what the will of the Lord is.' There is the over-ruling principle which governs everything. What does he mean? Understanding what the will of the Lord is does not mean that you seek a special guidance about everything that you do and say. There are people who interpret it like that, you know, and they never move without praying and waiting for some immediate guidance. But you need not do that. Here is the guidance in the Bible before you. Read your Bible instead. There are very exceptional circumstances in which one needs some special guidance, but they are very few. Understanding what the will of the Lord is does not mean that.

What does it mean? It means the very thing the apostle has already been telling us in verse 10: 'Proving what is acceptable unto the Lord.' He says exactly the same in Romans 12 in the second verse. What then is the will of the Lord? Surely there should be no doubt about this. The fear of the Lord is the beginning of wisdom. What else, is His will? Well, 'This is the will of God, even your sanctification', says Paul in the First Epistle to the Thessalonians, chapter 4 and verse 3. He says it here in the Epistle to the Ephesians, chapter 1 and verse 4: 'According as he hath chosen us in him before the foundation of the world, that we should be holy and without blame before him in love.' Holiness is always the characteristic of the Christian. This is what the will of the Lord is. This is what he wants me to be. He wants me to be somebody who will act as light in this world, and the Bible is full of instruction to me about what to do and what not to do. Read the ten commandments, read the beatitudes, read the Sermon on the Mount. That is the will of the Lord. To know the will of the Lord, I say, you have to read your Bible. Meditate on the law of the Lord like the man in the first Psalm, whose delight is in it and who meditates in it day and night. Know it thoroughly and then apply it.

In other words, I would like to put it like this. Here is a man whose chief desire in life is to please the Lord. Like Count Zinzendorf, he, as it were, looks at the picture of the cross of Christ and reads that inscription – I did this for you, what have you done for me? – and he gets up and serves obediently. He is a man who, having realised what God has done for him in Christ, feels that he does not belong to himself. 'Ye are not your own, ye are bought with a price', therefore serve God with your body, with your spirit, with the whole of your being. This is his one desire and he knows that the Lord's desire is that he should show to the world that the Lord has delivered him from sin, has made him holy and is preparing him for heaven. If you keep that in your mind, you cannot go wrong. Everything then will be determined by that.

If you want something further, here it is. Look at the Son of God as he lived in this world. We are to try to live like that, to follow his steps who did no wrong. 'When he was reviled, he reviled not again but committed himself to him that judgeth righteously.' There it is all before us. 'Be ye imitators' – Paul has already said that to these Ephesians – 'Be ye imitators of God.' Imitate the Lord Jesus Christ, not to make yourselves Christians, but because you are Christians. As he is, so are we in this world. We are to follow in his steps. We are to deny ourselves, to take up the cross and to follow Christ. And as we do so, our lives will be holy, they will be steady. They will be calm and serene, they will be a rebuke to sin in every shape and form. They will be an attraction to poor sinners who are beginning to realise their state and their need. 'Always knowing', he says, 'and understanding what the will of the Lord is.' Here is His will: 'Let your light so shine before men that they may see your good works and glorify your Father which is in heaven.' That is the exhortation in Ephesians 5, verses 15 to 17. 'Let your light so shine'!